LOAD UP

A Youth Devotional by
Kenneth and Gloria Copeland

KENNETH
COPELAND
PUBLICATIONS

Load Up

ISBN 1-57562-905-4   21-0015

11 10 09 08 07 06   12 11 10 9 8 7

PRESENTED TO

_____

ON

_____

BY

_____

Your Mission

Now unto him that is able to do exceeding abundantly above all that we ask or think, according to the power that worketh in us.
Ephesians 3:20, KJV

We are living in the greatest and most challenging days of history—days in which God has begun doing mighty works in young men and women all over the world. He is continually doing more than we could ever ask or think. He is empowering those who give Him first place in their lives and commissioning us to a mission that will bring victory. You are a part of what God has started.

He has called you to a higher place; a place where you can soar far above the everyday ups and downs most people experience. He has placed a mission before you that can only be accomplished with His power. When you open His manual and accept this mission, His presence and power will become real to you and you will realize the truth of who you really are.

Who are you? You are an elite member of God's team. You are an overcomer in this present world. You have access to a level of spirituality that will open up the supernatural to you as you follow His directives. You are a believer, and God has chosen you to embark on a journey that can change the world as you know it.

For more than thirty years Gloria and I have been in this journey and we're being changed to be more like Him every day. It's an ongoing process that lasts our entire lifetime, as it will yours.

While we have changed, the process that changes us never has. To this day, we must continue to accept whom God has made us, and fulfill the mission. Now, we pass this assignment to you.

This mission is not for the faint or the weak in heart. Your success depends on the empowerment you receive from the Word of God. Every day, you will receive a charge designed to take you to a higher level, to teach you, challenge you and encourage you. It is important that you receive into your spirit the things you will read. As you do, God's Word will change you forever, and your mission will be accomplished.

Kenneth and Gloria Copeland

Your *Load Up* Instructions

1. Start each devotion by reading the Scripture verse at the top of the page. Ask yourself what God is saying and allow the Holy Spirit to speak to you.

2. Read the devotion. Then take a moment to think about what you read and how it applies to your life today. You can write notes directly on the page if you want.

3. Read the passages marked *b a c k u p* at the bottom of the page. These "extra bytes" will help you get the most out of each devotion.

4. By following the *d o w n l o a d* scriptures, you'll read a portion of the Bible every day. By year's end, you'll have read all of God's Word.

5. Put action behind what you have just read by speaking the *v o i c e a c t i v a t e*. *Speak it* in faith and meditate on it all day long!

6. If there's a specific topic you want to find out more about, check out the TOPICAL INDEX in the back of the devotional. Here you will find all of the devotions listed by topic. It's an excellent tool to find the answers you need right away.

That's it! Enjoy your new *Load Up* devotional. Use it to its fullest and receive all that God has for you!

"For God so loved the world that he gave his one and only Son, that whoever believes in him shall not perish but have eternal life."
John 3:16

january 1

kenneth

Eternal Love, Eternal Life

Something's missing. You feel it. You know it, but...inside you're still unsure. How can you know that He'll come through *every time?*

To answer that question, you need a deeper understanding about Who God is. You need a personal *relationship* with Him. You need daily interaction with His love.

So what is God's love like? Well, as today's verse says, *"For God so loved the world, that he gave...."* His love is always giving. It's everlasting, unconditional and never-failing. Our minds can't grasp it. The Apostle Paul said in Ephesians 3:19 that he wants us to *"know this love that surpasses knowledge—that you may be filled to the measure of all the fullness of God."* How is that possible? How can we comprehend the incomprehensible?

We can't! Not with our simple human understanding. If we want to know something as vast as God's love, He will have to show us Himself through the Holy Spirit. This is because most of the things you learn go from your head down into your heart, but when the Holy Spirit shows you something, it goes from your heart up into your head.

If you've never known God's unconditional love, start the new year off right—ask the Holy Spirit to help you understand. If you've never asked God to be the Lord of your life, you can right now. Just pray a prayer like this:

"Father God, please forgive me for the things I've done wrong. Come into my life and save me. Be the biggest part of my life—be my Lord. I give myself to You. I receive You into my life. Thank You, God. Thank You for saving me."

Now, receive the unconditional love He has for you. Allow the Holy Spirit to show you just how great it is as you enter into God's presence every day. Yes, God really does love *you!*

b a c k u p :
1 John 4:8-19

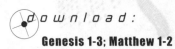
d o w n l o a d :
Genesis 1-3; Matthew 1-2

v o i c e   a c t i v a t e :
God loves me so much He gave His only Son for me. Because I believe in Jesus, I will not perish. I have eternal life. John 3:16

"Christ in you, the hope of glory."
Colossians 1:27

The Power Inside You!

I believe you are about to receive a truth that will turn you inside out and upside down. It's in today's verse: *"Christ in you, the hope of glory."*

Do you *really* realize what that verse is saying? Do you *really* realize that Jesus Christ lives *in* you?

You and I aren't just Jesus' representatives. We're His actual, physical Body on earth! If kids in your school are going to see Him, they'll have to see Him through you and me. That's truly a shocker—but 1 Corinthians 12:27 says it so plainly, anyone can understand it: *"Now you are the body of Christ."*

When you or I pray for someone, Jesus is in us to bring them the answer. When we open our mouths to speak, He's in us to give us the words to say. The Bible says, *"He who unites himself with the Lord is one with him in spirit"* (1 Corinthians 6:17).

Think about that! You are one with Jesus—and Jesus hasn't changed. He is all powerful and is the answer to everything in life! He is in you, and He is able to do the same things He did when He walked the earth 2,000 years ago.

So how can we do miracles like He did? How can we be sure that His power will show up in our lives? We do it by giving our faith a work-out, believing what His Word says about us.

That shouldn't surprise you. After all, nothing heavenly just drops in your lap. To receive healing, you have to believe God is a healer. To receive salvation, you have to believe that He is a Savior. Everything we get from God takes faith. So, for Jesus to show up in everything you do, you're going to have to believe He's inside you, ready to work through you.

So start doing it. Grab hold of this truth: *The power is in you...and Jesus is ready to move in your life!*

backup:
Mark 16:15-20; Romans 12:4-5; 1 John 4:4

download:
Genesis 4-5; Matthew 3

voice activate:
Jesus Christ lives in me. He is my hope of glory. Colossians 1:27

gloria

"Do not conform any longer to the pattern of this world, but be transformed by the renewing of your mind. Then you will be able to test and approve what God's will is—his good, pleasing and perfect will."
Romans 12:2

january 3

gloria

Take a Crash Course

If you've just started to move ahead with God, you may be wondering exactly how you walk by faith. It's simple. Romans 10:17 says faith comes by hearing God's Word.

When Ken and I first learned about the Christian life, we were so hungry to live for God that we took a crash course in living by faith.

For the most of that first year, we hardly did anything but read and study God's Word. We were so tired of being failures that we weren't interested in anything else. We were in our own little world, but God was moving!

You may think that's extreme—but it's all right to be extreme. Fill your life so much with God's promises to you that there's not room in your thinking for unbelief, doubt and fear. Fill your heart until the truths of the Bible naturally begin to come out when you speak. Let God's Word completely take over and change the way you think.

Then, when Satan lies to you and tells you that God isn't listening, that your friends hate you, or that you won't ace that test, don't listen to him. Instead, tell him, "The Lord is good to everyone. He's full of compassion and mercy. In fact, I'm one of God's favorites!"

If you've been afraid to ask God for what you need, take time to stop and think about His goodness today. Stop and think about all the good He wants to put into your life. Then, by faith, let it in!

Take a crash course in living by faith and let His goodness come into your life. Then expect more...because God is good all the time!

backup:
Psalm 1

download:
Genesis 6-7; Matthew 4

voice activate:
I am not conformed to this world. My thinking is changed as I renew my mind to God's Word. I experience God's good, pleasing and perfect will. Romans 12:2

"I can do all things through Christ [the Anointed One and His Anointing] which strengtheneth me."
Philippians 4:13, KJV

Get Ready for Power

Notice in today's verse Paul didn't say, "I can do all things through Christ *who* strengtheneth me."

He said, "*which* strengtheneth me."

He wasn't just talking about Christ, *the Anointed One of God*. He was also talking about the abilities He has—or, *the anointing!*

As a Christian, God has provided you with the ability to do everything He has called you to do—no matter how great or how small the task. He has given to you His power. That power is the anointing that is inside you, ready to empower you to do whatever God has called you to do.

When you understand that, it will change the way you read and understand the instructions God has given us about how we're to live.

In Ephesians 4, for example, Paul says, "*Walk worthy of the vocation wherewith ye are called...Endeavoring to keep the unity of the Spirit...sin not...Let no corrupt communication proceed out of your mouth...grieve not the holy Spirit of God...be ye kind one to another, tender-hearted, forgiving one another, even as*

God for Christ's sake hath forgiven you" (verses 1, 3, 26, 29-30, 32, KJV).

Why is it so important that we follow these instructions from Paul? He says it's for *Christ's* sake. It's for the sake of the anointing – the power He has given you to accomplish His will! In other words, it's our job to keep ourselves in a place where God can anoint us with His power, so we can bring Jesus' love to those around us.

When you realize that, you'll begin to protect that anointing and will not allow anything to hinder the power of God inside you.

b a c k u p :
   Ephesians 4:26-32

d o w n l o a d :
   Genesis 8-9; Matthew 5

v o i c e   a c t i v a t e :
   I can do all things through the Anointed One and His Anointing which strengthens me! Philippians 4:13

january 5

gloria

"But the worries of this life, the deceitfulness of wealth and the desires for other things come in and choke the word, making it unfruitful."
Mark 4:19

Deny Your Impulses

Most people don't think much about worry. To them it's *normal*. They think loving their family or caring about their friends *means* worrying about them.

But Jesus considered it deadly! He listed it as one of the few things that can stop the Word from working in your life.

No doubt, this year will fly by as quickly as last year, but you can make it the best year of your life. How? By making the decision right now to quit worrying!

You may think that this year offers more reasons than ever to worry. However, this year you have more reasons *not* to worry than ever—because God's Word can overcome any problem in your life—at school, at home, wherever. If you'll plant His truth into your heart and let it grow, it will soon become greater in your life than any problem you'll ever face!

You may be ready to quit worrying right now, but let me warn you—worrying is a habit. You'll have to be diligent to get rid of it. I know that from experience.

I'll never forget the verse that helped me kick the habit: *"Roll your works upon the Lord—commit and trust them wholly to Him; [He will cause your thoughts to become agreeable to His will, and] so shall your plans be established and succeed"* (Proverbs 16:3, AMP).

When I read that verse, I decided to believe it. Once I did, I began to quit worrying—one moment at a time. Every time I had a worried thought, I'd give it to the Lord. I did that over and over and *over*. As I continued to resist worried thoughts and remind myself of God's promises to me, those thoughts were fewer in coming. Today, I hardly ever have a worried thought!

So kick the habit! Put Proverbs 16:3 into practice every time worry beats at your door. Pretty soon, it'll be normal for you *not* to worry!

backup:
Psalm 55:22; 1 Peter 5:7

download:
Genesis 10-11, Matthew 6

voice activate:
I will not allow the worries of this life or the deceitfulness of wealth or the desires for other things to enter my heart and choke the Word. I determine to bear much fruit. Mark 4:19

"All these blessings will come upon you and accompany you if you obey the Lord your God."
Deuteronomy 28:2

Dominion Over Failure

When I say God's Word can bring you victory in every area of your life, not everyone believes me. Most don't admit it, but it's true.

They don't mean to doubt the God, of course. They're just so overwhelmed by the problems in their own lives, they're not sure anyone can help.

Sometimes they look at others and think, *Sure it's easy for them to live by faith, but what can God do with a life as messed up as mine?*

If you struggle with that question, let me tell you, God can do way more for you than you can imagine. After more than thirty years of teaching this, I can say that—not only because it's in the Bible, but also because it's reality for me.

I haven't always done so well. When I first learned about having faith in God, I was a failure. Then one day I read Deuteronomy 28, and I discovered all the good things God's people are supposed to have in their lives.

Quite honestly, I got mad. *Where are all these things that are supposed to belong to me?* I thought. At the time, I

didn't have even one of them. Yet I realized that the Bible clearly said I was supposed to have them all.

Now, some people may try to tell you that you're not supposed to have these things. Even your friends and family may think you're being extreme...but do what I did: Give your attention to what God says in His Word. Get out from under that barrel and dare to believe God will take care of your every need. Receive Deuteronomy 28 as God's will for your life, and watch God do more—much more—than you can imagine!

backup:
Haggai 2:7-9

download:
Genesis 12-13; Matthew 7

voice activate:
I obey the Word of God. All the blessings of the Word come on me and accompany me! Deuteronomy 28:2

"Everything is possible for him who believes."
Mark 9:23

january 7

kenneth

Nothing is Impossible!

Have you ever felt hopeless...ready to give up? Maybe you've already given up and felt that there were no answers and that you were simply trapped right where you sit. Well, here's good news: You don't have to stay there.

According to the Bible, hopelessness isn't caused by lack of money. It isn't caused by lack of education. It isn't caused by negative circumstances. Hopelessness comes from being a stranger to God's promises (Ephesians 2:12). Anybody anywhere can have hope if they know Jesus and the promises of God.

There is one country in Africa where the government wanted a tribe to die out, so they just stopped the flow of food and began to starve them to death. However that plan failed because some African Christians refused to give up hope. They knew God's promises, so they prayed "Give us this day our daily bread." Do you know what happened? The people were fed and the government went under!

The Apostle Paul said in Philippians 1:20 (NKJV), "*According to my earnest expectation and hope that in nothing I shall be ashamed....*" The terms "earnest expectation" and "hope" both mean the same thing.

So hope is *earnest expectation*. It isn't dependent on the world's way of doing things. It's based on what God has promised me. Because He said it, I earnestly expect it! I have hope because of His promises. If you need hope today, resist Satan and throw hopelessness into the dumpster. Everything is possible to him who believes!

b a c k u p :
Ephesians 2:11-18

d o w n l o a d :
Genesis 14-15; Matthew 8

v o i c e   a c t i v a t e :
I am a believer. Everything is possible to me! Mark 9:23

"The [Holy] Spirit comes to our aid and bears us up in our weakness; for we do not know what prayer to offer nor how to offer it worthily as we ought, but the Spirit Himself goes to meet our supplication and pleads in our behalf with unspeakable yearnings and groanings too deep for utterance. And He Who searches the hearts of men knows what is in the mind of the [Holy] Spirit...because the Spirit intercedes and pleads [before God] in behalf of the saints according to and in harmony with God's will."
Romans 8:26-27, AMP

Plug Into the Spirit

Most Christians don't realize it, but praying in the spirit is a spiritual exercise that strengthens you inside. Praying in your God-given prayer language builds you up just like barbells build up your arms. If you'll do it faithfully, it will help to keep your old sinful nature in line.

Many people wonder why they can't just pray in their known language.

The reason why is because the Bible says your "weakness" gets in the way. Many times your brain doesn't have a clue how to pray prayers that will strengthen you against coming temptations. Your brain may not have any idea what you need.

Your mind just isn't informed like your spirit is. Your spirit is in constant contact with God. That's why, as Romans 8:26-27 says, the Holy Spirit helps us because we don't know how to pray as we should.

Praying in the spirit enables you to pray for exactly what God wants for your life. It enables you to pray for exactly what you need, no matter how weak you may feel.

Praying in the spirit is the tool God has given you to tap into what the Holy Spirit knows. When you pray in the spirit, you help your spirit to see things differently—as the Holy Spirit shows you the truth.

Be warned, nothing will happen unless you make an effort. The Holy Spirit isn't a bully. He's not going to grab you by your shirt collar and make you pray in the spirit. He's going to wait for you to *want* to start.

So begin to pray in the spirit every day and build yourself up. Tap into what the Holy Spirit knows. You'll see...you'll have the strength, ability and answers you need for whatever comes your way!

backup:
1 Corinthians 14:1-4

download:
Genesis 16-18; Matthew 9-10

voice activate:
The Holy Spirit comes to my aid and bears me up in my weakness when I do not know how to pray on my own. He intercedes on my behalf according to the will of God. Romans 8:26-27, AMP

gloria

january 9

kenneth

"For the Son of God, Jesus Christ...was not 'Yes' and 'No,' but in him it has always been 'Yes.' For no matter how many promises God has made, they are 'Yes' in Christ. And so through him the 'Amen' is spoken by us to the glory of God." 2 Corinthians 1:19-20

What's on Your Mind?

"Oh, God, I feel so sick. My head hurts. My stomach aches. I'm gonna miss a week of school. Heal me!"

Have you ever prayed like that? If so, don't ever do it again!

We need to go to God on the basis of *what He can do for us*—not on the basis of *what we need*. That's just the way faith works.

I learned this years ago when I needed healing. Now, I don't ever go to God and tell Him how sick I am, and then ask for healing.

Isaiah 53:5 proves that Jesus already provided for my healing when He died on the cross and rose again. So when my body is feeling sick, I pray:

"Thank You, Lord, for providing healing for me. By faith I receive it now, in Jesus' Name. I agree with Your Word which says, *By His wounds I have been healed*" (1 Peter 2:24).

Remember this: If you talk about what you need over and over again, it will be on your mind so much that it will put your faith in a headlock, and you won't

be able to receive what God has for you. If you talk about God's promises over and over again, *they* will be on your mind...and it will be the most natural thing in the world to simply reach out by faith and receive what He has for you!

b a c k u p :
Luke 13:11-17

d o w n l o a d :
Genesis 19-20; Matthew 11

v o i c e a c t i v a t e :
All God's promises to me are "yes" and "amen." 2 Corinthians 1:20

"He redeemed us in order that the blessing given to Abraham might come to the Gentiles through Christ Jesus, so that by faith we might receive the promise of the Spirit. If you belong to Christ, then you are Abraham's seed, and heirs according to the promise."
Galatians 3:14,29

God's Fortune

Have you ever been invited to an attorney's office for the reading of a will? I haven't. Where I come from, there was never enough money left for the relatives to fight over when somebody died.

Thank God that's not the case anymore. When I gave my life to Jesus more than thirty years ago in Little Rock, Arkansas, I became an heir to a fortune. At that moment I was reborn—into the richest family ever known. I received an inheritance so huge, it will take me all of eternity to fully realize all I have.

Some people get excited about tracing their natural family history. They like to know if they have great people in their family tree because it makes them feel like they come from good stock.

You and I ought to be that way about our heritage as Christians. Our ancestors are the greatest men and women who ever walked the face of the earth. We can trace our lineage all the way back to Abraham, Isaac, Jacob, Joseph, King David...and to Jesus. Think about that! Those are our relatives.

"Now wait a minute," you may say. "They lived in Israel and Canaan. You're an American from Arkansas! You're not part of that family."

No, not physically, but I am spiritually. According to the Bible, if you've made Jesus Christ the Lord of your life, you are too. Galatians 3 says so.

As a Christian, you are the seed of Abraham! That means everything God promised him belongs to you. It has been passed down to you through Jesus.

The gifts God gave Abraham are your inheritance! It has been willed to you in the Bible. While you need to read the will, the Bible, to find out what is yours, you can't receive the gifts without faith. Faith gives you access to God's favor...and it gives God access to your life. It opens the door to your inheritance.

So start reading the Bible with a new eye—not like a book of stories, but as the record of your ancestors. Read it and believe it like you would a will that detailed your inheritance. Enjoy the riches that are yours because you've become a Christian. Discover for yourself that you truly are an heir to the unlimited resources of the family of God!

backup:
Hebrews 6:13-20

download:
Genesis 21-22; Matthew 12

voice activate:
The blessing of Abraham comes on me through Jesus Christ. I receive the promise of the Spirit through faith. I am an heir to the promise! Galatians 3:14,29

"As we have therefore opportunity, let us do good unto all men, especially unto them who are of the household of faith."
Galatians 6:10, KJV

Members Only

When God gave you His faith, He didn't shortchange you. He put enough faith in you to blast through every mountain that gets in your way.

He expects you to use it. He will even help you develop it to the point where it can consistently empower you to keep your relationships strong and keep things going well for you.

If you haven't had much success in those areas, it's time to develop your faith. Start studying your Bible and spending time with the God and exercising your faith until you're a spiritual Schwarzenegger.

Then, the next time Satan comes bursting through your door, you can stand up, flex those faith muscles and say, "Back off, man! There's nothing for you in this house. It belongs to me and you can just keep your grubby hands off it. Stand back or I'll cut you up one side and down the other with God's Word. Now, get out and don't let me see your ugly face again!"

Now that's what I call being exactly who you are...a member of the household of faith!

b a c k u p :
Ephesians 2:4-10

d o w n l o a d :
Genesis 23-24; Matthew 13

v o i c e   a c t i v a t e :
My heavenly Father provides me with the measure of faith and I determine to build my faith by meditating on His Word. Romans 12:3

An Open Door for Miracles

When people came to Jesus and asked, *"What must we do to do the works God requires?" Jesus answered, "The work of God is this: to believe in the one he has sent."* (John 6:28-29) All through Bible, every time something awesome and miraculous happened, every time a life was touched, somebody had to act on his or her faith. Somebody had to trust God enough to act on what He said and open the door.

That's what happened to me the day I made Jesus my Lord. I read Matthew 6:26 and found out that God cares even for birds—and faith burst into my heart. I didn't know the first thing about becoming a Christian. Yet when I spoke that faith out— that I *believed* in Him—I opened the door just a crack and God's mercy and love flooded my heart and changed me forever.

It's still true today. However wide you open that door of faith is how much of God's mercy and goodness will flow into your life. I'm telling you, He's ready. He wants to do great things in your life. He wants to give you all the benefits of salvation.

When I say salvation, I'm not just talking about a ticket to heaven. Salvation means freedom. It is freedom from depression, poverty, sickness, danger, fear—anything you need freedom from!

Salvation also means "soundness, protection, liberty, health and restoration."

Psalm 68:19 says God loads us with the benefits of salvation daily. When you wake up in the morning, you can start thanking God for the salvation that's going to happen *today*.

Start each day by opening the door of faith. Don't just open it a crack—rip it off the hinges!

january 12

gloria

b a c k u p :
Psalm 103:1-12

d o w n l o a d :
Genesis 25-26; Matthew 14

v o i c e a c t i v a t e :
I have gained access by faith into the grace of God. Romans 5:2

"Why are you so afraid? Do you still have no faith?"
Mark 4:40

january 13

kenneth

Good Luck?
Bad Luck?
Yeah, Right.

"It doesn't matter how hard I try, everything still turns out wrong!"

Have you ever felt that way? I have. There was a time in my life when everything I tried fell apart. Back then, I chalked it up to "bad luck."

I've found out since then that there's no such thing as luck—good or bad. It's not luck that determines how things turn out in our lives—it's *choices.* When we make good ones, things go well for us. When we make bad ones, things go wrong.

There is only one way you can be absolutely sure you've made the right choice, but it is not according to how things operate in this world. You have another, far more powerful option.

Take the record in Mark 4:36-41 for example. The disciples were in a boat, facing a raging storm. No doubt they were doing everything *in the world* to keep their boat afloat. They were bailing; they were paddling.

They didn't say a word to Jesus, even though He was right there in the boat with

them! They didn't ask Him for help until the boat was full of water and they were about to sink. Why? They made a wrong choice. They chose to look to natural solutions instead of supernatural ones. Putting their faith in Jesus never even entered their minds until they were about to drown!

Many well-meaning Christians make that same mistake today. Jesus is right there in the boat with them, but they're depending on natural resources to get them through. They're making wrong choices, and chalking it up to bad luck.

If you're living like that, stop! Get in the Bible. Start living according to His promises. Then, when the storms of life come, you'll know what to do.

b a c k u p :
Mark 4:36-41

d o w n l o a d :
Genesis 27-28; Matthew 15

v o i c e   a c t i v a t e :
I have faith in God. I will not be afraid.
Mark 4:40

Change
Your Mind

When Jesus came preaching the good news, He said to people, *"Repent, for the kingdom of heaven is near."*

What did Jesus mean by this?

He means, *Change your mind and come My way. Turn around and go a different direction. Come into the kingdom of heaven.* He was offering life, but for the people to receive it, they had to repent— or change their ways. They had to choose God's way of doing things.

That's what it means to repent. It's not just being sorry for something you've done, or sad about a situation. It's changing your mind. It's changing your direction. It's choosing God and His way over your own. It's turning back to God when you realize you've done wrong.

It doesn't matter what you've done...or what you may do in the future. If you repent, God will forgive you and receive you cleansed and made new (1 John 1:7). Then you can live obedient to Him.

Don't live with a constant feeling of guilt. Repent! That's all you have to do. Just ask God for forgiveness, and change. Go the other way. Go toward God!

january 14

gloria

backup:
Luke 15

download:
Genesis 29-30 ; Matthew 16

voice activate:
I repent and turn away from sin because the kingdom of heaven is near. Matthew 4:17

21

"We have this hope as an anchor for the soul, firm and secure."
Hebrews 6:19

january 15

kenneth

Realize the Truth

It may seem like you are in deep trouble, but if the Bible says you have hope, then you have hope!

You may think your circumstances are tearing you apart, but I have news for you. Your circumstances are not the problem! All circumstances—I don't care what they are—must surrender to God when faced with faith, hope and love.

When circumstances are bad, fill your heart and mind with the Word of God until you stop those negative thoughts from bombarding you. Take time during study hall or skip that TV program.

No matter what happens, stand your ground. To keep from slipping, toss aside every thought that does not line up with the truth of God. Make every thought agree with that truth—*every thought!*

You can do it! The Bible says you can (Philippians 4:8). The Bible tells you to choose what you think, and trash what you shouldn't be thinking. When you do that, hope can do its work. In fact, if you'll guard your mind, hope will suddenly rise up. Add faith and God's love,

and that's all you need! Suddenly you can walk right out of that trouble you were in.

backup:
Psalm 71

download:
Genesis 31-33; Matthew 17-18

voice activate:
Hope is the anchor of my soul. Hope keeps me firm and secure. Hebrews 6:19

"Fear the Lord, you his saints, for those who fear him lack nothing."
Psalm 34:9

Total Respect

What does it mean to fear the Lord? It means to give Him total respect and to honor Him. If you fear the Lord, whatever He says, you do it. When you find something in His Word, you make it happen in your life immediately. You're quick to make the necessary changes right away.

God says people who live that way lack nothing. *Nothing!* That's a pretty big statement, but if you'll read the Bible, you'll see it's true. God has always taken total care of His people. When Israel followed Him, the whole nation had everything they needed. They were strong. They were living well. No enemy could stand before them. They had no sickness or disease.

God doesn't have any problem backing up His promises. The only problem He's had has been finding people who would do what He says.

God knows exactly how to get you out of trouble. He hasn't forgotten how to part the Red Sea. He never changes. When God finds somebody who is fully committed to Him, He's fully committed to him or her.

Second Chronicles 16:9 says, *"For the eyes of the Lord range throughout the earth to strengthen those whose hearts are fully committed to him."*

God isn't just willing to rescue you from trouble, He *wants* to rescue you. He is constantly searching for opportunities to do great things for you, but He won't force it on you. You'll have to fear Him—give Him total respect and honor Him in the way you live around your parents, your classmates and your friends. If you want to walk in His power, you'll have to want it enough to let God be God in your life every day.

gloria

b a c k u p :
Proverbs 2:1-6

d o w n l o a d :
Genesis 34-35; Matthew 19

v o i c e   a c t i v a t e :
I reverently fear the Lord. Because I respect and honor Him, I lack nothing! Psalm 34:9

january 17

kenneth

"By the grace of God I am what I am, and his grace to me was not without effect. No, I worked harder than all of them—yet not I, but the grace of God that was with me."
1 Corinthians 15:10

God's Favorite

Did you know that you are God's favorite? Well, you are! The Apostle Paul wasn't just using a figure of speech when he talked about "the grace of God" in today's verse. He was referring to a very real power that was operating in his life. That power can also be called favor.

Even though we've disobeyed Him and done wrong, He hasn't turned away from us. God is determined not to lose us.

He said He would personally help you do everything He's called you to do—*more than you can imagine*—if you'll allow Him to be Lord of your life. That's what grace is all about!

I'm really just scratching the surface here, but study your Bible and you'll get what I'm saying—so much so that the truth will become very real to you and make you very bold. The longer you spend time studying it, the bolder you will get.

I've had people accuse me of being on an ego trip because I talk boldly about what God will do for me; but I'm not bragging on me, I'm bragging on God.

When you start to really understand grace, you'll have that same kind of boldness. You'll just reach out and grab God's

promises by faith because you know they're promises to you. Romans 4:16 says, *"The promise comes by faith, so that it may be by grace and may be guaranteed to all Abraham's offspring."* Who are Abraham's offspring? Galatians 3:29 says, *"If you belong to Christ, then you are Abraham's seed, and heirs according to the promise."*

God's promises belong to you just as much as they belong to Jesus!

How can that be? By grace—that's how!!

You want to see great power? You want to see miracles happen in your school? You want to see the your classmates taking hold of the Word? Then, reach out for a true understanding of grace. It will shake your life!

backup:
Ephesians 2:8-10

download:
Genesis 36-37; Matthew 20

voice activate:
God has given His grace to me. By His grace, I am what I am. 1 Corinthians 15:10

"All authority in heaven and on earth has been given to me. Therefore [you] go...."
Matthew 28:18-19

Satan is Under Your Feet

God has given you authority over the things in your life—but if you don't exercise your authority, Satan will come in and try to take over.

When Ken and I first became Christians, we didn't understand that. We just kept bumping around in the same old ruts we'd been in before we were Christians. We stayed just as broke and as sick as everybody else in the world.

Sure, we knew God worked miracles. Ken saw them firsthand when he was working as a co-pilot for an evangelist.

When they arrived at meetings, it was Ken's job to get the people in the invalid tent ready before the evangelist came in to minister to them. The invalid tent was where the people went who were too sick to go into the regular meeting. Most of them were on stretchers or in the last stages of some terminal disease.

Yet, as the man of God placed his hands on those people, Ken saw amazing miracles. One woman with cancer spit the cancer up, right in the middle of the floor. A girl, who'd come in strapped to a board because she was totally paralyzed, jumped up when the evangelist touched her, and ran around the tent, totally healed.

Ken saw those miracles with his own eyes, but they didn't do anything for us. It was when we discovered that Jesus had already healed *our* sicknesses and *our* diseases that our personal lives changed.

After we saw in the Bible that we had authority over sickness and began to say so, we got free. When we realized that we weren't the sick trying to get healed—no, Satan was trying to steal our *health*—we began to stand up and take our authority saying, "Satan, get out in Jesus' Name!"

Sure, it's exciting to see God work miracles, but you can't live day in and day out on miracles. What will change your life is when you take hold of the authority that belongs to you and speak it out. If you'll do that, you can keep Satan where he belongs: under your feet.

b a c k u p :
Genesis 2:15-17, 3:1-6

d o w n l o a d :
Genesis 38-39; Matthew 21

v o i c e   a c t i v a t e :
All authority in heaven and on earth has been given to me by Jesus Christ. Matthew 28:18

january 19

kenneth

"And when you stand praying, if you hold anything against anyone, forgive him, so that your Father in heaven may forgive you your sins."
Mark 11:25-26

Forgive–Period

Unforgiveness is downright dangerous. It will make your spirit weak and your prayers ineffective. It will pull the plug on your faith so much so that you won't have enough power to effectively live as a Christian.

In Mark 11, Jesus didn't say, "When you stand praying, *try* to forgive" or "When you stand praying, *forgive if you can.*" He simply said, "*Forgive.*" Period.

Jesus made forgiveness a command. It wouldn't be right for Him to command us to do something we couldn't do. So you can be sure it's within your power to obey His command and forgive—no matter how badly you've been hurt.

Most people don't realize it, but unforgiveness is actually a form of fear. Quite often we don't forgive because we're afraid of getting hurt again. We're afraid we're never going to recover from the damage that person has done to us.

If you want to forgive, get rid of those fears. How? By filling your mind and heart with God's promises that apply to your situation (Psalm 119:11).

If you'll do that, I can assure you, your feelings will change. It may not happen overnight...but it will happen. One of these days, almost without thinking, you'll throw your arms around that person, give them a big hug and say, "I love you, friend." What's more, you'll mean it from the bottom of your heart.

backup:
Luke 6:27-36, 17:3-4

download:
Genesis 40-41; Matthew 22

voice activate:
I forgive those I have anything against so God can forgive my sins. Mark 11:25-26

"I will give you every place where you set your foot."
Joshua 1:3

Access Your Healing

If you need healing, you need to possess it like Joshua and the Israelites possessed the land God promised them. To get it, they had to put their feet on what belonged to them.

As a Christian, healing already belongs to you. Isaiah 53 says Jesus has taken our sickness, weakness and pain, and that by His wounds we are healed. So healing is yours. You just have to take hold of it. You have to possess it!

Now, that's not always easy. It wasn't easy for Joshua to possess the land God promised him. God told him he would have to be *"strong and very courageous"* (Joshua 1:7). The people of Israel had to arm themselves and fight their enemy. They had to put their feet on the land that belonged to them.

In the same way, taking the land of healing requires spiritual strength and courage. Why? Because you don't always find yourself instantly healed. Sometimes it takes time.

When you think about it, that's not so unusual. After all, in most cases, sickness and disease do their destructive work gradually. They don't just appear one moment, and kill you the next. They take time. So it's not surprising that healing often destroys them gradually as well.

If you need healing today, you need to step out on God's promise of health for you and say, "Healing is mine. Satan is not going to steal it from me. No one is going to talk me out if it. It belongs to me. Today, I receive my healing!"

Once you've said that, don't ever say anything different. Don't let time or feelings change your mind. Just stay with it. Continue to take God's medicine—the Word—every day and you will continually improve.

When Satan comes back next week and tells you you're not going to get your healing, just laugh and say, "Too late! I put my foot on healing ground last week and it's mine." Then refuse to give up. Your healing will come—every time!

backup:
Isaiah 53:1-5

download:
Genesis 42-43; Matthew 23

voice activate:
God has given me every place I set my foot. Because of that, I have victory over sin, sickness and lack. Joshua 1:3

january 21

kenneth

"The Spirit of the Lord is on me, because he has anointed me to preach good news to the poor. He has sent me to proclaim freedom for the prisoners and recovery of sight for the blind, to release the oppressed, to proclaim the year of the Lord's favor."
Luke 4:18-19

Power Surge

The message Jesus preached was this: *"The Spirit of the Lord is on me, because he has anointed me...."* That may not mean a great deal to you right now, but if you'll keep reading, that one verse will get you pretty excited!

The word *anoint* actually means "to pour on, smear all over or rub into." So Jesus was preaching that, "God is poured on, smeared all over and rubbed into Me." He was telling people that He had come with the bondage-breaking power of Almighty God all over Him.

He didn't just make that statement either. He preached a sermon saying: "Hey, I have good news for you! Poverty is bondage and I'm anointed to destroy it! Broken heartedness is bondage and I'm here to destroy it! Being a captive to sin, sickness, demons or fear is bondage, and I'm here with the bondage-destroying power of God. I'm here to get that trouble off your back! I'm here to set you free!"

That's the truth Jesus preached. It is the good news of the anointing!

That same anointing is available to you today. You don't have to put up with what Satan is throwing your way. If you'll draw on God's anointing power, you can be free. It is available to break you out of every bondage of Satan. It can tell you things you never knew before. It can destroy the bondage you've fought for years. It can utterly annihilate every bit of guilt, fear, poverty, abuse, addiction, torment, hatred and anger—just to name a few.

Whatever it is you want to be free from, the Anointing of Jesus is what will free you. If you've made Jesus the Lord of your life, it's on the inside of you—no matter what your age. Receive it. Activate it! Receive the good news of the anointing!

backup:
Luke 4:14-19

download:
Genesis 44-45; Matthew 24

voice activate:
The Spirit of the Lord is on me. He has anointed me with the same anointing Jesus has. The anointing in me destroys every bondage in my life. Luke 4:18; Isaiah 10:27

"God has dealt to each one a measure of faith."
Romans 12:3, NKJV

The Force is With You

Everyone who has made Jesus their Lord has been given a measure of faith—the same measure—but not everyone takes the time to develop it into a powerful force.

Your faith grows stronger when you hear God's promises. That's because whatever God promises you in the Bible, you can be sure it will happen. He is *"alert and active, watching over [His] word to perform it"* (Jeremiah 1:12, AMP).

So, if you want some faith, start finding out what God has said. Open your Bible and discover what He has promised to you.

Then keep that Word in front of you. Put it in your locker. Put it in your organizer. Speak it aloud. Proverbs 4:20-22 puts it this way: *"My son, pay attention to what I say; listen closely to my words. Do not let them out of your sight, keep them within your heart; for they are life to those who find them and health to a man's whole body."* The force of faith comes when you *pay attention* to the Word of God!

It comes when you do what God told Joshua to do—let the Word of God *"not depart out of your mouth, but...meditate on it day and night, that you may observe and do according to all that is written in it. For then you shall make your way prosperous, and then you shall deal wisely and have good success"* (Joshua 1:8, AMP).

So do what it takes to develop your faith into a powerful force. Then, when trouble comes and you need help, you'll be ready. You can speak that promise, and watch your faith go to work. Or, better yet, learn to use your faith ahead of time and all the time, and you can avoid most of those troubles in the first place!

gloria

b a c k u p :
2 Timothy 1:1-5

d o w n l o a d :
Genesis 46-48; Matthew 25-26

v o i c e   a c t i v a t e :
God has given me the measure of faith. I have the God kind of faith. Romans 12:3

january 23

kenneth

"Ask of the Lord rain in the time of the latter or spring rain. It is the Lord Who makes lightnings, which usher in the rain and give men showers and grass to everyone in the field."
Zechariah 10:1, AMP

Focus

Some years ago, the Lord showed me a vision of the glory that would be released on the earth before Jesus' return. It was vast and very heavy, and it was being held back by what looked to me like a thin, elastic sheet of some kind.

As I looked at it, I was reminded of a balloon filled so full of water that the pressure of the water made it stretch thin and appear to be ready to burst.

That's what the glory looked like to me. It was hanging over the earth and had a big swag in it. When I saw it, I asked the Lord what it was.

That membrane is filled with My glory, He said. *In it are more signs and wonders, an outpouring of the Holy Spirit, the gifts of the spirit, and more souls to be won than the human race has ever seen. All that will have to happen is for that membrane to get one little hole in it, and it won't be able to hold back the glory anymore. So continue to pray. Keep poking at that spiritual membrane with prayer and with faith until it breaks and spills the glory all over the earth.*

In the years since, many have prayed about that glory. Then a few years ago something happened. That "balloon" burst—and lately there have been spiritual breakthroughs on every hand. People who had preached on the streets for years suddenly saw more people turn to God than they'd ever seen in all their lives. People whose hearts had been hardened toward God began to turn to Him in staggering numbers.

That's good news! The membrane that held back the glory has burst! A powerful change has taken place in the spirit world. The storm of God's glory has been released in the earth. The earth is now filling up with that glory.

It has only just started. It's only going to increase more and more in these days before His return. Pray about it. Ask God for His glory to be seen in your life...then look out! It's going to come.

backup:
Deuteronomy 11:13-15

download:
Genesis 49-50; Matthew 27

voice activate:
I expect the glory of God to be poured out on my life like the rain. Zechariah 10:1

"Do not be so deceived and misled! Evil companionships (communion, associations) corrupt and deprave good manners and morals and character." 1 Corinthians 15:33, AMP

Choosing to Be Different

A lot of people don't understand Christians. They say we are unusual and have no fun. They don't understand that we do the things we do simply because we love God—and because God says it is right. They don't understand how rewarding living for God is. We have good health, wealth, godly friendships, things working right at home, at school, and at work. People in the world don't feel like they have anything in common with you. They've never experienced God's peace.

They think, *Why, when you could drink without your parents finding out, do you choose not to? Why, when all your classmates can get away with smoking or experimenting with drugs, do you stay away from it? Why, when "everyone else" is sleeping around, do you choose to stay pure? Don't you want to have any "fun"?* They don't understand that sin brings death (Romans 6:23).

First Corinthians 15:33 tells you that you'll be influenced to do wrong if you stay friends with wrongdoers. Now that you're a Christian, you shouldn't want to hang out in the same places you once did. You're living a new life.

Later on, as you grow stronger, you might be able to be around some of that old stuff without temptation. However, you have to be very careful until you learn how to walk completely free of your old lifestyle. Many times you have to break off old friendships. You have to listen to God about where you're to go and whom you're to hang around. You can love your old friends and people in the world, but you can't spend time with them in same way you once did.

You know the way to peace. You know the right way to live. You know in your heart where you should spend your time, and the places you need to avoid. So follow your heart. It doesn't matter that no one understands. It's okay to be called strange or different—especially when you're full of God's peace.

gloria

backup:
2 Corinthians 6:14-18

download:
Exodus 1-2; Matthew 28

voice activate:
I refuse to be deceived or misled by having evil associations or companions. I choose to fellowship with those who believe in the Lord Jesus Christ. 1 Corinthians 15:33, AMP

january 25

kenneth

"This is the blood of the covenant, which is poured out for many for the for-giveness of sins."
Matthew 26:28

Freedom Was Paid For

Jesus' death and rising again pro-vided us with complete freedom from the curse of sin and death. Until we learn what that means and what to do with it, we won't know how to take hold of all He has for us.

To walk completely free of sin, guilt, condemnation and defeat is like an unat-tainable dream to some people. They have no idea what freedom and joy is already theirs—if they only knew how to tap into it.

When Jesus died, His shed blood was the final sacrifice for all we've done wrong. You don't have to "do" things to make up for your sins. You don't have to punish yourself, or offer a sacrifice like they did in the Old Testament.

Back then, they had to sacrifice animals. When the animal's blood was shed, it covered for their sin...but it didn't destroy it.

With Jesus it was different.

The blood of Jesus did not just cover up our sin. It completely wiped it out. Colossians 2:14 explains that Jesus' blood canceled the note against us. It

took it away. Under the Old Covenant, the note would have just been stamped "paid in full." Under the New Covenant, there's no more evidence that there ever *was* a note. The note is not only paid, it doesn't exist anymore. The blood of Jesus destroyed it.

Do you see the difference? It means when you confess your sins, the blood of Jesus wipes them out. You mention them to God the next day, and He doesn't even know what you're talking about. The marks against you have been obliterated! They're no longer in existence. So why worry about something that doesn't exist anymore? If you are, you're living under the pressure of something that isn't even there. You've been set free!

b a c k u p :
Colossians 1:9-23; 1 Peter 1:18-25

d o w n l o a d :
Exodus 3-4; Mark 1

v o i c e   a c t i v a t e :
Jesus poured out His blood for the for-giveness of my sins, and now they no longer exist. Matthew 26:28

"For those whom He [God] foreknew—of whom He was aware and loved beforehand—He also destined from the beginning (foreordaining them) to be molded into the image of His Son [and share inwardly His likeness], that He might become the first born among many brethren."
Romans 8:29, AMP

Fulfill Your Destiny

It's no secret: The end of this age is very near. You can sense it in your heart. Time is running out, and God is fulfilling His plan in us. He is preparing us to be the people He has called us to be—making us ready for eternity with Him! God is getting Christians together who will fulfill the destiny prepared for them since the beginning of time. That destiny is spelled out clearly in Romans 8:29. Our destiny as Christians is to grow up in Jesus. It's to be fully molded into His image, which was put within us the moment we made Him our Lord.

It's staggering to think that you and I could ever truly be changed into His image. It seems almost impossible that we could be like Jesus, yet God says we can be. In fact, the Bible says He has equipped us with everything we need to continue growing and developing and becoming more like Him (Ephesians 4:13).

Not only is God able to do that, but He wants to. It's His plan, and it's up to us whether or not it'll happen in our lives. If we want to *be* a part of God's plan, we must *do* our part of God's plan. Our part is simply this: *to walk pleasing before Him— to think His thoughts, to speak His Words. In other words, to walk in His ways.*

When we do that, we're fulfilling His desire, and then He can show up in our lives just as He did in Jesus' life.

If we truly want to fulfill our divine destiny and see the power of God in our lives, we must determine to start living every moment of every day to please our Father. We must walk out the prayer that Paul prayed for the Colossians: *"Asking God to fill you with the knowledge of his will through all spiritual wisdom and understanding...in order that you may live a life worthy of the Lord and may please him in every way: bearing fruit in every good work, growing in the knowledge of God, being strengthened with all power according to his glorious might"* (Colossians 1:9-11).

Make your decision today...and fulfill your destiny!

b a c k u p :
Daniel 1:8-17

d o w n l o a d :
Exodus 5-6; Mark 2

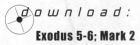
v o i c e   a c t i v a t e :
I am filled with the knowledge of God's will in all spiritual wisdom and understanding. Colossians 1:9

january 27

kenneth

"So that by his death he might destroy him who holds the power of death—that is, the devil—and free those who all their lives were held in slavery by their fear of death."
Hebrews 2:14-15

Spiritual Navigation

If you were the navigator of a ship, you'd be at a great disadvantage if you didn't know south existed, wouldn't you? If the only direction you were aware of was north, you'd get off track very easily.

That sounds silly, but many Christians are trying to do that very thing in their spiritual lives. They're trying to navigate by faith without taking into consideration the contrary force that can take them in the opposite direction if they don't guard against it. What is this contrary force? It's the force of fear.

Just as *"faith is the substance of things hoped for"* (Hebrews 11:1, KJV), fear is the substance of things you *don't* hope for. Faith reaches into the unseen realm of the spirit and brings about God's promises. Fear reaches into the unseen realm and brings about Satan's threats. Faith is the power God uses to create. Fear is the power Satan uses to destroy.

Hebrews 2:14-15 says Jesus came to destroy the power of death and rescue those held captive by it. He knew it was the fear of death that keeps us captive. He came to free us from that fear—which includes the fear of sickness, poverty, failure and so on.

If you have grown up in a poor family, for example, you might spend your lifetime captive to the fear of poverty. You might even try to apply God's principles of giving and tithing—but if you hold on to the underlying fear of being poor, it won't matter how much wealth you receive. Satan will rob you every time you turn around. You have to get free!

So how do you do it? You have to stand against fear by standing on God's promises to you. Simply go before God and turn things around. Then, in faith, you can stand in your freedom. You can speak the truth of Psalm 118:6 (KJV) where David said, *"The Lord is on my side; I will not fear."*

b a c k u p :
Psalm 118:1-6

d o w n l o a d :
Exodus 7-8; Mark 3

v o i c e   a c t i v a t e :
Jesus came and destroyed the power of death and the works of the devil in my life. He has delivered me from the slavery of fear of death. Hebrews 2:14-15

"I urge you, brothers, in view of God's mercy, to offer your bodies as living sacrifices, holy and pleasing to God—this is your spiritual act of worship. Do not conform any longer to the pattern of this world, but be transformed by the renewing of your mind. Then you will be able to test and approve what God's will is—his good, pleasing and perfect will."
Romans 12:1-2

The Final Frontier

Today we are standing at the edge of a great frontier. I believe it is the final frontier that stands between us and the greatest move of God this earth has ever seen. What is the last great, spiritual frontier?

Holiness.

That's right. Holiness is the final frontier, and we will cross it before Jesus returns. I know we will because the Bible says that He is coming for a Church without spot or wrinkle (Ephesians 5:27). In other words, He is coming for a Church that is holy.

Holiness is what allows God's power to explode in the earth. The more we walk in holiness, the more God will be able to touch the world and show Himself through us! In fact, that's what holiness is. It simply means "being separated to God for His use."

Knowing that should make us hunger for holiness. It should make us more eager than ever to separate ourselves from worldly things, and make godly things the biggest part of our lives. It should give us an intense desire to obey today's verses, Romans 12:1-2.

So commit yourself to being holy. Give yourself completely over to God for His use. Then get ready to see God's power explode in your youth group, your school, your workplace and your home. Get ready to cross the final frontier!

gloria

backup:
Ephesians 5:23-33

download:
Exodus 9-10; Mark 4

voice activate:
I offer my body to God as a living sacrifice. I will live a holy life, acceptable to Him, which is my reasonable service. Romans 12:1

"You are the Christ [the Anointed One, with Anointing power], the Son of the living God."
Matthew 16:16

january 29

kenneth

Think About It

Did you know that when the Bible was translated into English, the translators never translated the Greek word *Christ?* It's true. The word *Christ* is a Greek translation of the Hebrew word *Messiah.* Translated into English it means "anointed" or "the Anointed One."

Now, this is something you're going to see me referring to a lot in this devotional, because it's such an important key. If you want to see just how much this lack of translation has cost us, read through the New Testament and find every time the word Christ is mentioned. (It will take awhile because it's in there 341 times!) In each instance translate Christ into *the Anointed One and His Anointing.* Then think about each scripture with that translation completed.

Take, for example, Colossians 1:27, *"Christ in you, the hope of glory."* Translate that and think about it. It's really saying, *"The Anointed One and His Anointing in you, the hope of glory."* Wow! It's the anointing in us—the same death-destroying power that Jesus has—that gives us the expectation of seeing God's glory and power in our lives! *Did you get that?* Read this paragraph again!

So, when the New Testament refers to the good news of Christ, it's talking about the good news of the anointing—the good news of the sin-annihilating, sickness-crushing, poverty-pulverizing, bondage-breaking, death-destroying power of God! Jesus brought that anointing to us. That's why it's called *good news.*

Can you see how this translation can change the way we look at things? Can you see what a powerful truth has been kept from us? Get your Bible out. Go through the New Testament. Every time you see *Christ,* mark it. Translate that word, then stop and think about what it's really saying: *Christ, the Anointed One and His Anointing.* You'll never see it the same again.

backup:
Matthew 16:13-25

download:
Exodus 11-13; Mark 5-6

voice activate:
Jesus is the Anointed One, the Son of the living God. He removes every burden and destroys every yoke of the devil. Matthew 16:16; Isaiah 10:27

> "Be constant in prayer."
> **Romans 12:12, AMP**

No Voice Mail in the Throne Room

Have you ever called out to God and received His voice mail? "Hello, this is God. I'm away from the throne right now. If you'll leave a brief message at the beep, I'll return your call."

Of course not! God is on call 24 hours a day, every day. He is always ready to talk to you. You'll never get voice mail. Never! Even at 3 o'clock in the morning, He is right there, ready to visit with you.

In fact, He sent His Spirit to live in you so He could communicate with you every moment of the day.

If you haven't already, wake up to this fact and started taking advantage of it! Set aside special time to pray and talk with God every day.

I'll never forget when I first began to do that. It was after God spoke to me through a man of God. At that time my son, John, was just a teen, and I was concerned about him. He wasn't a total rebel, but he was doing things I knew he shouldn't do.

That Word from God said that if we'd spend just an hour or two with the Lord each day, all would be well.

Just an hour or two a day is not very much to invest in order to have everything in your life be well. I can vouch for the fact that it really works, because today all is well in our lives. All of our children, including John, are dedicated to the Lord and serving Him with us in ministry.

So make a final decision to spend time with God every day. Find time to spend with Him amid your schoolwork, activities and everything else you're doing—He will help you get it all done. I guarantee when you call out to Him, you won't get voice mail!

b a c k u p :
John 16:5-16

d o w n l o a d :
Exodus 14-15; Mark 7

v o i c e   a c t i v a t e :
I am constant in prayer. Romans 12:12, AMP

january 31

kenneth

"The tongue has the power of life and death, and those who love it will eat its fruit."
Proverbs 18:21

Power Containers

Words have intense effects on our lives. Many Christians think words just communicate information, but words are far more powerful than that. They actually serve as containers for spiritual power. According to today's verse, they have the ability to carry the power of life or death.

People sometimes speak empty words, but God never does. Every word He has ever spoken has been filled with faith, power and life. In fact, God's Word actually contains within it the power to do exactly what it says it will do (Isaiah 55:11).

Every word God has ever spoken is backed by His faith and is as full of power today as it was the moment He said it. So when you believe something He has said by faith, the Holy Spirit goes into action, and that Word explodes into this natural realm and becomes a reality in your life!

That's what happened when you made Jesus your Lord. You heard or read Romans 10:9—*"That if you confess with your mouth, 'Jesus is Lord,' and believe in your heart that God raised him from the dead, you will be saved."* You believed that word, spoke it in faith and the power

of the Holy Spirit was released, transforming your dead, fallen spirit into a reborn spirit, re-created in the image of Jesus Himself.

If His Word can save you, it can accomplish everything else you need: healing, finances, spiritual growth, a job, restored friendships, a new car, better grades, courage.... Whatever it is you need, you can speak His promises in faith. Then, as spiritual containers, they will begin to go to work—and eventually show up right before your eyes.

Yes, you have the power to makes changes in your life, by *speaking*, because your words contain power. So get started. Speak God's Word. Speak out His promises. Speak words of life and power. Things will never be the same!

backup:
James 3:1-6

download:
Exodus 16-17; Mark 8

voice activate:
Death and life are in the power of my tongue. I am determined to only speak words of life. Proverbs 18:21

> "You will receive power when the Holy Spirit comes on you."
> Acts 1:8

A Spiritual Upgrade

If you want to be baptized in the Holy Spirit but have hit a brick wall, hang on. Help is on the way! The promise of receiving the Holy Spirit is for all Christians—so it's for you!

God wants you to have it. He knows the Holy Spirit will empower your walk with Him. He knows praying in the spirit helps you get the answers you need for day-to-day living. God wants you to have this gift. It's not hard to receive (like some say) because God *wants* to flood your life with His power!

If you've made Jesus your Lord, you can be filled with the Holy Spirit (Ephesians 5:18). It's the Holy Spirit's job, not only to put God's nature inside you when you become a Christian, but also to come live in you and teach you. Jesus said in John 14:26 that God would send us the Holy Spirit to teach us "all things."

When you receive the Holy Spirit, you receive God's power in your life. The word *power* in today's verse is translated from the Greek word *dunamis,* which means "ability" and "might." So, it is the Holy Spirit living in you that gives you the ability and might to be a powerful example to your classmates and family.

If you haven't received the Baptism in the Holy Spirit, pray a prayer like this one, believing God. He is faithful!

"God, I am Your child and You are my Father. Jesus is my Lord. I believe with all my heart that Your Word is true. Your Word says that if I ask, I will receive the Holy Spirit. So in the Name of Jesus Christ, I ask You to fill me with the Holy Spirit. I believe that I now receive the Holy Spirit and I thank You for Him. I believe that the Holy Spirit is within me now. Holy Spirit, I believe I will speak in other tongues as You give me the words. Amen."

Now begin to praise God. Worship Him and let His Spirit rise up within you as you speak in other tongues. Just receive and get in on the power!

backup:
Acts 2:1-13

download:
Exodus 18-19; Mark 9

voice activate:
I have the Holy Spirit in me; therefore, I have power! Acts 1:8

february 2

"So, since Christ suffered in the flesh for us, for you, arm yourselves with the same thought and purpose [patiently to suffer rather than fail to please God]. For whoever has suffered in the flesh...[has stopped pleasing himself and the world, and pleases God]."
1 Peter 4:1, AMP

gloria

Sold Out to God

God was able to say to Jesus, *"You are my Son, whom I love; with you I am well pleased."* (Mark 1:11). As Christians, there is no reason why we can't please God as much as Jesus did. We have a completely new spirit made in His image. We have the same right-standing with God. We've been filled with the same Holy Spirit. Because He lives in us, we have all the ability that Jesus had in the earth to be just like Him and to do the things He did (Colossians 1:27).

He was totally sold out to God. He didn't sin. The Bible tells us many times He ministered all day and then prayed all night, yet He had a flesh-and-blood body just like you. He enjoyed a good night's sleep just as much as you do. But He said no to doing His own thing, and yes to what God wanted.

"Well, Gloria, I know Jesus did that, but God doesn't expect that kind of self-sacrifice from us."

Yes, He does. Today's verse says so. It's time for us to live for God, regardless of what the rest of the world is doing.

It doesn't matter how dark this world gets, we are still the light. We need to fight against compromise and commit to "suffer in the flesh" rather than fail to please God. Suffering in the flesh is when you obey God and make your flesh do something it doesn't want to do. When you do that, you'll go beyond simply "not sinning" and into a life truly pleasing to God. You'll be ready to give up even those things you enjoy—activities, TV shows, music, video games—things that aren't necessarily bad, but can hinder your walk with God.

If you want to walk in the best life God has for you, those are the kinds of sacrifices you must make. You have to step into that higher life by faith. You have to lay down your life because the Word says do it. Then, and only then, will you discover the amazing things God has waiting for you!

backup:
1 Peter 4:1-7

download:
Exodus 20-21; Mark 10

voice activate:
I choose to suffer in the flesh rather than fail to please God. 1 Peter 4:1, AMP

"Do not let your hearts be troubled."
John 14:1

God 24/7

People everywhere—including Christians—run around pulling their hair out, worrying about what to do, but there's no need to panic. After all, Jesus told us what to do. He said, *"Do not let your hearts be troubled."*

When Jesus said those words to His disciples, they were about to face more trouble than most of us can imagine. Jesus was about to be crucified before their eyes. Peter was about to deny Him. Who can even imagine how stressful those days must have been?

Yet Jesus said to them, *"Do not let your hearts be troubled."*

He went on to teach *how* to have an untroubled heart even in the most troubling times.

He said, *"Remain in me, and I will remain in you. No branch can bear fruit by itself; it must remain in the vine. Neither can you bear fruit unless you remain in me. I am the vine; you are the branches... If you remain in me and my words remain in you, ask whatever you wish, and it will be given you. This is to my Father's glory, that you bear much fruit..."* (John 15: 4-5, 7-8).

When you *remain* in Jesus, He's not just God on Sundays. He's not just the One you think about when you get in trouble or have a hard test. No, when you *remain* in Him, He's God from Monday through Sunday. He's your school-life God and your home-life God. He's involved in your life 24/7.

Remain in Jesus by talking to Him throughout the day and remembering His Word to you. For if His Word remains in you, it will constantly teach you God's ways and wisdom. His promises will keep your heart from being troubled!

backup:
Proverbs 8:10-17

download:
Exodus 22-23; Mark 11

voice activate:
I do not let my heart be troubled because I trust and remain in Jesus. John 14:1

41

"A righteous man may have many troubles, but the Lord delivers him from them all."
Psalm 34:19

Set Your Angels Free!

I don't think it's any exaggeration to say that every one of us, or someone we know, is facing some kind of problem today—some kind of trouble we can't escape without God's help. For one person, that trouble may be a disease that medical science can't cure. For another, it may be schoolwork problems, an addiction or a family crisis.

No matter what kind of wall Satan has backed you up against, you can count on one thing: God has promised to rescue you. That's right. The Bible says you may have many troubles, but the Lord delivers you from them all. Yes, *all!*

Psalm 91:9-11, AMP says, *"Because you have made the Lord your refuge, and the Most High your dwelling place, There shall no evil befall you, nor any plague or calamity come near your tent. For He will give His angels [especial] charge over you, to accompany and defend and preserve you in all your ways [of obedience and service]."*

God gives His angels charge over you, to protect you and to minister to you. Does that surprise you? It shouldn't.

As Hebrews 1:14, AMP says, *"Are not the angels all (servants) ministering spirits, sent out in the service [of God for the assistance] of those who are to inherit salvation?"*

If you're a Christian, angels are here help to you. So how can you get them to help? By being faithful to God and watching your words. When you speak words of defeat instead of victory, the angels assigned to you are stopped by your words of unbelief. They have been charged to listen to God's Word—words of faith (Psalm 103:20).

So give the angels the Word they need to protect you. When you're tempted to discuss how bad your situation is, stop. Remember what God has promised you. Then open your mouth, speak out that promise from the Word and put your angels to work!

backup:
Daniel 3

download:
Exodus 24-25; Mark 12

voice activate:
The Lord delivers me from all my troubles. Psalm 34:19

"I tell you that if two of you on earth agree about anything you ask for, it will be done for you by my Father in heaven."
Matthew 18:19

Power Tools

Agreeing together in prayer is one of the most powerful tools God has given us. Jesus said praying like this would bring results every time.

However, sometimes when agreeing in prayer, people don't seem to get results. Maybe you've prayed about something with your parents, brother, sister or a best friend, but nothing appears to be happening. I have found, when that occurs, we need to remind ourselves of the four basic "power tools" of agreeing in prayer:

1) *Be in harmony.* When a band is tuning their instruments, the sound isn't much to hear, but when they all begin to harmonize, the sound they make is powerful. The same is true in prayer. Christians in harmony are a powerful, unstoppable force. That's why Satan fights Christian families. That's why he tries to split them up and set them against one another. He wants us fussing and fighting all the time because he knows it will hinder our prayers (1 Peter 3:7).

2) *Establish your heart on God's Word.* Agreeing in prayer should be based on God's promises. Find scriptures that cover your request. Those scriptures are the basis of your prayer and place you in agreement with what God has said.

3) *Fix your mind on God's Word.* Keep those promises before your eyes. When Satan tells you something contrary to your prayer, tell him what God said about it. Make your thoughts agree with His promises (2 Corinthians 10:5).

4) *Act as if it's done.* This is where many people miss it. You have to act on what you believe. Don't get up from your knees and start worrying and speaking out of fear. Only speak about what you expect to see in the end. Refuse to act like the issue is a problem anymore. When someone asks you about it, say: "That's taken care of. So-and-so and I agreed in prayer. As far as we're concerned, that problem is history."

Agreeing in prayer is a powerful force. So don't lose hope if you're not seeing results. Go through this list and check your heart. Use your power tools!

b a c k u p :
Matthew 18:18-20

d o w n l o a d :
Exodus 26-28; Mark 13-14

v o i c e a c t i v a t e :
When I agree with someone in prayer about anything we ask for, it will be done for us by our Father in heaven. Matthew 18:19

"And when he thus had spoken, he cried with a loud voice, Lazarus, come forth. And he that was dead came forth, bound hand and foot with graveclothes: and his face was bound about with a napkin. Jesus saith unto them, Loose him, and let him go."
John 11:43-44, KJV

Dare To Be Supernatural

Do you remember in John 11 when Jesus raised Lazarus from the dead? Go back and read it and you'll see that when Jesus stood before the tomb, He shouted, *"Lazarus, come forth!"* Sure enough, Lazarus did, but the Bible says he was still bound up in grave clothes. So Jesus said, *"Loose him, and let him go!"*

It's the same way with us. When we made Jesus our Lord, our spirit came out of the grave. We were alive in God, but like grave clothes, the self-centered habits of our old life were still in place. They still had us bound.

Well, Jesus wants the same thing for us that He wanted for Lazarus. He not only wants us alive, He wants us free! He wants us walking in love because then the new life He put in us can get out!

When we walk in love, we step into a supernatural way of living. Nothing can hold us back. The grave clothes, those deadly habits of unforgiveness, impatience, irritation and selfishness, have to go.

Do you want to be free from bad habits? Then agree with Jesus and say to each one of those bad habits, *"Loose me and let me go! I'm going on with God. I refuse to be held back. I will walk in love.*

I put hate and unforgiveness and self-ishness behind me. I'm going forward in God. LOOSE ME AND LET ME GO!"

It doesn't take weeks or months to switch over from natural to supernatural living. For a Christian, all it takes is a decision to let love rule in your life. After all, God has already placed love within you, but it won't do any good if you keep it locked inside.

"Put on the new self, created to be like God," Ephesians 4:24 says. Don't leave him trapped inside. Bring him to the outside. Dare to release what God has put in you. Strip off those grave clothes and live the life He has called you to live.

Dare to step into the supernatural. Dare to give yourself over to love!

backup:
Galatians 5:13-15

download:
Exodus 29-30; Mark 15

voice activate:
Deadly habits of unforgiveness, impatience, irritation and selfishness, loose me and let me go. I choose to walk free by the power of God's Word. John 11:43-44; Romans 8:2-6

"God did this so that, by two unchangeable things in which it is impossible for God to lie, we who have fled to take hold of the hope offered to us may be greatly encouraged."
Hebrews 6:18

Settle It at the Table

God has never changed. The only ones who need to change are you and me. If things aren't going right, we need to make some adjustments. We need to get into the Bible and find out what God has promised us. Then we need to receive those things by faith.

To do that, we need to put our faith in what today's verse calls the "two unchangeable things in which it is impossible for God to lie." We need to put our faith in *the body* and *the blood* of Jesus.

That's what you're dealing with when you take Communion. Bread and wine—body and blood. Through Jesus' body and blood, God made an oath with us. Jesus' sacrifice was the sealing of a covenant. His body and His blood were the sealing of God's promises to us. They were the sealing of the New Testament.

Now, when you want something settled once and for all, you can go to God about it. Go to Him with all the promises you find in the Bible about your situation. Share them with Him. Agree with them. Then seal it with Communion.

I can tell you from experience, that's a powerful thing to do. Gloria and I have done it many times over some very serious issues. It helped us seal our faith in what He promised so completely that at the moment of Communion, those things stopped being issues for us. They were settled.

If you're facing something today that looks overwhelming, go to the Communion table. Whether it's cancer, a bad habit to be broken or direction you're needing, settle it once and for all in the body and blood of Jesus.

backup:
Matthew 26:26-29

download:
Exodus 31-32; Mark 16

voice activate:
As I receive Communion, I put myself in remembrance of what Jesus did for me through His death on the cross. Because of Jesus, I am redeemed from the curse of the law. 1 Corinthians 11:25-26; Galatians 3:13

kenneth

gloria

"But if ye have bitter envying and strife in your hearts, glory not, and lie not against the truth. This wisdom descendeth not from above, but is earthly, sensual, devilish. For where envying and strife is, there is confusion and every evil work."
James 3:14-16, KJV

Toxic Strife

You read it here first: One of the most toxic weapons Satan uses against us is strife. *Strife* is vigorous or bitter conflict, discord and antagonism; to quarrel, struggle or clash; competition; rivalry. Strife gives Satan the license to bring trouble into your life. That's why he's always pushing for us to argue with one another and get offended or critical. It gives him access to our lives!

When you made Jesus your Lord, the Bible says you were rescued out of the control of darkness (Colossians 1:13). Right then, Satan lost his right of lordship over you when you received salvation. Now, salvation doesn't just include going to heaven. It includes all kinds of benefits on earth, too, like peace, healing, well-being and help for every area of your life.

Satan doesn't want you to enjoy those things. He doesn't want you to be peaceful and healed and happy, because if you are, other people will notice and want what you have. They'll want God.

In order to stop that from happening, Satan tries to steal those things from you, but since he has no rule over you anymore, he has to trick you into opening your life to him. So what does he do? He tries to get you into strife.

I remember when Ken and I first found that out. We realized that if we wanted to walk in all God has for us, we would have to stay out of strife. We wouldn't be able to argue with people. We wouldn't be able to fight back when people criticized us or wronged us. We'd have to respond in love.

So we made up our minds to get strife out of our lives. When we did mess up and exchanged harsh words, we were quick to repent so Satan wouldn't get even a foot in the door.

You must do the same thing. Don't let Satan into your life. Put strife out of your life. Put it out of your family. Put it out of your friendships. When you do, you'll enjoy life like never before!

backup:
Romans 13:11-14

download:
Exodus 33-34; Luke 1

voice activate:
I refuse to allow envy and strife into my heart. I refuse to give the devil a license to bring confusion and every evil work into my life. James 3:16

"Seeing then that we have a great High Priest who has passed through the heavens, Jesus the Son of God, let us hold fast our confession."
Hebrews 4:14, NKJV

Voice Activate

Your confession is what you say. It is the way you act and talk continually—not just once in a while when you need to, but all the time.

Jesus said, *"Whoever says to this mountain, 'Be removed and be cast into the sea,' and does not doubt in his heart, but believes that those things he says will be done, he will have whatever he says."* (Mark 11:23, NKJV). Notice He said "those things," not just "that one thing."

Everything you do and say all day long ought to be an answer to the mountainous situation you're facing. What do you do when no one is watching? What do you say when you first get up in the morning? How do you talk about that situation when there's nobody around to hear you? That's your confession.

If your confession isn't full of faith, then get into the Bible and find God's promises that apply to your situation. Think and pray about those scriptures until they become as real as God Himself speaking to you (because it is God speaking to you!). Then hope will rise up inside you. Your faith will be established on God's promises!

Let me tell you, when you speak His promises with faith like that, mountains move and Satan runs for cover. Why? Because Jesus will make it happen. He is ready, willing and able to move on your faith-filled words and actions. So speak what you expect to see and nothing more. Then continually thank God for the answer.

Jesus, I know You'll take the words I've spoken about this situation and put them into action. I'm standing on Your promises and I refuse to stop. I know Your Word will never change. So that means Satan and this situation will have to change. God, I thank You for it. From here on out, I consider this problem solved. Amen!

february 9

kenneth

backup:
Matthew 17:14-20

download:
Exodus 35-36; Luke 2

voice activate:
Jesus is the High Priest of my confession and I will hold fast to it. Hebrews 4:14

47

"But the fruit of the spirit is love, joy, peace, patience, kindness, goodness, faithfulness, gentleness and self-control. Against such things there is no law."
Galatians 5:22-23

february 10

gloria

Keep Line Clean

Could you imagine what it would be like if God's power flowed through you all the time? Wouldn't it be excellent if you could walk in His supernatural might every day of your life?

There's no question about it. That would be a great way to live, but is it possible? Of course it is. God has put supernatural power within us that is continually ready. He put mighty forces in our spirit that can enable us to overcome anything Satan throws our way.

Galatians 5:22-23 calls these unbeatable forces the fruit of the spirit. They include love, joy, peace, patience, kindness, goodness, faithfulness, gentleness and self-control.

Contrary to popular belief, the fruit of the spirit aren't *just* nice qualities that make us pleasant people. The fruit of the spirit actually release God's supernatural power into our lives!

Love, for example, is God's power to overcome every obstacle, for as 1 Corinthians 13:8 says: *"Love never fails."* Joy fortifies you with supernatural power when you start to weaken, for Nehemiah

8:10 says, *"The joy of the Lord is your strength."* Peace undergirds you and helps you make correct decisions, for Colossians 3:15, AMP says, *"Let the peace...from Christ rule (act as umpire continually) in your hearts—deciding and settling with finality all questions that arise in your minds...."*

God provided the fruit of the spirit for the strength of your character to be developed, so you can win in all circumstances. Study them. Let them rule in your life. Watch them come out of you and put you on top!

backup:
2 Peter 1:5-11

download:
Exodus 37-38; Luke 3

voice activate:
I flow in the fruit of the spirit. I allow love, joy, peace, patience, kindness, goodness, faithfulness, gentleness and self-control to grow and develop in my life. Galatians 5:22-23

"Finally, be strong in the Lord and in his mighty power."
Ephesians 6:10

Dare to Be Courageous!

In the face of impossible challenges, God gives us the same instructions He gave to Joshua and Solomon. "Be strong and very courageous."

He does not say, "Pray and I'll make you strong."

He says, "Be strong—not in your own power, but in mine."

Clearly, being courageous is our responsibility, and it's not a choice we have. It's a command.

Many Christians today have a lack of courage. For instance: They know the Bible says that by the wounds of Jesus we were healed (1 Peter 2:24). They believe it. They've even been taught that if they'll fill their hearts and mouths with that promise—and stick with it long enough—healing will be certain to show up in their bodies.

Why then don't more people take hold of that truth and stay with it until they're healed? No courage.

The same problem exists in the area of finances. Christians everywhere want to be debt free. They know the truth. They say God supplies all their needs, but when it comes time to buy a car or pay for college tuition, they wilt. "Oh, my, that's a lot of money. There's no way in the world I could believe God for that much money."

What makes people back off their faith like that? A lack of courage.

You may be facing some serious circumstances today. It may be your health, your family, your education. Whatever it is, being courageous to believe God's promises can put you over, but you have to choose to stand up to the fear and the doubt that will come. Boldly declare, "Fear, you have no place in my life. I won't serve you. I dare to believe God! I dare to stand on His promises to me and not back off! I dare to be courageous!"

backup:
Psalm 31

download:
Exodus 39-40; Luke 4

voice activate:
I am strong in the Lord and in His mighty power. Ephesians 6:10

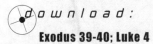

february 12

gloria

"A new command I give you: Love one another. As I have loved you, so you must love one another."
John 13:34

Love—Our Secret Weapon

Have you ever wondered why Jesus commanded us to love? It's because He desires for us to succeed in every area of life, and He knows love is the key to that success.

If we actually understood the benefits that walking in love brings, we wouldn't be so willing to stop loving when we're pressured or aggravated. If we knew, for example, that worry and resentment would keep us from discovering spiritual truths, we might be more willing to lay them aside.

"What does love have to do with discovering spiritual truths?"

Plenty! Read Colossians 2:2 and you can see for yourself how closely they are tied together. The benefits of love don't stop there. They also include divine power. Jesus said in John 14:21 that He will reveal Himself to the person who walks in love.

I think this verse in John is very interesting, especially in light of how much we want Jesus to show His power to us. We long for Him to shower down signs and wonders and miracles, but those things show up among those who walk in love. That's what happened in the book of Acts. God poured out His Spirit in mighty power, not on people who were squabbling with one another, but on people who *"joined together constantly in prayer"* (Acts 1:14).

He shook the building and filled everyone with the Holy Spirit and boldness—not when they were fussing, but when they were *"one in heart and mind"* (Acts 4:32).

Do you need God's power in your life today? Do you need harmony with your parents, your brothers and sisters and with your friends? Then walk in love at all costs. Walk in love and decide that, for your life, love is a command, not an option.

backup:
1 Corinthians 13:1-3

download:
Leviticus 1-3; Luke 5-6

voice activate:
I am obedient to the command of Jesus. I love others as He has loved me. John 13:34

"Oh, give thanks to the Lord, for He is good! For His mercy *[hesed]* endures forever."
Psalm 136:1, NKJV

Do You Know What *Hesed* Is?

What I'm about to share with you has changed my life more than anything else. It changed the way I read the Bible. It settled every question I ever had—or could have—about the good things God wants for us.

The truth I'm referring to is summed up in one small, Hebrew word: *Hesed.* That word may mean nothing to you right now, but once you understand it, you'll take off like a bird out of a cage.

What truth could be that powerful? It's the word *mercy* in today's verse— which is translated from the Hebrew word *hesed* (pronounced kheh'-sed). It means "mercy, kindness, tender mercies, lovingkindness and fidelity." It also means "unconditional love."

To be quite honest, people don't truly understand what these words mean. You talk to them about unconditional love or real mercy, and they just bat their eyes at you like a frog in a hailstorm. Yet, if we don't understand these words, we can't even begin to grasp the truth about our relationship with God...because He loves us with *hesed*.

Take some time and read Psalm 136. *Hesed* is mentioned in all of the 26 verses.

Obviously the psalmist was making a point. He was telling us that the driving force behind all God's actions is *hesed*. *Hesed* is God's very nature.

Hesed can be compared to that tender yet fiercely protective love a mother has for her baby. It's the love that causes her to say, "I'll nurse you and care for you. I'll teach you all that I know. I'll see to it that no one harms you." It's a picture of God Almighty saying to you, "I'll never leave you—ever."

No matter how you feel today, you are loved. Your feelings may tell you otherwise, but God loves you with His *hesed*—unconditionally, just the way you are, every day of your life. He never changes...He never leaves. Never.

Receive His love today and let it change your life!

backup:
Psalm 136

download:
Leviticus 4-5; Luke 7

voice activate:
I give thanks to the Lord for He is good. His love and mercy endure forever. Psalm 136:1

february 14

gloria

"Love never fails."
1 Corinthians 13:8

The Greatest Quest

What is the number one goal in your life? What's your dream?

Maybe you want to build a successful business. Or be a teacher. Or join the Armed Forces. Or maybe you're called into the ministry.

Those are all great goals, but something even more important should be *"your aim, your great quest"* (1 Corinthians 14:1, AMP).

What is it? Living a life led by and filled with God's love.

Human love is changeable and unpredictable. On the other hand, God's love, which is the kind of love you and I should walk in, is entirely different. It doesn't act one way today and another way tomorrow. It doesn't let circumstances or emotions alter it. It is sure and consistent.

First Corinthians 13:4-8 tells us precisely what its characteristics are. This passage of Scripture sets a very high standard for love—so high that you might be tempted to think it's beyond your reach, but it's not. In fact, if you're a Christian, it's natural for you. It's in your heart. You may not be letting it out, but it's there. When you made Jesus your

Lord, God put His love inside you (Romans 5:5).

Without time with God and His Word, however, you'll naturally pull toward selfishness. We all have a natural mind that has been trained to believe things like, "You have to look out for yourself...and stick up for your own rights." Plus, Satan continually tries to draw us out of love, because he wants to steal the answers to our prayers.

The bottom line: Love is the foundation for your new life. When you walk in love, you put yourself in a place where God Himself can protect you—and then nothing can stand against you (Romans 8:31-34). Love is the key to God's wisdom, power and protection. No wonder the Word says, *"Make it your aim, your great quest!"*

backup:
1 Corinthians 13:4-8

download:
Leviticus 6-7; Luke 8

voice activate:
I eagerly desire and follow the way of love. I make it my aim and my great quest in life. 1 Corinthians 14:1

"God is love, and he who dwells and continues in love dwells and continues in God, and God dwells and continues in him. In this [union and communion with Him] love is brought to completion and attains perfection with us... because as He is, so are we in this world."
1 John 4:16-17, AMP

You Can Do It!

If you've made Jesus your Lord, you can walk in love with others all the time! (Yes, even those people who really get to you.) Did you know you have the power to do that?

You can if you continually stay in contact with God by talking with Him and reading His Word. You do it by letting His love flow through you.

Christian writer Donald Gee says, "Fruit is the result of life. Loss of communion is the explanation of most of our failure in spiritual fruit-bearing, and no amount of Christian work, or even exercise of spiritual gifts, can ever be a substitute for walking with God. It is encouraging to remember that sustained [continual] communion with Christ in our daily walk produces the fruit of the spirit unconsciously."*

Jesus Himself taught us how important it is to spend time with Him. He said, *"Just as no branch can bear fruit of itself without abiding in (vitally united to) the vine, neither can you bear fruit unless you abide in Me. I am the Vine; you are the branches. Whoever lives in Me and I in him bears much (abundant) fruit. However, apart from Me—cut off from vital union with Me—you can do nothing"* (John 15:4-5, AMP).

Actually, the more we spend time with God, the more we are changed by His presence and empowered to walk in love. The more we walk in love, the more intimate our time with Him becomes.

Do you want more of God's power in your life? Then aim to walk in love with everything within you. Determine above all else to do what you believe God's love would do. You *can* do it!

b a c k u p :
John 15:9-11

d o w n l o a d :
Leviticus 8-9; Luke 9

v o i c e a c t i v a t e :
God is love. As I dwell and continue in God, He dwells and continues in me; and love is brought to completion and attains perfection in me. 1 John 4:16-17, AMP

* Donald Gee, *The Fruit of the Spirit* [Springfield: Gospel Publishing House, 1928], p. 60, used by permission of the publisher.

gloria

february 16

gloria

Have faith in God. For assuredly, I say to you, whoever says to this mountain, 'Be removed and be cast into the sea,' and does not doubt in his heart, but believes that those things he says will be done, he will have whatever he says. Therefore I say to you, whatever things you ask when you pray, believe that you receive them, and you will have them.
Mark 11:22-24, NKJV

It's Not What You Know...

Notice Jesus didn't say we should believe we've received what we ask for *when we see it?* He said to believe you receive *when you pray.*

Now, if you follow His instructions, how do you think you're going to act? Are you going to walk around depressed? Are you going to mope around worrying?

No! You're going to be thrilled and thank God for the answer to your prayer. You're going to act like you've already received it.

That's where most people miss it. They know God's Word works, but they don't act on it.

You may have been studying the Bible since you were five years old. You may be the Bible trivia buff at a Christian school. You may know how to live the Christian life better than anyone around. But remember, it's not what you know that will bring you through—it's what you do.

You can walk through ten trials and have great success. Yet on the eleventh one, if you don't act on what the Word says, you'll fail. Although you've had a string of great victories, it's what you do *today* that will get you through today's trouble.

So set your heart and mind on doing what the Bible says...in every situation. Believe you receive your answer when you pray...and enjoy the victory!

backup:
1 John 3:19-22

download:
Leviticus 10-11; Luke 10

voice activate:
Whatever things I ask when I pray, I believe I receive them, and I will have them! Mark 11:24

"For surely, O Lord, you bless the righteous; you surround them with your favor as with a shield."
Psalm 5:12

A Firewall of Favor

It doesn't matter what kind of trouble you may find yourself in at school, at home or at work. God's favor is always strong enough to get you out! All you have to do is tap into it...by faith.

If you want to enjoy God's favor in your life, start believing it's there. Get into the Bible. Put His promises into your heart and speak them aloud. Begin to believe what God's Word says and act on it.

If you'll do that, you won't be defeated in any area of your life. Because there is no situation, no circumstance, no disaster—nothing Satan has ever done or can do—that is stronger than God's favor.

The Apostle Paul proved that. He faced more trouble than most of us could ever imagine. He gives a list of the things that happened to him in 2 Corinthians 11:23-29—beatings, stonings, jail, shipwrecks.

Paul said those things came to him because an evil spirit had been sent to stop him. This evil spirit came to stop him from preaching the truth. Paul called the spirit *"a thorn in my flesh"* (2 Corinthians 12:7).

That demon worked hard to shut Paul's mouth and throw him off course,

but nothing worked. Why? God's favor was with Paul.

Remember that when troubles come against you. When Satan is trying to mess up your life and it looks like there's absolutely no way out of a problem, don't lose hope. God's power comes through in those situations. His favor is always enough to bring you out on top.

So speak to that trouble you're facing today. Say: *"I'm a child of God and I know the Bible says His favor surrounds me like a shield. It can easily pull me out of this trouble. So I put my faith is this promise from God to me. I believe His favor is surrounding me and I'm coming out of this a winner!"*

backup:
Acts 7:8-10

download:
Leviticus 12-13; Luke 11

voice activate:
The Lord blesses me because I am righteous. He surrounds me with His favor like a shield. Psalm 5:12

"Jesus stood up and commanded the wind and the waves to stop. He said, 'Quiet! Be still!' Then the wind stopped, and the lake became calm."
Mark 4:39, NCV

Say What You Want to See

For years I have believed that Christians need to speak directly to the situations in their lives that they want to change, but what do you say to those situations?

The answer is simple. You say what you want to see. Nothing more. Look at today's verse. *"Quiet! Be still!"* is all Jesus had to say to end a violent storm.

We need to follow His example.

There's no telling what you or I would have said to that storm, but Jesus just spoke what he expected to see happen— and He never looked back.

How could He be so certain? Well, He knew how strong His words were. He knew without question that Almighty God backed Him and caused what He said to happen.

When you speak in faith, you can be just as confident. God is backing your faith just as surely as He backed Jesus' faith. So speak to your situation with confidence today, and say what you expect to see.

backup:
Mark 11:13-14,20-21

download:
Leviticus 14-15; Luke 12

voice activate:
As I speak in faith, I don't doubt in my heart. I believe that what I say will happen. It is done for me. Mark 11:23

"Glory and honour are in his [God's] presence; strength and gladness are in his place."
1 Chronicles 16:27, KJV

God Is a Heavyweight

You can see the signs all around you—we are nearing the end of time. God's getting ready to move—and His glory will be seen. We need to *expect it!*

When I say we need to expect God's glory, most Christians nod their heads and say, "Yes, sure," without having any idea of what I am talking about.

To them, God's glory is just a vague, religious term or some kind of spiritual thrill that leaves them with goose bumps every now and then.

Listen, God's glory isn't a goose bump. It's much more than that, and before we can begin to expect it, we must know what it is.

First Chronicles says glory and honor are in God's presence. However, the word *glory* in the English language is really kind of pitiful. It can mean splendor, but it can also refer to boasting and pride. Those things have nothing to do with God's glory.

In the original Hebrew, this word translated *glory* means "desire, adornment, honor, beauty, majesty, cleanliness, purity, preciousness, rarity, weight and heaviness." So when you say God is glorious, you're really saying that God is a heavyweight—heavy with everything good. He is heavy in love. Heavy in healing. Heavy in rescuing power. Heavy in salvation. If you need to be rescued from anything, God is heavy enough to do it!

What we're talking about here is *living* in the heavy weight of God's goodness, desire, adornment, honor, beauty, majesty, cleanliness, purity, preciousness and rarity.

In these end times, those things are going to be seen more and more. We're going to see God's glory right here on earth! In our homes! In our schools! In the streets! Expect it! Who knows, you may even get some goose bumps.

b a c k u p :
Matthew 17:1-8

d o w n l o a d :
Leviticus 16-18; Luke 13-14

v o i c e a c t i v a t e :
In the presence of God there are glory and honor and strength and gladness. 1 Chronicles 16:27

february 20

kenneth

"You will be blessed when you come in and blessed when you go out."
Deuteronomy 28:6

Dreaming Beyond the Possible

People always talk about one day building their "dream home." Did you know that you can build dreams out of God's Word? Oh, yeah! A good foundation for them is Deuteronomy 28. I can tell you from experience, the truth found here is good dream-building material.

God intended for us to be dreamers. He made us that way. He didn't intend for us to be limited by the things around us. He meant for us to dream beyond them. He meant for us to dream about doing things—today and tomorrow—that are far beyond what naturally seems possible.

That's what Abraham did. He locked into God's dream—and it was bigger than anything he could have thought up on his own.

It will be that way for you, too. God's dream is bigger than your dream for yourself. It is *way more* than you could ask for or even think up! (Ephesians 3:20)

Once you get that dream inside you, things will begin to change. No, all your problems won't disappear overnight. But you'll react to them differently.

When trouble rises up in front of you and threatens to defeat you, God's dream will stir in your heart.

You'll start saying, "Wait just a minute. I'm on top of this thing, not stuck underneath. I don't have to put up with this situation. I happen to be a child of God! No weapon used against me can defeat me!" (See Deuteronomy 28:13 and Isaiah 54:17.)

Building your dream home is great...but building God's dreams inside of you, and then seeing those dreams come to pass, is even better.

b a c k u p :
Psalm 23

d o w n l o a d :
Leviticus 19-20; Luke 15

v o i c e   a c t i v a t e :
I am blessed when I come in and blessed when I go out. Deuteronomy 28:6

"For if because of one man's trespass...death reigned through that one, much more surely will those who receive [God's] overflowing grace...and the free gift of righteousness...reign as kings in life through the One, Jesus Christ, (the Messiah, the Anointed One)."
Romans 5:17, AMP

Superabundance

In Deuteronomy 28, God told the Israelites that if they would listen carefully to Him and do what He said, He would set them high above all nations. He told them to carefully follow His Word because He knew Satan was out there, continuously working to destroy them.

If they obeyed God, He promised to bless them—not just a little here and there, but in every area of their lives. He said they'd be blessed wherever they went. Their children would be blessed. Their crops and livestock would be blessed. All their work and savings would be blessed. He said their enemies would run away at the sight of them. God didn't leave anything out!

In spite of Satan's rulership over the world at that time, God made a way— through His Word—for His people to live the most wonderful life anyone could imagine: The life of a king! He desired for His people to be so blessed the whole world would know, just by looking at them, that they belonged to God.

Think about that. When God's people are doing well, even the ungodly are forced to say, "Hey, those people serve a living, powerful God!"

Today's verse clearly says He wants us to live like kings. Now, because of what Jesus did for us, and the power of the Holy Spirit inside us, we *can* live like kings—not just physically, but spiritually too. He wants us to know that He is willing and able to do for us *"superabundantly, far over and above all that we [dare] ask or think—infinitely beyond our highest prayers, desires, thoughts, hopes or dreams"* (Ephesians 3:20, AMP).

He wants us to believe His Word and act on it. He wants us to walk upright before Him. He wants our lives to astonish the world. He wants us to be so assured of His goodness that we can stop being concerned about ourselves and start reaching out to others. He wants us to live like kings!

backup:
Psalm 67

download:
Leviticus 21-22; Luke 16

voice activate:
I have received God's overflowing grace and the free gift of righteousness. I reign in life as a king through Jesus Christ. Romans 5:17, AMP

gloria

february 22

gloria

"Be self-controlled and alert. Your enemy the devil prowls around like a roaring lion looking for someone to devour. Resist him, standing firm in the faith, because you know that your brothers throughout the world are undergoing the same kind of sufferings."
1 Peter 5:8-9

Talk...Talk... Talk

Satan is a salesman. He makes a presentation and tries to sell you his line of products. He tells you God doesn't really love you. He tells you God's promises are just words. He tells you that you don't have the strength to go on. He'll even try to sell you on the idea that it would be easier for you just to curl up and die than to see this trouble through.

All he does is talk...talk...talk, and lie...lie...lie. His talking can get very annoying, but remember, that's all he can do! He doesn't have any real power over you.

According to 1 Peter 5:8, he *"prowls around like a roaring lion looking for someone to devour."* It doesn't say he *is* a lion. He just acts like one. Therefore, he can't devour you—unless you let him.

First Peter 5:9 says we are to resist Satan and stand firm. That means you have to use patience to resist him. He is, after all, very persistent. He may pester you a thousand times a day, but if you'll patiently resist him every time, he will tuck his tail and run (James 4:7).

He and all the low-level demons he sends to aggravate you have already

"come to nothing" (1 Corinthians 2:6). Jesus has ripped away all their power and authority and left them with nothing. (See Colossians 2:15.)

So the next time Satan starts his sales pitch, *talk back.*

"I am brand new in Jesus. I am filled with the Holy Spirit. I have been given the Name of Jesus, which is *'far above all rule and authority, power and dominion, and every title that can be given, not only in the present age but also in the one to come.'* (Ephesians 1:21). Greater is the One in me, than the one who is in the world (1 John 4:4). So, Satan, leave me alone in Jesus' Name!" (James 4:7).

b a c k u p :
Psalm 112

d o w n l o a d :
Leviticus 23-24; Luke 17

v o i c e a c t i v a t e :
I resist the devil and stand firm in faith. He will not devour me, because the One Who is in me is greater than the one who is in the world! 1 Peter 5:8-9; 1 John 4:4

"There is therefore now no condemnation to those who are in Christ Jesus, who do not walk according to the flesh, but according to the Spirit."
Romans 8:1, NKJV

Free From Condemnation

There's one serious mistake we often make that trips us up and keeps us from winning in life: Letting Satan put us under condemnation.

Condemnation will weaken your spirit. Yet we use condemnation on ourselves and each other all the time.

That's what happened to me. I fought cigarettes with everything I had. I threw away more than I smoked. I knew I shouldn't be smoking them, but after I became a Christian, I went from one and a half packs a day to three packs a day.

Some people would say that was proof I wasn't a Christian, but they'd be wrong. I was a Christian. I knew it!

Two and a half months later, I received the Holy Spirit. Still, I was fighting those cigarettes with both hands and feet. Why? My spirit was trying to get me to quit, but my body was fighting to keep doing what it had been trained to do. Every time I lit up a cigarette, it would tear me up inside. I felt so condemned!

I finally went to a meeting in Houston and heard someone preach that Jesus was coming back. You know, the Bible says when you put your hope in Jesus' return, it will purify you, and that's what it did for me. I walked away from that meeting without any desire for tobacco. Years have come and gone since then and I haven't had any desire for it at all.

If you're struggling with something, strengthen your spirit by not putting up with condemnation. Learn to say, "There is no condemnation to those who are in Jesus—and that's me. So I'm not condemned. I'm not just going to do whatever my old sinful nature wants to do." Before long, you'll be free of that thing...and free of condemnation.

kenneth

backup:
Hebrews 10:1-17

download:
Leviticus 25-26; Luke 18

voice activate:
I am in Christ Jesus. I do not walk according to the flesh, but according to the Spirit. I am free of condemnation. Romans 8:1

february 24

"My son, pay attention to what I say; listen closely to my words. Do not let them [the Word of God] out of your sight, keep them within your heart; for they are life to those who find them and health to a man's whole body. Above all else, guard your heart, for it is the wellspring of life. Put away perversity from your mouth; keep corrupt talk far from your lips."
Proverbs 4:20-24

gloria

The Healer

There is a medicine so powerful it can cure every sickness and disease known to man. It has no dangerous side effects. It's safe even in massive doses, and when taken daily, it can prevent illness altogether and keep people in perfect health.

I can tell you by God's Word and by my own experience that such a medicine exists. You don't have to call your doctor to get it. You don't even have to hitch a ride to the pharmacy. All you have to do is reach for your Bible, open it to Proverbs 4:20-24 and follow the instructions there.

As simple as they might sound, those five verses contain the supernatural pre-scription to divine health. It's a powerful prescription that will work for anyone who will put it to work.

If you know someone who needs healing, it will give them strength until they are completely healed. Also, it will help you stay healthy for the rest of your life.

These five verses teach people how to keep their attention trained on God's Word—not the way their body feels—so that they can be like Abraham who *did not consider his own body*" (Romans 4:19, NKJV). Instead

of focusing on circumstances, the person who has symptoms of sickness can focus on what God has said in His Word.

You can show them how to see themselves well and healed in every way.

The things we focus on determine what we believe in our heart and what we do. With this in mind, show those who are sick how to make God's Word their number one priority. Show them how to keep taking God's medicine as directed and trust the Great Physician to do His healing work!

backup:
Deuteronomy 7:8-15

download:
Leviticus 27; Numbers 1; Luke 19

voice activate:
I pay attention to what God says and listen closely to His Word. I don't let God's Word out of my sight. I keep it within my heart, for it is life to me and health to my whole body. Above all else, I guard my heart for it is the wellspring of life. I choose to allow that life to flow from me to others around me. I put per-versity from my mouth and keep corrupt talk far from my lips. Proverbs 4:20-24

"But Christ [the Anointed One and His Anointing]...was faithful over His [own Father's] house as a Son [and Master of it]. And it is we who are [now members of] this house, if we hold fast and firm to the end our joyful and exultant confidence and sense of triumph in our hope [in Christ]." Hebrews 3:6, AMP

Draw on the Power

Did you know that you could live near something and never take part in it? Sure you could. You could live right across the street from a baseball field and never watch a game. You could go to school with a hundred drama students and never enjoy a play. It's no different with God's power. As a Christian, you can live with it, but never draw on it.

So how can you be sure to tap into God's power? By faith, of course!

"Well, I don't have much faith."

Yes, you do. If you've made Jesus the Lord of your life, you have great faith. To consider just how great it is, read Hebrews 11. That's where all the Old Testament heroes of faith are listed. Usually when we read about those people, we want to be like them, but Hebrews 11:40 says God has *"planned something better for us!"*

That means you have more faith than those Bible heroes did. Think about that. You have more faith inside you than

Moses did when he split the Red Sea! God gave it to you when you made Jesus your Lord. First John 5:4 says, *"for everyone born of God overcomes the world. This is the victory that has overcome the world, even our faith."*

You're born of God. You have His spiritual genes and they include world-overcoming faith! What's more, according to Hebrews 3:1-6, you have the power to use that faith. You live in it...now take part in it!

b a c k u p :
Hebrews 11

d o w n l o a d :
Numbers 2-3; Luke 20

v o i c e a c t i v a t e :
I am born of God and I overcome the world! 1 John 5:4

gloria

"As the One Who called you is holy, you yourselves also be holy in all your conduct and manner of living."
1 Peter 1:15, AMP

Set Apart for God

Let me ask you a question. Do you want to see God move in your life, your school, your household and your world like never before? Then you must live a holy life.

That's just the truth and we all need to know it. As wonderful and vast as the coming great move of God is going to be, the fact is, not everyone will be a part of it. He will only use those who have set themselves apart to Him.

In other words, if you and I want in on this great move of God, we must follow after holiness!

Holiness is separation unto God. It also describes the conduct of those who are separated. To be separate means to be set apart or to disengage as cream separates from milk and rises to the top. If we want to be holy, we must be disconnected from the world and its ways—and connected to God and His ways.

"We're just human beings. Is it really possible for us to be holy?"

Yes, it is, because we've made Jesus our Lord. When that happened, we were separated to God on the *inside*. Now God expects us to live out that separation so it can be seen on the *outside*. Holiness isn't a strange thing that just a few people achieve. Holiness is the way all Christians should walk.

We shouldn't look, talk and act like the world. We should look, talk and act like God! We've been commanded: *Be holy! In all your conduct and manner of living.* So set your way. You can do it. Live from the inside out. Walk holy before God.

backup:
2 Timothy 2:19-21; Hebrews 12:14

download:
Numbers 4-6; Luke 21-22

voice activate:
Because God is holy, I am also holy in all I do. 1 Peter 1:15

"I will show wonders in the heaven above and signs on the earth below, blood and fire and billows of smoke. The sun will be turned to darkness and the moon to blood before the coming of the great and glorious day of the Lord."
Acts 2:19-20

Sitting on the Edge of His Seat

All my life, my Mama said, "Kenneth, Jesus is coming this year."

I would say, "Is that right, Mama?"

"Yes," she'd say, "He's coming this year, so you had better get yourself straightened out!"

Even though Jesus didn't come when Mama said, she was right—JESUS IS COMING! I don't know when, but I *do* know He's coming—sooner than most people think.

We are living in a whole new time frame. From the very beginning, God has given us the time frame in which He will work with mankind. It's a seven-day time frame—where a day is as a thousand years. For example, we see in Genesis that God created the earth in six days, and rested on the seventh. Then He gave mankind a 6,000-year lease on the earth. Jesus was born 4,000 years into that time frame—or on the fourth day. For all practical purposes, 2,000 years have come and gone since Jesus' ministry—which is 6,000 years since Adam was created.

Where does that put us on our spiritual clock? We have entered that sliver of time between Adam's lease on earth and the period of time we read about in today's verses. You and I are being squeezed between 6,000 years of time behind us and another 1,000 years ahead of us. The 1,000 years facing us is the time when Jesus will reign over the earth, which is the first time since Adam's fall that humanity will be totally and completely out of contact with Satan.

I'm telling you, Jesus is coming! He's about to rise off His heavenly throne and return to earth. He may not have stood up yet, but I guarantee you, He is on the edge of His seat!

backup:
1 Thessalonians 4:13-5:11

download:
Numbers 7:1-48; Luke 23

voice activate:
Jesus is coming soon! He will show wonders in heaven above and signs on the earth below. I prepare myself for that great and glorious day. Acts 2:19-20

february 28

gloria

"For we are members of His body, of His flesh and of His bones."
Ephesians 5:30, NKJV

The Greater One Lives in You!

Today, if anyone is going to see Jesus, they'll have to see Him through Christians. We're His physical Body! If His Body doesn't preach the good news, the good news doesn't get preached. If His Body doesn't reach out to the hurting, then His ministry to them is cut short.

That thought surprises some people. They think Jesus changed somehow after He rose again and went to heaven. They think He stopped being interested in ministering personally to people like He did when He was on earth, but Jesus didn't change. He is the same yesterday, today and forever (Hebrews 13:8). He still wants to preach the good news to people. He still wants to cast out demons and heal the sick. He still has the power to do all those things—and even more! (John 14:12)

How does He get them done? Through you and me.

Point your finger at yourself right now and say out loud, "I am the Body of Jesus. He is living in me right now!"

When that truth comes alive in you, impossible tasks won't overwhelm you anymore. You won't give up, because you'll know that God is in you, and He has the power to get the job done. When He calls you to preach and you can't talk very well, you'll just say, "Well, that's all right. Jesus is in me and He'll give me the words." When someone who's sick comes to you for prayer, you won't want to bolt and run. You'll be eager to pray for that person because you'll know the Healer lives in you.

The Greater One lives in you! Now believe it! Live like it!

backup:
1 John 4:1-6

download:
Numbers 7:49-78; Luke 24

voice activate:
The One Who is in me is greater than the one who is in the world! 1 John 4:4

"The one who sent me is with me; he has not left me alone, for I always do what pleases him."
John 8:29

You Are Under His Training

Jesus lived by faith. Did you know that? Some people don't realize that. They think that because He was the Son of God, He just floated through life, but He didn't. Jesus lived by faith—and He got that faith the same way we get it. *"Faith comes by hearing, and hearing by the word of God"* (Romans 10:17, NKJV).

How do you think His mother knew to tell the leaders of the Cana wedding feast to do whatever He told them? (See John 2:1-11.) How did she know He could solve the problem? Because even though He hadn't yet performed a miracle, He had always lived by faith.

Year by year, He grew in faith, just as He grew physically. He wasn't born a faith giant. He had to develop, just as we do. He said, *"As my Father taught me, I speak these things"* (John 8:28, NKJV).

Jesus had to be taught. How was He taught? By the Holy Spirit through the written Word! Luke 4:16 says that when Jesus came to Nazareth, *"on the Sabbath day he went into the synagogue, as was his custom."*

Jesus was a Bible reader! That was His custom. He studied. He learned. He preached what the Bible said. He knew the truth and the truth made Him free!

Now, more than ever, we need to follow in His footsteps. Our Father needs us to grow up in Him. He needs people who will dare to stand on His Word and develop their faith. When you do, you won't just start following after the miracles someone else performs...you'll be the one God uses to perform the miracles! *That* is the greatest thrill of all, and that is the day we're living in.

backup:

John 2:1-11

voice activate:

Without faith it is impossible to please God. I determine to live by faith so I will always please Him. Hebrews 11:6

kenneth

"For anyone who speaks in a tongue does not speak to men but to God. Indeed, no one understands him; he utters mysteries with his spirit."
1 Corinthians 14:2

march 1

gloria

Unlock the Mysteries

What are mysteries? Mysteries are things we don't know. Sometimes we don't know exactly what steps to take and what moves to make each day to fulfill the plan God has laid out for us, and nobody in the world can tell us!

As 1 Corinthians 2:9-10 says, *"No eye has seen, no ear has heard, no mind has conceived what God has prepared for those who love him'—but God has revealed it to us by his Spirit."*

When you pray in the spirit, you'll get answers. The answers to your circumstances will rise up inside you. You'll get a word. A sentence. You'll begin to understand things you've never understood before!

God has things for us that are so much better than what we can imagine, that we can't even figure them out. If we pray in the spirit, we'll get beyond what little we know and get into what God knows. Spend time praying in the spirit every day. Tap into what God knows. Receive wisdom from heaven, and unlock the mysteries of God's plan for your life!

backup:
Jude 1:17-21

download:
Numbers 7:79-89, 8; John 1

voice activate:
When I speak in other tongues, I don't speak to men, but to God. I unlock the mysteries of God and receive wisdom from heaven. 1 Corinthians 14:2

"Is not this the kind of fasting I have chosen: to loose the chains of injustice and untie the cords of the yoke, to set the oppressed free and break every yoke?"
Isaiah 58:6

The Flood Is on Its Way!

The fast mentioned in today's verse is talking about a *lifestyle*. It is more than just a refrain from eating. It is a commitment that says, "I'm putting aside the worldly things and focusing on God. I'll get down on my knees and pray until I'm 100 percent committed to Jesus. Then, once I'm free, I will pray for others so they can get free too!"

Do you know what that kind of fast will do for you? To get an idea, all you have to do is look at Jesus. He went out, led by the Holy Spirit, into the wilderness for forty days. While He was out there, He fasted and prayed just as Isaiah described.

When Jesus left that place of fasting, His service to God was empowered. From the earthly perspective, it looked like people being healed of sickness and disease. It looked like the dead being raised. It looked like people's needs being met in supernatural ways. In the spiritual perspective, it looked like a dam had broken and a flood of spiritual power had been released. The same can happen in your life!

Right now, God is calling you and me to the same place of fasting that He called Jesus. He's calling us to separate ourselves to Him. He's calling us to develop a deep hunger to know Him and follow Him.

Don't wait another moment. Answer that call right now. Get down on your knees and say, "Lord, I'll do anything You want me to do. I'll be everything You've made me to be. No matter what it takes, I want You to move through me."

Now get ready...the dam has broken and the flood is on the way!

kenneth

backup:
Matthew 4:1-11

download:
Numbers 9-10; John 2

voice activate:
I am putting aside the worldly things that have kept me bound. I am like a well-watered garden, like a spring whose waters never fail. Isaiah 58:11

"**If anyone does not remain in me, he is like a branch that is thrown away and withers.**"
John 15:6

Overloaded With His Spirit

Jesus said if we want to bear fruit we must remain in Him. The word *remain* simply means staying somewhere continually.

Contrary to what many people think, you cannot live from Sunday to Sunday without spiritual food. You can't spend time with the Lord once a week at church or youth group, ignore Him the rest of the time, and still expect Him to be Lord of all you're doing. John 15:6 makes that clear.

The moment a branch is broken off the vine, it begins to die. It doesn't matter how close they are to one another. You can lay that branch beside the vine, but if they're not connected, there will be no life flow of sap traveling from the vine into the branch.

The same is true for us. When we get too busy to spend time with God in prayer and in His Word, when we get preoccupied with everyday things and disconnect from spending time with Him, we immediately begin to wither. We begin to lose spiritual energy when we aren't living in close contact with the Lord. Even though we still belong to Him and have His life within us, His energy is not flowing through us so we can't produce anything.

Suddenly, even when we know the right thing to do, we find ourselves lacking the power to do it. We need strength to bear fruit!

On the other hand, when you do remain in the Vine, you're sure to bear fruit. It *has* to happen! The Holy Spirit's power flowing through you will just naturally make what God has placed within you come out, and you will begin to act like the loving, joyful, peaceful, patient, kind, good, faithful, gentle and self-controlled person you really are! You will overflow with His fruit!

b a c k u p :
John 15:1-8

d o w n l o a d :
Numbers 11-12; John 3

v o i c e   a c t i v a t e :
I remain in Jesus and I overflow with His fruit! John 15:5

"It shall come to pass in that day That his burden will be taken away from your shoulder, And his yoke from your neck, And the yoke will be destroyed because of the anointing oil."
Isaiah 10:27, NKJV

The Yoke Destroyer

Ever since Adam blew it, Satan has been using people as slaves. He has clamped his yoke around their necks and burdened them down with sin, sickness, failure, poverty and every other thing hell could devise.

Everyone has felt the terrible weight of that burden. We've all experienced the pain and frustration that comes from struggling free of one thing, just to have Satan yank us around and pile on even more.

For thousands of years, that yoke of bondage was the inescapable tragedy of man's existence. It looked as though there would never be a way out, but the prophet Isaiah looked forward to a time when a redeemer was coming. One Who would finally free us from Satan's oppression.

To fully appreciate just how good that news is, you must realize that Isaiah doesn't say the yoke of bondage will be broken because of the anointing. Many people read the verse that way, but that's not what it says. It says the yoke will be *destroyed*.

When you look it up in the Hebrew, you'll find the word translated *destroyed* means "absolutely useless." It's possible that a broken yoke could be repaired and put back. However, Isaiah said this anointing would annihilate Satan's yoke so completely, there would no longer be any evidence that it was ever on your neck!

That means every time you allow God's Anointing to destroy a yoke in your life, whether it's for your health, your finances, your relationships or your past, it is literally, utterly destroyed and cannot be repaired to be used again. Satan can't pick it up and hold you in bondage with it again. Now, that's good news!

b a c k u p :
Isaiah 61:1-3

d o w n l o a d :
Numbers 13-14; John 4

v o i c e   a c t i v a t e :
The anointing of Jesus has destroyed every yoke of bondage in my life.
Isaiah 10:27

"'Do not be afraid, Abram. I am your shield, your very great reward.'"
Genesis 15:1

march 5

gloria

A Child of Promise

God promised Abraham many things. Genesis 12:2 records God's first promise to him: "'*I will make you into a great nation and I will bless you; I will make your name great, and you will be a blessing.*'"

To fully grasp what God was saying here, you must realize that when He blesses someone, He's not just telling them to have a good day. He is giving them the power to do well in every area of life. It was actually God's blessing that made Abraham rich and caused him to do great wherever he went. It also made him a winner. Abraham could conquer any enemy that came against him or his family.

Genesis 14 tells of the time when Lot and his family were taken captive by wicked kings who made war on Sodom and Gomorrah. Abraham and his servants single-handedly whipped four kings and their armies, then recovered everything and everyone that had been taken captive!

What gave Abraham the boldness to go after those kings? He knew God had promised to be an enemy to his enemies, and he dared to believe and act on that promise. Abraham understood that God was *God!* Abraham took God at His Word

when God told him not to be afraid in Genesis 15:1.

We need to do the same thing. We need to take that promise and put our name in it. After all, we're Abraham's descendants, so that promise is for us!

Years ago, when Ken and I first started following the Lord, we were facing overwhelming debts and problems. So I took that promise and put my name in it. I read: *Don't be afraid, Gloria. I am your shield, your very great reward!*

I decided that those words were just as true for me as they were for Abraham. Since then, God has rewarded me beyond anything I could ask. He has been as faithful to me as He was to Abraham. He will be just as faithful to you!

God keeps His promises. Whatever you need today, His Word has a promise to cover your need. Find it and put *your* name in it. Then receive it!

backup:
Genesis 14:12-15:1

download:
Numbers 15-17; John 5-6

voice activate:
I am not afraid because God is my shield and my very great reward. Genesis 15:1

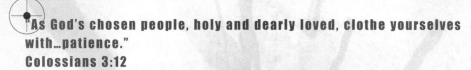

The Zero Hour

The most critical time when you're believing God for something is *after* you pray...but *before* you actually see the answer.

This is the critical time when things are being set in motion by your faith, even though you can't *see* anything. It's the time when you're the most tempted to say, "Nothing is happening. I prayed and believed, but I don't have it. It looks like I never will. I guess I just don't have enough faith."

You may *want* to say that—but don't! The Bible says that every believer has received *"the measure of faith"* (Romans 12:3). You don't need more faith. What you need is something to strengthen and undergird the faith you have, so it will continue working until the answer comes. What you need is *patience*.

Patience is one of the characteristics God placed inside you when you became a Christian. It does not give in to tough times. It doesn't quit believing. Patience undergirds faith to keep it stable and strong when circumstances say, "It's impossible!"

Patience is the opposite of hopelessness. Ephesians 2:12 says that people who are not Christians are *"without hope"* and are *"without God in the world."*

We are not in the world without a Savior. We have *"the hope held out in the gospel"* (Colossians 1:23), and patience is associated with hope. Patience, you see, will hold on. It knows, "I have a promise from God, and I *will* stand. I *will* endure until the answer comes."

The force of patience is so powerful that it cannot be overcome. If you'll exercise the patience inside you, it will be there when you need it to help you stand. It will undergird your faith to keep you believing until the answer comes.

So, the next time you're tempted to say, "It's not working," give way to the force of patience instead. Faith and patience working together will make you a winner...and help you through the critical times!

⊕ *b a c k u p :*
Psalm 128

⊕ *d o w n l o a d :*
Numbers 18-19; John 7

⊕ *v o i c e   a c t i v a t e :*
Because I have God, I am not without hope. My hope is in the gospel. I will be patient and endure until my answers come. Ephesians 2:12; Colossians 1:23

"I tell you the truth, anyone who has faith in me will do what I have been doing. He will do even greater things than these, because I am going to the Father."
John 14:12

march 7

gloria

Turn the World Right-Side Up

If you want to receive God-given spiritual gifts, it won't happen until you start reaching out to others. As much as you might want, you can't wait until you receive the gift of healing, for example, before you go and pray for someone who's sick.

God's power shows up as you reach out. When you step out and do things like Jesus did, the Holy Spirit will back you up with His power.

When it comes down to it, power is what people of the world are looking for today. They have problems with no answers. They're sick. They're abusing alcohol and drugs. They're failing. Satan has turned their lives so upside down, they don't know where to go or what to do to fix things.

People like that don't care very much about what you believe. They don't care if you pray in the spirit and dance in the aisles, or sit up straight and sing out of a hymnal. If you have the power to get their bodies healed and their lives straightened out, they'll show up wher-

ever you are. Not only that, they'll listen to what you say.

God wants us to have the same reputation Jesus had when He was on the earth. He wants people to say about us what they said about the disciples: "If you get around them, you can get healed."

Now that's exciting. In fact, you haven't had any excitement until you've started doing things like Jesus did. It's a blast to be on fire, going all-out for God. When you live like that, you never know what's going to happen. You don't know where you'll wind up or who you'll touch or what amazing things the Holy Spirit will do next, but you will know this: You're doing what God created you to do. You're destroying Satan's works, and turning this upside-down world right side up again!

backup:
Luke 10:17-20

download:
Numbers 20-21; John 8

voice activate:
I do the works of Jesus because I have faith in Him. John 14:12

"God has said, 'Never will I leave you; never will I forsake you.' So we say with confidence, 'The Lord is my helper; I will not be afraid. What can man do to me?'"
Hebrews 13:5-6

Shatter the Fear

Without courage, you'll never be able to believe God for anything. You won't be able to receive what God has promised you, because fear will come and steal the faith right out of your heart.

The moment you fear is the moment you fail. When fear begins, faith ends. It takes courage to shatter that creeping fear and push it back further and further until "I will not fear" is a reality in your life.

I can't count how many times I have had to break away from fear. One memorable time was when God told us to start our TV broadcast. I really struggled with it. I wanted it, but I knew how expensive it was, and I couldn't even figure out where to start—much less how.

So Gloria and I began to pray and talk about what God said about it. We studied His promises to us and focused on His ability instead of our inability.

This went on for a long time. Then one morning, as we ate our breakfast and discussed the television ministry, the faith I needed dropped into my heart. I looked at Gloria and realized by the look

on her face that the same thing had happened to her.

"Gloria," I said, "tomorrow is Monday. Let's make arrangements to go on television."

Suddenly, it looked easy. We didn't have the money, but we had the faith, and if you have the faith, the money will come.

The courage came as I spent time discovering God's promises in the Bible. As I thought and prayed about what He said, my capacity for faith grew, until one day I thought, *There's not any reason not to do this! I can do all things through Him!* I broke through—from fear to faith. It takes courage to do that...courage that comes from God's Word.

backup:
Psalm 27

download:
Numbers 22-23; John 9

voice activate:
The Lord is my helper and I will not be afraid, for what can man do to me? The Lord will never leave me and will never forsake me. Hebrews 13:5-6

march 9

gloria

"For this very reason, make every effort to add to your faith goodness; and to goodness, knowledge; and to knowledge, self-control; and to self-control, perseverance; and to perseverance, godliness; and to godliness, brotherly kindness; and to brotherly kindness, love. For if you possess these qualities in increasing measure, they will keep you from being ineffective and unproductive in your knowledge of our Lord Jesus Christ...Therefore, my brothers, be all the more eager to make your calling and election sure. For if you do these things, you will never fall."
2 Peter 1:5-8,10

The Real You

When I realized what these verses were saying, I determined to have the fruit of the spirit in my life—because I want to be a winner!

Many people may not realize that the fruit of the spirit can be a part of our lives, but as a Christian, these qualities are supernaturally a part of who you are. When you made Jesus your Lord, you became *"a new creation"* (2 Corinthians 5:17). Your spirit was remade in the image of your heavenly Father. You began to share in His divine nature (2 Peter 1:4).

- God is loving by nature. First John 4:8 says, *"God is love."*
- God is joyful by nature. Psalm 16:11 (NKJV) says, *"In Your presence is fullness of joy."*
- God is good by nature. Exodus 34:6 (NKJV) says the Lord is *"abounding in goodness."*
- God is peaceful by nature. Philippians 4:9 says He is *"the God of peace."*
- God is patient by nature. Numbers 14:18 (NKJV) says, *"The Lord is longsuffering [patient] and abundant in mercy."*

- God is gentle by nature. David said to Him in Psalm 18:35 (NKJV), *"Your gentleness has made me great."*
- God is faithful by nature. Psalm 119:90 says, *"Your faithfulness continues through all generations."*
- God is humble by nature. Jesus—Who is exactly like the Father—said, *"I am... humble"* (Matthew 11:29, NIV).

We know that by nature, God has self-control, because if He did not, none of us would be here.

The reason I made this list is because I wanted you to see that all the fruit of the spirit are part of God's nature. Since you've been re-created in His image, they are also part of *your* nature! It's who you really are!

backup:
Psalm 101

download:
Numbers 24-25; John 10

voice activate:
I am not ineffective and unproductive in my knowledge of Jesus, because I make every effort to possess the fruit of the spirit in increasing measure in my life. 2 Peter 1:5-8

"How much more is done by the blood of Christ. He offered himself through the eternal Spirit as a perfect sacrifice to God. His blood will make our hearts clean from useless acts. We are made pure so that we may serve the living God."
Hebrews 9:14, NCV

When You Make a Mistake

Christians make mistakes. Sometimes we flat-out miss God. That doesn't mean we're looking for a way to sin and get out of it. No, we're looking for a way to get sin out of our lives and grow in God.

That's why it is so vitally important to realize the Bible is not a religious book. It is the copy of an unbreakable promise—a covenant—between you and God.

It's sworn in blood. Both the Old Covenant and the New are blood-sworn oaths to us, but there is a big difference between them.

The Old Covenant, first recorded in Genesis, was between Abraham and God, and sworn in the blood of animals. God told Abraham to kill specific animals and lay them out a certain way. God walked in the blood and passed between those animals, and that convinced Abraham God was serious about doing what He had promised for Abraham and his descendants.

Later, under Old Testament Law, a priesthood was set in motion in order to continue to sacrifice animals. Galatians 3 says it was done because of man's sin—he kept breaking the covenant.

That's why Jesus came and established the New Covenant. Jesus is called the Lamb of God because He was the final sacrifice under the Old Covenant. When His sinless blood was shed, that settled sacrificing for sins forever. Under the old covenant, the blood of animals could only "cover" for sins, but the blood of the Lamb of God obliterates them.

When you become a Christian, the blood of Jesus does not cover up your sins, it completely annihilates them. They no longer exist. His blood washes you clean. After that, God sees you as clean. You don't have to sacrifice an animal to get forgiveness—or do anything else. You simply have to repent...and the blood of Jesus will cleanse you. He paid the price for your sin. You don't have to pay any price. You can't! There's nothing you can do to be forgiven, except ask for forgiveness and have faith in the blood.

In the same way, if Satan is making you feel guilty, you don't have to take it. Just plead the blood, like you would plead your case before a judge. Because of the blood, you're innocent, as though you'd never sinned. You've been rescued. You've been reconciled. You've been bought with the blood of Jesus.

backup:
1 John 1:7-9

download:
Numbers 26; John 11

voice activate:
Because of the blood of Jesus, God forgives my sins and purifies me from all unrighteousness. 1 John 1:9

march 11

gloria

Endure Hardship

There are no "ifs" about it. Hard times are going to come. There will be times at home, at school and at work, when circumstances seem dark. There will be times when you face seemingly impossible obstacles, times when defeat seems inevitable.

In 2 Timothy 2:3, Paul didn't tell Timothy, *"If* hard times come, endure them." He simply said, *"Endure hardship."*

Some Christians get confused when those times come. "What's happening?" they cry. "I thought Jesus rescued me from Satan!"

He did, but you can rest assured, Satan will challenge that fact. He will try his best to mess your new life up by pulling you off your walk of faith. Jesus warned us about that in Mark 4:15. He said, *"Satan comes immediately and takes away the word that was sown in their hearts"* (NKJV).

Satan will not sit by while you sail through life. He'll pressure you with hard times. He'll attack you with sickness or trouble, then he'll lie to you and tell you

that God doesn't care. He'll try to convince you that God is not going to answer your prayer this time. He'll try to talk you into believing there's no way out and that you will end up a miserable failure.

When those hard times come, don't cave in. Don't give up. Stand on God's promises to you and endure hardship like a good soldier until things turn around!

backup:
2 Timothy 2:1-7

download:
Numbers 27-28; John 12

voice activate:
I endure hardship as a good soldier of Jesus Christ. I stand on God's promises because he has given me the victory. 2 Timothy 2:3

Not Guilty

All of us struggle with bad habits at some time or another. We work hard to change them. There may be some things in your life today where it's a little hard to get control. You may have to resist Satan in those areas. You can take God's Word and put him out of commission.

In the meantime, do not allow yourself to be harassed by him or made to feel guilty. It's dangerous.

Don't let yourself or anyone else say things like, "I'm so messed up. I'm so bad. I'm so worthless." That's directly opposite of what God says. If Jesus walked through the door and stood right there for the next 20 years talking every minute of every day, He would never call you worthless. It's proven in Hebrews 2.

Jesus is not ashamed of you. Therefore, you don't have any business being ashamed of yourself!

Start believing what the Bible says. Believe that you're God's special workmanship, created in Jesus. Start saying that. Instead of talking about what a messed-up person you are, start agreeing with what God says and know that you are in right-standing with God (2 Corinthians 5:21).

Practice seeing yourself that way. Practice seeing yourself without those bad habits. After all, Jesus has already beaten them for you. So believe it today by faith!

march 12

kenneth

backup:
Hebrews 9:11-28

download:
Numbers 29-31:24; John 13-14

voice activate:
Jesus is not ashamed of me; therefore, I am not ashamed. Hebrews 2:11

"If you forgive anyone, I also forgive him. And what I have forgiven—if there was anything to forgive—I have forgiven in the sight of Christ for your sake, in order that Satan might not outwit us. For we are not unaware of his schemes." 2 Corinthians 2:10-11

march 13

gloria

Conquering the Enemies of Love

Love is the secret of our success. That's why Satan is working day in and day out to pressure us to stop loving. It's very important that we see what Satan's trying to do, because if we pretend he's not doing anything, we're more likely to fall into his traps.

We must study the Bible to know what love is. We also need to know what the enemies of love are, so when Satan tempts us with them, we can quickly recognize his strategies and say, "No, Satan! I refuse to do that."

Some people don't realize that resisting temptation is that simple, but it is! Temptation is nothing more than *an invitation to do evil*. In times of temptation, Satan comes to you like a salesman and makes you a presentation. He puts an opportunity in front of you to sin. One reason we fail to reject Satan's schemes is because we don't recognize temptation for what it is. We buy Satan's sales pitch before we even realize he's selling something to us. So we must learn his strategy.

The enemies of love are things such as *envy*. Envy is the feeling of discontent and ill will because of the advantage and success of another person.

Jealousy is also an enemy of love. To be *jealous* is to be resentfully envious and apprehensive of rivalry.

Pride, too, is listed in 1 Corinthians 13 as an enemy of love. It is an overly high opinion of yourself, exaggerated self-esteem or conceit—and it shows itself through arrogant behavior. We have to watch out for pride.

Other enemies of love include bitterness, resentment and unforgiveness. Those three things are among the biggest obstacles to walking in love, especially for people who have truly been hurt or abused.

Examine your heart. Are you walking in love, or do you see the enemies of love in your life? Love is the real secret to your success in relationships, in school, in your activities—everywhere. Make a firm decision today: I will walk in love!

backup:
Romans 13:8-10; 1 Corinthians 13:1-8

download:
Numbers 31:25-54, 32; John 15

voice activate:
I am aware of Satan's schemes. I determine to walk in love and refuse to let him outwit me. 2 Corinthians 2:10-11

> "Now about spiritual gifts, brothers, I do not want you to be ignorant.... There are different kinds of gifts, but the same Spirit....To one there is given through the Spirit the message of wisdom, to another the message of knowledge by means of the same Spirit, to another faith...."
> 1 Corinthians 12:1,4,8-9

Make the Distinction

Have you ever wondered why some people get healed while others don't? It's a very good question, one that often leaves people confused. Even ministers can get off track when they step into a meeting and God simply drops His gifts upon them. Suddenly they find themselves operating in power beyond anything they've ever experienced and they say to themselves, *I didn't do anything to get this. God just gave it to me. So maybe I should quit trying to develop faith and just let God give it as He wills.*

The reason people start thinking that way is because they fail to make the separation between the kind of faith God gives every Christian, and the special gift of faith that is described in 1 Corinthians 12.

It is a wonderful thing when God's gifts are working. It's awesome when God moves in on the scene and does things that none of us are developed in faith enough to accomplish, but here's the truth: Those special gifts of faith were not given to us for day-to-day living. It's our own faith that has to be developed and used for that purpose.

Why then does God sometimes meet day-to-day type needs through the ministry gifts? Years ago, I asked the Lord about it.

He explained, *I have sick spiritual babies all over the world. They don't know to walk in the Word. They don't know what you know about living by faith. Some of them are so lazy they will never know it, but I want them well anyway.*

So learn to make the separation between the faith you are developing and the gift of faith. Because both are needed!

backup:
1 Corinthians 12:1-11

download:
Numbers 33; John 16

voice activate:
I live by faith and not by sight. I allow God to move in my life by faith. 2 Corinthians 5:7

"For surely, O Lord, you bless the righteous; you surround them with your favor as with a shield."
Psalm 5:12

march 15

gloria

A Firewall of Favor

What would life be like if you were one of God's favorite people? Think about that for a moment. How would it be to have His favor wrapped around you like a firewall, protecting you from every outside entity?

It would relieve all your anxieties. It would calm all your fears. It would save your life. I know it would because the Bible says in Ephesians 2:8 that *"by grace you have been saved, through faith."*

Now, *grace* is a word many people use and don't understand. This word actually means "favor." Unconditional favor. God's favor saves you. To be *saved* actually means "to be delivered, preserved, healed and made sound and whole."

If you are a Christian, you know that God's grace at work in your life enabled you to become a Christian, but did you know that grace didn't stop working the moment you made Jesus the Lord of your life? That was just the beginning! God will minister grace to you every day if you'll let Him. Psalm 5:12 ensures that.

If you're a Christian, today's verse is talking about you. Through Jesus' blood, you've been placed in right-standing with God and His favor is there for you constantly. Whether you need to be rescued from something, healed or made complete in any way...call upon God's favor by faith. Say, "Surely, O Lord, You bless the righteous! You surround me with a firewall of favor! I am one of God's favorites!"

backup:
Psalm 5

download:
Numbers 34-35; John 17

voice activate:
God surrounds me with His favor as a shield. I am one of God's favorites! Psalm 5:12

"This is the message we have heard from him and declare to you: God is light; in him there is no darkness at all. If we claim to have fellowship with him yet walk in the darkness, we lie and do not live by the truth."
1 John 1:5-6

You Are Either In Or Out

Many times people think forgiveness is only for those major resentments they've been carrying against someone. True forgiveness is also for all those "little" hurts and offenses that cause you to go out of your way to avoid someone. It's those memories that cause you to treat someone with less warmth and love than usual because they have injured you in some way.

I'm talking about any attitude you have that's less than loving someone with the love of God Himself.

Some people don't want to give up those attitudes. They'll say that they love God and get along fine with Him. They just claim to have trouble getting along with those who may have offended them.According to the Bible, people who feel that way are not walking in truth. They're trying to walk in darkness and light at the same time, and today's verse tells us it can't be done. Period.

The sad thing is, many Christians who are walking in unforgiveness don't know they're in darkness. They think that because they read their Bible and attend their youth group that everything's cool with God, but 1 John 2:11 says, *"But whoever hates his brother is in the darkness and walks around in the darkness; he does not know where he is going, because the darkness has blinded him."* A person who does not forgive is *hating* his brother.

"I don't hate him," you may say. "I just don't like him very much!"

How far outside of love do you have to go before it can be called hate? As far as God is concerned, just one step outside of love is hate. To Him there are no shades of gray. In His eyes, anything less than love is sin.

So make the decision today to forgive—everything and everyone.

b a c k u p :
1 John 2:7-11

d o w n l o a d :
Numbers 36; Deuteronomy 1; John 18

v o i c e   a c t i v a t e :
I determine to walk in love and compassion toward others and forgive them, just as in Christ God forgave me. Ephesians 4:32

"I have set before you life and death, blessings and curses. Now choose life."
Deuteronomy 30:19

march 17

kenneth

Rock Solid

"Oh, God, please...give me more faith...make me a better Christian...take these evil thoughts away from me! Oh, God, help me walk in love!"

How many times have you heard (or prayed) prayers like that? Plenty, I'd guess. Everyone, including me, has prayed that way at one time or another, but these prayers don't do squat. You can pray them all day and all night and end up just as faithless as you were when you started.

There's a crucial key missing in prayers like that. A key that, if present, will link you to God's power—and, if absent, will leave you as helpless as can be.

The key I'm talking about is what I call the *Rock-Solid Decision*.

A rock-solid decision is a decision from which there is no retreat and about which there is no argument. It's deliberate—something you choose to do. What's more, it's the one thing God will not do for you. He has done everything else. He's even gone as far as to say, *"I have set before you life and death, blessings and*

curses. Now choose life." The actual choosing—the decision—is up to you.

If you make a rock-solid decision that you will walk by faith and live by what the Bible says, that you will stop smoking cigarettes, that you will walk in love, that you will think pure thoughts, then you will...because you've connected yourself to God's power. You aren't making a decision that you'll have to carry out on your own. God will back you up and enable you to be a winner. So whatever your battle is today, whatever area you want to win over, make a rock-solid decision, and don't look back!

backup:
Joshua 24:14-18

download:
Deuteronomy 2-3; John 19

voice activate:
God has set before me life and death, blessings and curses. I choose life. I choose God's blessings. Deuteronomy 30:19

Healing Power

Not so long ago it was just as tough to get people to make decisions for Jesus as it is to get them healed today. Religious tradition had convinced people that salvation just couldn't be obtained by the average person. Then, a man named Dwight L. Moody started preaching something new. He started telling people that Jesus took their sins upon Himself, and if they'd simply receive the gift of salvation, He would be their Lord!

Whole denominations preached that message to anyone who'd listen. You'd hear it in every church service. If you walked in the door and admitted you weren't a Christian, somebody would grab you and tell you that Jesus died for your sins! They would tell you to trust Him and He will change your life forever.

Well, what do you think would happen if everyone picked up on the truth about healing in the same way? I can tell you what would happen. Healing would become as easily received as salvation, and we'd wonder why we had so much trouble with it for so long!

If you're sitting there right now wishing such a move of God would begin, stop wishing and start your own! Dig into the Bible. Study and think about God's promises about healing. Listen to messages by men and women who understand healing. Then start sharing the healing power of God to others who need to hear it.

I'm not saying all this will be easy. It won't be. Not in this world. No, you'll have to stand strong for it in order to win. When you stand strong in faith, you will see God's healing power touch through you!

march 18

kenneth

backup:
1 Peter 2:21-24

download:
Deuteronomy 4-5; John 20

voice activate:
Jesus took up my infirmities and carried my diseases. By His wounds I have been healed! Matthew 8:17; 1 Peter 2:24

"If anyone destroys God's temple, God will destroy him; for God's temple is sacred, and you are that temple."
1 Corinthians 3:17

gloria

You Are That Temple

"Nobody could be as holy as God."

Have you ever heard people say that? You might even think that way yourself. If so, it's time to change your thinking.

If you've made Jesus your Lord, God has called you to be holy. That's your destiny. That's where you're headed. Romans 8:29 says God *"predestined [us] to be conformed to the likeness of his Son."*

As a Christian, you have been made holy. Now you are called to live on the outside what you are on the inside. To be like Jesus, you have to give yourself completely to Him. That's how you're changed to be like Him.

Becoming more like Him—living like Jesus would—is a process. Your spirit has been completely changed, but your soul—your mind, will and emotions—and your body are changed to be more like Him over time.

You are on a journey. The Bible says you are changed by the Holy Spirit to be more like Him, as you look at Him in the Word (2 Corinthians 3:18, AMP).

Many people become Christians, but they never disconnect from their old life. They never spend enough time reading the Bible, praying or listening to the Holy Spirit within them, allowing Him to teach them how to separate from the world. As a result, they never change on the outside.

Your freedom comes when you change on the outside. That's when you experience all that God provided for you when He saved you. That's when you'll walk in holiness.

b a c k u p :
Leviticus 20:7; 2 Corinthians 6:14-7:1; Hebrews 12:14

d o w n l o a d :
Deuteronomy 6-8; John 21; Acts 1

v o i c e   a c t i v a t e :
I do not destroy the temple of God. I walk in holiness. 1 Corinthians 3:17

kenneth

> "By day the Lord went ahead of them in a pillar of cloud to guide them on their way and by night in a pillar of fire to give them light, so that they could travel by day or night."
> Exodus 13:21

Massive Glory

The glory of God is hard to put into words. But God gives glimpses of it throughout the Bible. The first time the glory is mentioned is in Genesis, and it's referring to God's wealth. So, God's glory includes His wealth, but it's much, much more than that.

In the book of Exodus, God's glory could be seen leading the Israelites in a cloud pillar by day and in a fire pillar by night. Habakkuk saw God's glory and described it as lightning—like shafts of splendor that streamed from His hands (Habakkuk 3:4, AMP).

The word *glory* actually means "heavyweight." God is *heavy* with everything you could ever want or need. He is so heavy with healing, that if everyone in the world believed Him for healing at once, no one would have to wait until tomorrow to be healed because God was tired.

In Acts 5:15, this heavy, weighty glory was flowing out of Peter. As he walked by, people were healed: *"People brought the sick into the streets and laid them on beds and mats so that at least Peter's shadow might fall on some of them as he passed by."* It wasn't Peter's shadow that healed them. It was God's massive glory that surrounded him.

If you need healing today, expect the glory. If you need a job, expect the glory. If you need relationships restored, expect the glory. It's heavy, man, and it's all you'll ever need.

backup:
Exodus 13:15-22

download:
Deuteronomy 9-10; Acts 2

voice activate:
My God meets all my needs according to His glorious riches in Christ Jesus. Philippians 4:19

"For the battle is the Lord's, and he will give all of you into our hands."
1 Samuel 17:47

march 21

gloria

The Four-Point Battle Plan

I've seen it happen time and again. Someone finds out that if they'll base their prayers on God's promises in the Bible, they can have anything they ask from God. They read Mark 11:24 where Jesus said, *"whatever you ask for in prayer, believe that you have received it, and it will be yours,"* and they're quick to obey. They pray, believe God for the answer and then...Satan comes and knocks them flat on their backs.

Why? Because they weren't properly prepared to defend themselves against Satan's attacks. The moment you take a stand in faith, he gets more aggressive than ever, but don't let that throw you. You can whip him every time if you'll use this four-point fight plan to defeat his attack.

1) Make the decision. You must make a decision to take a stand in faith. When you pray, and then stand believing, you must determine not to get flustered until your answer comes—no matter what.

2) Resist Satan. When he comes at you and wants you to see yourself failing— toss those thoughts aside instantly. Jerk your mind back to what God has promised you and say the scriptures out loud that apply to your situation.

3) Spend time in the Bible. Spend time in God's Word every day. I know it sounds simple. Yet this is where so many Christians miss it.

4) Speak the Truth—and only the Truth. Satan can't do anything to you if you won't open the door to him with your words. Satan doesn't have any rulership over you. Jesus Christ is your Lord. Satan can't rob you unless you let him, and you let him in or keep him out by the words you say.

That's the four-point fight plan. If you follow it, it will work for you every time. I like what Ken says: "A good fight is the one you win." So go ahead and enjoy the fight—it's already been won for you!

backup:
2 Chronicles 20:14-17

download:
Deuteronomy 11-12; Acts 3

voice activate:
I fight the good fight of faith. It is a good fight because Jesus has already won it for me. 1 Timothy 6:12

"And being not weak in faith, he [Abraham] considered not his own body now dead, when he was about an hundred years old, neither yet the deadness of Sarah's womb: He staggered not at the promise of God through unbelief; but was strong in faith, giving glory to God; And being fully persuaded that, what he had promised, he was able also to perform."
Romans 4:19-21, KJV

Consider Jesus

Over and over, young Christians have come to me and said, "Kenneth, I know it's right to put my faith in God, and I've made a decision to believe what God promises in the Bible, but every time I take a step, all hell breaks loose.

"I start believing God will heal me and I break out in a rash. I get healed of that and my eyes cross! I pay off my car and the engine blows up. Then my stereo goes on the fritz and I lose my job. It seems like I get over one wall only to hit a bigger one behind it!"

No, it doesn't *seem* like that. It *is* like that!

When you just start making faith your lifestyle, you have more problems now than you will a few years down the road. Because you're just getting started, obstacles that one day won't be any threat at all, can send you sprawling.

How do you get through all these things and keep going? How do you "keep the power on?" You *consider* the right things. You change the focus of your attention. Today's verse says that when believing for a son, Abraham didn't consider his own body. You must not focus on the things that contradict what God has promised. You can't consider your cir-

cumstances. What you must consider is *Jesus.* What does considering Jesus really mean?

1) It means focusing on what He has said. The Holy Spirit will show you exactly Who Jesus is as you study the Bible.

2) It means realizing Jesus is, as Hebrews 3 says, the Apostle—the "Sent One." He is sent to you to fill your life with *life.*

3) It means understanding Jesus is watching over your words and actions—and He's making those faith-filled words and actions happen.

4) It means knowing Jesus is faithful. He will do what He has said!

So keep believing—keep considering Jesus—and eventually you'll realize that you are more than able to face anything that comes your way.

b a c k u p :
Hebrews 3:1-6

d o w n l o a d :
Deuteronomy 13-14; Acts 4

v o i c e   a c t i v a t e :
I am not weak in faith, considering my own body. I consider Jesus. I believe the promise of God. Romans 4:19-21

"[The Father] has delivered and drawn us to Himself out of the control and the dominion of darkness and has transferred us into the kingdom of the Son of His love."
Colossians 1:13, AMP

march 23

gloria

Citizens of Heaven

Where do you live? The first place that may come to mind is the spot on earth where you wake up each morning. I want you to think deeper than that. I want you to see that you are in this world, but not of it. You are a citizen of heaven. Even here and now, you are living in that kingdom.

That statement startles many Christians. They've been taught all their lives that they won't reach God's kingdom until they die and go to heaven. However, today's verse says we've already made it into God's kingdom.

Because God lives in us, His kingdom is with us right now. Jesus said it this way: *"For behold, the kingdom of God is within you [in your hearts] and among you [surrounding you]"* (Luke 17:21, AMP).

Certainly we'll go to heaven one day, but since we're already citizens of the kingdom now, we can enjoy many of the benefits of heaven right here on earth. We can live our lives in love, peace, joy, well-being, health and victory.

"If Christians can enjoy all that," you may ask, "why don't they?"

It's because often, they have been so absorbed in this world—the world that they see and touch—they haven't given much thought to God's kingdom.

We can change that! We can obey Colossians 3:1-2: *"Aim at and seek the [rich, eternal treasures] that are above, where Christ [the Anointed One] is, seated at the right hand of God. And set your minds and keep them set on what is above—the higher things—not on the things that are on the earth"* (AMP).

By studying what the Bible has to say about the kingdom of God, it will become more real to us daily. The Bible says so much about the kingdom of God. I challenge you to study it. Get a concordance and look up all the references to the kingdom of God or the kingdom of heaven. Let the reality of that kingdom get down in your heart so that it becomes part of your thinking...and part of your life!

b a c k u p :
Matthew 6:33, (AMP); Luke 17:20-21; John 3:3-21

d o w n l o a d :
Deuteronomy 15-16; Acts 5

v o i c e   a c t i v a t e :
God has rescued me from the dominion of darkness and brought me into the kingdom of the Son He loves. Colossians 1:13

"Since the children have flesh and blood, he [Jesus] too shared in their humanity so that by his death he might destroy him who holds the power of death—that is, the devil—and free those who all their lives were held in slavery by their fear of death."
Hebrews 2:14-15

No Fear

Every fear that exists springs from that one basic fear: The fear of death.

The Bible says Jesus destroyed Satan's authority over death, pulling the plug on fear forever. It doesn't have any rule over you. If you allow fear in your life, it will stop your faith, cut you off from God's power and put you back in slavery to your old way of doing things.

"Well, Kenneth, sometimes I just can't help being afraid."

Yes, you can! Sure, Satan is roaming around like an outlaw, killing, stealing and destroying (John 10:10), but he can't just come storming in anywhere he wants. In fact, without fear, it's impossible for him to do anything…because, in this old world, fear plays the same role as faith does in the supernatural world of light.

The bottom line is, if you stay with God, and stay with His promises, you can stop the fear.

That's what Jesus told Jairus to do in Mark 5. Jairus had run into an impossible situation. His daughter was dying and there was nothing he could do to save her. So, by faith, he connected to the supernatural. He came to Jesus and said, "If You'll put Your hands on her, she'll live."

However, before Jesus reached the little girl, Satan took a shot and killed her. Someone even told Jairus, "Your daughter is dead. Why bother Jesus anymore?"

Do you know what Jesus said to him? *"Don't be afraid; just believe."* In other words, don't let fear unhook you, Jairus. Just be strong with faith, stay connected to the supernatural and everything will turn out all right.

Now if Jesus told Jairus not to be afraid, that means Jairus had the *ability* to stay unafraid. If he could throw out fear in the face of his own daughter's death, you can do it in your situation.

Just remember, God is on your side. What do you have to be afraid of?

backup:
Mark 5:21-24,35-43

download:
Deuteronomy 17-18; Acts 6

voice activate:
Jesus has destroyed him who holds the power of death. I am no longer held in slavery to the fear of death. Hebrews 2:14-15

"For the eyes of the Lord range throughout the earth to strengthen those whose hearts are fully committed to him."
2 Chronicles 16:9

March 25

gloria

He's Waiting on You

"I'm just waiting on God...waiting for Him to give me what I need... waiting for Him to heal me...waiting for Him to rescue me."

Sounds spiritual, doesn't it? The truth is, people who make statements like that don't know much about God. I know they don't, because the Bible clearly says that when it comes to God's blessings, we're not waiting on Him. He's waiting on us! What is He waiting on? Obedience.

The world tries to convince us it's more exciting to sin than to obey God. Jesus proved that it's not. He lived the most exciting life in history.

Obeying God isn't going to doom you to a life of boredom. No! Obedience will lead you into the most thrilling life you could ever imagine.

So how do you become obedient like that? One day at a time. You don't sit around for years waiting for God to tell you to go to Africa as a missionary. You learn to do the little things He tells you to do. You learn to follow His directions on a daily basis—just going about your day doing what pleases Him.

He will give you His direction through the Bible and by the voice of His Spirit. Many Christians are eager to hear God's direction, but they don't want to take time to study the Bible or be quiet enough to listen to the inward witness—which is the voice of their own spirit directed by the Holy Spirit.

Even Jesus, Who was more sensitive to God's voice than any man had ever been, studied the Bible. In fact, He studied so much that at age 12, the temple teachers were *"amazed at his understanding and his answers."* (Luke 2:47).

So study the Word! The Bible will retrain your mind to think like God thinks so that you recognize His directions. When He speaks, you'll know it's Him because what you are hearing is right in line with His written Word. Then you can walk in obedience with nothing to stop you from receiving what you need.

Remember, you're not waiting on God. He's waiting on you!

backup:
Genesis 12:1-4, 13:1-4

download:
Deuteronomy 19-20; Acts 7

voice activate:
Because I obey God and am fully committed to Him, He strengthens me.
2 Chronicles 16:9

"'In a surge of anger I hid my face from you for a moment, but with ever-lasting kindness I will have compassion on you,' says the Lord your Redeemer. 'To me this is like the days of Noah, when I swore that the waters of Noah would never again cover the earth. So now I have sworn not to be angry with you, never to rebuke you again. Though the mountains be shaken and the hills be removed, yet my unfailing love for you will not be shaken nor my covenant of peace be removed,' says the Lord, who has compassion on you."
Isaiah 54:8-10

God Is Not Mad at You!

I have six simple words for you today. Six words that are contrary to popular belief: *God is not mad at you!*

I remember the first time I found that out. I was shocked. I hadn't been a Christian very long, and I had heard all my life about the terrible things God would do to you. He would make you sick and keep you poor. He would bring you trouble to make you strong. I heard He did bad things to you, but it was all right for Him to do them because He was God.

Then one day I was reading the Bible and I came across Isaiah 54. It changed everything. *God is not mad at us!* That's earthshaking news, though you don't hear about it much. It's such good news, some people have a hard time believing it. They start thinking of all the sin they've allowed into their lives, all the wrongs they've done.

"There's no way God is going to over-look all that!" they say. "Surely He's going to do something about it."

He already did. He sent Jesus to the cross.

Read Isaiah 52. All of us have seen paintings of the Crucifixion. Yet none of them come close to the horror of what happened to Jesus that day. When He took the sins of mankind into Himself, His body became so marred, He didn't even look human.

Yet it was this very event that freed us forever from God's wrath. The sacrifice of Jesus' death on the cross was enough to pay for your sins and mine. As far as God is concerned, it's all over. We just have to accept it.

So study Isaiah 52, 53 and 54. Let that eye-opening news sink into you. Let it change the way you think. God isn't mad at you! He loves you! Just the way you are, right where you are!

backup:
John 3:9-17

download:
Deuteronomy 21-23; Acts 8-9

voice activate:
Though the mountains be shaken and the hills removed, God's unfailing love for me will not be shaken and His covenant of peace will not be removed from me. Isaiah 54:10

"Is any one of you in trouble? He should pray."
James 5:13

march 27

gloria

Drawing Strength From Him

It's wonderful to have a good youth pastor, and it's wonderful to have friends who can pray with power—and I certainly do ask for prayer from others occasionally, but it's a Christian's own prayers that are most important.

James 5:13 doesn't say, "If anyone is in trouble, he should ask his youth pastor to pray." No, it says if there is trouble in your life, *you* need to pray.

That's because prayer is more than just asking for something. When you pray, you're spending time with your Father. You talk to Him. He talks to you. He strengthens you.

I was reminded of that at a family gathering once. One of our family members had gone to be with the Lord unexpectedly and it was a challenging time. After some time, one of my cousins said, "It just strengthens my faith to be around this family."

I knew exactly what she meant. I know people who are more mature in faith, and have been walking with the Lord longer than I have. When I talk with those people, it makes me stronger too.

As I thought about that, it struck me. *If a person who is full of faith can strengthen me, how much more does it strengthen me to spend time with God Himself every day in prayer?* Think about that!

You have the privilege any time, day or night, to go to God and spend time with Him. You can talk to Him all day long. You can continually draw strength from Him.

He is always ready to listen and respond to you. It's perfectly fine to have your youth pastor or friends pray. However, it's more important that you pray...that you have intimate time with your Heavenly Father. Call out His Name. He is always available. He's waiting to hear from *you!*

backup:
1 John 5:13-15

download:
Deuteronomy 24-25; Acts 10

voice activate:
When I am in trouble, I pray. God delivers me out of all my troubles. James 5:13; Psalm 34:19

"His [God's] divine power has given us everything we need for life and godliness through our knowledge of him who called us by his own glory and goodness."
2 Peter 1:3

What Do You Want Me to Do for You?

God isn't holding back on giving us anything good. That's what I finally realized in 1967 when, as a young Christian, I saw His Word as a love letter to me—a letter filled with promises He had made to me. I began to see that God was honorable, His Word had integrity and He was committed to doing those things He had promised—to make me the spiritually, emotionally, physically, financially and relationally successful person He had created me to be.

I found out He'd do anything in the world for me. You start telling Him you love Him and start keeping His commandment of love, and He'll get all over you like a fur coat!

I remember one afternoon, I was driving down the road when the first real understanding of God's love hit me. I had to pull my car over and stop. It was the first time in my life I had come to God without trying to get something in return.

"I just can't drive this car any farther," I cried out to God. "I had to stop to raise my hands and tell You how much I love You, worship You and care for You! Father, my needs are met according to Your glorious riches in Christ Jesus.

"It just dawned on me a few days ago, that the whole world is running against you," I said. "I want to run with You! I want to do something to give you a good day. I want to do everything I can for you in a big way. Your slightest whim is my command. Just tell me what you want me to do!"

After I said all of that, He still wouldn't tell me what He wanted me to do! Instead, He said, *Son, what do you want Me to do for you? Is there anything?*

That's God's heart toward you. He's given you everything you need to succeed. He's given you every edge. Take hold of it. Be all He created you to be. Read His love letter to you...start telling Him how much you love Him...and let Him get all over you just like a fur coat!

backup:
Psalm 36:7-10; Proverbs 8:17-21

download:
Deuteronomy 26-27; Acts 11

voice activate:
God has given me everything I need for life and godliness. 2 Peter 1:3

"Withstand him [the devil]; be firm in faith [against his onset]—rooted, established, strong, immovable, and determined."
1 Peter 5:9, AMP

march 29

gloria

Put Hell on the Run

We live in an evil day. Actually, the days have been evil ever since Adam sinned in the Garden of Eden. Today, that evil is intensifying because the end of the age is near. Jesus is coming soon, and Satan is doing everything he can to stop Him. He is killing, stealing and destroying as fiercely and as rapidly as he can. Never have I seen a time when it was more crucial for us to heed the instructions God gives us in today's verse.

We can do it, if we'll obey the instructions God gives us in Romans 12:21 and *"Do not be overcome by evil, but overcome evil with good."* After all, God has given us so many good things, so much supernatural power and ability that no matter what happens in this dark world, we can come through it squeaky clean. He has given us weapons that aren't of the world. Instead, they have divine power to demolish strongholds (2 Corinthians 10:4).

In fact, if we'll shake off the sluggishness of everyday living and start living supernaturally, we can win in life and put hell on the run! We just need to wake up to what God says in the Bible, to prayer and to the Holy Spirit's guidance. Believe it today: God has given us all the power, strength and wisdom we need to come out on top!

backup:
Titus 2:11-15

download:
Deuteronomy 28-29; Acts 12

voice activate:
I am firm in faith. I am rooted, established, strong, immovable and determined to triumph over the devil. 1 Peter 5:9, AMP

"The ones sown among the thorns are others who hear the Word; Then the cares and anxieties of the world and distractions of the age, and the pleasure and delight and false glamour and deceitfulness of riches, and the craving and passionate desire for other things creep in and choke and suffocate the Word, and it becomes fruitless."
Mark 4:18-19, AMP

Keep It Simple

Over the years, I've noticed how easy it is to get caught up in day-to-day living. In fact, it sometimes seems as though this world is like an octopus, always trying to grab you with its tentacles. If you don't watch out, it will wrap itself around you until you're completely tied up in the trivial things of this world.

Those trivial pursuits can hold you down and keep you from soaring on into the things of God. They can choke the Word out of your heart and leave you without faith and without power. That's what Mark 4:18-19 is talking about.

Here in America, we must be especially alert, because we have so many material possessions! We can easily spend all our time taking care of them.

As the Lord told a friend of mine in prayer one day, this nation has become a nation of maintenance men. We maintain our houses. We maintain our cars. We maintain our hair, our nails and our clothes. The problem is, by the time we've done what it takes to maintain all the "things" in our lives, we often don't have any time left to maintain our spirit.

There's only one thing to do: *Simplify your life.*

There's nothing more important than spending time with God. So make whatever adjustments you must to spend time with Him. Whenever you take on anything new, count the cost—not just in money, but in time. Ask yourself, *Can I afford this spiritually? Can I spare the precious hours and minutes this activity or thing will require and still have plenty of time to spend with the Lord?*

If the answer is no, then set that thing aside. I realize that may mean passing up some things you enjoy. Remember, your aim is not to please yourself. It's to please God. Believe me, when you make sacrifices for Him, He always makes sure you're well-rewarded. Now, that's "the good life."

b a c k u p :
Luke 12:22-31

d o w n l o a d :
Deuteronomy 30-31; Acts 13

v o i c e   a c t i v a t e :
I throw off everything that hinders and easily entangles me. Hebrews 12:1

gloria

"Seek the Lord while he may be found; call on him while he is near. Let the wicked forsake his way and the evil man his thoughts. Let him turn to the Lord, and he will have mercy on him, and to our God, for he will freely pardon."
Isaiah 55:6-7

march 31

kenneth

Built on the Rock

When hard times come, they're never as hard as they look. That's a spiritual law that is important to remember. Hard times are not as hard as they look—unless you are looking in the wrong place, through the wrong eyes, thinking the wrong thoughts or imitating the wrong people.

Wrong thoughts paint the wrong pictures in your mind. They tell you things are worse than they are. They tell you that you don't have what it takes to succeed in life, or that the right opportunity won't come to you. I'm here to tell you, you can succeed!

Of course, as Christians, our motive to do well during hard times isn't so we can rub it in other people's faces. No, we want to do well in order to help others get back on track. We want to say, "Hey friend, let me teach you how to live successfully. Get over here in my house. No depression is going to tear it down. It's built on the Rock!" (Matthew 7:24-25).

If people are sick, we can say to them, "Don't let sickness and disease knock you down. Come on over to my house. By God's power, we can show you how to be well!" That's what the good news is really all about.

So how do we change our thinking? Isaiah 55:6-11 tells us. We're to take up God's thoughts and God's ways. If we want to live the kind of life God has in mind for us, we must exchange our thoughts for His thoughts. We must lay down the way we look at things and instead pick up the wisdom of God—the Bible. Through God's written Word, we'll learn what reality is. We'll learn what's really going on in the world and His plan for getting through it.

The answer to every problem is in the Bible. Let it change your thinking. Remember, times are not as hard as they look when you look from God's eyes!

backup:
Isaiah 55:9-11

download:
Deuteronomy 32-33; Acts 14

voice activate:
I live the kind of life God intends for me to live by exchanging my thoughts and ways for His. Isaiah 55:6-11

"'The Spirit of the Lord is on me, because he has anointed me to preach good news to the poor. He has sent me to proclaim freedom for the prisoners and recovery of sight for the blind, to release the oppressed, to proclaim the year of the Lord's favor.'"
Luke 4:18-19

A Staggering Truth

I have some good news. So good, you'll want to jump up and shout. You'll be inspired to jump out of bed in the morning, grin real big and holler, "Look out, Satan! I'm up again, and I'm going to whip you all day long!"

The good news is: You have God's power moving through every part of you...in other words, *you are anointed!*

I can almost hear someone thinking, *Well, Ken, I would never go so far as to assume I was anointed.*

You mean you aren't a Christian?

"Why certainly I'm a Christian!" Well, if you're a Christian, then you're anointed because the very word *Christian* comes from the Greek word *Christ* which means "the Anointed One." Translate the word *Christian* and you'll find out it means to be anointed like Jesus!

In fact, to say you're anything less than anointed is to reject what Jesus bought for you with His precious blood. Jesus didn't pay the price for sin just so you could get eternal fire insurance. He

did it so you could be cleansed, and be filled with His own anointing (1 John 2:27). Jesus laid down His life so that He could equip you to do the same things He did, and more! (John 14:12)

The very thought of doing the same things Jesus did staggers the minds of most Christians. When we think about being witnesses for "Christ," we usually think about passing out tracts. As wonderful as that is, there is more for us to do. You're to preach the good news to the poor, proclaim freedom to the prisoners, recovery of sight to the blind, release the oppressed and proclaim that it's the time of God's favor. Why? Because He said so, and He has anointed you to do it!

Yes, you can do it! You're ANOINTED!

b a c k u p :
Ephesians 1:17-23

d o w n l o a d :
Deuteronomy 34; Joshua 1; Acts 15

v o i c e   a c t i v a t e :
The Spirit of the Lord is on me. He has anointed me! Luke 4:18

"In the beginning God created the heavens and the earth. Now the earth was formless and empty, darkness was over the surface of the deep, and the Spirit of God was hovering over the waters. And God said, 'Let there be light,' and there was light."
Genesis 1:1-3

kenneth april 2

The Eternal Word

God is all-powerful. Therefore, His Word is all-powerful. In fact, His Words contain the power to create. You can see that in the first three verses of the Bible. You'll notice in those verses that the Holy Spirit was moving before God spoke, but nothing happened until *God said.* Creation did not take place until God released words of faith.

Everything in creation, everything you can see, touch, taste or smell came into existence as a result of God's Word. That means God's Word is the substance of all matter. Think of it! The paper in this devotional came from a tree that came from a seed that came from a tree that came from a seed, all the way back to God's Word "Let there be..."

Knowing that, do you think His Word *still* has the power to change this physical world? Do you think the Word that created the dirt your physical body was made from has enough power to heal that body? Do you think the Word that brought into being all the silver and gold in this earth has enough power to supply you with the resources to pay your college tuition?

Of course! God's Word is eternal. It cannot be changed. Psalm 119:89, NKJV says, *"Forever, O Lord, Your word is settled in heaven."*

This material universe, on the other hand, is temporary. It changes. So whenever you take God's Word and apply it in faith, the things in this material universe must give in and conform to the Word.

Jesus lived His life by this truth. He had such faith in God's Word that when He spoke it, this material creation obeyed Him. You can live by this truth, too! You can speak the Word in faith and disease will leave. You can speak to your college tuition and it will be paid. You can speak to any circumstance, and know that the Word spoken and acted on in faith will change the changeable...all because you are standing on the *unchangeable* Word of God.

b a c k u p :
Genesis 1

d o w n l o a d :
Joshua 2-4; Acts 16-17

v o i c e   a c t i v a t e :
God's Word stands firm in the heavens. It will never change. Psalm 119:89

"Peace I leave with you; my peace I give you. I do not give to you as the world gives. Do not let your hearts be troubled and do not be afraid."
John 14:27

He's Given You Peace

Some people have the idea that if you live by faith, you can float through life without any problems. Forget it. It will never happen.

Just look at Jesus. If anyone should have been able to float through life, it was Jesus. He had perfect faith. Yet, He had the toughest time of any man who ever walked on earth. He was persecuted, criticized and plotted against. He was tempted with every sin mankind has ever known. Yet He resisted it all.

If you think that's easy, think again. There's nothing tougher than feeling the pressure of sin or sickness, and then standing, refusing to let it take over. There's nothing tougher than standing up at those times and saying, "No! I won't receive this sickness on my body. I won't give in to this circumstance! I've been set free by the blood of Jesus, and I will live free by faith in Him!"

If you want to see just how much pressure such a stand of faith can bring, look at Jesus before He went to the cross. The pressure of the temptation He faced put such a strain on His physical body that drops of blood poured through His skin like perspiration. Even then, sin could not conquer Him.

None of us will ever face that much trouble. We'll never have to stand against that much pressure. Yet we have available to us the same power and peace that took Him not just through the pressure, but through the whipping, the mocking and the Crucifixion. We have the peace that took Him all the way through!

"Peace I leave with you," He said. "My peace I give you.... Do not let your hearts be troubled and do not be afraid."

He's given you His peace...far more than you'll ever need. So don't rehearse the problem over and over in your mind. Instead, receive the peace He provided for a day like today.

backup:
John 16:29-33

download:
Joshua 5-6; Acts 18

voice activate:
Jesus has given me His peace. I don't let my heart be troubled. I am not afraid. John 14:27

"'No one knows about that day or hour, not even the angels in heaven, nor the Son, but only the Father.'"
Matthew 24:36

april 4

gloria

Sooner Than We Think

Some time back, the Holy Spirit spoke to Ken and said, *I am coming sooner than you think.*

Many people just don't believe that truth. Just as the Scripture says, they scoff saying, *"Where is this 'coming' he promised? Ever since our fathers died, everything goes on as it has since the beginning of creation"* (2 Peter 3:3-4).

Those people are mistaken. Jesus *is* coming back. We know that's true because Jesus said it in Matthew 24:36. At an appointed time, He will catch away those of us who are prepared for His coming and take us to heaven with Him to celebrate for seven years. Then He'll bring us back with Him when He comes to rule over the earth.

What a day that will be!

It's coming. There's no doubt about it. Will you be ready?

If you're not, the thought of the Lord's return may not be very exciting to you. It may even fill you with anxiety. If so, you need to make some changes.

First, you need to make Jesus the Lord of your life. Then you need to focus your attention and your love on the things of God instead of the things of this world (Colossians 3:2).

After all, this world is not our home. It's not our final destination. We're just passing through this place, looking forward to being with God for eternity. We need to constantly remember that, so we don't get tangled up in the things going on in this world. We need to constantly look toward heaven so when the time comes to go, we'll be ready.

So get your thinking right. Set your heart on godly things. Look forward to His coming. It will happen sooner than we think!

backup:
2 Peter 3:1-14

download:
Joshua 7-8; Acts 19

voice activate:
I will be ready when Jesus comes. I set my mind on things above, not on earthly things. Colossians 3:2

Spiritual Hunger

Within every Christian, there's a hunger that cannot be satisfied by the things of this world. It's a hunger that grows stronger the more we walk with God.

The Apostle Paul walked in more supernatural understanding than any man except Jesus, yet he expressed a spiritual hunger that was so powerful it completely overshadowed everything else in his life: *I consider everything a loss compared to the surpassing greatness of knowing Christ Jesus my Lord...I want to know Christ and the power of his resurrection* (Philippians 3:8-10).

When you read those words, you can see exactly what Paul desired: A deeper relationship with Jesus, and to know the power of His resurrection.

What is "the power of His resurrection?"

According to Romans 6:3-4, Jesus was raised from the dead by the glory of God. So "the power of the resurrection" is the same thing as "the glory of God." Paul's burning desire was to know Jesus...and to know God's glory!

So what is God's glory? It's His goodness. In Exodus 33:18, when Moses wanted to see His glory, God replied, *"I will cause all my goodness to pass in front of you"* (verse 19). God's glory is Himself!

That spiritual hunger we have is a hunger for God's glory—His goodness and His life.

The Bible says all of us have *"sinned and fall short of the glory of God"* (Romans 3:23).

Well, that's true, but Jesus took our sin and bore the penalty of it. He made it possible for us to fill our spiritual hunger. He made it possible for us to know the glory. He made it possible for us to know God Himself.

So let God's glory—His goodness and His life—run through your life and change everything today. It will satisfy your hunger!

kenneth **april 5**

b a c k u p :
romans 6:3-4

d o w n l o a d :
Joshua 9-10; Acts 20

v o i c e   a c t i v a t e :
I determine to know Christ and the power of His resurrection. Philippians 3:10

"'The Lord be exalted, who delights in the well-being of his servant.'"
Psalm 35:27

april 6

kenneth

God's Happy When You're Happy

If you're like me—and many other Christians—you want to please God every day. The good news is, we know exactly how to do this. Hebrews 11:6 tells us that it is impossible to please God without faith.

Faith pleases God because it gives Him access into your life. He needs access in order to remove troubles, free you from bondage and make you a living example of His desire to bless people. He has it only when we believe that He exists, and believe that He rewards those who earnestly seek Him (Hebrews 11:6).

Acting on His Word is acting in faith. It gives Him the opportunity to heal your body, to bless you, to save your family, to rescue a loved one from drugs—whatever it is you want and need. Faith not only gives Him access into your life, but it gives you access into His divine favor.

Third John 2, NKJV says, "I pray that you may prosper in all things and be in health, just as your soul prospers."

God wants you to excel in everything in life: spirit, soul, body, financially and socially. He wants you to be learning about faith and walking by faith. He wants to change your way of thinking to where you agree with what He says about you. He wants you walking in His wisdom.

His desire is that you know His healing power and walk in divine health. He loves it when you have your financial needs met and have extra to give. He wants you to be a strong witness and example of His love to your family, your friends and your classmates.

God has committed Himself to your success in every area of life. Think about that. Keep this thought in your mind all the time: *God receives pleasure when I—by faith—do well in every area of my life.* Think about today's verse all day and live it! You'll be sure to please Him!

backup:
Galatians 3:6-11; Hebrews 10:38; 1 John 3:22

download:
Joshua 11-12; Acts 21

voice activate:
The Lord delights in my well-being. I prosper in every area of my life. Psalm 35:27

"The apostles performed many miraculous signs and wonders among the people….[And] more and more men and women believed in the Lord and were added to their number."
Acts 5:12,14

God-Generated Boldness

If Christians today would get a true understanding of what happened when Jesus was raised from the dead, the same thing would happen to us that happened to the people in Acts 5. We'd get bold. Not with "faking-it" boldness that falls flat on its face, but with God-generated boldness that brings miracles on the scene.

If you want to see what can take place when that kind of boldness is around, go ahead and read Acts 5. There were miracles, decisions to follow Jesus, sick were healed and lives were changed.

For years I read this and thought only the apostles were involved in this great move of God. That wasn't the case. All the Christians were. They were all filled with the Holy Spirit and spoke God's Word with boldness.

This group preached about Jesus' rising all over town until thousands of people made Jesus their Lord. Then those people filled the streets, bringing in the sick to be healed!

You can have that kind of boldness. Your church and youth group can have that kind of boldness. You get it by faith, just like the Christians in Acts 4 and 5. Want to turn your school upside down for God? Then get hold of the Word. Dare to believe it. Then preach it in faith with boldness. Soon, people will be waiting at your locker, because they'll know that's where they can be saved, healed and rescued.

backup:
Acts 5:12-16

download:
Joshua 13-14; Acts 22

voice activate:
I open my mouth fearlessly and make known the mystery of the gospel. Ephesians 6:19

"If you are willing and obedient, you shall eat the good of the land."
Isaiah 1:19, AMP

april 8

gloria

Get Aggressive!

God has always promised that if you are willing and obedient, you will "eat the good of the land." Being willing means more than just saying, "Well, Lord, if You want me to do well, I will." Being willing means that you determine to receive by faith what God has promised, no matter how things look.

That's what Ken and I had to do. When we saw in the Bible that wealth belonged to us, we were so deep in debt it looked like we would never get out, but we became willing anyway. We said, "In Jesus' Name, we will do well. We won't live in poverty. We receive all God has provided for us now!"

For years, I didn't understand that we needed to make a stand like that, so without realizing it, I allowed Satan to come in and give me a hard time over finances. Then one day, God showed me that I needed to use the same kind of stand for finances as for healing.

I had already learned to be aggressive about healing. Once Ken and I found out that Jesus took away our sickness, we refused to put up with it. We realized sickness was our enemy and we stood against it. We'd tell it, "No! God has rescued us from sickness. So don't come near us!"

One day God said to me, *Why don't you treat poverty the same way? Why do you put up with it? You say you've been rescued from it, but you haven't resisted it like you do sickness and disease.*

When I heard that, I determined to make a change. I began to aggressively resist poverty the same way I resisted sickness, and it made a big difference!

I must warn you though, it wasn't easy. It takes effort and determination to resist it. If you want to do well financially now or in the future, you'll need to keep God's promises in your heart. You'll need to think about what God says all the time. You'll need to get aggressive!

backup:
Galatians 3:13-14

download:
Joshua 15; Acts 23

voice activate:
I am willing and obedient. I always eat the best from the land. Isaiah 1:19

> "Then he said to Thomas, 'Put your finger here; see my hands. Reach out your hand and put it into my side. Stop doubting and believe.'"
> John 20:27

Walk by Faith, Not by Sight

Eight days before Jesus said the words in today's verse, Thomas had refused to believe that the other disciples had seen Jesus alive. He told them, "Unless I see him and feel his wounds myself, I won't believe."

Jesus said that kind of believing has no faith in it. Faith comes from your heart—your spirit—not your mind. Many Christians today don't realize that. They think if Jesus would appear to them before their eyes, their faith would sky-rocket, but it wouldn't. If you depend more on what you see or feel than you do on what the Bible says, seeing something astounding like that will only set your faith back. That's why Jesus did what He did on the road to Emmaus (Luke 24:13-35).

Two of His disciples were walking down the road, sad about Jesus' death. So Jesus, walked up alongside them and said, "What's up? What's the matter?"

They thought He was a stranger. Well, when Jesus began preaching to them, they realized Who He was. At once, He disappeared. Why?

He did it because He wanted them to keep their faith in His Word, instead of simply believing He was alive because they had seen Him. He didn't want to set their faith back.

Some years ago, when I didn't understand that, I used to pester God to appear to me. "Lord, I want You to show up right before my eyes!"

One day, He said to me, *Kenneth, if you keep asking Me to appear to you, I'm going to have to do it. I'm warning you though, it will set your faith back five years.*

Had I kept on like that, I would have suddenly started relying on what I saw instead of my faith in God's Word.

The fact is, Jesus would like to appear to every one of us. It would thrill Him to just walk into the room and sit down with us. He's had to restrain Himself, because He is training us to live our lives by the God kind of faith—not by sight (2 Corinthians 5:7).

backup:
Luke 24:27-32

download:
Joshua 16-18; Acts 24-25

voice activate:
I live by faith and not by sight.
2 Corinthians 5:7

"Have faith in God."
Mark 11:22

Fact vs. Truth

Jesus commanded us to operate in the same kind of faith He has. He also told us that anyone who did it would have the same results.

That being the case, how do we deal with the fact that so many Christians are being defeated by sickness, poverty and every other kind of problem? By understanding that those defeats are "fact," but they are not "truth."

Facts can be changed. Truth can't. Truth supersedes fact. Spiritual law supersedes natural, physical law.

The law of gravity, for example, is a fact. But did you know there is a higher law than the law of gravity? Those in the aeronautical industry know it as the law of lift. If you do certain things—make an airplane, build the wing right and engine powerful enough and so on—you'll be able to put the law of lift into motion and make an airplane fly.

How does that happen? Does gravity cease to be a fact? No. The law of lift simply supersedes it.

In the same way, sickness and disease are facts. Yet, those facts can be superseded by the truth in Isaiah 53:5, "By

his [Jesus'] wounds we are healed." It's a truth that can never be changed. What's more, if you'll apply that truth, it will overcome sickness every time!

Truth changes facts. The key is applying it. You can put on your finest traveling clothes, pack your luggage and go sit down in a perfectly good airplane...but you won't get six inches off the ground unless somebody turns on the engines and begins to put the law of lift into motion.

What we need to do is apply our faith just like Jesus did. We need to learn to supersede our natural circumstances by activating the supernatural law of faith. So apply truth to your facts today. Speak Isaiah 53:5 to your body. Speak Proverbs 2:6 over your schoolwork. Speak Philippians 4:19 to your needs, and watch the truth change the facts!

b a c k u p :
Matthew 21:17-22

d o w n l o a d :
Joshua 19-20; Acts 26

v o i c e a c t i v a t e :
I have faith in God. I walk and live by faith. Mark 11:22; 2 Corinthians 5:7

"My God will meet all your needs according to his glorious riches in Christ Jesus."
Philippians 4:19

You Are God's Business

Whatever you need today, God is able to provide it. Whether you need a car, a job or good Christian friends, He knows how to get you what you need. All you have to do is receive what you need by faith. You don't have to figure out how He's going to get it to you.

For example, remember when Moses and the Israelites were wandering in the desert? Remember how God supplied them manna to eat? Then they began to complain. They grew tired of manna. They decided they wanted some meat (Numbers 11).

Well, Moses tried to figure out how God was going to get enough meat to feed all of the people. Moses began reasoning with God. He said, *"Would they have enough if flocks and herds were slaughtered for them? Would they have enough if all the fish in the sea were caught for them?"* (verse 22).

God said to Moses, *"Is the Lord's arm too short?"* (verse 23).

Clearly, God didn't appreciate Moses' questioning. Moses was saying, "Lord, it will take all the cattle we've got to feed this bunch. It can't be done."

Not only did God not appreciate Moses' attitude—God got hot! *"Is the Lord's arm too short?"*

You need to remember that when you need something. You have no business reasoning out how God is going to get something to you. *Well, I wonder if He's going to have someone in the church give it to me. I wonder if somebody's gonna die and leave me a bunch of money.*

God is not limited by the things you know. His arm is not too short. He has ways that you've never even thought about (Ephesians 3:20). He knows how to get it to you. That's His business.

God might just drop a best friend next door to you. He might leave a brand new car in your driveway one night. He can. He's God! He can do it however He wants. So stop reasoning, release your faith and receive. God will get it to you!

b a c k u p :
Numbers 11:18-23

d o w n l o a d :
Joshua 21-22; Acts 27

v o i c e   a c t i v a t e :
My God meets all my needs according to His glorious riches in Christ Jesus. Philippians 4:19

"In him we have redemption through his blood, the forgiveness of sins, in accordance with the riches of God's grace."
Ephesians 1:7

kenneth april 12

Case Dismissed

I went for years not knowing anything about the blood of Jesus. I heard people plead the blood, saying: "I plead the blood." I knew it was powerful, and I could tell they knew what they were doing, but I didn't have the foggiest idea what *pleading the blood* actually meant.

I don't know why I didn't make the connection based on my American Indian background. I should have. Indian life is based around blood covenants. When I finally did realize that God, in the blood of Jesus, has promised Himself to us, I knew exactly what those people were saying and doing.

Satan has to respect the blood. When you say, "I plead the blood of Jesus in this situation," that's the blood by which God's promises to us were sealed. Satan can't touch it.

When you plead the blood, you have laid down your case and put your entire confidence in an oath sworn by God. When Jesus took the Communion cup in the upper room, He said, "Take this and drink it. This is the new covenant in My blood, ratified for you."

That blood guarantees certain things. It guarantees that every word in the Bible is a blood-sworn oath. That blood-sworn oath is your anchor. It says God is your Father and Jesus is your blood Brother. Everything that's His is yours and everything that's yours is His.

Jesus' blood shed for you obliterated your sin on the cross. When you received Jesus as your Lord, you took your place in your part of the New Covenant and you activated your freedom. Every time you repent of sin, it is destroyed forever and you are cleansed of it. That's why you can be free of guilt. So when you feel like you're in front of a judge and he asks, "How do you plead?" say, "I plead the blood! I'm innocent of that sin."

The case will be dismissed because of lack of evidence!

Yes! Even Satan has to honor that blood.

backup:
Hebrews 9:11-10:23

download:
Joshua 23-24; Acts 28

voice activate:
In Christ I have been redeemed through His blood and my sins have been obliterated. Ephesians 1:7

"For you were bought at a price; therefore glorify God in your body and in your spirit, which are God's."
1 Corinthians 6:20, NKJV

Live a Holy Life

Your body is not your own. Therefore, what you do with it is not totally up to you. You've been bought with a price. Jesus paid for you through His sacrifice on the cross. Your body belongs to God. It is the temple of the Holy Spirit (1 Corinthians 6:19). *The Amplified Bible* says it is His sanctuary.

God gave us the Holy Spirit to help us walk in holiness. We are separated from the world—separated to God. It is the Holy Spirit within you that prompts you to do what God wants you to do. God's own Spirit came into you when you made Jesus your Lord. To do what? *To promote holiness and separation of our lives, our hearts, our very lifestyles and every action unto God.* Read that sentence again.

Some people say not doing certain things will make you holy...like you can't wear certain clothes, you can't wear your hairstyle a certain way or you can't wear makeup, and so on. The truth is, none of those things will make you holy. They only affect the way you look.

Only God's Spirit will make you holy. We are united with God in such a way that the Holy Spirit is leading us, guiding us and directing us.

God has paid a high price for you. So worship Him in the way you treat your body. Honor Him with your lifestyle. Obey the peaceful voice of the Holy Spirit within you. Choose to live a holy life.

kenneth

backup:
1 Corinthians 6:9-20

download:
Judges 1-2; Romans 1

voice activate:
I am bought with a price. I glorify God in my body and in my spirit, which are His.
1 Corinthians 6:20

"I tell you that if two of you on earth agree about anything you ask for, it will be done for you by my Father in heaven."
Matthew 18:19

april 14

kenneth

An Unstoppable Force

A symphony is composed of many instruments which, when played together, seem to be a single voice. If you've ever heard a symphony, you know that when the individual instruments are tuning up—each one playing separately from the other—it's not much to hear. But when the conductor raises his baton and all those instruments begin to harmonize, the sound they make is powerful. This is what it means to have agreement.

Christians agreeing together in prayer is a powerful, unstoppable force. That's why Satan fights Christian families and Christian friendships. That's why he wants us fighting and fussing all the time—because he knows it will hinder our prayers (1 Peter 3:7).

Any time you don't get results when agreeing in prayer, run a harmony check. Ask the Holy Spirit to show you if you're in strife with someone. Then follow the instructions in Mark 11:25 where Jesus tells us, *"When you stand praying, if you hold anything against anyone, forgive him, so that your Father in heaven may forgive you your sins."*

It's not enough for you to simply agree with someone about what you're praying about. You must also be in harmony in other areas as well. So run a harmony check!

backup:
1 Peter 3:7-12

download:
Judges 3-4; Romans 2

voice activate:
When I agree with someone in prayer about anything we ask for, it will be done for us by our Father in heaven. Matthew 18:19

"If ye then be risen with Christ, seek those things which are above, where Christ sitteth on the right hand of God. Set your affection on things above, not on things on the earth."
Colossians 3:1-2, KJV

Check Your Affections

Separating yourself from the ways of the world doesn't always mean just leaving bad habits behind. It often means simply getting rid of those things that don't build you up.

Hebrews 12:1 says as we run the race that is set before us, we are to throw off everything that hinders us. You may have things in your life that are slowing you down spiritually. They may not be bad things in themselves, yet they are draining you. You may be so wrapped up in your computer, for instance, that you spend all your time thinking and talking about it. Or you may have joined a club or taken up a hobby that has become the center of your attention.

The problem with things like that is not that they are sinful, it's that they've captured your affection. It's time to check your affections. The Bible says in Colossians 3 that we're to set our affection on things above, not on things on the earth.

God wants you to set the affection of your heart on Him. Why? So that He can pour out His affection on you!

You can't give anything to God without His giving you more in return. When you set your affection on Him, He will give you more than you can imagine!

gloria

backup:
Hebrews 12:1-4

download:
Judges 5-6; Romans 3

voice activate:
I seek those things which are above. I set my affection on things above, not on things on earth. Colossians 3:1-2

"Then Moses said, 'Now show me your glory.' And the Lord said, 'I will cause all my goodness to pass in front of you.'"
Exodus 33:18-19

april 16

kenneth

Overwhelming Evil With Good

God's goodness and His glory are one. That's why, after Moses asked to see God's glory, God showed it to Him...by making all His *goodness* pass in front of Moses.

If you read all of Exodus 33, you'll also find that God told Moses He would have to hide him from that glory, because if he saw God's face, he would die.

Why? Because good overwhelms evil. Remember, Moses' heart had never been re-created, so he had sin in him. (His heart couldn't be re-created, because Jesus hadn't come to earth yet.) God doesn't have to try to kill darkness. He doesn't have to bash it in the head with His fist. When God walks on the scene, His goodness is released in its full force—and it's so powerful, it just blasts evil into nothingness.

That's the reason God and man had to be separated after Adam messed up. God had to protect man from the power of His glory.

I want you to know, God isn't separated from us any longer. He is living inside our re-created spirit—and, in these end times, He's going to show up not only in our spirit, but on our bodies, too!

Think about that. Satan thought he had our bodies locked up for himself. For years he did, but not any more. Sickness and disease have begun disappearing from human bodies like never before.

Now, you just can't play around with this glory. It is power. It's the kind of power that will lead many people to Jesus. It's the kind of power that makes Satan pack his bags and run! That's the reason He is calling on us to get the sin out of our lives. If He pours out His glory and you're hanging on to sin, it will destroy you. So get the sin out!

backup:
Exodus 33:12-23

download:
Judges 7-9; Romans 4-5

voice activate:
The Lord shows me His glory. He causes all His goodness to pass in front of me.
Exodus 33:18-19

"But nothing that a man shall devote to the Lord of all that he has, whether of man or beast or of the field of his possession, shall be sold or redeemed; every devoted thing is most holy to the Lord.... And all the tithe of the land, whether of the seed of the land or of the fruit of the tree, is the Lord's; it is holy to the Lord."
Leviticus 27:28,30, AMP

Devoted to Blessing

"Behold, what a drudgery and weariness this is!" (Malachi 1:13, AMP).

Have you ever had that thought when you were giving your tithe to God? Have you ever wanted to hide your money from God so you wouldn't have to give? If so, you need to change your attitude quick, or it will prevent you from receiving the financial blessings God has for you.

We ought to be like a little child when it comes to giving. Have you ever seen how excited kids get when their parents give them money to put in the offering? They can hardly wait to give it.

We ought to be that way. We ought to look forward to giving God 10 percent of what we make—from our jobs, our allowances and from gifts.

Just as tithing opens the door to God blessing you, stealing God's tithe and using it on yourself opens the door to Satan stealing from you. You'll never come out ahead by keeping the tithe.

Ken and I know that from personal experience. When we became Christians, we tithed for a while...but then we decided we needed the money more than

God. Soon, our finances got worse. We kept getting deeper in debt.

Things only turned around when we began to obey God's Word. We made a rock solid decision to tithe before spending money on anything else, no matter what. That's when our finances took an upturn—and things have been great ever since! It just keeps getting better and better!

If you're not experiencing the kind of blessings the Bible says belongs to a tither, then check your attitude. Check your heart. When your heart is right, you'll have a hard time *not* getting excited about it! You won't want to hold God's ten percent from Him. You'll thank Him for letting it pass through your hands. You'll just love to tithe!

backup:
2 Corinthians 9:6-11

download:
Judges 10-11; Romans 6

voice activate:
I honor the Lord with my wealth and with the first fruits of all my increase. My barns are filled to overflowing and my vats brim over with new wine. Proverbs 3:9-10

"The Lord will grant that the enemies who rise up against you will be defeated before you. They will come at you from one direction but flee from you in seven." **Deuteronomy 28:7**

The *Hesed* of God

Do you know what the Ten Commandments mean? Most people just think they mean "Don't do this and don't do that." However, to a covenant-minded person who understands God's mercy—His *hesed*—they mean something much different.

Hesed is a word of promise. In Hebrew, it describes God's mercy, kindness, tender mercies, His lovingkindness and fidelity. It's His unconditional love for you.

So, God is saying in the Ten Commandments, "Listen, children, there isn't any need for you to steal, or murder or covet anything. Just bring your problems to Me. You have a covenant with Me. I'll take care of you. All you need to do is live in love and faith. I'll take care of the rest."

I can just hear your mind working. *Oh, Ken, that sounds great. But I've done some rotten things since I've been a Christian. I've messed up my part of the covenant pretty badly.*

No, you haven't. You can't mess up this covenant because it's not between you and God. It's between God and Jesus.

You can't break it. You can turn your back on it and refuse to receive its benefits. It will still be there when you repent.

"Yeah, but I just don't understand how God could still love me after all I've done."

Listen, the *hesed* of God isn't affected by what you do or don't do. He loves you because He *wants* to love you. He loves you because you and He are connected by the pure covenant blood of Jesus—and there's nothing you can do to change that. That's what *hesed* is!

So don't let Satan deceive you. You are worthy to receive God's unconditional love. The blood of Jesus has given it to you. It's yours. Remember: He loves you because He *wants* to!

backup:
1 John 4:16-21

download:
Judges 12-13; Romans 7

voice activate:
I am worthy to receive God's unconditional love because of the blood of Jesus. I receive and walk in that love today. 1 John 4:16-21

"'And I will ask the Father, and he will give you another Counselor to be with you forever—the Spirit of truth. The world cannot accept him, because it neither sees him nor knows him. But you know him, for he lives with you and will be in you.'"
John 14:16-17

Press In

God has set things up for your success. It's true! He has given you everything you need to succeed in life. He's given you His Word, the blood of Jesus and the power of the Holy Spirit...just to name a few.

Even with all of that, you still have to do your part. Some people waste a great deal of time by not understanding this. When they find themselves in a hard situation, they often sit back and wait for God to rescue them.

You won't get anywhere by just waiting for God to do everything. As one minister says, "The Holy Spirit is your Helper, and if you don't do what you're supposed to, He doesn't have anything to help!"

So don't just sit there—do something!

Put God's promises in your heart and speak them out. No, that's not always easy—especially when you're facing a hard situation, but you can do it!

I think it was great that Ken and I were in an impossible financial situation when we first heard about faith. (I didn't think it was great then, of course, but I do now!) Our finances were really bad. We didn't have anything but debt!

We were so desperate, we *had* to believe God. It was the hardest believing we ever did, too. Because we didn't know very much, we got aggressive with our faith and God's promises.

If you want to walk in the supernatural, you aren't going to do it by slouching on the couch. You must press in. Jesus said, *"The good news of the kingdom of God is being preached, and everyone is forcing his way into it"* (Luke 16:16).

Press in. That's so important! So take what God has given you. Get His promises in your heart and speak them out. Plead the blood of Jesus over your circumstances and your friends and family. Get aggressive and give the Holy Spirit something to help!

b a c k u p :
2 Kings 7

d o w n l o a d :
Judges 14-15; Romans 8

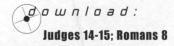
v o i c e   a c t i v a t e :
**As I press in and lay hold of God's promises for my life, the Holy Spirit helps me.
John 14:26**

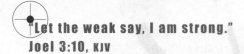

april 20

kenneth

Watch Him Move!

Your confession is what you say—not just with your lips, but with your actions. The Bible says Jesus is the High Priest of your confession (Hebrews 3:1). That means He has the authority to make anything you say by faith happen—as long as it's in line with His Word.

That means when you're broke and you say by faith, "My God will meet all my needs according to His glorious riches in Jesus" (Philippians 4:19), Jesus has the authority to deliver the finances to you. Or, when you are sick and you say by faith, "I'm healed by Jesus' wounds" (Isaiah 53:5), you put yourself in a position to receive that healing from Him.

Some people say, "Oh, I couldn't say I was healed when I was actually sick. That would be lying!"

If that were the case, then the prophet Joel told people to lie because he said, *"Let the weak say, I am strong."*

No, Joel wasn't telling people to lie. He was sharing a spiritual principle. He was telling God's people they should say what God says about them, instead of what the circumstances say about them.

The reason that seems strange to most people is because they're so selfish. They see everything from their own viewpoint. When you speak about what God has promised, instead of speaking about the way things look around you, you're setting aside your own viewpoint and speaking from God's viewpoint.

So speak God's Words over your circumstances today. Speak His Words in faith...and watch Him move!

backup:
Proverbs 18:20-21

download:
Judges 16-17; Romans 9

voice activate:
I am strong in the Lord and in His mighty power. Ephesians 6:10

> "Bring all the tithes...into the storehouse, that there may be food in My house, and prove Me now by it, says the Lord of hosts, if I will not open the windows of heaven for you and pour you out a blessing, that there shall not be room enough to receive it."
> Malachi 3:10, AMP

A Prosperity Surplus

Christians need to prosper. We need to have enough not just to meet our own needs, but to see to it that the good news is preached around the world. Jesus is coming back soon! We don't have time to sit around wishing we had enough money to do things right. We need to be able to give now!

How do we get on that road? Through tithing. Tithing opens the door for God to be directly involved in our finances. It is a two-way exchange in which we honor God by giving Him 10 percent of our income and He, in return, provides us with a *"surplus of prosperity"* (Deuteronomy 28:11, AMP).

"Gloria," you may say, "I know Christians who have been tithing for years and they are not wealthy!"

Actually, you don't. You just know people who have put ten percent of their income into the offering bucket. They went through the motions, but they weren't doing true Bible tithing.

Tithing isn't just a matter of taking money out of your purse or wallet. It is a matter of the heart. That's the way it is with everything as far as God is concerned. He always looks on the heart. So

when we tithe as a religious routine—not in faith—just because we're supposed to and not as a genuine expression of our love for God, we miss out on the benefits of it.

That's what happened to the people in Malachi's day. They were going through the motions of tithing, but they were not seeing God move in their lives.

What they were missing was honor! They weren't giving God their best. Because they didn't love and honor God in their hearts, they were offering Him their leftovers.

So are you ready to take the limits off? Then tithe the right way. Remember to honor God with your tithe...honor Him from your heart. Soon, you'll enjoy the supernatural prosperity God has promised you!

backup:
Malachi 3:8-12

download:
Judges 18-19; Romans 10

voice activate:
I bring the whole tithe in to the storehouse. The Lord throws open the floodgates of heaven and pours out so much blessing on me that I don't have room enough for it! Malachi 3:10

gloria

"But for you who revere my name, the sun of righteousness will rise with healing in [His] wings. And you will go out and leap like calves released from the stall. Then you will trample down the wicked; they will be ashes under the soles of your feet on the day when I do these things,' says the Lord Almighty." Malachi 4:2-3

april 22

kenneth

Blazing Glory

I imagine you are probably just as tired of having Satan get in the middle of your affairs as the next guy. You're tired of him causing trouble in your family and messing with your friendships. It doesn't have to be that way, you know. Read today's verse again.

Notice that this scripture says *"S-U-N of righteousness,"* and not *"S-O-N of right-eousness"*? That's not a mistake. Malachi was talking about a bright, blazing glory. The wings he refers to aren't bird's wings, they're flames of fire that are shaped like wings.

Most exciting of all is the fact Malachi didn't say that "He will go out." He said, *"You* will go out."

You and I are the ones who will ensure Satan's defeat in our lives. We have all the power we need to destroy Satan's works, and to kick him out of our affairs.

The words you say coupled with your faith are going to pull the glory out of you, and you'll walk in that glory right in the face of all the trouble hell can give you.

You are the one who will go out into the world with this blazing glory...the same glory that raised Jesus from the dead. It's that same glory that you'll use to trample down Satan like ashes under your feet!

backup:
Mark 16:14-19

download:
Judges 20-21; Romans 11

voice activate:
I go out and leap like a calf released from the stall. I trample down the wicked one and he is ashes under the soles of my feet. Malachi 4:2-3

"You are still worldly. For since there is jealousy and quarreling among you, are you not worldly? Are you not acting like mere men?"
1 Corinthians 3:3

Being an Overcomer

It's bad enough that strife opens us up to confusion and evil (James 3:14-16, KJV). That alone should make us resist it with everything we've got. But that's not all the Bible has to say about strife.

In his letter to the Corinthians, Paul gave us even more information about the damaging effects of strife. He wrote:

"Brothers, I could not address you as spiritual but as worldly—mere infants in Christ. I gave you milk, not solid food, for you were not yet ready for it. Indeed, you are still not ready. You are still worldly. For since there is jealousy and quarreling among you, are you not worldly? Are you not acting like mere men?" (1 Corinthians 3:1-3).

Worldly Christians are miserable people. They've made Jesus their Lord and they know enough about God not to enjoy sin, but they aren't committed enough to stay out of sin.

If you don't want to find yourself trapped in that condition (and I know you don't) then stay out of strife, because strife will keep you worldly! It will stop up your ability to really understand the deep things in God's Word, which will keep you from growing into a strong, winning Christian. If you fuss and bicker with others, your spiritual growth will be stunted. You'll stay in a continual state of spiritual babyhood and Satan will run over you time and again!

So grow up. Don't stay a baby. Get out of strife and into the Word. Soon you'll be the overcomer God says you are!

gloria

backup:
2 Timothy 2:24-26; 1 John 5:4-5

download:
Ruth 1-3; Romans 12-13

voice activate:
I walk in love and grow up in every way and in all things. Ephesians 4:15, AMP

"For the word of God is living and active. Sharper than any double-edged sword, it penetrates even to dividing soul and spirit, joints and marrow; it judges the thoughts and attitudes of the heart."
Hebrews 4:12

His Word Is His Bond

april 24

kenneth

The Word of God is not just a book! It is not just a black leather book you carry to church on Sunday and then leave hidden in your gym locker the rest of the week. God's Word has been recorded in a book...but the Word itself is what God has said and is saying to you personally!

That's powerful. That means the Word of God is living...and active every time you put it to work. That's because God's Word is His bond.

You've heard people say that about others: "A man's word is his bond." That means a person's word is the measure of his character. If a man honors his word by keeping it, then he is an honorable man. If he dishonors his word by breaking it, he is a dishonorable man. Like it or not, everyone's integrity—including God's—is judged on the basis of whether or not he keeps his word.

That may sound funny, but God set it up that way. He invented the integrity of words. He taught us to judge integrity on that basis. He set the standard.

God and His Word are one—not because we say so, but because He said so. He has made it clear that we cannot separate Him from His Word. Just as He never changes, His Word never changes. They are both the same—yesterday, today and forever.

That means that if you've been believing God for something based on a promise in His Word, you can rest assured He will keep His Word. He won't fail you. His Word is living...it is working for you every time you speak it aloud and act on it in faith. So stand up strong today. Put your trust in Him. Don't cave in to doubt. Remember, His Word is His bond.

backup:
John 17:1-6

download:
Ruth 4; 1 Samuel 1; Romans 14

voice activate:
God's Word is alive and full of power. It is active, operative, energizing and effective in my life. Hebrews 4:12, AMP

"Jesus said to it [the fig tree], 'Let no one eat fruit from you ever again.' And His disciples heard it…. Now in the morning, as they passed by, they saw the fig tree dried up from the roots."

Mark 11:14,20, NKJV

Hit It From the Source

You can't wipe out a weed simply by mowing it down. If you want to get rid of a weed, you must destroy its roots. That's Biology 101.

Did you know that's true in every other area of life? If you want to change a situation permanently, you must tackle it at its root. You can lose hundreds of pounds, for example, and you'll regain every one of them (and probably more) if you don't solve that weight problem at the root.

That is what's so awesomely powerful about faith. If it's founded on a promise from God to you, it will change things in your life from the roots up.

Read Mark 11 and you'll see what I mean. Jesus was walking from Bethany to Jerusalem with His disciples. He was hungry, but when He saw a fig tree that didn't have any figs, He *said to it, 'Let no one eat fruit from you ever again'. And his disciples heard it* (verse 14).

Jesus *answered* the fig tree because it spoke to Him first! By the very fact that it had no fruit, that tree was saying to Jesus, "Forget it, buddy. You aren't getting anything to eat here."

Your circumstances talk to you in the same way. Do you realize that? If you're standing against sickness, that sickness is talking to you. When you get up in the morning, it says, *You haven't received your healing. You're hurting all over. This faith stuff isn't working. You might as well go back to bed.*

Your situations will talk to you all the time. So do what Jesus did. Answer them! Get to the root. Say, "By His wounds I was healed! I am more than a conqueror in Christ Jesus!"

Speaking words in faith like that will change things. Jesus took on the fig tree at its root…and it made a permanent change. You have the same power. If you'll release your faith, you can hit even the most stubborn problem and dry it up at the source. You can get rid of it from the roots up!

b a c k u p :
2 Corinthians 4:13-18

d o w n l o a d :
1 Samuel 2-3; Romans 15

v o i c e   a c t i v a t e :
I have the same spirit of faith as Jesus. I believe and therefore I speak. 2 Corinthians 4:13

kenneth

123

"After beginning with the Spirit, are you now trying to attain your goal by human effort?"
Galatians 3:3

april 26

gloria

Stay Connected

Wouldn't life be wonderfully simple if there was only one thing that truly mattered? Wouldn't it be great if only one factor determined your success? All the confusion and complexity that clutters your life would suddenly disappear. Instead of constantly juggling priorities, you'd always know what to put first.

Well, here's a bit of news that may surprise you. There is, in fact, only one real key to victory in life. That's right. Just one. *A continual connection with God.*

In years past, I used to say, "If things aren't going well, check to see if you're walking in love." Or sometimes I'd tell people, "If you're not getting your prayers answered, make sure you aren't harboring any unforgiveness." I had learned that by checking those spiritual gauges, you could track down the causes for failure.

Even though such gauges are very helpful, after more than years of living by faith, I've come to realize that ultimately our success stems solely from our vital, continual contact with God. That one factor rules all others.

If you're in contact with the Lord, those other qualities will flow naturally from you. If you keep a prayerful connection with God, you will walk in love and joy. You will walk in forgiveness.

So what exactly is a continual connection with God? It simply means keeping the lines of communication open between the two of you. It means going about your daily activities in such a way that you're always ready to hear from Him.

Just think: The real key to consistent victory is just one thing! You don't have to memorize a list of dos and don'ts. All you have to do is keep in continual contact with God. He's always speaking to our hearts. Keep your ear tuned to Him. Keep your heart lined up with His Word. Just keep the line open!

b a c k u p :
1 John 1:1-7

d o w n l o a d :
1 Samuel 4-5; Romans 16

v o i c e a c t i v a t e :
After beginning with the Spirit, I stay in the Spirit and attain my goal.
Galatians 3:3

"Those who belong to Christ Jesus have crucified the sinful nature with its passions and desires."
Galatians 5:24

Winning the Battle

Do you know what it is like to be in a losing battle with your own body? I do...and I can tell you, it's miserable.

There have been times in my life as a Christian when I wanted with all my heart to behave one way, and my body seemed absolutely intent on doing exactly the opposite. Times when I desperately wanted to lose weight, yet kept on stuffing myself with all kinds of junk food. There was even a time when I wanted to quit smoking so much that I threw my cigarettes out the car window...then turned the car around to go back and get them.

You know what I'm talking about. You've been there too. It's a battle with your old sinful nature.

So how do we get things right? Well first, you need to realize when we make Jesus our Lord, we're not half God and half devil. Jesus paid the price for our whole being on the cross—spirit, soul and body. So we need to take charge over our old nature and train it to obey God through practice (Hebrews 5:14). We practice training ourselves by obeying God's Word and the Holy Spirit as He speaks to our hearts. Galatians 5:16 reveals the key. It says when we live by the spirit, we will not indulge the desires of the sinful nature.

If you'll develop your spirit and put it in charge of your body, instead of being dominated by your old nature, eventually you'll train that body to work with your spirit instead of against it. That's good news!

backup:
Galatians 5:16-18

download:
1 Samuel 6-7; 1 Corinthians 1

voice activate:
I am Christ's. I crucify my sinful nature with its passions and desires. Galatians 5:24

"Command those who are rich in this present world not to be arrogant nor to put their hope in wealth, which is so uncertain, but to put their hope in God, who richly provides us with everything for our enjoyment. Command them to do good, to be rich in good deeds, and to be generous and willing to share."
1 Timothy 6:17-18

april 28

kenneth

Freely Give

God created us in His image. We have His giving image planted deep within us, and because of that, giving is one of the most basic spiritual needs we have. We *need* to *give*—and this need to give that's inside us is far greater than the need to keep.

The key to enjoying all things God has given us, as mentioned in today's verse, is being *"generous"* and *"willing to share."*

To just hold on to everything you accumulate for your own security, your own retirement, your own "cushion" or whatever you want to call it, is to be earthly minded.

Obviously, saving is not a bad thing. What I'm talking about here is the "hold-on-to-everything-I've-got" mentality. It doesn't let faith in. It doesn't allow for God to supply your needs according to His glorious riches in Jesus (Philippians 4:19).

The world says, "Hey, I've worked hard for this. I may not have another opportunity to have this much again, so I'd better hold on to it as long as I can...'cause you never know." That's living in fear! Suddenly, the need to give is overridden by the need to keep. You've never had so little in all your life until you've had a lot of money that you're afraid to spend.

Faith, on the other hand, says, "I received all these riches by believing God, and as long as God is around, there is always more where this came from."

Faith doesn't have to hold on to everything it gets. Faith freely gives...because faith is not in a mindset of expecting to do without.

So how are you handling your money? In faith, or fear? Give in faith. Give freely. Give of yourself, your time, your talent and your money. Give as an expression of who you really are...someone created in the very image of God...the greatest giver of all!

backup:
Matthew 6:19-20

download:
1 Samuel 8-9; 1 Corinthians 2

voice activate:
I put my hope in God, Who richly provides me with everything for my enjoyment. 1 Timothy 6:17

"'Go home to your family and tell them how much the Lord has done for you, and how he has had mercy on you.'"
Mark 5:19

Put Your Reputation on the Line

God is a good God. In most circles, that's still shocking news. Do you remember what Jesus told the madman from Gadara after He cast out the demons that had possessed him? Jesus told him to tell his friends about all the great things the Lord had done for him.

Jesus was concerned about God's reputation. He wanted it corrected. Everywhere He went He taught people that God was not Who they thought He was. He taught them that God is a good God, and that's the job He gave us when He left the earth (Mark 16:15).

Mark 5:25-34 tells the account of a woman with a blood condition who put her reputation on the line. It was against the Jewish Law for a woman with a sickness like this to be in public at all. Yet, she risked public humiliation, even arrest, and fought her way through the crowd to touch the hem of Jesus' garment.

Why? Because she was more interested in Jesus' reputation than her own. She knew she couldn't get healed by staying at home doing what the religious community of her day said she should do. To receive her healing, she had to hang on to Jesus' reputation—and let go of hers. She wanted healing so desperately and believed in Jesus' goodness so fully, she was willing to risk it all.

That's how you have to be if you're going to see God work miracles in your life at home, at work, at school and at church. You have to become so confident about how good He is that you'll dare to lay everything on the line. Choose His reputation over yours every single time.

gloria

backup:
Luke 8:43-48

download:
1 Samuel 10-11; 1 Corinthians 3

voice activate:
The Lord has done great things for me. He has compassion and mercy on me. Mark 5:19

"But in a great house there are not only vessels of gold and of silver, but also of wood and of earth; and some to honour, and some to dishonour. If a man therefore purge himself from these, he shall be a vessel unto honour, sanctified, and meet for the master's use, and prepared unto every good work."
2 Timothy 2:20-21, KJV

april 30

kenneth

Destined for Greatness

You are destined for greatness! God's plan and desire is for you to be so full of His power, that it overflows to others, changing their lives forever!

"Well, now, Kenneth, you know not everyone is destined for greatness. As the Bible says, some vessels are gold and silver...others are wood and earth. I guess I'm just one of those little mud vessels."

If you are, it's your own fault! God isn't the one who decides if we're to be vessels of honor or not. We make the decision ourselves.

If you want to be a vessel of honor, you can be. According to 2 Timothy 2:19-21, you simply have to purge yourself from sin and dishonor. Notice I said purge *yourself*. God won't do it for you. He cleansed you from sin the moment you made Jesus your Lord, but it's your responsibility to keep yourself pure. It's up to you to admit your sins and walk in holiness day by day. God will give you power, but you're the one who must put that power to work.

The Bible doesn't say Jesus will drag you away from sin, it says you are to *depart* from it. You are to cleanse yourself from sin as well as from the phony faith tactics many Christians use.

Don't ever be like the fellow who went down to the altar and knelt down right next to the richest man in the church and began praying: "Oh, God, pleeeease, I need a car. How will I ever get around without one?! Oh, God, You know I've given away all I have for You...."

When the rich man yielded to the pressure and gave him a car, that fellow said he got it by faith. That wasn't faith! It was a religious con.

We must back away from such dishonorable ways. We need to be a people of honor who would rather take a bus than resort to begging. We need to be the kind of people who go off in a corner where no one can hear us and pray to God in secret, believing He will answer! Then, we can fulfill all of His plans for greatness...plans for us to overflow into other people's lives with all of His power!

backup:
Matthew 6:5-8

download:
1 Samuel 12-14; 1 Corinthians 4-5

voice activate:
I am a vessel of honor, sanctified, and fit for the Master's use. 2 Timothy 2:21

It Takes Courage

Do you know it takes courage to obey the Bible? It really does, because when you obey the Word and believe God in a situation, you're swimming upstream. You're going against the current of the world.

Whether you're standing strong while waiting for a college acceptance letter, or working toward funding a missions trip with your youth group, it always takes courage when you obey. It takes courage, strength and determination to stay with something, especially when the world seems to offer an easier, quicker way to get there.

When people and circumstances are screaming in your ears, it takes courage to stand on God's promises to you and not be moved.

Once you make the decision to stand and be courageous, you'll be in position and ready to activate God's three-part formula for success.

You'll find it spelled out in Joshua 1:8, AMP:

1) "This Book of the Law shall not depart out of your mouth...

2) "But you shall meditate on it day and night...

3) "That you may observe and do according to all that is written in it; for then you shall make your way prosperous, and then you shall deal wisely and have good success."

There they are. Three simple steps directly from God. They are the steps that enabled Joshua to conquer the land of Canaan and bring the Israelites into their inheritance.

They are also the steps that will enable you to live like the conqueror God created you to be. So don't give up. That acceptance letter will come. You'll go on that missions trip. Things will change...as long as you stand, continuing to be courageous.

may 1

gloria

backup:
Joshua 23:1-11

download:
1 Samuel 15-16; 1 Corinthians 6

voice activate:
I am strong and very courageous.
Joshua 1:7

"You are a chosen people, a royal priesthood, a holy nation, a people belonging to God, that you may declare the praises of him who called you out of darkness into his wonderful light."
1 Peter 2:9

Jesus Isn't the Only One!

May 2

Kenneth

God's power is increasing in Christians everywhere. They are flowing in the anointing—ministering to others and seeing miracles. Despite all that, there's still a bunch of religious people who say, "Oh, no. I'm not anointed. I'm nothing more than an unworthy sinner. Jesus was the only One truly anointed."

That's an ungodly lie! Jesus isn't the only one anointed anymore! It was never God's intention to simply give Jesus His power and leave it at that. God knew that wasn't enough!

That's why He sent Jesus to the cross and then raised Him from the dead. He wanted to open the way for us all to receive His power. That's been God's plan from the beginning. Through Jesus the Anointed One, He raised up a whole nation of kings and priests and called them His Church.

That's who today's verse says we are! We are a chosen people, a royal priesthood! We are anointed with the Anointing of the Anointed One!

We are to be living proof that Jesus is alive and anointed with bondage-destroying power because His Anointing is on us.

In His Name, we pray for the sick and they recover. We cast out devils. We speak His promises in faith and set captives free! We're not unworthy sinners. The Bible says we are sons of the Most High God.

If a classmate asks you, "Do you mean to tell me you have the power to heal?" We should answer them boldly and say, "Yes! Because the One Who is in me is greater than the one that is in the world. The Holy Spirit within me does the work!" After all, Jesus isn't the only anointed One!

backup:
Acts 10:38-39

download:
1 Samuel 17-18; 1 Corinthians 7

voice activate:
I am a part of a chosen people, a royal priesthood, a holy nation. I declare the praises of Him Who called me out of darkness into His wonderful light.
1 Peter 2:9

"Make every effort to live in peace with all men and to be holy; without holiness no one will see the Lord."
Hebrews 12:14

Looking Deep Inside

Holiness is living for God. Unlike the way the world lives, holiness isn't easy. You can't just coast along doing what everybody else is doing and be holy. It takes effort. It takes grit. It means doing what God wants you to do even when you might want to do something else. The rewards are tremendous when you obey Him.

Today's verse says that without holiness, no one will see the Lord. Does that mean if you're holy, you will see Him? Yes!

Jesus Himself said, *"Whoever has my commands and obeys them, he is the one who loves me. He who loves me will be loved by my Father, and I too will love him and show myself to him"* (John 14:21).

In other words, if you live the way I'm talking about right now—doing things that are pleasing to God—Jesus will show Himself to you. He can become so real to you through the Bible, that it will be as if He's standing right in front of you. You can be closer to Him than you are to your best friend.

That's enough reason to live holy...but there are even more rewards!

According to 1 John 5:18, Satan can't touch you. Can you imagine what life would be like if Satan couldn't lay a finger on you? Well, that's the way God wants your life to be. He wants you so free that Satan can't hurt you in any way.

Furthermore, if you're living holy, when you pray you won't feel guilty for things you've been doing. First John 3:21-22 says that if our hearts don't condemn us, then we have confidence before God. Do you know why so many people's prayers fail to be answered? It's not because God doesn't do His part. It's because the people had no confidence when they went before God in prayer. They couldn't ask in faith because their hearts condemned them about the sin in their lives. .

Deep inside, you know whether or not you're giving God top priority— whether or not you're living a holy lifestyle. Make a decision today to live for God and live holy. The rewards are great!

backup:
1 John 3:21-24

download:
1 Samuel 19-20; 1 Corinthians 8

voice activate:
I make every effort to live in peace with all men and to be holy, and I shall see the Lord. Hebrews 12:14

"He who by charging excessive interest and who by unjust efforts to get gain increases his material possession gathers it for him [to spend] who is kind and generous to the poor."
Proverbs 28:8, AMP

May 4

gloria

Who's Wealth?

As I've studied about financial success, one point is always clear: God is a God of justice as well as mercy.

His mercy is evident by His giving us the handbook—His Word—on how to live a godly life, which is the basic key to living well. When we obey and follow His commands, He takes care of us and blesses us.

His justice is evident in the outcome for those who don't follow Him: *"The Lord delights in justice and forsakes not His saints; they are preserved for ever, but the offspring of the wicked [in time] shall be cut off"* (Psalm 37:28, AMP).

Now, some people may feel that God isn't just or merciful because they don't see Him fulfilling His promises right away. He's actually both! *"The Lord does not delay and be tardy or slow about what He promises, according to some people's conception of slowness, but He is long-suffering (extraordinarily patient) toward you, not desiring that any should perish, but that all should turn to repentance"* (2 Peter 3:9, AMP).

God is giving unbelievers plenty of time to repent. However, He is well aware of what they are doing (Proverbs 5:21, 15:3). They may appear to be successful even though they're living wrong, but their success will be short-lived (James 5:1-4; Psalm 37:7-9). The Bible indicates that in the last days, wealth will be transferred from the wicked to the just (Proverbs 13:22). The sinners are actually just storing up wealth for Christians (Ecclesiastes 2:26)!

That wealth will come to the Church in different ways, but one thing is for sure: The riches will be given to those who know how to give.

We need to determine to be one of those givers, so we can receive the wealth and use it to reach people. Get ready today by getting your words and actions in line with God's Word. Believe for what He promises you. Use your faith. Learn to give, and watch for the wealth of the world to come to you!

backup:
Proverbs 13:22; Ecclesiastes 2:26; Mark 10:29-30

download:
1 Samuel 21-22; 1 Corinthians 9

voice activate:
The wealth of the sinner is stored up for me. It finds its way into my hands. Proverbs 13:22, AMP

"Honor the Lord with your wealth, with the firstfruits of all your crops; then your barns will be filled to overflowing, and your vats will brim over with new wine."
Proverbs 3:9-10

He Wants Your Heart

Have you ever wanted God to bless you? Well, sure you have! God has already given us more than we ever dreamed possible. He has rescued us from darkness. He has provided healing for us. He has blessed us in a thousand different ways. That's what we should remember every time we tithe. We should give with a thankful attitude.

If you'll read Deuteronomy 26, you'll see that's what God instructed the Israelites to do. He didn't want them to simply toss their tithe into the offering plate. He wanted their hearts in what they were doing. He wants the same from us.

When we give our tithe, we should worship God and say, "Father, once I was lost, a prisoner of sin with no hope, but You sent Jesus to rescue me. You sent Him to die so I could live. Thank You, Lord, for rescuing me from the darkness and bringing me into the Light. Thank You for receiving my tithe as an act of my worship to You."

Don't stop there! Just like the Israelites, say, "Lord, here's my tithe. I haven't kept it for myself. I've given it just as You commanded. So look down from heaven and bless me!" (Deuteronomy 26:13-15)

Does that kind of talk make you nervous? Do you think God will be offended if you tell Him to bless you? He won't! He'll be delighted. After all, it's His idea to bless us in the first place! It's what He's wanted to do all along.

So don't be shy. Tithe boldly! Tithe gladly! Give God 10 percent of what you make, and give Him 100 percent of your heart. Then shout, "The Lord be exalted, who delights in the well-being of his servant!" (Psalm 35:27).

may 5

gloria

backup:
Deuteronomy 26

download:
1 Samuel 23-24; 1 Corinthians 10

voice activate:
I honor the Lord with my wealth, with the first fruits of all my increase. My barns are filled to overflowing and my vats brim over with new wine. Proverbs 3:9-10

"Until we all reach unity in the faith and in the knowledge of the Son of God and become mature, attaining to the whole measure of the fullness of Christ." Ephesians 4:13

may 6

kenneth

Faith Is Not a Fad

Living the faith life for more than 30 years, I've become convinced that faith is not just a fad. It's much more than that.

God is moving. He is calling people from all denominations to move into a life of power. He is showing us a way to live successfully—day in and day out, in good times and bad times. Isn't that what we want? Isn't that what we need?

He is teaching us that faith in His Word works, even when nothing else does. He is calling us to live by faith, not just temporarily, but as Ephesians 4:13 says, *"until we all reach unity in the faith and in the knowledge of the Son of God and become mature, attaining to the whole measure of the fullness of Christ."*

If God is calling you to live a life of faith, and you've been tiptoeing around it...wondering if it's real or not...jump in now! Faith is not a fad. Faith is how God operates and lives...it's how He wants you to live.

Faith will open the door to success for you, and it will keep you there—safe and healed and wealthy in all areas of life. It will keep you armed and dangerous to Satan. It will keep you free from sin and enable you to grow into a man or woman of character. Faith will enable you to please God. Faith is a permanent way of life, and it's here to stay.

backup:
Colossians 2:6-7

download:
1 Samuel 25-26; 1 Corinthians 11

voice activate:
I develop and attain oneness in faith with other believers. I am perfect and complete in Christ. Ephesians 4:13, AMP

> "You will do well to pay close attention to it as to a lamp shining in a dismal (squalid and dark) place, until the day breaks through [the gloom] and the Morning Star rises (comes into being) in your hearts."
> 2 Peter 1:19, AMP

Keep Your Eyes on the Light

Do you know what the most important thing in your life is? It's not where you go to school. It's not even your family. The most important thing in your life is keeping your heart full of the light of God's Word.

You can have faith strong enough to change circumstances in your life. You can live in success instead of defeat, but you'll only do it on a continual basis by spending time in the Bible.

Proverbs 4:20-23 spells out this key to success in no uncertain terms: *"My son, pay attention to what I say; listen closely to my words. Do not let them out of your sight, keep them within your heart; for they are life to those who find them and health to a man's whole body. Above all else, guard your heart, for it is the wellspring of life."*

If your heart is full of the Word, you can do well in school and be at the top of your class! You can pray for the salvation of your family and see results. When you give your attention to the Bible, every other area in your life will be successful. It is the answer to everything.

God's Word shows you how to live successfully, even in a dark world. When you walk according to what God has said, His wisdom shines a light on your pathway.

Continually focus your attention on God's Word, and you can win even when negative circumstances surround you. Keep your eyes on the light, and it will bring you through to victory!

backup:
Psalm 91:9-10,14-16

download:
1 Samuel 27-29; 1 Corinthians 12-13

voice activate:
I pay attention to the Word of God. I keep it within my heart. It is life to me and health to my whole body. Proverbs 4:20-22

"There is no truth in him [the devil]."
John 8:44

may 8

kenneth

The Original Versus The Counterfeit

You might as well face it. As long as you are on this earth, Satan is going to talk to you. He has a right to test your faith by bringing you tough situations and lies to see if you'll go along with them.

When he does, refuse them. Throw aside those fearful ideas and every thought that is opposite of what God has promised you (2 Corinthians 10:5). Say, "The Lord is on my side. I WILL NOT FEAR!"

Then open your mouth and speak God's promises. Use the Word to contradict Satan's lies. If he tells you, *You won't have enough money to make it on your own,* don't start worrying. Speak up. Say right out loud, "I will too have the money I need. I know I will because my God supplies all my needs according to His glorious riches in Christ Jesus!"

I found out a long time ago that when my mouth speaks, my mind has to stop and listen to what it's saying. Maybe you won't fully believe what you're saying the first time you say it, but if you'll keep saying it, you'll keep hearing it, and what you hear, you'll believe. Eventually your faith will be so strong and your heart will be so full, you'll start speaking with total confidence.

That's when Satan will run for cover—because fear has no chance when faith comes on the scene. Faith is the original and fear is the counterfeit. The real thing overcomes the phony every time.

backup:
1 Peter 5:6-9

download:
1 Samuel 30-31; 1 Corinthians 14

voice activate:
The Lord is with me. I will not be afraid! Psalm 118:6

"Keep out of debt and owe no man anything, except to love one another."
Romans 13:8, AMP

A Two-Part Promise

I used to think it was my job to worry. I spent a lot of time thinking things like, *What are we going to do about our bills?* Then I found out God doesn't want us to worry. He wants us to believe He will take care of us. I also learned that as Christians, we're not to seek after material riches. We're not to pursue money like worldly people do. They *have* to pursue it. They don't have a covenant with God. So if they don't seek material goods, they won't get them!

We're not like those people. We're not in the world without God and without a covenant—an unbreakable promise (Ephesians 2:12-13). We have God's promise that He will take care of us and even give us *more* than we need.

It's important for us to remember, however, that a covenant is always between two parties. It has two sides. It says, *If you do this, then I'll do that.*

God's part of the covenant is to bless us. Our part is to seek after Him, not the things He gives us! Our part is to say, "Lord, I'll do whatever You tell me to do— even if it looks like it will cost me." It's always worth it.

I'll be honest with you, though. Years ago, when we first read today's verse, we weren't too excited about it. At that time in our lives, it looked like we'd never be able to do anything without borrowing money. We thought, *How will we ever buy a car? How will we get a home? How will we finance our ministry? We're doomed!*

We had already decided to obey God no matter what the cost, so we committed ourselves to get out of debt. Of course, that decision has turned out to be one of the wisest decisions we've ever made.

That's the way it always is. Obeying God always works to your advantage in the end! So start giving Him first place in your life. Commit to God that you will never get in debt. Keep your side of the covenant!

b a c k u p :
Psalm 37:21-40

d o w n l o a d :
2 Samuel 1-2; 1 Corinthians 15

v o i c e   a c t i v a t e :
I am out of debt and owe no man anything except to love him. Romans 13:8, AMP

"Their [Our] hearts...are knit together in love."
Colossians 2:2, AMP

may 10

kenneth

I Love You Regardless...

Our hearts are knit together in love. That's what God says about Christians. The word translated "love" in today's verse is from the Greek word, *agape*. *Agape* never means "I will love you if..." *Agape* means "I will love you regardless." That's the unconditional love of God. We are brought together by that love. We are in Him and He is in us.

Now, you may have some classmates or family members, or you may work with some people with whom you don't want to be knit together. They may give you serious challenges, but you are commanded to walk in love. So do it. Start releasing the love *(agape)* that's been placed in your heart by the Holy Spirit. Throw fear out. Throw worry out.

Love, love, LOVE! The Bible says love NEVER fails. When you put love into a situation, you have put God into that situation. Think about that. When you do that, Jesus becomes responsible for its success.

The person who refuses to love is missing out on the very best God has to offer. Don't you miss out on any of it.

Release love every moment into every situation, every prayer and every thought until it totally takes over your life.

Go for it! It will strengthen you. It will throw fear to the wind. It'll drive Satan out of your life and set you free from every torment of darkness.

Be still before the Lord and sense His flow of love in your heart. Then love others with His love. If it seems too hard, remember, once you start putting love into a situation, Jesus becomes responsible for its success. Love never fails, and Jesus never fails. So love your way to success!

b a c k u p :
John 13:34-35

d o w n l o a d :
2 Samuel 3-4; 1 Corinthians 16

v o i c e   a c t i v a t e :
I walk in love and I never fail because love never fails! 1 Corinthians 13:8

"Again, I tell you that if two of you on earth agree about anything you ask for, it will be done for you by my Father in heaven."
Matthew 18:19

Reject Strife

Satan hates it when Christians stand together. Standing in agreement opens heaven to us, and it closes the door on every destructive thing Satan can do. So he will continually try to disrupt that agreement by causing strife and division in the two places where Christians come together in the most powerful way: the family and the church.

Until now, you may not have thought of your family as a powerful force for God, but it is if you're in agreement with one another. So make it your goal to stay out of strife and walk in love *at home.*

Oddly enough, home is often the most difficult place to be loving. I think that's because we don't have our guard up when we're at home. We're not worrying about our reputation or trying to impress anyone. At home, nothing will stop you from being selfish—except your commitment to walk in God's love.

Don't be fooled into thinking it doesn't matter how you act at home. It matters a great deal. In fact, years ago, the Lord said this to me and I have never forgotten it: *If you allow Satan to stop you with strife at your front door, you'll be no threat to him anywhere else.*

So make the commitment to keep strife out of your home. Learn to live a lifestyle of agreement with your parents and your brothers and sisters. See to it that your prayers are strong by being in harmony with the members of your family. The moment you mess up and get in strife, make it right. Don't be afraid to say, "Please forgive me. I love you. I don't want to be in strife with you." Then say to the Lord, "Father, I repent of that. I choose to live in love."

It may be hard at first, because you've probably developed habits that will take awhile to change. Don't give up. Get in agreement and keep strife out of your home!

b a c k u p :
Proverbs 17:1; Mark 11:25-26; 1 Peter 3:7

d o w n l o a d :
2 Samuel 5-6; 2 Corinthians 1

v o i c e   a c t i v a t e :
I keep strife out of my life by acting on the Word. My prayers are effective and not hindered. 1 Peter 3:7

may 11

gloria

"The threshing floors will be filled with grain; the vats will overflow with new wine and oil. I will repay you for the years the locusts have eaten…. And afterward, I will pour out my Spirit on all people'."
Joel 2:24-25,28

Get Ready... It's Beginning to Rain

If you're like me, right now you're thinking, *Oh man, I want to be in on what God's doing in the last days. I want to be smack dab in the middle of it!* You can be, if you'll get yourself ready by doing these three things...

First, prepare yourself for the greatest criticism you've ever experienced. There has never been a time God has moved when there hasn't been criticism. If Jesus couldn't avoid it, neither can you.

Second, get the sin out of your life. Make a change. Just ask God's forgiveness and turn from that sin! We're free people, but we are never free from obeying God's commands. Third, pray for the "rain." Zechariah 10:1 tells us to pray for the rain of God's power and love to hit the earth in these end times.

To do these things, we must take time to pray. We must go before God and turn off the pleasures of this world. Turn off the music, shut off the movies, stop playing the video games. All that entertainment is only meant to do one thing: to distract you away from your time with God. Don't let it succeed. Instead, start praying and using your faith. It's time to pray until God's power and love is seen around the world.

What a sight it will be when it is! Years ago, when I was praying about these end times, the Lord said to me, *I've been manifested as the rain. I've been manifested as the fire or as lightning. I've been manifested as the wind, but I've never been manifested as all four at the same time. Now, in the time of the former and latter rain, you're going to see all of Me for the first time ever.*

Think of it! A spiritual storm of God's power is coming now. Get ready for it...it's beginning to rain!

b a c k u p :
2 Chronicles 5:11-14

d o w n l o a d :
2 Samuel 7-8; 2 Corinthians 2

v o i c e   a c t i v a t e :
It's beginning to rain! The Lord is pouring out His Spirit on all people! Joel 2:28

"Out of the overflow of the heart the mouth speaks. The good man brings good things out of the good stored up in him, and the evil man brings evil things out of the evil stored up in him."
Matthew 12:34-35

Your Future Is Determined by You

Your future is stored up in your heart! It's not ruled by what's happened to you, or by your current circumstances. Your future is determined by you!

In today's verses, Jesus said that what's in a person's heart is what comes out of him. So consider this: Who's responsible for what goes in your heart? You are! You're the only one who can put God's Word into your heart. Your friends can't do it for you. Your parents can't do it for you. Your youth pastor can't do it for you. Even God can't do it for you.

God has already done His part to help you. He's the One Who made your heart into a place that could store His promises. He's the One Who opened your heart to His Word. As the Scripture says, *"God has dealt to each one [the] measure of faith"* (Romans 12:3, NKJV). The moment you made Jesus your Lord, He put faith in your heart—but you're the only one who can make that faith increase.

You can do that by taking God's Word and putting it into your heart. Each time you put His promises in your heart, your faith grows and your future gets brighter. Isn't that exciting? There is no limit to the amount of His Word you can put into your heart!

The more you put in, the better things are, because that is where you will draw from to change the circumstances in your life. Your heart holds all the faith you'll need to cover any discouragement Satan tries to send your way. If he tries to put sickness and disease on you, you can draw from the Word about healing and it will put you over in that area. If you've just been released from a detention center, you can draw from the Word about God's plans for your life and have peace that you can make it just fine.

Your future really is bright! The Lord says in Jeremiah 29:11, *"For I know the plans I have for you...plans to prosper you and not to harm you, plans to give you hope and a future'."* Put God's Word in your heart. Speak it out in faith, and watch everything change!

backup:
Psalm 119:33-40

download:
2 Samuel 9-10; 2 Corinthians 3

voice activate:
Out of the overflow of my heart my mouth speaks. I bring good things out of the good stored up in my heart. Matthew 12:34-35

may 13

gloria

"Crave pure spiritual milk, so that by it you may grow up in your salvation."
1 Peter 2:2

may 14

kenneth

Well, Overcome It!

One time a fellow came up to me and said, "Kenneth, I'll tell you what my problem is. It's my old, sinful nature."

I said, "Well, overcome it."

"But, you don't understand!"

"No, but Jesus does," I answered. "He said He's already overcome the world. So go get in the Bible, pray, believe God and walk away from that problem. The power is within you to do it."

Suddenly it hit him what I was saying. He stopped being hung up on the problem and started focusing on the answer.

That's what you need to do. Quit seeing yourself defeated by your old nature and start seeing yourself like the Word says you are—raised up with Jesus and seated with Him in heavenly places (Ephesians 2:6)! Start seeing things the way He does.

Study God's Word and give your spirit something to grow on. As 1 Peter 2:2 says, crave the pure spiritual milk (of the Word) that you may grow up in your sal-vation. Then move on to the *"solid food*

[of the Word which] is for the mature, who by constant use have trained themselves to distinguish good from evil" (Hebrews 5:14).

Give your spirit rule over your mind and your body. You'll still have to fight with your faith to keep them in line, but if you're following God's Word, you'll win every time.

b a c k u p :
Ephesians 2:1-7

d o w n l o a d :
2 Samuel 11-13; 2 Corinthians 4-5

v o i c e a c t i v a t e :
I overcome my old nature by seeing myself as the Word says I am—raised up with Christ and seated with Him in the heavenly realms. Ephesians 2:6

Power From On High

After Jesus' resurrection, about 120 of God's servants were gathered in a room, praying together in agreement (Acts 1:14-15). They were ready to move into the streets as soon as God's power came to them. They were doing exactly what Jesus told them to do.

The shameful part of it was, only about a third of those who had been invited were present. Jesus had appeared to more than 500 of them and told them all the same thing...to stay in the city until they received power.

Apparently 380 of them decided to stay home!

What's the difference between the 380 who didn't follow Jesus' instructions and the 120 who did?

Those in the first group were merely Christians. Those in the second group were God's *servants*.

The Word translated "servants" in Acts 2:18 is the Greek word *doulos*. It refers to someone who has voluntarily given himself over to another person's will. It describes someone who could be free if he wanted to be, but chooses instead to be wholly submissive to another because of his love for that person.

If you are a servant, you will be committed to the Lord. He doesn't force you into that commitment. It is one you make by choice because you love Him.

When you made Jesus your Lord, you literally became a *child* of God. You were made free and *"if the Son sets you free, you will be free indeed"* (John 8:36).

If you truly love the One Who set you free, you will trade that freedom for a life of service to Him. That's what the Apostle Paul did, for in Romans 1:1, AMP he calls himself *"a bond servant of Jesus Christ."*

Choose today to be a bond servant...one who longs to stay close to the Master's side...serving Him wholeheartedly from a heart of love and devotion.

may 15

kenneth

backup:
Luke 10:38-42

download:
2 Samuel 14-15; 2 Corinthians 6

voice activate:
I am not a slave to sin. I am free to be a servant of Jesus Christ. I choose His will above my own. John 8:34-36

143

"When the day of Pentecost came, they were all together in one place. Suddenly a sound like the blowing of a violent wind came from heaven and filled the whole house where they were sitting. They saw what seemed to be tongues of fire that separated and came to rest on each of them."
Acts 2:1-3

may 16

kenneth

Fiery Power

A time is coming when God's glory won't just radiate out from God, it will radiate from us! It will burn within us and upon us with such power that Satan will be like ash under our feet!

It is almost unthinkable to him that such glory and power could flow through mere flesh-and-blood bodies. Yet the Bible tells us it will happen.

We've seen the beginning of this...on the Day of Pentecost. To grasp the impact of that day, you have to forget those Sunday school pictures depicting tiny flames hovering over the heads of the disciples. You need to get the images of God as described in Habakkuk 3:3-4, Ezekiel 1:1-28 and Malachi 4:1-3...you need the images of God's glory as seen in His fire and His light.

Go through these passages of Scripture and think about His blazing fire of glory! When you read them, you will realize what really happened in Acts 2. God Himself came in!

Everything was shaken so much that it sounded like a freight train was coming through the room. It was the glory! It roared in and filled the whole place. Then a blazing fire appeared, and He enveloped each disciple one by one!

On that day, God was able—at last—to embrace His people. Because of Jesus' sacrifice and resurrection, sin was defeated. They were re-created and placed in right-standing with God. So He could come to them without any covering of any kind. He could come to them as His own Glorious Self!

Now it is our time to walk in that radiating, fiery power that is so full of God's presence that Satan can't withstand it. It is God's plan for us to walk in the light as He is in the light, to walk in the glory as He is in the glory (1 John 1:5-7). It is time for us to shine!

So stretch yourself and what you believe. Study what the Bible says about the glory. Make it your aim to walk in the light—and you will see the glory of God!

backup:
Ezekiel 1:1,4-5,26-28; Habakkuk 3:3-4

download:
2 Samuel 16-17; 2 Corinthians 7

voice activate:
I walk in the light, as He is in the light. I walk in the glory, as He is in the glory. 1 John 1:7

"Consider it pure joy, my brothers, whenever you face trials of many kinds, because you know that the testing of your faith develops perseverance. Perseverance must finish its work so that you may be mature and complete, not lacking anything."
James 1:2-4

Consider It What?

Usually, when you're in the middle of a trial, the last thing you feel like doing is considering it pure joy. Usually, you're not in the mood to jump and sing and see it as an opportunity to develop patience.

The truth is, you should. If you'll let patience finish its work, you'll receive what you need to beat that trial. You will receive whatever God has promised you in His Word!

Hebrews 10:32-36 confirms that. Addressing a group of people who had been through an extremely fiery trial, it says: *"Remember those earlier days after you had received the light, when you stood your ground in a great contest in the face of suffering. Sometimes you were publicly exposed to insult and persecution; at other times you stood side by side with those who were so treated. You sympathized with those in prison and joyfully accepted the confiscation of your property, because you knew that you yourselves had better and lasting possessions. So do not throw away your confidence; it will be richly rewarded. You need to persevere so that when you have*

done the will of God, you will receive what he has promised."

You might as well know right now that if you want to enjoy the health and well-being God has promised you, you'll have to develop patience. You'll have to believe God when it's hard. You'll have to keep walking in faith when everything in you just wants to quit.

I'm not trying to be negative. It's just the truth. If you know that truth, you can prepare yourself for those hard times by deciding that when they come, you won't give up. You can train yourself for success by starting right now to develop the patience you'll need to make it through when the going gets tough. In the end, you might just surprise yourself. You'll be considering it pure joy without giving it a second thought!

backup:
Romans 5:1-5

download:
2 Samuel 18-19; 2 Corinthians 8

voice activate:
I consider it pure joy whenever I face trials. I let patience and perseverance finish their work in me so that I may be mature and complete, not lacking anything. James 1:2-4

gloria

"Have faith in God...I tell you the truth, if anyone says to this mountain, 'Go, throw yourself into the sea,' and does not doubt in his heart but believes that what he says will happen, it will be done for him."
Mark 11:22-23

may 18

kenneth

Speak to the Problem

"I just don't know what I'm going to do. This is just a mess...."

That is a classic example of speaking *about* the problem and not *to* the problem...and it will get you nowhere except deeper into trouble!

Now speaking *to* your problems, out loud, may sound strange to you, but God instructed us to in today's verse. He said to speak *to* the mountain. The mountain represents any problem in your life. You can change your circumstances by speaking to them. Romans 4:17 refers to such talk as *calling "things that are not as though they were."*

It's important to note that *calling things that are not as though they were* is quite different from *calling things that are as though they are not.* Doing this doesn't mean you're denying the problem exists. It means you're smart enough to call on God's help by faith.

I remember one Sunday morning many years ago when I had to speak to a mountain of sickness that was trying to prevent me from preaching. I was so sick that as I stood behind the pulpit and started to read the Word, I began to pass out.

Now, I had already gone to God earlier that morning by faith and believed I

received my healing. It wasn't yet evident in my body. So I told the congregation I would be right back. I went to another room and started speaking to that mountain.

I told Satan that I was healed by Jesus' wounds. I told him his power over me had been destroyed. I commanded him in Jesus' Name to get his filthy hand of sickness off me. When I walked out of that room, I didn't feel any better physically, but I knew I'd done what the Bible instructed me to do. So I went right back in and started preaching on healing.

At first my voice sounded bad. My body ached all over. Then suddenly, God's power hit me, healed me and gave me so much strength, I was able to preach all morning long! I had spoken to the mountain in faith, believing, and it was cast into the sea!

backup:
Mark 11:22-26

download:
2 Samuel 20-21; 2 Corinthians 9

voice activate:
I believe what I say will happen and I do not doubt in my heart. It will be done for me. Mark 11:23

"You, however, know all about my teaching, my way of life, my purpose, faith, patience, love, endurance, persecutions, sufferings—what kinds of things happened to me in Antioch, Iconium and Lystra, the persecutions I endured. Yet the Lord rescued me from all of them."
2 Timothy 3:10-11

Identify the REAL Enemy

Persecution comes through people... sometimes through those we love the most, but despite how it looks, those people are not the source of your problem.

According to Mark 4, it's Satan himself who stirs up persecution. It's one of the strategies he uses to steal God's promises out of your heart.

So when persecution comes your way, don't get sidetracked by getting angry with the people involved. They aren't operating on their own. They're being driven by Satan's influence.

Instead, use the authority Jesus has given you and put Satan in his place. Then pray for the people he has been using, that they'll be free to know the truth.

Once you understand who the real enemy is, and pray accordingly, the next thing God says to do is this: Continue doing good. *"For it is God's will that by doing good you should silence the ignorant talk of foolish men"* (1 Peter 2:15).

Your mission in life isn't to argue. You're not called to defend your position or your name when someone talks about you behind your back. Just leave all that in God's hands and continue doing what God has called you to do.

That's what Jesus did. He didn't quit. When He was hated, He didn't start hating back. He just kept right on preaching the good news, healing the sick and rescuing those captive to sin. He kept right on walking in success!

I know it's tough to be quiet in hard times, but you can do it if you're confident that God will ultimately rescue you. That's why Paul was able to live so triumphantly. In 2 Timothy 3:11, he said God rescued him from *all* of his persecutions!

We're not in this alone! Right in the middle of persecution, God is there with us. So trust in Him. Listen to what He says. Obey Him when it seems like all hell has broken loose. He'll rescue you from those persecutions—not just some of them, but *all* of them!

b a c k u p :
Matthew 5:10-16

d o w n l o a d :
2 Samuel 22-23; 2 Corinthians 10

v o i c e   a c t i v a t e :
The Lord rescues me from all my persecutions. 2 Timothy 3:11

may 19

gloria

"Then Peter came to Jesus and asked, 'Lord, how many times shall I forgive my brother when he sins against me? Up to seven times?' Jesus answered, 'I tell you, not seven times, but seventy-seven times.'"
Matthew 18:21-22

may 20

kenneth

No Whining Please

We need to face the fact that we can't walk with God and be even a little unforgiving or a little offended. If we're going to walk with God, we must allow His love to drive out every trace of unforgiveness.

"But you just don't know how badly they treated me!"

Has God forgiven your sin?

"Yes."

Then you forgive them. Period.

Quit whining about how hurt you are. Maybe you have been mistreated, but if so—get over it! Everybody has been mistreated in some form or another.

The reason I can talk so straight to you about this is that God has already said these things to me. I remember one day when I was moping around at home because my wife had said something to me I didn't like.

"Oh, she doesn't care about me anyway," I muttered in self-pity.

Right then, the Lord said to me, *It isn't any of your business whether she cares for you or not. It's your business to care for her.*

Then He added something I'll never forget. He said, *I'm the One Who cares whether you hurt or not. Your hurts mean everything in the world to Me, but they ought to mean little or nothing to you.*

As His children we need to learn that. We need to quit paying so much attention to our own hurts and give them to God. We need to take a lesson from the pioneers of the faith like Peter and John and look at troubles as opportunities.

When you have that attitude, it's not hard to forgive, because you're not focusing on yourself. You're focusing on God and His purposes, God and His love. If you want to discover the secret to real forgiveness, that's where your focus has to be—on God. Then we'll find it easy to forgive others—in the same way God forgives us.

backup:
Matthew 18:21-35

download:
2 Samuel 24; 1 Kings 1; 2 Corinthians 11

voice activate:
I forgive others, just as in Christ God forgave me. Ephesians 4:32

> "As you sent me into the world, I have sent them into the world."
> John 17:18

Fulfilling Your Destiny

"What's God's plan for my life?" We've all asked that question at some time or another. We're all eager to fulfill the divine purpose for our lives, but we need direction in finding out what that plan is.

The truth is, God never intended for us to be in the dark about His plan for us. He left us clear, written instructions. What's more, He gave us a pattern to follow so we could see how to carry out those instructions.

The pattern is Jesus. Our call is to continue His ministry. I know that sounds like a tall order, but it's true. Jesus said so in John 17:18.

Once we realize Jesus is the pattern, we need to find out exactly what Jesus was sent to do. Well, the Bible's pretty clear: *"The reason the Son of God appeared was to destroy the devil's work"* (1 John 3:8).

Think about that. You're called to finish what Jesus began: to destroy Satan's work on the earth. That is the job God wants us to do, and we do it the same way Jesus did. After all, He promised, *"Anyone who has faith in me will do*

what I have been doing. He will do even greater things than these, because I am going to the Father" (John 14:12).

In short, Jesus' ministry was comprised of three functions: 1) He healed the sick, 2) He cast out demons, and 3) He preached the good news.

Now, I know it's easy to do the preaching and not the other two works. However, the Bible was never designed to be preached without proof that Jesus is alive today. Jesus didn't just say, "God loves you." He demonstrated it. He proved the truth of what He was saying by operating in the supernatural power of God.

He expects us to do the same. *That's* God's plan for your life!

may 21

gloria

b a c k u p :
Matthew 8:16, 9:35

d o w n l o a d :
1 Kings 2-4; 2 Corinthians 12-13

v o i c e   a c t i v a t e :
I believe in Jesus. I am sent by Him. I fulfill God's plan for my life. John 17:18

"Whoever believes in me, as the Scripture has said, streams of living water will flow from within him.' By this he meant the Spirit, whom those who believed in him were later to receive."
John 7:38-39

may 22

kenneth

A Flood is Coming

A flood is coming! In fact, it has already started to fall. God's prophets have been forecasting this rain for thousands of years. This rain is called "the former and latter rain." It is an outpouring of the Spirit that combines the power of the old covenant with the power of the new covenant—both at the same time.

Now, let me ask you this: According to today's verse, where did Jesus say the rivers of the Spirit would flow? *From within Christians.* Where does the Holy Spirit live? *Within Christians.*

So, where will this final supernatural flood of power come from? You've got it— *from Christians! From you and me!*

"But, wait a minute," you say. "We're talking about miracles. We're talking about the whole earth being flooded with God's glory. How could something that huge come from one person like me?"

It won't. It will come from all of us together. It will come as the Holy Spirit river flowing out of you joins up with the Holy Spirit river flowing out of me. Then our rivers will come together with the rivers of millions of others. It will come when we stop fussing with one another and unify in faith.

You might have a hard time grasping that such a thing is even possible, but it is. What's more, it will happen because the Bible says so (Ephesians 4:13). When it does happen, we'll see the same things the early church saw when they were in agreement—and greater things.

I'm telling you...it will be a rain of the Holy Spirit like we have never seen!

backup:
Jeremiah 17:7-13

download:
1 Kings 5-6; Galatians 1

voice activate:
I believe in Jesus and in the Spirit of God. Therefore, streams of living water flow from within me. John 7:38-39

"The Lord will send a blessing on your barns and on everything you put your hand to."
Deuteronomy 28:8

More Than Enough

God doesn't promise just to meet your basic needs. He says He'll give you more than enough. Some religious people would argue about that, but the truth is, there's nothing to argue about because the Bible makes it perfectly clear. Look back at today's verse from Deuteronomy.

Now check this out: If you don't have more than you need, why would you need barns?

If that's not clear to you, verse 11 of that chapter says point-blank *"the Lord shall make you have a surplus of prosperity"* (AMP). I want you to remember those words—*a surplus of prosperity*—because that's what God's wants for you. When you made Jesus the Lord of your life, God's blessing came upon you, not so you could just "get by," but so you could have a surplus of prosperity.

That shouldn't really surprise you. After all, if you look at God's history with man, you'll see that when He had His way, man always had more than enough. Everything in the Garden of Eden, for example, was good. The temperature was just right. The food was right there on the trees. All you had to do was pull it off and eat it. Talk about fast food! Adam and Eve lacked nothing.

In the same way, God cares just as much about how well you do. He wants you to have more than enough. He wants you to have good things, a good home, good food...everything! He's the God of more than enough!

backup:
Psalm 35:27; Proverbs 3:9-10

download:
1 Kings 7-8; Galatians 2

voice activate:
The Lord will bless everything I do. God cares for me and wants me to have more than enough! Deuteronomy 28:8

"Grace and peace to you from God our Father and the Lord Jesus Christ."
Ephesians 1:2

may 24

kenneth

Beyond the Obvious

Have you ever stopped to think what that phrase *"Grace to you"* actually means? I think most people just read over these opening words by Paul, assuming they're just some sort of greeting.

Well, it's far deeper than that. Paul said, "I am what I am *by the grace of God!"* (1 Corinthians 15:10).

Acts 14:3 says that God's Word is the word of His grace. Then in Acts 20:32, it says that the word of grace is able to build you up and give you an inheritance among all them which are sanctified.

Man, that is far too powerful to just be a greeting on a letter!

Most Christians have treated the subject of God's grace too lightly. For some reason, most people just see it as something vague with no real definition, other than maybe God's favor.

It certainly is that, all right, but it's more than just that. The Word says we should grow in grace (2 Peter 3:18). No one can grow in anything from God without spending time in His Word (1 Peter 2:2). God's grace is mentioned more than 120 times in the New Testament alone!

That should be enough to let us know that we should be spending a whole lot more of our time studying it. After all, it has been put in the re-created spirit of every person who has made Jesus the Lord of his or her life (1 Corinthians 1:4).

Grace is powerful. It is God's willingness to enter into covenant with you, letting you live in Him and giving you the right to let Him come live in you, and through you. Read that last sentence over and over until you get understanding of it in your spirit.

Grace is a powerful force that you need to do the things God has called you to do. So dig into the Word. Let the Holy Spirit show it to you. Let grace become far more than a greeting on a letter.

backup:
Romans 5

download:
1 Kings 9-10; Galatians 3

voice activate:
Grace and peace have been given to me from God my Father and from the Lord Jesus Christ. Ephesians 1:2

"Continue in what you have learned and have become convinced of, because you know those from whom you learned it."
2 Timothy 3:14

Destroy Those Incoming SCUDs

Jesus warned us that distractions—the deceitfulness of riches and lusts of other things—can creep in, choke the Word and make it ineffective in our lives (Mark 4:19). Right next to that verse in my Bible, I've written the letters S-C-U-D. They stand for the phrase, "Satan Continually Uses Distractions." He's always sending those SCUD missiles at you to discourage you and draw you off course.

Hey, he'll whisper, *have you noticed you don't have any money? Have you noticed your body is in pain? Have you heard all the ugly things people are saying about you?*

How do you fight distractions like that? Just *"continue in what you have learned and have become convinced of, because you know those from whom you learned it."*

The thing that brings you defeat is failing to do what you already know. So whenever you reach a hard place, continue to do what you know and you'll make it through, a winner.

You have everything it takes to be a winner. You have everything you need.

Get aggressive. Press in. That's the price you pay to win this race. Yet one thing is sure, you not only have the present victory, but the eternal victory you gain will be worth it all.

Satan won't ever stop in his relentless efforts to distract you. However, you have the power to overcome. You have the power and the knowledge to continue to do what God has already told you to do. It's that simple. *Continuing* will put you over. Don't quit believing and acting on God's Word. You have what it takes to destroy those incoming SCUDs!

may 25

gloria

b a c k u p :
Mark 4:14-20

d o w n l o a d :
1 Kings 11-12; Galatians 4

v o i c e   a c t i v a t e :
I am not distracted. I continue in what I have learned and have become convinced of. 2 Timothy 3:14

"Endure hardship with us like a good soldier of Christ Jesus."
2 Timothy 2:3

may 26

kenneth

A Soldier's Victory

Make no mistake about it. There are hardships involved in being a soldier of Jesus Christ. However, there is no hardship, no problem, no suffering and no onslaught of persecution that can conquer you. Nothing hell can devise is powerful enough to overcome the Name of Jesus.

You are thoroughly equipped for victory. Yet to win that victory, you will have to go into battle. You will have to face the fact that you are a soldier.

Some Christians whine, "I don't feel like fighting in faith today. It's hard!"

That doesn't make any difference. You don't ask a soldier if he'd like to get up and go to combat each morning. You don't say, "Sir, could I bother you for a few moments? I hate to interrupt your checker game, but we're having a war about 10 miles up the road and I just wondered if you'd like to go?"

No! You don't ask a soldier to go to the battlefield. He is under authority. He does what he is ordered. A good soldier is willing to serve.

God is looking for soldiers like that. He is looking for people who are as eager to get in on the action as the boys were in my fifth grade football team. I'll never forget that team. There were about 14 of us and every one of us was constantly hanging on the coach's arm, begging him to let us in the game.

"Put me in there, Coach. I can whip that guy! Just let me have the ball!"

One thing about that bunch of boys, we were eager. We weren't any good, but we were ready.

If you'll be ready spiritually, if you'll be a good soldier, if you'll endure the hardship, God will put you where the action is. He'll give you more excitement than you ever dreamed you'd have. He'll help you turn tragedies into triumphs and temptations into testimonies...if you'll give Him an opportunity.

backup:
Romans 8:35-39

download:
1 Kings 13-14; Galatians 5

voice activate:
I endure hardship like a good soldier of Christ Jesus. 2 Timothy 2:3

"For you know very well that the day of the Lord will come like a thief in the night."
1 Thessalonians 5:2

A Thief in the Night

We all know that Jesus is coming back someday, and I believe it's much sooner than we all think. So we need to be ready.

It's our responsibility to be prepared. God has given us everything we need. He has put His own Spirit within us. He has given us His written Word. He has given us teachers, preachers, pastors, evangelists, apostles and prophets to help us learn how to live by faith, how to live separated from the world and how to operate in the power of God. We must decide to make those things the priority in our lives.

One way to keep them a priority in our lives is by expecting Jesus to return soon. Just start studying what the Bible says about His return.

Even though God hasn't told us the exact time, according to the Bible, if we're alert, we will know the season of His return. In fact, Jesus Himself said in Matthew 24 that His coming would be like the Flood in Noah's day.

That flood took the world by surprise, didn't it? The people were just going about their natural business, not expecting anything unusual, when suddenly they were swept away. They were completely in the dark about what was happening.

Noah wasn't caught by surprise. He'd been building the ark for years. He'd been expecting the Flood. He didn't know the day or the hour, but he knew it was coming and he was ready. When it started to rain, Noah wasn't in the dark—he was in the ark!

That's how we're supposed to be. We're to be aware of the season (1 Thessalonians 5:1-6). If you're watching and listening to the Holy Spirit, you won't be in the dark. You won't be unaware at the time of Jesus' coming. You'll know when He's ready. You won't be caught by surprise.

may 27

gloria

backup:
Matthew 24:32-44

download:
1 Kings 15-16; Galatians 6

voice activate:
I stand and lift up my head because my redemption is drawing near. Luke 21:28

"I call heaven and earth to record this day against you, that I have set before you life and death, blessing and cursing: therefore choose life, that both thou and thy seed may live."
Deuteronomy 30:19, KJV

kenneth   may 28

Eternal Health

Tradition has taught that God uses sicknesses, trials and tribulation to teach us. This idea, however, is not based on the Bible. God has never used sickness to discipline His children and keep them in line. Sickness is of Satan, and God doesn't need Satan to straighten us out!

"Kenneth, I see Christians that are sick all of the time. Why does God allow it?"

God allows it because we do. Why? Because He's given us the right to make our own choices, along with authority over the kingdom of darkness.

According to Deuteronomy 30:19, He has put life and death before us. Then He instructed us to choose life. It's up to us to make the decision.

You have the power to live after God's ways and resist sickness, or not to. You have the choice to let Satan run over you, or use the authority you have been given. Good gifts come from God. No matter what tradition has taught, sickness and disease simply don't fall into the category of good gifts—ever.

So make a decision today. Resist Satan's sicknesses and diseases. Give way to life!

⊕ *b a c k u p :*
James 1:12-17

⊕ *d o w n l o a d :*
1 Kings 17-19; Ephesians 1-2

⊕ *v o i c e   a c t i v a t e :*
God has set before me life and death, blessings and curses. I choose life!
Deuteronomy 30:19

Success is Hunting You

How much do you want to succeed in life? Enough to change what you're saying? Enough to change where your attention is focused? Enough to act on God's Word even when the rest of the world is telling you it will never work?

If you want it that much, the Bible guarantees you'll get it.

I must warn you, though. Satan won't like it. He'll try to talk you out of it, and since he knows God's success formula, he knows exactly what tactics to use.

He'll pressure you to say negative things. He'll try to distract you from the Word and get your attention on anything—it doesn't matter what it is, as long as it isn't the Word.

His goal is to stop your faith. He knows it's the only force that can cause impossible situations to change. He also knows that it comes from God's Word. So when he sees that Word going in your heart and hears you speaking it, he doesn't just sit there. He starts talking. Doubtful thoughts will come into your mind, thoughts that are just the opposite of what God has said.

It is important to remember that those thoughts don't become yours unless you believe them and speak them. That's what he wants you to do, of course. If the Bible says you're healed, he'll tell you you're sick. If the Bible says you're forgiven, he'll say you're still guilty. If the Bible says your needs are met, he'll tell you they're not.

However, if you hold on to your faith, and keep the Word in your mouth and in your heart, you can't lose. There's no force Satan can bring against you that is stronger than God's Word. It will make you a winner every time.

So if you've been wanting true success and it's been eluding you, quit wondering if you have what it takes to make it—and remember instead Who is with you and in you. Then turn to the Bible and put God's success formula to work in your life. Soon, you won't be hunting for success...it will be hunting you!

may 29

gloria

b a c k u p :
Romans 8:31-34

d o w n l o a d :
1 Kings 20-21; Ephesians 3

v o i c e   a c t i v a t e :
The blessing of the Lord brings me wealth, and He adds no trouble to it. Proverbs 10:22

"But my righteous one will live by faith. And if he shrinks back, I will not be pleased with him.'"
Hebrews 10:38

May 30

kenneth

Are You on Standby?

Did you know God doesn't want you sitting around waiting for a thunderbolt from heaven to stir you into action? Did you know He wants you to step out in faith and power just because the Bible says you can?

Now, you may be concerned that you would be out there all alone, but would that be so bad? After all, you've been given a new life. God's love is in your heart. You have a covenant with Jesus—in His blood.

God didn't do all of that for nothing. He didn't re-create you so you could sit around like a puppet, afraid to take any initiative on your own.

He created you to be His partner, working together with him (2 Corinthians 6:1). That means you have a part. You have responsibilities, and to fulfill them, you must take your place.

When people come along and say, "Do you mean to tell me you have the power to heal?" you shouldn't shake your head and say, "Oh, no. I'm just a nobody."

You should say, "Yes, because the Father is in me and He does the work! Jesus said when Christians lay hands on the sick, they'll recover"

Faith is the force God has given us to direct our personal lives day in and day out. He expects us to take that force—the same force He used to create the world—and change circumstances, heal our physical bodies and keep our lives in line with His Word. He expects us to take our stand and *to imitate those who through faith and patience inherit what has been promised*" (Hebrews 6:12).

So the next time you have an opportunity to step out, do it! What are you waiting for?

backup:
Hebrews 6:9-15

download:
1 Kings 22; 2 Kings 1; Ephesians 4

voice activate:
I live by faith. I do not shrink back.
Hebrews 10:38

"O Lord, our Lord, how majestic is your name in all the earth! You have set your glory above the heavens. From the lips of children and infants you have ordained praise because of your enemies, to silence the foe and the avenger."
Psalm 8:1-2

Power in Praise

When you've prayed and believed God to change circumstances, then you should praise and thank Him in the middle of those circumstances while you wait for them to change.

There's power in praise. If you praise God, you'll be able to triumph over every attack. Psalm 8:1-2 confirms that. Satan is not going to hang around listening to you praise God. Praise shuts his mouth. So put it to work.

Praise God that the trouble is gone even while it's still there. Praise Him for setting you free.

Praise Him for the blood of Jesus that paid the price for your sin and rescued you from every curse.

Praise Him in the morning. Shout your way to school every day.

Praise Him at noon.

Shout your way home every afternoon.

Praise Him at night.

Praise Him when you don't feel like praising Him! It will make a difference.

Gloria and I have applied truths like this for more than 30 years, and God has brought us out on top every time. He'll do the same for you!

may 31

kenneth

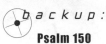
backup:
Psalm 150

download:
2 Kings 2-3; Ephesians 5

voice activate:
My continual praise and thanksgiving to God gives Him the opportunity to intervene in my circumstances and bless me. Psalm 145

"We demolish arguments and every pretension that sets itself up against the knowledge of God, and we take captive every thought to make it obedient to Christ."
2 Corinthians 10:5

june 1

kenneth

The Biggest Problem Isn't Big Enough

It doesn't matter what you are facing today...no problem is too big when you factor in God's power! Take hold of His power by expecting something good to happen to you. Grab hold of hope—because you're believing God's promises.

Don't be a stranger to His promises. Dig them out of the Bible. Find out what God has said about your situation. Then start saying, "I expect something good to happen because God promised it!"

Think about those promises. Let them build an image inside you until you can see yourself healed and doing well in every way.

If you'll do that, you'll eventually get bigger on the inside than you are on the outside. Your hope will grow so strong that Satan himself won't be able to beat it out of you.

When we're confronted by impossible situations in this world, we just need to factor in Jesus...His Word...His power!

Some say, "That sounds too easy." Easy?! I don't think so. When Satan throws the noose of hopelessness around your neck with some terrible situation, you have to fight hard. The way you fight hard is by grabbing hold of your hope in God's promises and using it to destroy every thought that contradicts them.

"We demolish arguments and every pretension that sets itself up against the knowledge of God, and we take captive every thought to make it obedient to Christ" (2 Corinthians 10:5).

The battleground where hope is won or lost is in your thoughts. So take your stand on that battleground and take control of your thoughts. Begin to expect God's power to destroy the bondage in your life. Begin to expect God to keep His promises to you.

backup:
Hebrews 6:16-20

download:
2 Kings 4-5; Ephesians 6

voice activate:
I will break down what people think and every big idea that tries to stop people from knowing God. I make every thought a prisoner to obey Christ. 2 Corinthians 10:5

Extreme Confidence

Many years ago, before I understood much about living a holy lifestyle, I prayed to God for the money to buy a house. At the time, it seemed like a big request. After all, Ken hadn't been in the ministry very long, and we'd never owned a house before. What's more, we'd committed to God not to borrow money, so the amount of cash we needed seemed gigantic.

It took me awhile—six years to be exact—but I got it by faith. Some years later, I found another house I wanted. Once again, I prayed and believed God for it. This time was different. I had begun to live in the things I am teaching now, so when I prayed, I had confidence.

Somehow I just expected Him to give me what I asked for. I knew in my heart I'd been faithful to do the things He wanted me to do. I'd been faithful to Him—and I expected Him to be faithful to me, and He was. The second house only took three weeks!

God doesn't hold out on us. Many people's prayers are hindered because their hearts are affected by a lack of dedication. It keeps us from receiving what God wants to give to us.

Jesus was totally dedicated to pleasing God—which caused Him to have total confidence in the Father. If you'll totally dedicate yourself to the things of God, the same will happen for you. If you'll put God's Word in your heart and speak it out, soon you'll see results. Jesus will make Himself real to you, and your heart will be constantly confident toward God.

So make whatever adjustments you need to get your heart fixed on God. Dedicate everything you do to Him, and watch your confidence rocket!

june 2

gloria

backup:
Ephesians 4:17-24

download:
2 Kings 6-7; Philippians 1

voice activate:
I dedicate everything I do to God. I always do what pleases my Father. John 8:29

"Who [God] satisfies your desires with good things so that your youth is renewed like the eagle's."
Psalm 103:5

june 3

kenneth

The Auto Response of Faith

I love to talk about my youth being renewed! When someone talks to me about getting old and feeble, it's like waving a red flag in front of a bull because my faith knows better than that. When somebody starts the "old and feeble" routine, I say, "God satisfies my desires with good things so that my youth is renewed. You can do what you want, but I'm not falling apart in my old age."

You may think that's extreme, but I'll tell you something: Until you build up those kinds of faith responses, you'll just flow downstream with the rest of the world. You'll end up drifting into sickness, poverty, depression and all the rest of Satan's deadly stuff.

You can live above the rotten circumstances of the world if you'll guard your words. I have faith-building things I say every day of the year. I don't wait until I'm facing a crisis. I build my faith continually: "This is a ministry that is debt free...Thank God, we're a family without tragedy...." I say those things every single day. I even confess Psalm 103 when I brush my teeth!

God calls that putting up *"the shield of faith, with which you can extinguish all the flaming arrows of the evil one"* (Ephesians 6:16).

Every time you do that, your spiritual muscles get into shape. If you keep on exercising those faith responses, when Satan does send some deadly situation your way, you'll be ready for it. You'll be able to deliver the Holyfield blow that will put Satan on the mat.

Making it a habit to respond in faith isn't complicated. Anyone can do it. You train yourself, just like you trained yourself to tie your shoes when you were six years old. By practicing.

Practice responding in faith. Do it over and over until it becomes an automatic response. If you'll do that, your faith will be there when you need it most!

backup:
Isaiah 54:14-17

download:
2 Kings 8-9; Philippians 2

voice activate:
God satisfies my desires with good things so that my youth is renewed. Psalm 103:5

"Be self-controlled and alert. Your enemy the devil prowls around like a roaring lion looking for someone to devour. Resist him, standing firm in the faith, because you know that your brothers throughout the world are undergoing the same kind of sufferings."
1 Peter 5:8-9

"Get Out!"

Satan is an outlaw. God has given us laws to keep him in line, but he won't obey them unless we enforce those laws.

That's not really surprising. Things work the same way in everyday life. In the United States, for example, we have laws against selling drugs. We have laws against murder and stealing. If those laws aren't enforced, thieves and murderers continue to steal and kill. That is why the law must be enforced.

Once you understand that, you'll see why Satan works so hard to get you to talk about your problems instead of God's promises. He knows your ability to enforce God's law is in your words. If he can get your words going in the wrong direction, he can interfere with your life—even though it doesn't belong to him.

Satan doesn't care what belongs to him. He's a thief. He's a killer. He takes what he can get. So you have to use God's Word on him when he tries to come into your life and spoil it.

The first time Satan starts trying to make you doubt—*Do you really think God is going to heal you? Do you really think God is going to help you get that scholarship?*—we should just tell him to take his lies and get out of our lives!

How do you do that? Just say, "In the Name of Jesus, get out! I choose to believe what God's Word says instead!" Quote God's promises to you and don't stop. Refuse to listen to words that kill, steal and destroy (John 10:10).

Just keep on speaking and studying what the Bible says about your situation until you're more used to hearing it than you are the lies of Satan. When you're walking in the authority God's given you, and speaking God's Word, you'll have no trouble telling Satan to get out.

june 4

gloria

backup:
Acts 28:1-6

download:
2 Kings 10-12; Philippians 3-4

voice activate:
I am self-controlled and alert. I resist the devil, standing firm in faith. 1 Peter 5:8-9

"The name of the Lord is a strong tower; the righteous run to it and are safe."
Proverbs 18:10

june 5

kenneth

You Have a New Name

Did you know your name has been changed? Well, if you've become a Christian, it certainly has. When you make Jesus the Lord of your life, you are brought into a covenant relationship with Jesus and your name is changed!

To fully appreciate what that means, you'll have to think about the blood covenant. When a person enters into this unbreakable promise with another person, they become one with each other. They exchange their coats saying, "All that I have and all that I am is now yours."

Actually, when someone enters a covenant of blood, he is giving himself completely away. He is no longer his own. His assets and his debts, his strengths and his weaknesses belong forever to his covenant partner. To provide a symbol of this, at the close of the covenant ceremony, the families exchange names.

When you accepted Jesus as your Lord, He took your name. Your name was sin. Your name was weakness. Your life was ruled by fear, and hell was your home destination.

Then you accepted Jesus. He gave Himself to you. You gave yourself to Him. His life became yours. Your life became His. You turned loose of natural man as your father and received God as your Father.

Ephesians 3:15 says the Church has been named after Him—that's you and me! Philippians 2:9 says He has been given the Name that is above every name.

You've been given that Name!

When poverty calls, don't answer "Yes." Answer "No!" When your body calls itself sick, answer "No! That's not my name. I am healed." When Satan tries to tell you you're alone and discouraged, answer him out loud, "That's not in my covenant. I am loved and strong in the Lord."

No matter what Satan tries to throw against you, the Name of the Lord is stronger. Whatever He has called Himself in His Word is who you are now!

b a c k u p :
Hebrews 8:6-13

d o w n l o a d :
2 Kings 13-14; Colossians 1

v o i c e   a c t i v a t e :
The name of the Lord is a strong tower. I run into it and am safe. Proverbs 18:10

> "Therefore, since we are surrounded by such a great cloud of witnesses, let us throw off everything that hinders and the sin that so easily entangles, and let us run with perseverance the race marked out for us."
> Hebrews 12:1

Back to Basics

Several years ago, our ministry went into debt—we were behind by nearly $6 million in bills! It didn't look like there were any easy answers. We thought about selling everything so we could pay off the deficit. Then, we wouldn't have had any place to house the ministry operations.

Things looked dark, but do you know what got us through that situation? It wasn't some new insight from God. It wasn't some flash from heaven bringing us an instant solution.

What overcame that debt was the same thing that put food on our table more than thirty years ago when we first began to live by faith: patiently putting God's Word into practice.

We began listening to teachings from people who really ministered to us. We went back to basics—learning about the words we say and how to use our faith. Where we discovered we'd slipped, we corrected ourselves. We put God's Word in our hearts and spoke out His promises.

In other words, we did what James 1:4 says. We let that trial work patience in us, and when it was done, we had everything we needed. What's more, others saw how God helped us through and it has showed them the way, too.

That's the risk Satan always takes when he puts you through a trial. He takes the chance you'll come through stronger than you were before, instead of weaker. He takes the chance of you becoming a living example of God's power.

If you're facing a challenging situation, and Satan is up to risky business, just put into practice the basic truths you've already learned. Do what you know to do and God will take care of the rest.

b a c k u p :
James 1:1-8

d o w n l o a d :
2 Kings 15-16; Colossians 2

v o i c e a c t i v a t e :
I throw off everything that hinders and the sin that so easily entangles me. I run with perseverance the race marked out for me. Hebrews 12:1

"Through whom we have gained access by faith into this grace in which we now stand. And we rejoice in the hope of the glory of God."
Romans 5:2

june 7

gloria

Faith Connects You

It is so important to develop your faith. Why? Because faith is what makes God's blessings appear in your life (Hebrews 11:1). It also pleases God (Hebrews 11:6).

It's faith that reaches into the supernatural, grasps God's promises and brings a tangible result. It brings that computer you need, or the healing for your body. It brings action.

Romans 5:2 says we have access by faith into the grace (favor) of God. Therefore, if you want God's favor in your relationships or any other area of your life, you must get it by faith.

I like to think of it this way: *When you believe the Bible, you open your life to God and give Him the opportunity to move in it.*

Oddly enough, that bothers some people. They can't understand why God needs *an opportunity*. After all, He is God. Can't He do anything He wants?

Yes, He can, and He wants to respond to our faith. God is not like Satan. He doesn't force Himself on you.

He waits for you to give Him an opening by believing His Word. When you believe His Word and make your stand, even in the middle of the most impossible situations, God moves.

Remember, faith speaks, and it doesn't speak gibberish. It speaks what God speaks. When cancer attacks, faith doesn't say, "I'm dying of cancer." Faith says, "I'm healed by the wounds of Jesus. Therefore I'll live healthy and strong." Faith mixed with God's very own words gives God an opportunity to work. It gives Him something to work with. It connects you with Him!

backup:
Luke 17:5-6

download:
2 Kings 17-18; Colossians 3

voice activate:
Through Jesus I have gained access by faith into this grace in which I now stand. I rejoice in the hope of the glory of God. Romans 5:2

"The Lord is gracious and compassionate, slow to anger and rich in love. The Lord is good to all; he has compassion on all he has made."
Psalm 145:8-9

A Picture of God

The amazing news that God is a good God is one of the greatest truths we have learned in recent times. Years ago, a man of God began preaching that message and it has changed countless lives. Until then, most people hadn't known that God wanted to do good things for them. They thought God made them sick to teach them something. They didn't know God wanted to heal them. They didn't even know He healed *anyone* anymore!

Imagine how shocked those people were when people boldly began to proclaim that God is a good God and He wants you healed. Because of this truth, attitudes changed, faith arose in people's hearts and great miracles happened.

Before that time, most people were afraid of God. Yet once they knew the truth about God, it was easy to receive good things from Him. That's why it's so important to know the Truth.

Psalm 145 tells the truth about God. He is:

- gracious

- compassionate

- slow to anger

- rich in love

- good to all

- and more!

That's the picture of God you should tack up in your heart. When you see God as He really is, it's no struggle to have faith. You don't have to memorize formulas. You just trust Him. He really is a good God!

june 8

gloria

backup:
Psalm 145

download:
2 Kings 19-20; Col. 4; Isa. 56-57; Ps. 56

voice activate:
The Lord is gracious and compassionate. He is slow to anger and rich in love. The Lord is good to me and has compassion on me. Psalm 145:8-9

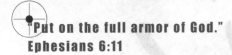

"Put on the full armor of God."
Ephesians 6:11

june 9

kenneth

Your True Destiny

Did you know that right here, in the middle of the same storms that are tearing the world apart, you and I and every other Christian can win in life?

We can put on the full armor of God, walk right into the middle of the worst circumstances the world has to throw at us, and none of them will be able to bring us down.

That's why God told us to put on His armor in the first place! He knew it would protect us. The Word of God and the full armor of God is bulletproof. It's sickness-proof, debt-proof, depression-proof. With it, you'll stand when everything around you is falling apart, but you have to get dressed!

You can't just give God's Word a passing nod and then go on watching what the world watches and saying what the world says. If you keep copying the world's ways, you're going to share in the world's destiny. But if you'll copy Jesus, you'll share His destiny. It's your choice.

Romans 12:2 says, *"Do not conform any longer to the pattern of this world,* but be transformed by the renewing of your mind. Then you will be able to test and approve what God's will is— his good, pleasing and perfect will."

You won't find God's will for your life by copying the world. You'll find it by copying Jesus. *"If you hold to my teaching, you are really my disciples. Then you will know the truth, and the truth will set you free."* (John 8:31).

So put on the full armor and stand strong. Being a winner is your true destiny!

backup:
Ephesians 6:11-20

download:
2 Kings 21-22; 1 Thessalonians 1

voice activate:
I put on the full armor of God and stand strong against the devil. Ephesians 6:11

168

"For the eyes of the Lord range throughout the earth to strengthen those whose hearts are fully committed to him."
2 Chronicles 16:9

He's Looking for You

God is looking for you. Ever since the world began He's been looking for people who would allow Him to bless them and demonstrate His power in their lives—people whose lives would be a walking advertisement of His love and power.

Look at the children of Israel in the Old Testament. God wanted them to be this kind of people. He prepared a marvelous land for them to enjoy (Exodus 3:8). It was a land of abundance where no enemy could stand before them and no sickness could stay on their bodies (Exodus 23:25).

In fact, as soon as they came out of slavery in Egypt, God wanted them to go to that land. It was a short journey, but they wouldn't go! Instead, they spent 40 years wandering around in the wilderness getting nowhere.

All this happened thousands of years ago, but God hasn't changed. He still wants to lead His people into a place of goodness and wealth.

The problem is that His people haven't changed that much. The same thing that kept the children of Israel out of the Promised Land is keeping most Christians out of their personal promised land today. The problem is unbelief.

"Gloria, that can't apply to me. I believe in God."

Israel believed in God too. Yet when their scouts went into the Promised Land, they came back and reported there were giants there—and the people became scared.

Now, if they had believed God, it wouldn't have mattered how big those giants were. They could have marched right in, expecting God to scatter the giants, but they didn't believe God!

Today, God is looking for *you*. Don't let the giants in your life scare you into hiding. Stand up and let God know you'll be faithful and obedient. Let Him know you'll trust Him no matter what things look like. Then get ready to enter your promised land!

backup:
Numbers 13:25-33

download:
2 Kings 23-24; 1 Thessalonians 2

voice activate:
I keep my heart fully committed to God and He strengthens me. 2 Chronicles 16:9

june 10

gloria

169

"Be patient, then, brothers, until the Lord's coming. See how the farmer waits for the land to yield its valuable crop and how patient he is for the autumn and spring rains."
James 5:7

kenneth june 11

Knowledge of His Glory

It is time for the glory. We've reached the end of the end times. We've come to the time the prophet Zechariah prophesied: *"Ask of the Lord rain in the time of the latter or spring rain. It is the Lord Who makes lightnings which usher in the rain and give men showers of it, to every one grass in the field"* (Zechariah 10:1, AMP).

In this verse, he wasn't just referring to natural rain. He wasn't just talking about natural lightning. He was referring to that bright, shining cloud of God's glory that would bring in the outpouring of the Spirit and open the way for millions to come to the Lord. He was pointing to the same day James referred to in today's verse.

Both Zechariah and James were looking ahead to the time immediately before the return of Jesus. That's today! We've reached that time. The glory is beginning to flash around us and the rain has started to fall.

It is awesome to think that God has chosen us—this generation of Christians—to be alive at this moment. He has chosen us to help bring in the glory. What a great privilege!

With great privilege comes great responsibility. We can't afford to just sit around and play church. No, we must follow the example of the Apostle Paul and determine to know God and His freeing power, and to know the power of His glory (Romans 6:5; Philippians 3:10). It's our responsibility to press in to Jesus until we come to understand and experience the glory (2 Corinthians 4:6)!

Some people shy away from that responsibility. They say, "Well, I don't want to mess with all that complicated stuff. I just want to follow the Lord."

You can't separate the two. You can't separate Jesus from His glory. The glory is the appearance of God Himself. So seek the Lord *and* the knowledge of His glory!

backup:
2 Corinthians 4:6-7

download:
2 Kings 25; 1 Chronicles 1-2; 1 Thessalonians 3-4

voice activate:
I am patient until the Lord's coming, for He waits for the land to yield its valuable crop. James 5:7

"Take no part in and have no fellowship with the fruitless deeds and enterprises of darkness, but instead [let your lives be so in contrast as to] expose and reprove and convict them.... Awake, O sleeper, and arise from the dead, and Christ shall shine [make day dawn] upon you and give you light. Look carefully then how you walk! Live purposefully and worthily and accurately, not as the unwise and witless, but as wise—sensible, intelligent people; Making the very most of the time— buying up each opportunity—because the days are evil."
Ephesians 5:11,14-16, AMP

A Wake-Up Call

As I was reading these scriptures some time ago, that phrase, *"Awake, O sleeper,"* seemed to jump out at me. It reminded me that the "regular-ness" of life can sometimes lull us to sleep spiritually.

I believe God is sending out a wake-up call. He is saying, as He did in this verse, "Wake up, sleeper! I'm returning soon!"

There are three things that will take us through these end times successfully:

1) The Word of God

2) Prayer

3) The guidance of the Holy Spirit.

You can beat every evil that comes against you if you'll keep your faith strong. The simple key to keeping your faith strong is this: *Stay in the Word of God.*

By being *faithful in prayer* (Romans 12:12), you can stay in communication with your Father. Just talk to Him throughout your day and listen. Being in touch

with Him will keep you strong, and you'll see your prayers answered.

If you *keep your ear listening to the Holy Spirit,* and obey His promptings in your spirit, you'll avoid the pitfalls and traps of Satan.

So wake up! Throw off those covers of laziness and indifference and take your stand in Christ. Get in the Word and in prayer and obey the Holy Spirit. Give God place in your life and He will keep you safe in these end times.

gloria

backup:

Ephesians 5:11-20

download:

1 Chronicles 3-4; 1 Thessalonians 5

voice activate:

I live purposefully and worthily and accurately. I live wisely and make the very most of my time, because Jesus is coming soon. Ephesians 5:15-16

> "'Don't be afraid,' David said to him, 'for I will surely show you kindness for the sake of your father Jonathan. I will restore to you all the land that belonged to your grandfather Saul, and you will always eat at my table.'"
> 2 Samuel 9:7

kenneth **june 13**

From a Dog to a Prince

Most people know the story of the blood covenant David and Jonathan made with each other (1 Samuel 18:3). What most people don't know is that after Jonathan died, the covenant relationship continued between David and Jonathan's son Mephibosheth.

David's unconditional love didn't end the day Jonathan was killed. It remained within him—even though he had become king. Even though he was wealthy and powerful, his covenant with Jonathan still burned inside him. Years later, he asked, *"Is there anyone still left of the house of Saul to whom I can show kindness for Jonathan's sake?"* (2 Samuel 9:1). One of Saul's former servants, Ziba, gave David his answer: *"There is still a son of Jonathan; he is crippled in both feet.... He is at the house of Makir son of Ammiel in Lo Debar."* (verses 3-4).

When David sent for him, Mephibosheth was afraid David would kill him. He came into the palace, threw himself at David's feet, and began to bawl about what an unworthy dog he was (verses 6-8). David didn't even acknowledge that nonsense. In his eyes, Mephibosheth wasn't a dog. He was a

rich man. He just didn't know it. David had kept his promise to Jonathan...and all of Jonathan's wealth had been set aside for an heir. All Mephibosheth's life, he had been covenanted to David, but he didn't know it. David was as much his father as Jonathan was because of the blood covenant between them.

That's the message of God's prosperity. Mephibosheth didn't do anything to become wealthy. Somebody just loved him—not because of anything he had done, but because he was the successor of a blood covenant.

Once you grasp that, you won't ever believe you don't deserve to be healed, blessed or rescued from anything. You didn't do anything to get where you are except receive Jesus. Because of a blood covenant, you are placed right in the middle of all the wealth God has for you. You are royalty!

backup:
2 Samuel 9

download:
1 Chronicles 5-6; 2 Thessalonians 1

voice activate:
God has made me a king and priest and I reign on the earth. Revelation 5:10

"My God will meet all your needs according to his glorious riches in Christ Jesus."
Philippians 4:19

More Than Enough!

Do you remember the older brother in the story of the prodigal son (Luke 15:11-32)? His younger brother had asked for his share of the inheritance, so the boys' father divided his estate between them. The younger brother ran off and squandered his share on a sinful lifestyle. The older brother stayed home and faithfully served his father. When the younger brother repented and returned, the father received him with open arms. He killed a calf for him so they could celebrate with a feast because he had come home. He put a robe on his back and a ring on his finger.

The older brother was furious. He pointed out that he'd always been faithful, yet the father had never killed a fat calf for him!

The father's answer to him is very important. He said: *"My son, you are always with me, and everything I have is yours."* (Luke 15:31). The father had divided his estate between his two boys. Therefore, after the younger brother had taken his goods and departed, everything that was left belonged to the older son. *Everything!* He could have eaten a fat calf every day if he'd wanted, but he didn't take advantage of his inheritance!

Many Christians are going to find themselves in the same situation when they get to heaven. They're going to find out after they get there what belonged to them down here. They're going to find out that God has always wanted His people to live in wealth, and all He has is ours.

God wants you to live in a good place. He wants you to attend the college of your heart's desire. He wants you to be so blessed you don't even have to think about those things.

Listen, God isn't anywhere near broke! He has enough wealth to give to *all* of His children. He doesn't have a problem with finances. His problem has been getting His kids to believe what He says about finances. So trust in Him and remember...He has more than enough!

june 14

gloria

backup:
Luke 15:11-32

download:
1 Chronicles 7-8; 2 Thessalonians 2

voice activate:
My God meets all my needs according to His glorious riches in Christ Jesus.
Philippians 4:19

"[Jesus] went on to tell them, 'Our friend Lazarus has fallen asleep; but I am going there to wake him up.'"
John 11:11

june 15

kenneth

Better Than Ever

Death.... We have to deal with it. Or do we?

Do you remember Jesus' friend, Lazarus? Jesus didn't wail and cry like a baby when He heard about His friend. No, today's verse says Jesus told His disciples, *"Our friend Lazarus has fallen asleep; but I am going there to wake him up."* His disciples misunderstood. They thought He was actually saying Lazarus was just sleeping. So Jesus had to come right out with it saying, *"Lazarus is dead"* (verses 13-14).

The Lord spoke to me about death one time after Gloria and I attended the funeral of a family member. I was walking to the graveside, talking to the Lord, when He said, *You're to be commended for saying that [your loved one] came home to be with Me. However, you are wrong when you say, "We're going out here to bury him." You're not going to bury him. You'll only bury his body—he's here with Me.*

Because that's the truth. The ceasing of life in that body is not *real* death. Real death is when God's presence is separated from your spirit—like you were before you became a Christian.

Then God said more to me out there by the graveside—and what He said *really* blessed me. He said, *You put it (the body) in the ground and commit it to Me because he's not there to do it for himself. Then at the last day, I'll raise it up for him—because he can't do that either—and give it back to him a glorified body, and he'll have charge over it for the rest of eternity.*

So don't feel overwhelmed at the death of a loved one. If they knew the Lord, soon they'll be better than ever!

backup:
John 11

download:
1 Chronicles 9-10; 2 Thessalonians 3

voice activate:
Jesus is the resurrection and the life. Because I believe in Him, I will see the glory of God. John 11:25,40

> "For the grace of God that brings salvation has appeared to all men. It teaches us to say 'No' to ungodliness and worldly passions, and to live self-controlled, upright and godly lives in this present age."
> Titus 2:11-12

It Is Possible To Live Holy

If we want to enjoy God's favor and power in our lives, we can't just obey Him in certain areas and not in others. We can't be holy in one area and not another. We have to give Him our entire lives.

Paul said, *"If you live according to the sinful nature, you will die; but if by the Spirit you put to death the misdeeds of the body, you will live, because those who are led by the Spirit of God are sons of God"* (Romans 8:13-14).

Paul is telling us that although we are free from having to follow a bunch of rules, we still have to obey the Lord. The Holy Spirit will never approve of sin in our lives. On the contrary, He will show us how to get rid of it.

When you spend time with God, the Holy Spirit will lead you into holiness. He will say to you, for example, *Stop cussing. Use words that glorify Me (God).* Or, *Stop reading those worldly novels and read the Bible more.*

Another part of God's favor is that you don't have to do everything by yourself. Whatever the Holy Spirit asks you to do, He empowers you to do. First Corinthians 10:13 says He gives us the strength to overcome every temptation.

That's why the New Testament speaks to us in such strong terms about holiness. Nowhere does it say, "Well, I know you've been sinning a lot, but, hey, I understand. Life is tough and at least you're trying."

No! It just says, *"Be holy in all you do"* (1 Peter 1:15). We have no excuse for living unholy lives. Because God not only tells us what we need to do to be holy—He also gives us the ability to do it!

It's time we started using that ability. It's time to get the slack out of our lives and become focused on God. It's time to drop everything that pulls us away from Him.

God has enabled you to succeed. It *is* possible to live holy...because He's given you His favor to see you through.

b a c k u p :

Romans 6:1-22

d o w n l o a d :

1 Chronicles 11-12; 1 Timothy 1

v o i c e a c t i v a t e :

I live a self-controlled, upright and godly life in this present age. Titus 2:12

"The kings of the earth take their stand and the rulers gather together against the Lord and against his Anointed One. 'Let us break their chains,' they say, 'and throw off their fetters.' The One enthroned in heaven laughs."
Psalm 2:2-4

june 17

kenneth

Just Laugh at Satan

God is moving like never before. More people are giving their lives to Jesus than we've ever seen. With all the power He's put in us, He's also given us great responsibility.

Today's verse helps us see what God is saying today. Psalm 37:12-13 says, *"The wicked plot against the righteous and gnash their teeth at them; but the Lord laughs at the wicked, for he knows their day is coming."*

As time draws to a close, I'm hearing the Lord say, *Hey! Give Me a couple of days here. There are a lot of things I've been wanting to do, but My hands have been tied. Now that they're untied, let's have some fun. Let's have a good time—and win billions of souls before we go!*

What do you think all this laughing is about, anyway?

Well, we just read it in the Psalms. Satan's time is up, and God is laughing at him! God is having one *BIG* time of it. The bottom line is, Satan's through! He's finished!

Hebrews 10:12-13 tells us that Jesus *"sat down on the right hand of God; from henceforth expecting till his enemies be made his footstool"* (KJV).

Notice that Jesus didn't sit down to do nothing. No, He sat down *expecting* until His enemies are made His footstool. He sat down. He rested.

Would you please tell me how in the world will Jesus defeat His enemies sitting down? It's simple: He has already defeated the enemy. What's more, God gave us authority over Satan, with the command to go into all the world and preach the good news and walk all over him.

So go ahead, laugh, and do it like Jesus did—*expecting*. Do it expecting, until the enemies you face in life are made your footstool.

backup:
Psalm 3

download:
1 Chronicles 13-14; 1 Timothy 2

voice activate:
The Lord sits in the heavens and laughs at the devil. I join in with God and laugh at the devil, too! Psalm 2:4

"God is able to make all grace abound to you, so that in all things at all times, having all that you need, you will abound in every good work."
2 Corinthians 9:8

Enough for Every Good Work

When Ken and I were first learning to believe for God's goodness in our lives, we didn't know very many of God's promises to us yet. We discovered them one by one. Every time we learned something new, we'd put it into practice.

Actually, it's much easier for us to walk in financial success now than it was back then. Today, we have to believe for millions of dollars just to pay our TV bills. That's not nearly as challenging as it was to believe God back then for food on the table. During those days I often had to pray just to pay my way out of the grocery store. That was the hardest time of all—when we were just learning.

You have to grow in these things. If you're just now hearing that God wants you to live well, you probably won't be able to get a million dollars in cash by this time next week.

Why? Because your faith isn't up to it yet. What you need to do is start where you are. Start believing God for money to go on a missions trip. Start believing God for money for your family to buy groceries. Start, and then grow.

That's what we did. We just kept growing. We kept listening to God and doing what we knew, and our faith grew bigger.

What's important is to just get started. Don't wait until next month. If you want a change, make a change. Start believing God for the things you need today. Start thanking Him for them. Tell Satan he has no hold over you. Grab God's promises and don't let go.

If you'll do that and stay with it, continuing to do what God tells you, you'll eventually have more than you need. You not only have enough to pay for necessities, but you'll also have more than enough to give into every good work!

b a c k u p :
Philippians 4:15-19

d o w n l o a d :
1 Chronicles 15-17; 1 Timothy 3-4

v o i c e   a c t i v a t e :
God makes all grace abound to me. I always have all that I need. I abound in every good work. 2 Corinthians 9:8

"Jesus took him by the hand and lifted him to his feet, and he stood up."
Mark 9:27

june 19

kenneth

Someone is Waiting on You

Mark 9 recounts the story of a father who brought his demon-possessed son to Jesus and asked for help. Jesus commanded the spirit to leave the boy.

Simple enough, we think. But if we look at verse 26, Jesus was suddenly in a situation where he could have undone everything with unbelief...or simply trust God. *"The spirit shrieked, convulsed him violently and came out. The boy looked so much like a corpse that many said, 'He's dead.'"*

What a situation! The man brings his son to Jesus for help. Jesus casts the spirit out, and now the boy appears to be dead! It sure looked like Jesus had just made the situation worse.

Well, it's a good thing Jesus had more faith in God's Word than He had in His natural senses. He didn't care how things looked. So, in verse 27, *"Jesus took him by the hand and lifted him to his feet, and he stood up."* He stood up!

If you've prayed for someone and they don't look healed, don't let that tempt you into unbelief that healing didn't come. Healing always comes. Your responsibility is to obey God's Word and pray for the sick.

Now, not everyone may be healed. Sometimes people are full of fear or doubt or unforgiveness, and they can't receive what God is giving them.

When that happens, the last thing you want to do is pull your faith away and say, "Well, I guess it didn't work." Don't do that! Your faith may be the only hope that person has! Keep believing God. Act like Jesus did. Don't be moved by what you see.

Once you do that, never back off again. Go forward in faith. Boldly place your hands on the sick and pray for them. Expect God to do exactly what He promised. Just like that little boy, there are people out there who need someone with enough faith to deliver their miracle—people who are waiting for someone just like you!

b a c k u p :
Mark 9:14-29

d o w n l o a d :
1 Chronicles 18-19; 1 Timothy 5

v o i c e   a c t i v a t e :
In Jesus' Name I lay hands on the sick and they get well. Mark 16:18

> "Everyone who hears these words of mine and puts them into practice is like a wise man who built his house on the rock. The rain came down, the streams rose, and the winds blew and beat against that house; yet it did not fall, because it had its foundation on the rock."
> Matthew 7:24-25

A Word to the Wise

I've been telling people to spend time in the Word for years now. Almost everywhere I preach, no matter what topic I'm talking about, it seems I always get back to the importance of putting God's Word first.

You may have heard me say it a hundred times, but hearing it isn't enough. It's doing it that will make you successful.

Jesus taught us that principle in Matthew 7. There He told about two men. Both of them heard the Word, yet Jesus said one of the men was foolish and the other wise. What was the difference between the two? The wise man acted on what he heard and the foolish man didn't.

You may know full well that you need to spend time reading your Bible, but unless you act on what you know, it won't do you any good when the storms of life come.

So take action! Start setting aside time to read your Bible each day. Begin making it the number one priority on your schedule. Don't wait until you're faced with some terrible, stormy situation.

Have you ever tried to build a house in a storm? Ken has been through several hurricanes. He has seen the wind blow so hard that coconuts shot through the air like cannonballs. Just think about some poor fellow out there trying to build his house with the wind blowing 120 mph!

Don't do that. Don't wait until you're desperate to make time for studying God's Word. Make the decision and start today.

Then, when the storms of life come against your house, you'll be totally cool, calm and collected. You'll be glad that you didn't let Satan talk you into being too busy for the Word.

backup:
Proverbs 1:1-9

download:
1 Chronicles 20-21; 1 Timothy 6

voice activate:
I am wise because I hear God's Words and I put them into practice. Matthew 7:24

"'Even now,' declares the Lord, 'return to me with all your heart, with fasting and weeping and mourning.' Rend your heart and not your garments. Return to the Lord your God, for he is gracious and compassionate, slow to anger and abounding in love."
Joel 2:12-13

june 21

kenneth

Don't Miss the Move!

The words "weeping and mourning" in today's verses are talking about repentance. *Repentance* means "to turn around, to change the way you're going." When you do, the blood of Jesus will take away that sin you're repenting about.

Remember: *Repentance is absolutely necessary for anyone who wants to be in on everything God is doing.*

"Well, there's certainly no hope for my church," you may say. "There's so much junk going on, we'd never get it all repented. Don't even get me started on the kids in my youth group. So I guess we'll just miss out on what God's doing."

Don't be so sure. If the bunch that was gathered after Jesus' resurrection could repent and get unified in just a few days, then your church can too.

"Wait—are you saying Peter, John and Mary, the mother of Jesus, and all the rest of the disciples had to repent before the Holy Spirit could fall on them?"

I certainly am. Think about it. The treasurer had been stealing and ended up committing suicide...the rest of the disci-

ples argued about who would be top guy...there was so much strife, John and James' mother got involved...Peter denied the Lord...and that's just to start.

Yet somehow, together in that room, they dropped their differences. Jesus' mother was there. James and his brothers were there. Peter and John were there. All those who had been fighting with each other were there...and the Bible says *"they were all with one accord"* (Acts 2:1, NKJV).

I'm telling you, they repented!

After they repented, God came on the scene. *"Suddenly a sound like the blowing of a violent wind came from heaven and filled the whole house where they were sitting"* (Acts 2:2). He will do the same for you!

backup:
2 Corinthians 7:9-10

download:
1 Chronicles 22-23; 2 Timothy 1

voice activate:
I turn to the Lord with all my heart. He is gracious and compassionate, slow to anger and abounding in love. Joel 2:12-13

"Praise the Lord. Sing to the Lord a new song, his praise in the assembly of the saints. Let Israel rejoice in their Maker; let the people of Zion be glad in their King. Let them praise his name with dancing and make music to him with tambourine and harp. For the Lord takes delight in his people." Psalm 149:1-4

Express Yourself

Some years ago, when I first found out about how powerful joy is, I did a Bible study on it. During that study, I discovered that one of the biblical words for *joy* is translated "to shine." Another word means "to leap." Another means "to delight." However, in every case, joy is more than an attitude. It's an action.

As I studied, I also found out that, as Psalm 149 says, joyful praise delights God. It doesn't offend Him when we praise Him with all we've got. He likes it. It pleases Him to see us shine and leap and express our delight in Him.

"Let the saints rejoice in this honor.... May the praise of God be in their mouths and a double-edged sword in their hands" (verses 5-6).

I know that by today's standards, expressive praise doesn't look very cool. However, acting "cool" kept me from being as free as I should be with the Lord for a long time.

As Christians, we need to get past caring about that. Instead, we need to focus on pleasing God. We should have such a desire to please Him that we don't care how we look to other people.

"Gloria, that's easy for you to say. You're comfortable with expressing yourself to God in praise."

I haven't always been. I held back so much when I first became a Christian that it took me a long time to even begin expressing myself in praise, but I broke through that "coolness" and so can you!

backup:
Psalm 149

download:
1 Chronicles 24-25; 2 Timothy 2

voice activate:
I praise the Lord. I sing praises to God. I praise the Lord with dancing. I make music to Him with instruments, for the Lord delights in me. Psalm 149:1-4

"And it shall be that if you earnestly obey My commandments…to love the Lord your God and serve Him with all your heart and with all your soul, then I will give you the rain for your land in its season, the early rain and the latter rain, that you may gather in your grain, your new wine, and your oil."
Deuteronomy 11:13-14, NKJV

kenneth june 23

The Rain is Coming

God Himself says He is coming to us as rain (Hosea 6:3). Not just as rain, but specifically as the *former and the latter rain.*

What is the former and latter rain? In everyday speaking, the Israelites knew the former rain as the fall rain that prepared the soil for planting, and the latter rain as the spring rain that moisturized the soil to bring forth a good harvest.

In spiritual terms, the former and latter rains represent the move of the Holy Spirit under the Old and New Covenants.

The Bible calls the former rain of the Spirit, under the old covenant, a "moderate" rain. Under that covenant, people would go hundreds of years without hearing God's voice or seeing anyone whom He was miraculously working through. If there was anyone whom He was working through, it would be some prayer warriors somewhere who didn't draw much attention to themselves, so people didn't see them.

Eventually, however, a little rain would fall: A prophet of God, a great priest or a king would be raised up in the land. The Holy Spirit would be upon that person and miracles would flow through them. If you could get near them, you could be healed,

have your needs met supernaturally and hear the voice of God.

To understand how powerful that "moderate" rain was, you have to realize that even Jesus' ministry was under the old covenant. He was the Son of God sacrificed under the old covenant. So, as powerful as the ministry of Jesus was, it did not show the fullness of the Holy Spirit's power.

He said it didn't! Just before He went to the Cross, He told His disciples, *"Anyone who has faith in me will do what I have been doing. He will do even greater things than these, because I am going to the Father"* (John 14:12).

How could Jesus say such an astounding thing? He knew the latter rain was on the way!

b a c k u p :
Hosea 6:1-3

d o w n l o a d :
1 Chronicles 26-27; 2 Timothy 3

v o i c e a c t i v a t e :
I expect the anointing and the miracle power of Jesus to flow through me because Jesus sent the latter rain of the Holy Spirit when He returned to the Father. John 14:12

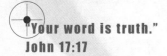

"Your word is truth."
John 17:17

The Word Is Truth

Notice that today's verse doesn't say, "Your Word is fact." Truth goes beyond facts. The fact may be that you're having relationship troubles. The fact may be that the doctor said you have an incurable disease. What does the truth have to say about it?

The truth is absolute. Truth doesn't give in. Truth doesn't change. So, facts are subject to truth.

It can be a fact that you are sick as can be, but God says you were healed by the wounds of Jesus when He died on the cross. That's the truth. Now you have a choice. You can apply the truth of God's Word to the fact that you're sick and the fact will change—or you can agree with the facts and things will stay the way they are.

I'll tell you right now, it will be much easier just to agree with the facts, because facts scream a lot louder than God's Word does. God's Word will be quiet—until you start speaking it out of your mouth.

Once His promises come out of your mouth in faith, they will be the final word.

If it is God's Word about healing, you'll be healed. If it's His Word about financial success, you'll be financially successful. If it's His Word about rescuing, you'll be rescued.

God has given you His contract. When you do your part by believing, speaking and acting, God's Word will bring results. No circumstance on earth and no demon in hell can stop it.

So forget all those stories you have heard about so-and-so who believed the Bible, but it didn't work for him. Quit asking questions and settle it once and for all. God's Word *is* truth.

kenneth june 24

backup:
Psalm 119:151-152,160

download:
1 Chronicles 28-29; 2 Timothy 4

voice activate:
God's Word is truth. I believe His Word and not my circumstances. John 17:17

183

"Remember that formerly you who are Gentiles by birth...you were separate from Christ [the Anointed One], excluded from citizenship in Israel and foreigners to the covenants of the promise, without hope and without God in the world. But now in Christ [the Anointed One] Jesus you who once were far away have been brought near through the blood of Christ [the Anointed One]."
Ephesians 2:11-13

june 25

kenneth

Breakthrough

Have you ever hit a brick wall? I know what you're thinking: *Ouch!* Don't worry, I'm not talking about a physical one. I'm talking about an emotional one. The kind that comes when you've chased every lead you knew to get a job, or understand geometry, or learn a new skill. You know the feeling. It's frustrating, and it usually drives *anyone* to cry out to God.

Well, there's one sure way to punch a good-sized hole in that wall and watch it crumble to nothing: I call it "factoring in the anointing."

According to the Bible, before you made Jesus your Lord, you were without the Anointed One (Jesus). Well, if you were without the Anointed One, you were also without the anointing, right? Today, you are *with* the Anointed One. His anointing is available to you for every wall you need to destroy. God's Anointing is literally "God on a person doing those things only God can do."

That's why you can have hope in the most hopeless situations. It doesn't matter who you are or what color your skin is. It doesn't matter where you live or if you never made it past the sixth grade. You can break out of that hopeless situation if you'll factor in the anointing.

The anointing factor is what the world always forgets. They say, "We'll build this wall so big nobody will ever get through it. We'll build it big enough to block out the Bible and keep the people under our thumb." They fail to figure in the anointing. It destroys walls. If you don't believe it, ask the Christians in Berlin (where the wall literally came down)!

So whatever wall you are facing today, begin factoring in the anointing in your life. If someone says to you, "Forget it. You can't expect to succeed," ask yourself, *Is there a wall holding me back?* Maybe your wall is a lack of education, the need for more confidence, or a sickness. If a wall is holding you back, then cheer up! Because the anointing will destroy it...completely!

backup:
Isaiah 10:24-27

download:
2 Chronicles 1-3; Titus 1-2

voice activate:
The anointing factor removes every burden and destroys every yoke and wall that tries to hold me back. Isaiah 10:27

"'The word is near you; it is in your mouth and in your heart,' that is, the word of faith we are proclaiming."
Romans 10:8

No Deposit—
No Return

Everything we could ever need is waiting for us. God has our name on it. All we need to do is get it—with faith.

Faith is the "currency" we use to transfer all God has for us from the unseen realm of the spirit to this natural, earthly realm. Or, as Hebrews 11:1 says, *"Faith is being sure of what we hope for and certain of what we do not see."*

The problem is, many Christians don't have a clue where faith actually comes from, where it's stored or how to get it out when they need it. That's critical information. In fact, without it, you're spiritually broke. So let's study this a moment.

Where does faith come from? Romans 10:17 (NKJV) says, *"Faith comes by hearing, and hearing by the word of God."*

Where is faith stored? *"'The word is near you; it is in your mouth and in your heart,' that is, the word of faith we are proclaiming.... For it is with your heart that you believe and are justified, and it is with your mouth that you confess and are saved"* (Romans 10:8, 10). Your faith is stored up in your heart—and since your faith (or lack of it) determines your future,

the truth is, your future is stored up in your heart as well.

How do you get it out? When you want to use your faith, "get it out" by speaking God's promises. Don't talk about the way things are. Don't "tell it the way it is" (or looks). Say what God says the outcome is going to be. Put your faith in *that*.

Let me ask you this: How much faith do you have in your heart right now? Is it enough to handle your current situation? Is it enough to make you win every day of your life? If not, you'd better start making some big deposits of God's Word. Remember: No deposit—no return.

backup:
Matthew 12:35-36

download:
2 Chronicles 4-5; Titus 3

voice activate:
The Word of God is near me. It is in my mouth and in my heart. Romans 10:8

"Weeping may endure for a night, but joy comes in the morning."
Psalm 30:5, NKJV

Joy Comes

Many Christians drag themselves around, all defeated, year after year. You've heard them. They say stuff like, "I just can't figure it out. I believe the Bible. I believe Jesus has set me free from this sickness. I believe He has set me free from this sin. But I still can't win."

The problem is, those people are too spiritually weak to receive what Jesus has given them. They need some muscle back in their believing. They need something to give them the spiritual might they need to knock Satan upside the head and take back what belongs to them.

That's exactly what the joy of the Lord will do. Nehemiah 8:10 says the joy of the Lord is our strength. That verse is literally true. To understand why, you must realize that joy is not happiness. Happiness is just temporary, based upon what you're doing. Joy, on the other hand, is a spiritual force. It's not based on what's happening, but upon the condition of your heart.

Happiness is wimpy. It disappears every time there's trouble. But joy is tough. If you'll let it, it will still be there in the middle of the most miserable situations. It will enable you to stand rock solid until the trouble is over.

I realize if you're sitting there right now in the middle of trouble, you probably feel like it will never be over, but believe me, it will! *"Weeping may endure for a night, but joy comes in the morning"* (Psalm 30:5, NKJV).

If you are a person of faith, it doesn't matter how bad things may be right now, you know a brighter day is on the way. That's because Satan can't keep up his attack forever. He doesn't have the power. So if you'll let the force of joy keep you strong, you will outlast him and he'll eventually have to give up.

Remember, the Bible promises that joy *comes*, and joy is your strength. It's tough. It will enable you to win...and it's inside of you. Give it place and your trouble will be over soon enough.

backup:
Psalm 30

download:
2 Chronicles 6-7; Philemon

voice activate:
The joy of the Lord is my strength. Joy comes to me! Nehemiah 8:10

"But in their distress they turned to the Lord, the God of Israel, and sought him, and he was found by them."
2 Chronicles 15:4

Welcome to Earth

If you're in trouble right now, you're not alone. At one time or another, everyone faces trouble. Welcome to earth.

Here's something you need to know: If you're a Christian, you can expect to come out of that trouble a winner. That's right. God brings His people out of trouble. In fact, coming out of trouble is part of your salvation.

The word *salvation* includes a whole lot more than becoming a Christian and going to heaven when you die. Salvation actually gives us the right to material and temporal deliverance from danger and apprehension. Because of salvation, we have preservation, pardon, restoration, healing, wholeness and soundness.

There's no doubt about it: coming out of trouble is part of our salvation.

"But the trouble I'm facing is my own fault," you say. "Will God rescue me from this mess even though I caused it?"

It's a good thing He does, because that's usually the way it is. We get into trouble by ourselves and then we turn to Him for help. Even so, He is always there. We can't wear out His mercy and patience. (If we *could* have, we already *would* have!)

Today's verse tells of a time when the people of Israel turned away from God and got themselves in trouble...and God found them.

The same will be true for you. When you turn to the Lord and look for Him, you will find Him. God won't say to you, "What are you doing here *now*? Why didn't you talk to Me *before* you got into this situation?"

That's what we deserve to hear, but—THANK GOD!—He is a God of mercy. He will always take you in. He will always listen to you. He will always take you from trouble to triumph!

gloria

backup:
2 Chronicles 15

download:
2 Chronicles 8-9; Hebrews 1

voice activate:
When I am in trouble, I turn to the Lord and seek Him, and I find Him.
2 Chronicles 15:4

"You made him [man] ruler over the works of your hands; you put everything under his feet."
Psalm 8:6

june 29

kenneth

You're in Charge

"Well, friend, you have to remember...God is sovereign."

You've probably heard someone say that at sometime, usually in religious-sounding tones, when circumstances seem to fall short of what God has promised they would be.

As spiritual as that phrase might sound, it really bothers me. It's not that I don't believe God is sovereign. Certainly He is. According to *Webster's Dictionary*, *sovereign* means "above or superior to all others; supreme in power, rank or authority." Without question, God *is* all those things.

All too often, when people refer to God being sovereign, what they're actually saying is, "You never know what God will do. After all, He's all-powerful and He does *whatever* He wants *whenever* He wants."

The problem with that is that it releases us of all responsibility. After all, if that's the case, God will do what He wants anyway, so we might as well kick back and watch professional wrestling for the rest of our lives and forget about everything, right?

Wrong. After more than 30 years of studying the Bible and preaching, I've come to realize that God does very few

things—if anything—in this earth without man's cooperation. Even though it belongs to God...it is His creation and He owns it.

According to Psalm 8:6, God Himself put mankind in charge. He doesn't intervene just whenever He wants. He respects the place He has given us. So, until man's time on this planet ends, God restricts His power, taking action only when He is asked to do so.

Since the people who do the asking are often very quiet people who do their praying in secret, it may appear at times that God simply acts on His own. The Bible teaches that God's connection with man is a prayer and faith connection. When you see Him act in a mighty way, you can be sure there was someone somewhere praying to bring Him on the scene.

backup:
James 5:13-18

download:
2 Chronicles 10-11; Hebrews 2

voice activate:
God has made me the ruler over all the works of His hands. He has put everything under my feet. Psalm 8:6

"His divine power has given us everything we need for life and godliness through our knowledge of him who called us by his own glory and goodness. Through these he has given us his very great and precious promises, so that through them you may participate in the divine nature and escape the corruption in the world caused by evil desires."
2 Peter 1:3-4

Find the Promise

If you're facing a challenge, the first thing you should do is go to the Bible and find a promise that covers your situation. (Today's verses are our assurance that there is such a promise for everything.) Once you have found the promise and believe it, keep it in the forefront of your thinking. My kids proved the power of this principle when they were very young.

They came to me and told me they wanted a boat so we could go out on the lake as a family and have some time to ourselves. "That sounds great," I said. "But your mother and I will not use our faith to get it. We'll agree with you, but you kids will have to get it by using your own faith."

So, off they went. Kellie opened the Bible and found promises that applied to them. (John was too young to read. He just listened and agreed.) Then they wrote out an agreement, signed it and taped it to the refrigerator door. From that day forward, every time they walked past the refrigerator, they would slap that agreement and say, "Thank God it is done!" They kept it constantly before them.

To make a long story short, 10 days later, a guy called me and gave me a fishing boat. Then, another guy called me and gave me a light cabin cruiser.

"Why *two* boats?" I asked the Lord.

Go read their agreement, He answered.

Those kids had agreed on the "perfect boat." To them that meant a boat we could use to fish, water ski and carry the entire family. Well, that took two boats!

Finding a promise from God made faith easy for John and Kellie, and it will make it easy for you, too. It's easy to believe someone will do something for you if you know they said they would—especially when it's someone like God.

kenneth **june 30**

backup:
Proverbs 4:20-27

download:
2 Chronicles 12-13; Hebrews 3

voice activate:
God has given me everything I need for life and godliness. 2 Peter 1:3

"Faith comes from hearing the message, and the message is heard through the word of Christ."
Romans 10:17

Faith Comes by Hearing

july 1

kenneth

One of the greatest healing evangelists I've ever known once said to me, "I don't understand it. I have prayed for more than 2 million people. I've seen all kinds of miracles, but I'm the last guy in the world to ever get healed."

Just think, that evangelist had seen Jesus face to face more than once. His hand had been set on fire with the healing touch of God, but he couldn't live on those experiences. He had to learn, just like you and I do, to walk one step at a time—speaking, believing and standing on God's promises in His Word.

"Well, maybe that's true," you say, "but I still think I would have more faith if Jesus would appear to me like He did to that evangelist."

No, you wouldn't. Jesus said, *"Blessed are those who have not seen and yet have believed"* (John 20:29). *Blessed* means "empowered." So, according to Jesus, you'll have more power if you'll believe *before* seeing Him face to face.

Why is that? It's because for you to believe something you don't see with your physical eyes, you have to turn inward. You have to see it with your spirit. When

you do that, the part of you that is like God rises up and gets stronger.

Am I saying you should avoid seeing miracles?

Absolutely not! Enjoy them all you want. Be a part of what God's doing, but don't drop your faith in the process.

First and foremost, keep standing on His promises. His Word will work when miracles are happening *and* when they're not. His Word will work in the daytime and in the dark. His Word will work for anyone who will put it to work—it doesn't matter if you're twelve or if you're 92.

Remember this: Faith—the everyday kind of faith you use for living—doesn't come from seeing miracles or even seeing Jesus Himself. It comes by hearing God's Word.

backup:
John 20:24-29

download:
2 Chronicles 14-15; Hebrews 4

voice activate:
Faith comes to me as I hear the Word of God. Romans 10:17

"Now I am writing you that you must not associate with anyone who calls himself a brother but is sexually immoral or greedy, an idolater or a slanderer, a drunkard or a swindler."
1 Corinthians 5:11

Choose Good Company

Honestly, I'm shocked at how some Christians live. When I see Christians who go to church on Sunday, then live like the world the rest of the week, it bothers me. Ken and I haven't been raised like that. The people we run with act the same all the time. When we take off on our motorcycles, we might look like the world with our helmets and our leathers on, but we talk straight and act in love just like we do when we're preaching at a convention.

If your friends don't do that, you need to find some new friends. If your friends are worldly, you need to separate yourself from them because they'll drag you down to their level.

It's good to bring the good news to sinners, but the Bible tells us not to associate with them on a continual basis. They'll start influencing you. Pretty soon, you'll be talking the way they talk and watching the movies they watch. Next thing you know, you'll be doing everything else they're doing too.

We're different! We don't need to be watching television sitcoms that make light of immorality. Over time, they just make sin seem like it's not as bad as it is.

Don't play around like the people in the world do. It will get you in trouble. (They are already in trouble.) You might start out doing something that seems small at first. You might indulge in just a sip of beer at a party so you can fit in with what everyone else is doing.

Compromising your standards for something as silly as a drink is foolish. Besides, why would you want to sacrifice God's power in your life just to "fit in" for a few minutes? Follow and obey God's Word by choosing your company wisely. Begin to associate with those who will compliment your life of holiness!

gloria

backup:
1 Corinthians 5:11; 2 Corinthians 6:14-18, 7:1

download:
2 Chronicles 16-18; Hebrews 5-6

voice activate:
I do not compromise my standards and walk the world's way. I walk in holiness.
1 Corinthians 5:11

"If you fully obey the Lord your God and carefully follow all his commands I give you today, the Lord your God will set you high above all the nations on earth. All these blessings will come upon you and accompany you if you obey the Lord your God."
Deuteronomy 28:1-2

july 3

gloria

Chased by Blessings

God promised Abraham that He would be his shield and his "very great reward" (Genesis 15:1). No question about it, that promise caused Abraham to be extremely successful and it will do the same for you. What is it like to be blessed in every way?

Deuteronomy 28:1-9 tells us. It says you can be blessed wherever you go. In fact, it says your whole family can be blessed. What you work on can be blessed and you'll always have more than enough. It says God will defeat your enemies, and on and on it goes. You'll be blessed in every area, from your school-work to your family to your possessions to your everyday business.

Sound too good to be true? Well, it's not. That's what Jesus bought for you on the cross. It will begin to happen in your life if you'll *obey the Lord your God."*

Notice I didn't say it'll happen just because you're a Christian. Ken and I were Christians for five years before we listened to what the Bible said to us about living well. So, during that time, we *weren't* living well. That curse (the oppo-site of living in God's blessings) came with all its force. No matter how hard we tried, we couldn't get away from it.

Then we began to believe God's Word—we became obedient because we wanted to—and good things started to happen. First a few. Then a few more. The longer we obeyed God and believed God, the more those good things happened.

Just like the curse once chased after us, now God's blessings chase after us. I like that much better.

The same thing will happen to you if you'll follow the instructions in Deuteronomy 28 to fully obey the Lord. Carefully follow all His commands. Then, all these blessings will come upon you!

backup:
Deuteronomy 28:1-9

download:
2 Chronicles 19-20; Hebrews 7

voice activate:
I fully obey the Lord and carefully follow all His commands. All God's blessings come upon me and accompany me. Deuteronomy 28:1-2

"It shall come to pass in that day That his burden will be taken away from your shoulder, And his yoke from your neck, And the yoke will be destroyed because of the anointing oil."
Isaiah 10:27, NKJV

Devil on the Run

Jesus is the Christ. The Greek word *Christ* means "the Anointed One." Since Isaiah 10:27 tells us the yoke of Satan is destroyed by the anointing, we don't have to run scared when Satan comes against us or someone we love. We can put him on the run with the yoke-destroying Anointing of Jesus Himself!

That's what Jesus expects us to do. He has already taken care of every kind of trouble that could ever come against us. He did it when He was put on the Cross, then raised from the dead. He stripped the powers of darkness of their authority. He stripped Satan of every last ounce of power.

Jesus has done His part. He has taken back Satan's authority over the earth and He has given it to us. Just before He went to heaven He said, *"All authority in heaven and on earth has been given to me. Therefore go..."* (Matthew 28:18-19). He gave His power and authority to us then *"after He had offered one sacrifice for sins forever, [He] sat down at the right hand of God, from that time waiting till His enemies are made His footstool"* (Hebrews 10:12-13, NKJV).

He expects us to stand up in the middle of the storms of life and rule over

them by speaking out our faith. He expects us to look sickness and trouble and terror in the face and say, "Get under my feet in the Name of Jesus!"

I realize you may not feel like you can do that today. You may be facing the greatest struggle of your life. It may really be hard right now, but, regardless of how you feel, you can do it because the Bible says, *"for everyone born of God overcomes the world. This is the victory that has overcome the world, even our faith"* (1 John 5:4).

You are destined to overcome. You have that anointing—the Anointed One—living on the inside of you. So stand up in the middle of the storm. Speak to it with all the power and authority that's been given to you. If you'll do that, you'll rule over the storm and put the devil on the run!

kenneth

backup:
Matthew 14:22-33

download:
2 Chronicles 21-22; Hebrews 8

voice activate:
Jesus has taken the burden from off my shoulder and the yoke from my neck. His anointing destroyed the yoke. Isaiah 10:27, NKJV

"May He [God] grant you out of the rich treasury of His glory to be strengthened and reinforced with mighty power in the inner man by the (Holy) Spirit [Himself]—indwelling your innermost being and personality.... That you may be filled (through all your being) unto all the fullness of God—[that is] may have the richest measure of the divine Presence, and become a body wholly filled and flooded with God Himself!"
Ephesians 3:16,19, AMP

july 5

gloria

God Is Able!

Can you imagine what it would be like to have the *"richest measure of the divine Presence, and become a body wholly filled and flooded with God Himself"*? I can! That's the glory. That's the totality of God's presence showing up in our lives and I want it!

I want not just my own life, but all of our lives to be filled with God's glory. In fact, I think we're falling short if we're satisfied with anything less.

We're not only cheating ourselves, we're cheating the world when we don't live with God's power in our lives. For when God's power shows up, the world is changed. Lives are forever altered.

Some people say we can't have a great move of God now because people just don't care about God anymore. Yet the greatest moves of God in the world have come in the darkest of days. They've come when men's hearts were like ice cubes.

Well, the world isn't getting better. People disrespect God all the time. Yet that just tells me we're ready for God to show up. It tells me we're ready for the glory!

You may not feel like God's glory can shine through someone as un-glorious as you, but He can. For in the closing words of Paul's prayer in Ephesians 3:20-21 he says, *"Now to him who is able to do immeasurably more than all we ask or imagine, according to his power that is at work within us, to him be glory in the church and in Christ Jesus throughout all generations, for ever and ever!"*

That verse plainly says, GOD IS ABLE! He not only wants to show Himself through you and me, He is *able!* You couldn't do it. I couldn't do it. A thousand of us couldn't do it, but *God* is able!

backup:
Philippians 3:7-11

download:
2 Chronicles 23-24; Hebrews 9

voice activate:
God grants me out of the rich treasury of His glory to be strengthened and reinforced with mighty power in my inner man. Ephesians 3:16, AMP

> "Strip yourselves of your former nature...And be constantly renewed in the spirit of your mind...put on the new nature...created in...true righteousness and holiness."
> Ephesians 4:22-24, AMP

Power Up

To live a life pleasing to God, you must have the spiritual strength to put aside some of your natural pursuits. How do you develop that strength? Mainly by spending time in the Bible and in prayer. As you do, the Holy Spirit will use the Word to separate you not only from sin, but also from the unnecessary things in life. He will give you the spiritual strength you need.

Today's verses tell us that righteousness and holiness are two different things. Righteousness is the right-standing with God you received when you made Jesus your Lord. The only thing you did to be put in right-standing was to make Jesus Christ the Lord of your life.

Holiness is another matter. You are not *made* holy. Holiness is the result of your choices. It's what you do with your time and your actions. It comes when you make a decision to live according to what God says. In short, holiness is doing those things that please God. To be *holy* is to be "set apart." Set apart from what? From the world! God wants us to be so caught up in spiritual things that we lose interest in worldly activities and pursue Him with all our heart.

According to Romans 12:1-2, being entirely dedicated to God is your "*reason-able service*" (KJV). God expects us all to live holy. He says, "*Be holy, because I am holy*" (1 Peter 1:16).

When God's power starts flowing through you, you won't regret you made those sacrifices. When you pray for a crippled person and see him walk instantly, you'll be glad you turned down that R-rated movie your friends went to see.

You may think I'm being dramatic, but I'm not. Those things are happening at the hands of everyday teens like you. They can happen in your life.

Determine to be a part of what God is doing. Make up your mind not to be sideswiped by doing petty things that please yourself. Give yourself entirely to God. Choose to live holy. Choose to live a life of power! Choose to live for God!

backup:
Romans 12:1-2

download:
2 Chronicles 25-26; Hebrews 10

voice activate:
I determine to put off my old self. I am made new in the attitude of my mind. I put on the new self, created to be like God in true righteousness and holiness. Ephesians 4:22-24

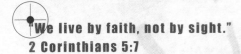

"We live by faith, not by sight."
2 Corinthians 5:7

kenneth *july 7*

Work Harder!

"We just need to get out of the way and let God work. After all, we can't do anything anyway. He's the One Who is in control."

Have you ever heard anyone say something like that?

I'm sure you have. In fact, you may have said it yourself. At the time, it probably sounded very good. Very church-like. Very humble.

Let me warn you, it's also very dangerous. It can leave you sitting around while Satan tears up everything around you. It can leave you in tears, begging God to fix a situation for you when He was saying all along, "Fix it yourself! I'll back you. I've given you everything you need. I've given you My own faith. Now, use it!"

Right now, especially, we must be on guard against such attitudes, because we are on the edge of a great move of God. During times like these, even Christians who know better can get lazy. They can look around them at the miracles and say, "I guess I don't need faith anymore.

It looks like God is taking care of everything Himself now."

Don't make that mistake. Even though God is moving mightily, He still expects His people to live by faith.

Don't get lazy just because God is moving. Work harder! Spend more time in the Word and develop your faith more than ever. Get yourself ready so that when someone gets healed, you'll be there beside them saying, "Now, friend, let me show you how to *stay* well."

These are the end times. God is moving more and more. God is wanting to use you in big ways. So don't get caught sitting around. Work harder!

backup:
Hebrews 10:32-39

download:
2 Chronicles 27-28; Hebrews 11

voice activate:
I am righteous and I live by faith.
Hebrews 10:38

God's Medicine

As you believe God for healing according to the promises in His Word (Proverbs 4:20-24), don't be discouraged if you don't see immediate results. Although many times healing comes instantly, there also are times when it takes place over time.

So don't let lingering sniffles or sneezes cause you to doubt. After all, when you go to the doctor, you don't always feel better right away. The medication he gives you often takes some time before it begins to work, but you don't allow that to discourage you.

When you take God's medicine you are really "treating" your spirit, which is the source of supernatural life and health for your physical body.

So release that same kind of confidence in God's medicine. Realize that the moment you begin to take it, the healing process starts. Keep your hope high and make up your mind to continue standing on what God has promised you until you can see and feel the total physical effects of God's healing power.

When Satan whispers words of doubt to you, when he suggests that the Word isn't working, deal with those thoughts immediately. Shoot them down (2 Corinthians 10:5). Speak out loud if necessary and say, "Satan, *whatever.* I'm throwing your thoughts far from my mind. I will not believe your lies." Then—for your own benefit—speak out what you believe. Something like "God has sent His Word to heal me, and His Word never fails. That Word went to work in my body the instant I believed it, so as far as I am concerned, my days of sickness are over. Jesus took my sickness, weakness and pain, and I am free!"

Then, *"after you have done everything, to stand. Stand"* until your healing shows up for all to see (Ephesians 6:12-14). Remember, your confidence is in God's Word—not in your sniffles.

july 8

gloria

backup:

Psalm 107:1-20

download:

2 Chronicles 29-30; Hebrews 12

voice activate:

When I have done everything to stand, I stand my ground. Ephesians 6:13-14

"You hold a sacred appointment, you have been given an unction— you have been anointed by the Holy One."
1 John 2:20, AMP

kenneth july 9

You Are Anointed

We've thrown around the word *anointing* in churches for years without really understanding what it means. If we're to walk in God's power, it has to become real to us.

The anointing is God's presence— who He *is*. It's the thing that makes God *God*. The anointing is God *on* you *enabling* you to do things that are impossible for you to do alone.

For instance, you can't heal anyone. Even Jesus as a physical man couldn't heal anyone. His physical being came from Mary. It was as human as she was. Yet His perfect, sinless being—speaking God's promises—caused God's Anointing to come on Him without measure (see John 3:34, KJV).

It's not hard for our minds to understand that God's Anointing was on Jesus. What's tough to comprehend is that the same anointing can be on *us*.

"No way! I'm not sinless."

No, but as far as God is concerned you are. That's what grace is all about—

giving us the anointing when we don't deserve it!

Just like Jesus couldn't heal in His own human-ness, neither can you. With the anointing, Jesus brought healing, and so can you. Everything you need to do today can be done in the Anointed One and His Anointing.

His Anointing is on you, in you and all over you. Because of it, you can do things you couldn't normally do...whether it's day-to-day responsibilities, or placing your hands on someone and zapping them with the healing power of God. You can be *and* do everything God created you to be *and* do in His Anointing. You *are* anointed!

backup:
Acts 8:5-8

download:
2 Chronicles 31-33; Hebrews 13; James 1

voice activate:
I am anointed and I know the truth. 1 John 2:20

"Make every effort to add to your faith goodness; and to goodness, knowledge; and to knowledge, self-control; and to self-control, perseverance; and to perseverance, godliness; and to godliness, brotherly kindness; and to brotherly kindness, love. For if you possess these qualities in increasing measure, they will keep you from being ineffective and unproductive in your knowledge of our Lord Jesus Christ.... Be all the more eager to make your calling and election sure. For if you do these things, you will never fall."
2 Peter 1:5-8,10

Your Supernatural Disposition

The character of God is so vital for our lives that if I had to choose between having His character or His supernatural gifts (which, thank God, I don't!), I'd choose His character. Why? Because you can have spectacular gifts in your life, yet still get so far off course you end up a spiritual failure.

When you have God's character in your life, however, you will never fall!

That may sound extreme—but it's true. The Bible makes that very promise in today's verses. Yet we've all discovered that living out His character in our lives is no piece of cake. It's hard! Galatians 5:17 tells us the desires of our old sinful nature are contrary to the desires of the Spirit. So when we decide to obey the desires of our re-created spirit, our old nature still wants control.

The way to keep from losing that battle is found in Galatians 5:16: We're to live in the spirit every day. Hebrews 5:14 tells us that our old nature is trained by practice.

Sometimes when I tell people that living in the Spirit is the secret to having God's character in their lives, they think I'm telling them to do something impossible. Actually, it's quite simple. You walk in the spirit by putting God first place in your life. You do it by spending time with Him, reading His Word, praying and obeying Him every opportunity you get.

As you give way to His character within you, something happens to your own character. It is changed. You are changed. You develop what I call your natural *supernatural* disposition. It's the disposition of character that you were originally created to have. It's what God intended for you all along...not what you've developed in life through the world's influence.

Keep in mind that it won't come automatically. You'll have to spend time with God. You'll have to choose to give way to love and joy and peace, and so on. When you do, you'll become the best you've ever been!

backup:
Galatians 5:22-26

download:
2 Chronicles 34-35; James 2

voice activate:
I am eager to make my calling and election sure by walking in the fruit of the spirit. I will, therefore, never fall. 2 Peter 1:5-8,10

"Your sins have been forgiven on account of his name."
1 John 2:12

kenneth *july 11*

On Account of His Name

How is it that God has forgiven us? First John 2:12 tells us the answer: our sins have been forgiven *"on account of his name."* In other words, God has put His Name on an agreement. He has given us His oath that, because Jesus died and paid the price for sin, all men are forgiven in His sight. He has put His Name to a document which says, because of what Jesus did, He is no longer holding anyone's sin against them (2 Corinthians 5:18-19).

Why did God put His Name on that document? Because of the blood Jesus shed. God forgives our sin because *He honors the blood.* He has said, *I will accept any man, any woman, any child from any place in the world regardless of any sin they have committed. I swore it in the blood and I will do it because of My Name.*

Considering our sin, it would be understandable for God to say to us, "Get out of My sight. What are you doing walking in here wanting to be a part of My family? Just look at yourself! Who do you think you are?"

The good news is, He doesn't think twice about our sin. He only thinks about the blood of Jesus. Because He honors that blood, He has wiped all our sins out. The Bible says He doesn't even remember them!

Let me tell you, when I sin there is no way in the world I would go to God and ask Him to forgive me because I've been in the ministry. I wouldn't pull a dumb stunt like that. Instead, I'll just go in and plead the blood of Jesus, because I know God honors the blood.

That's where my faith rests. I don't have to wonder what God is going to do. I don't have to wonder if He will forgive me. I know He will because He swore it in the blood of His own Son.

b a c k u p :
Romans 3:19-26

d o w n l o a d :
2 Chronicles 36; Ezra 1; James 3

v o i c e a c t i v a t e :
My sins are forgiven on account of the Name of Jesus and His blood. 1 John 2:12

"Therefore, as God's chosen people, holy and dearly loved, clothe your-selves with compassion, kindness, humility, gentleness and patience. Bear with each other and forgive whatever grievances you may have against one another. Forgive as the Lord forgave you. And over all these virtues put on love, which binds them all together in perfect unity. Let the peace of Christ rule in your hearts, since as members of one body you were called to peace."
Colossians 3:12-15

Revolutionary Love

How much do we really know about love? We've talked about it. We've heard about it. We've heard many sermons about it. If we're not watchful , the message of love will just go in one ear and out the other.

In spite of all that, most of us don't know the first thing about the real power of love. For instance, researchers have found that hostility and the stress it causes are physically damaging, but walking in love is good for your health, and the benefits don't end there.

God's love puts you in control of every situation. As long as you walk in love, you cannot be hurt and you cannot fail. No one even has the power to hurt your feelings, because you are not ruled by feelings but by God's love.

This love is revolutionary. If we fully understood how good it is for us to walk in God's love, we'd probably be competing with each other, each of us trying to love the other more. Without a doubt, everyone would end up winning!

Think about that. When you're acting in love, you're enjoying the best God has to offer. Love. Joy. Peace. Everyone in your school is chasing after those things. Many are trying to get them through drugs and alcohol and pre-marital sex, but they can't. In fact, those things pull them further away.

The only way to achieve true love, joy and peace is to make Jesus your Lord and then allow God's love to work through you. It's really rather simple. You can live in hostility and be stressed out...or you can walk in love and have supernatural peace.

b a c k u p :
John 14:27-31

d o w n l o a d :
Ezra 2-3; James 4

v o i c e a c t i v a t e :
As God's chosen, I clothe myself with compassion, kindness, humility, gentle-ness and patience. I forgive those who offend me. I forgive as God has forgiven me. The most important piece of cloth-ing is love, which binds us all together in perfect unity. Colossians 3:12-14

"Anyone who lives on milk, being still an infant, is not acquainted with the teaching about righteousness. But solid food is for the mature, who by constant use have trained themselves to distinguish good from evil."
Hebrews 5:13-14

kenneth july 13

Never Play Fair!

Look at today's verses again. How do they say you train yourself to be a mature Christian? First by becoming *"acquainted with the teaching about righteousness,"* and second, by *"constant use"* or practice.

You have to practice living for God. Practice living by faith. Practice walking in love. Practice, practice, practice!

At first, your old nature will rebel against it. It just hasn't been trained and it will throw a fit for a while. Some people don't realize that—and that's why they get discouraged when they try to live by faith and then stumble.

Keep practicing though. Pick out some kid you know that's nearly impossible to love and start practicing on him. If you strike out the first time at bat, don't worry about it. There are more than three strikes in this game. Just keep swinging until you hit.

Somebody once asked me, "Don't you ever have any failures?"

No, I don't...because I don't play nine-inning games. I play until I win. Sure, I've fallen on my face many times, but I don't count that as failure. I just count that as practice. When I win, you'd better believe that's for real!

"But Kenneth, that's not playing fair."

You show me in the Bible where it says we have to play fair with Satan. I don't play fair with him. I go in with a stacked deck. I go in with God on my side. There's nothing fair about that, but that's okay because Satan has already lost. We don't have to play fair with him anymore. We just step up to the plate and get ready for a home run!

backup:
Hebrews 5:12-14

download:
Ezra 4-5; James 5

voice activate:
I train myself to win as I practice walking in the things of the Spirit.
Hebrews 5:13-14

> **"For my thoughts are not your thoughts, neither are your ways my ways,'** **declares the Lord. 'As the heavens are higher than the earth, so are my** **ways higher than your ways and my thoughts than your thoughts.'"** **Isaiah 55:8-9**

Take the High Way

If you want to accurately hear when God is leading you, then you have to get to know His ways better than you know the world's ways. You have to spend some serious time in prayer and reading His Word.

That's the way Jesus lived. The Bible says He got up early in the morning to pray. He rose before the sun did. Sometimes He spent all night talking to God.

Spending time with God was the number one priority in Jesus' life. That's how He knew what God wanted Him to do. That's how He perfectly pleased Him. Jesus' disciples knew that His power was connected to the time He spent praying. They saw it was part of His daily lifestyle. That's why they asked Him, *"Lord, teach us to pray"* (Luke 11:1).

The things God told Jesus to do in those times weren't always easy. As you remember, in the Garden of Gethsemane, He sweat blood and said, *"My Father, if it is possible, may this cup be taken from me. Yet not as I will, but as you will."* (Matthew 26:39).

You may be in a hard place like that right now. God may be telling you to do something that's hard to do. He may have been telling you for months to get up early every morning so you can spend more time in prayer or reading the Bible. Maybe for months you've been thinking, *Yes, I really should do that...*but that snooze button is just too easy to hit.

Perhaps God has been speaking to you about other adjustments you need to make in your life. He may be saying, *Here's someone I want you to help*, or *Here's something you need to get out of your life.*

If He's saying something like that to you, take His instructions seriously. What may seem no big deal right now may help you more than you know in the future. God's direction is always in your best interest. His ways are higher!

backup:
Matthew 26:36-46

download:
Ezra 6-7; 1 Peter 1

voice activate:
As I spend time in the presence of God, His thoughts become my thoughts and His ways become my ways. Isaiah 55:8-9

july 14

gloria

203

"Just as Christ was raised from the dead through the glory of the Father, we too may live a new life."
Romans 6:4

A Force-Field of Glory

When Ezekiel saw God in His glory, he said His whole body was like fire (Ezekiel 8:2). God's glory is His supernatural life and essence...His very presence.

"Well, that's awesome, but hey, He's God. He alone has that kind of glory."

Says who? According to the Bible, in Psalm 8:5, when man was first created, he also had that glory. That's right! In the Garden of Eden, man and woman weren't walking around naked. God had enveloped them with the same fire and flame of beauty that was on God Himself.

God had put His own presence and glory on them so that they would shine like God shines. They weren't standing out there vulnerable to everything. They were surrounded and protected by a shimmering force-field of glory.

Then Adam sinned and that glory was lost. Most people know that. What they don't realize is that the glory was restored when Jesus rose from the dead! Romans 6:4 says so.

According to the Bible, you and I are supposed to be walking around with His glory shining through us. Everything we need is in the glory. Your healing, your relationships, your heart's desires and more are in the glory. So expect God's presence to show up in your life. Expect the glory!

backup:
Psalm 8; Ezekiel 8:1-4

download:
Ezra 8-9; 1 Peter 2

voice activate:
I live a new life by the same glory that raised up Christ from the dead.
Romans 6:4

"Dear friend, I pray that you may enjoy good health and that all may go well with you, even as your soul is getting along well."
3 John 2

Build Your Foundation First

Never try to build a house without first laying a foundation. I don't care how eager you are to get it finished. If you don't put down a good foundation, that house will be so unstable, it will soon come crashing down.

That's simple advice, isn't it? Of course it is. Yet, people make that mistake all the time in their spiritual life. They see something God has promised them in the Bible, and they are so eager to have it, they ignore the foundations of godly living and go after just that one thing.

That's especially true in the area of finances. Often, people are so desperate for a quick fix, they just pull a few financial scriptures out of the Bible and try to believe them—without allowing God to change anything else in their lives. Of course, it doesn't work, and those people end up disappointed.

It's important to truly grasp what John was saying in today's verse. He didn't just say, "I want all to go well with you." He said, "I want all to go well with you, even as your soul is getting along well."

He tied financial wellness to the "wellness" of our mind.

God's plan is for us to grow financially as we grow spiritually. He knows it's dangerous to give wealth to people who are too immature to handle it. He wants us to outgrow our old nature's foolishness so our finances will bring us good and not harm.

"But Gloria, I need financial help fast!"

Then get busy building your spiritual foundation! How? By finding out what God says in the Bible and doing it. Of course, keep in mind that this foundation is a *lifestyle.* It's putting God's Word first place in your life—in all you say, think and do.

So start building a strong foundation today...and get ready for financial success!

backup:
Luke 6:47-49

download:
Ezra 10; Nehemiah 1-2; 1 Peter 3-4

voice activate:
As my soul gets along well, I enjoy good health and all goes well with me. 3 John 2

"Now, Lord, consider their threats and enable your servants to speak your word with great boldness."
Acts 4:29

july 17

kenneth

True Boldness!

Have you ever noticed that miracles most often occur around people who are bold about God?

Boldness and miracles are so closely tied together that some people try to act bold just to get things to happen. Of course, it doesn't work. I've seen people pray as loud as they could in a restaurant just to prove they were bold about God, and all they did was make everyone choke on their French fries.

Yet someone with *true* boldness can do the same thing and great power will be released. Early 1900s preacher Smith Wigglesworth had that kind of boldness. One day, before Mr. Wigglesworth sat down to eat in a cafeteria, he looked around and in his powerful, booming voice said, "I didn't notice anybody praying over this meal and giving God thanks." Then he began to pray.

Everybody dropped their forks and bowed their heads. When he got through, people all over the room said, "Amen!" His prayer brought that whole café to a standstill because he had boldness from God.

Most people hear that and say, "Oh, I could never be that bold."

Yes you can! The secret is in Acts 4. In that chapter, the boldness of God came on a whole group of Christians as an answer to a specific prayer.

Here's the situation: Peter and John had ministered healing to a crippled man in front of the temple. He was completely healed...and that miracle stirred the city so much that the religious leaders arrested Peter and John and threatened them severely, ordering them to never preach about Jesus again.

Well, the first thing that group of Christians did was give God praise. They'd just been threatened, but they went to a Higher Authority! Then, they asked for boldness to speak God's Word!

These Christians didn't focus on the threats. They focused on the Word. Every word they prayed came from the Bible.

We can learn from that. When there's a threat, preach the Word. When there is sickness, preach the Word. When there is lack, preach the Word. When Satan tries to rough you up, preach the Word, and do it with boldness!

backup:
Acts 4:23-33

download:
Nehemiah 3-4; 1 Peter 5

voice activate:
God enables me with great boldness so I can speak His Word. Acts 4:29

"You have need of endurance, so that after you have done the will of God, you may receive the promise."
Hebrews 10:36, NKJV

A Spiritual Workout

Contrary to what you might think, you don't have to wait until a major problem comes to develop patience. There are great opportunities in all those small but irritating situations that hit us every day.

In fact, developing your patience a little at a time, in all those everyday situations, will strengthen you so when a major trial hits, you'll be ready.

I ran into one such situation in the grocery store. I was in a hurry, so I chose the express line. There were only a couple of people in line and they just had a few items to buy, so I didn't think it would take long.

Still, the clerk was so slow! So slow in fact, that as my frustration mounted I thought, *They ought to put a sign here that says "Slow-Motion Line"!*

That was a great opportunity to give my patience a workout.

Such opportunities are important, because when you exercise patience, it grows. If you'll use it for the small things, it will be strong enough to handle the big things when they arrive. Godly character—love, joy, peace, patience, kindness, goodness, faithfulness, gentleness and self-control—all increase in you when you exercise them.

Remember that the next time you're waiting in your school's lunch line, or waiting for your little sister to play the flute right, or some other little aggravation arises that makes you want to lose your temper. Instead of saying, "I've had it," give the character of God in you a workout...and build those spiritual muscles!

gloria

b a c k u p :
2 Peter 1:3-8

d o w n l o a d :
Nehemiah 5-6; 2 Peter 1

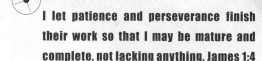
v o i c e   a c t i v a t e :
I let patience and perseverance finish their work so that I may be mature and complete, not lacking anything. James 1:4

"God did not give us a spirit of timidity, but a spirit of power, of love and of self-discipline."
2 Timothy 1:7

Get the Right Perspective

When the Israelites came out of Egypt, they had just seen God move in miraculous ways. Yet, as they faced the Red Sea with the Egyptian army on their tail, they turned on Moses and said, "Was it because there were no graves in Egypt that you brought us to the desert to die?" (Exodus 14:11).

What could possibly have caused these people to doubt God and make such a traitorous statement after all He had already done for them? Fear. They began to fear what the enemy could do to them, and all they could think about was trying to save themselves.

That seemingly innocent desire you have to protect yourself will cost you dearly when it comes to living for God. It infected the Israelites so much that they forgot the miracles. Suddenly they saw themselves as just ordinary people again...not people with Almighty God on their side.

If you don't watch out, Satan will try to make you look at things that way too. He will try to tell you you're just a nobody. He'll tell you that you can't trust God's power to pull you through. He'll get you into a "natural" rather than a "super-

natural" perspective. Instead of walking in faith with God, you'll walk in fear of Satan and what he might do. Those fears will keep you from hearing and obeying God.

That's why you need to start thinking the way God thinks. You need to live with your thoughts on the things of God instead of the things of the world.

God wants us to know Him so well and trust Him so much that when Satan bears his fangs—when he tells us no one cares or we're going to die or fail or whatever he says—we just laugh.

Start practicing that today. Believe God's promises to you. Speak God's Word to your problems...and watch faith rise up. Then you'll have the right perspective and you're sure to win every time!

backup:
Exodus 14:8-14

download:
Nehemiah 7-8; 2 Peter 2

voice activate:
God has not given me a spirit of timidity, but of power, of love and of self-discipline. 2 Timothy 1:7

"Let us continually offer to God a sacrifice of praise—the fruit of lips that confess his name."
Hebrews 13:15

Bring God on the Scene

Many times we think about praising God, but because we don't feel like it, we shrug off the thought and don't do it. I want you to remember this: God is worthy of our praise—whether we feel like praising Him or not. We must realize that our emotions don't have the last word when it comes to praising God. Hebrews 13:15 says we are to praise Him continually.

Under the Old Testament promise, when people had problems, they went to a priest and he would offer a sacrifice to God. That would bring God on the scene.

Today, under the New Testament promise, we can do the same. Only now we are the priests (Revelation 5:10). As we give sacrifices of praise to God, it brings Him on the scene. Psalm 22:3 says God inhabits the praises of His people (KJV).

So bring God's presence into your situation. When you need something, praise Him. Praise Him regardless of how you feel. Obey the Word and praise Him continually. He is worthy to be praised!

backup:
Revelation 5:7-10

download:
Nehemiah 9-10; 2 Peter 3

voice activate:
I offer the sacrifice of praise to God continually. The fruit of my lips gives thanks to His Name. Hebrews 13:15, KJV

"Be strong in the grace that is in Christ Jesus."
2 Timothy 2:1

july 21

gloria

Strong in Grace

In today's verse, you see that Paul instructs us to be strong in grace. What is grace? What does it do? Titus 2 tells us, *"For the grace of God that brings salvation has appeared to all men. It teaches us to say 'No' to ungodliness and worldly passions, and to live self-controlled, upright and godly lives in this present age"* (verses 11-12).

Grace teaches us. It teaches us how to live in freedom.

Whenever the Holy Spirit corrects you, whenever He points out a mistake you're making or speaks to you about something you're doing that is hurting Him, don't get upset. Get excited! It's God's grace teaching you something to make your life better.

Grow strong in that grace by spending time every day in prayer. Live each day expecting the Holy Spirit to teach you how to live in freedom.

Expect to hear from Him. If you don't, you won't be listening for Him, and you're not likely to hear Him because He speaks in a still, small voice. As a rule, His

words are quiet words. They're not thundering, overwhelming words. If you don't have an ear tuned toward heaven, you'll miss them.

So, every morning spend time praying, talking to God and reminding yourself that the Holy Spirit is inside you, constantly teaching and guiding you. Become strong in God's grace!

backup:
Psalm 32

download:
Nehemiah 11-12; 1 John 1

voice activate:
I am strong in the grace that is in Christ Jesus. 2 Timothy 2:1

"For the word of God is living and active. Sharper than any double-edged sword, it penetrates even to dividing soul and spirit, joints and marrow; it judges the thoughts and attitudes of the heart."
Hebrews 4:12

The Living Word

How can the Bible help one person in one way, and help another person in another way?

Because it is alive! The Word of God is full of life. Full! It infuses life wherever it is planted. It doesn't matter how dark your circumstances may be. There is enough life in God's Word to totally obliterate all the death that the world, Satan or circumstances can bring you.

The Bible says the Word is like a seed. Every seed has within it all the DNA required to produce whatever kind of plant it came from. If it's a peach seed, everything needed to be a peach tree is in the seed.

In the same way, God's Word has the supernatural life within it to fulfill God's promises in your life. You plant it in your heart as a seed, but when it comes up, it creates salvation, success, healing— whatever God has said belongs to you!

If you have a need in your life today, go to the Bible. Find a promise to stand on...and begin planting that seed in your heart. Say it aloud over and over as you

let that promise take root inside you. Let it become real to you, and then watch it come alive!

backup:
Psalm 119:50,93

download:
Nehemiah 13; Esther 1; 1 John 2

voice activate:
The Word of God is living and active. It judges the thoughts and attitudes of my heart. Hebrews 4:12

"So the man gave them his attention, expecting to get something from them."
Acts 3:5

july 23

kenneth

Stick Your Neck Out

When the Bible talks about hope, it's not talking about wishing. It's talking about intensely expecting that what God has said *will* happen.

How do you hope like that? You stay in the Word until your neck stretches out!

"Say what?!"

You read right...till your neck stretches out! I particularly like this definition of hope because I know what it means to have my neck stretched.

When I was a little boy, my grandfather was my hero. He was a full-blooded Cherokee Indian and I wanted to act like him, look like him, curse like him and spit like him—much to my mother's dismay. When my mother would tell me that he and my grandmother were coming to see us, I could hardly wait.

Every minute or two, I'd run to the window to see if they had arrived. I tell you, my neck was stretched out in anticipation. I expected him any moment.

That may sound like a simple example, but the Lord once told me if people would just expect Him to move as much as a child expects his grandparents to arrive, He could move in their situation and change things fast.

That's what happened in Acts 3 to the crippled man at the gate. He had been sitting by that gate begging, his head down and his eyes to the ground. When Peter and John walked by and said, *"Look at us!"* that man lifted his head and began to expect. Hope rose up in him. He was *"expecting to get something from them."*

What are you hoping for? Health? Friends? A better home life? Something you know you're called to do? What you're hoping for is what you're thinking about, talking about and praying about. Line your faith up with it. Begin to expect God to do something. Expect Him to come on the scene...just like a little child expects his grandparents to arrive.

b a c k u p :
Acts 3:1-11

d o w n l o a d :
Esther 2-4; 1 John 3-4

v o i c e   a c t i v a t e :
I give my attention to God, expecting to receive from Him. Acts 3:5

"The hour has come for you to wake up from your slumber, because our salvation is nearer now than when we first believed. The night is nearly over; the day is almost here. So let us put aside the deeds of darkness and put on the armor of light."
Romans 13:11-12

The Right Place at the Right Time

We are living in an exciting time. Jesus is coming soon! It's also a serious time. It is not the time to be lazy about spiritual things. This is not the time to ride the fence...there won't be anybody on the fence much longer anyway. God is separating the light and the darkness, and you'll either have to choose to go on with God or to backtrack.

In the story of the 10 virgins in Matthew 25, five of them didn't even start getting ready until they heard their groom coming. *"But while they were on their way,"* it says, *"the bridegroom arrived"* (verse 10).

Have you ever noticed that some people's timing is always off? If you listen to the Holy Spirit, you'll be right on time—and in the right place. *"While they were on their way to buy the oil, the bridegroom arrived. The virgins who were ready went in with him to the wedding banquet. And the door was shut."*

Are you ready...or not?

We must get to the place where we hear God and do what He says—where we're always ready for Him to move through us. It won't work to wait until the last moment and then try to get ready. We are the Church. We have a job to do before He comes.

Matthew 24:44-45 says, *"So you also must be ready, because the Son of Man will come at an hour when you do not expect him. Who then is the faithful and wise servant, whom the master has put in charge of the servants in his household to give them their food at the proper time?"*

Right there in my Bible beside that question, *"Who then is the faithful and wise servant?"* I've written, *"Gloria!"* You should do the same thing. You are the only one who can make that decision in your life. Write your name by that verse and say, "Lord, I'm going to be a faithful and wise servant. I'm going to be ready!"

backup:
Matthew 25:1-13

download:
Esther 5-6; 1 John 5

voice activate:
I am a faithful and wise servant of the Lord Jesus Christ. Matthew 24:45

"Do not merely listen to the word, and so deceive yourselves. Do what it says."
James 1:22

July 25

gloria

More Than Mental Assent

One of the greatest enemies of real faith is a thing called "mental assent." People who have mental assent read the Bible and think they believe it, but when pressure comes, they don't act on it.

Mental assenters say, "I believe the Bible from cover to cover. I believe I'm healed by the wounds of Jesus because the Bible says so."

Then, when sickness actually comes and attacks their bodies, they stop saying, "By His wounds I'm healed" and start saying, "I'm sick."

Real faith believes what the Bible says even though your eyes and your feelings tell you something different. Faith doesn't care what things look like. It doesn't care what the circumstances are.

Faith in God's Word will change the situation. It will turn every defeat into victory. It is God's success formula! However, you have to give that faith an opportunity to work. You have to keep God's promises in your mouth and pray and think about them in your heart *"that you may observe and do according to all that is written in it. For then you shall make your way prosperous, and then shall you deal wisely and have good success"* (Joshua 1:8 AMP).

So determine today to speak God's Word—and God's Word *only*. Don't be a mental assenter. Be a mighty person of faith!

backup:
Matthew 7:24-29

download:
Esther 7-8; 2 John

voice activate:
I do what the Word of God says. I do not merely listen to it. James 1:22

"The mystery that has been kept hidden for ages and generations, but is now disclosed to the saints. To them God has chosen to make known among the Gentiles the glorious riches of this mystery, which is Christ in you, the hope of glory."
Colossians 1:26-27

Jesus Lives in You!

I'm always looking for insight from God that will change my life—aren't you? A few years ago, God gave me just such an insight. It was so vast that I've been thinking and praying about it ever since. I can tell it to you in five words: *Jesus Christ lives in me.*

"Well, Gloria," you say, "that's no jump-start. All Christians know that!"

No, they don't. Oh, they may know it with their heads, but not their hearts. If they did, the Church today would be an entirely different Church, so full of the God's power that sinners would be beating down our doors to get in and get saved. We would be a Church where miracles and healings were not unusual, but commonplace, a Church so full of God's power that even the world would be amazed at the power of God in our lives.

Well, here's the good news: As Christians, we can confidently expect God's presence in our lives. We don't have to just wish for it or read about other people who have experienced it.

We can live in God's presence ourselves. We can do this because Jesus, the Lord of glory Himself, lives inside every one of us!

I want you to think about it. Let the thrilling reality of it sink into your heart. Let it begin to dawn on you that Jesus—Who rose from the dead and defeated darkness once and for all—really lives in you!

backup:
2 Corinthians 2:14-17

download:
Esther 9-10; 3 John

voice activate:
The resurrected Jesus lives in me! He is my hope and expectation of glory. Colossians 1:27

"Anyone who comes to him must believe that he exists and that he rewards those who earnestly seek him."
Hebrews 11:6

The Key to Pleasing Is Receiving

As a young adult, there were many times before I left home that I came to my father, A.W. Copeland, with things that seemed messed up in my life. What a relief it was to hear him say, "Well now, it's not as bad as it looks."

As we would talk about the situation, my father would bring up things that I hadn't considered and didn't know. Soon relief would hit me, and I would think, *Whew, I'm going to get out of this. Thank God...and thank Daddy!*

Why did that happen? I became comfortable in the middle of my circumstances when I'd listen to Daddy. I put my confidence in his desire for my success. My willingness to make decisions that honored his word and his commitments to me, gave him the opportunity to do what was always in his heart.

If I had continued to talk to him like that as I grew older, instead of thinking I was smarter than him, I could have been even more blessed in our father-son relationship. Unfortunately, I rebelled. I began to think I knew more than Daddy did—and I continually got deeper into trouble.

That was so stupid. Daddy already knew what I needed to do, but I wouldn't listen to him. Without faith in someone who knew better, I made decisions that continually worsened my situations.

The atmosphere this created drove a wedge between my daddy and me. Did his love for me change? No. Had my actions made him less willing to do everything he could to help me? Not at all. The choices I was making hurt him because he could no longer reach me, and I couldn't reach him. None of it was his fault—it was mine.

God is the same way. No matter what we do, His love for us never changes. When we get into a mess, He wants to help us get out. He is a loving Daddy Who delights in our well-being (Psalm 35:27).

So go to Him. Tell Him about your mess...trust Him with your life...and then watch Him unravel it all...and give you His perfect peace.

b a c k u p :
Psalm 46; Psalm 125:1-2

d o w n l o a d :
Job 1-2; Jude

v o i c e   a c t i v a t e :
**God rewards me as I earnestly seek Him.
Hebrews 11:6**

"'O Lord, God of Israel, there is no God like you in heaven or on earth—you who keep your covenant of love with your servants who continue whole-heartedly in your way.'"
2 Chronicles 6:14

Walking With a Whole Heart

If you are in trouble today, take heart. There is definitely a way out.

Second Chronicles 6:14 says God shows mercy to those who walk before Him with all their hearts. So, if you're in trouble today, take an honest look at your relationship with God.

Ask yourself, *Am I living for God wholeheartedly? Is there any area of my life that I'm keeping from Him? Is there any area I want to control and keep for myself?*

Let me tell you why that's important. It's not that God is holding out on you or holding back His help if you're not whole-heartedly living for Him. It's that your personal faith level is affected.

If you look at 1 John 3:20-22 (NKJV), you can see what I mean: *"For if our heart condemns us, God is greater than our heart, and knows all things. Beloved, if our heart does not condemn us, we have confidence toward God. And whatever we ask we receive from Him, because we keep His commandments and do those things that are pleasing in His sight."*

It's not what God knows about you that keeps your prayers from being answered. When you know you're not living for God and doing what you know to do, it causes you not to have confidence toward Him.

So check your heart today. If you're following Him with your whole heart, there's a great and mighty confidence that comes up within you. Satan can't shake that confidence. No one can talk you out of it, and no distress—no matter how great—can pressure you into letting go. No matter what happens, you remain certain that God will rescue you!

backup:
Psalm 37:3-11

download:
Job 3-4; Revelation 1

voice activate:
I walk before God wholeheartedly. He keeps His covenant of love with me. 2 Chronicles 6:14

"That at the name of Jesus every knee should bow, in heaven and on earth and under the earth, and every tongue confess that Jesus Christ is Lord, to the glory of God the Father."
Philippians 2:10-11

kenneth july 29

Named by His Name

If you've become a Christian, you belong to Jesus. You are joined together by covenant with God because of what Jesus did for you on the cross. You've been given Jesus' own Name—the Name that is higher in authority than any other name ever named, the Name at which every knee must bow.

For you to effectively use the Name of Jesus, you need to develop your faith in that Name.

Think about it this way. Gloria and I belong to one another. We are joined together by the covenant of marriage. She has my name. She writes it on a check without reservation. She has as much right to sign that name as I do. It's her name. It has been given to her. When somebody asks her who she is, she doesn't say, "I'm Gloria Neece operating in the name of Kenneth Copeland."

No, she says, "I'm Gloria Copeland."

That's the kind of confidence you need to have about the Name of Jesus. You need to know you've been named

after Him. Know that when you speak, you're speaking with His authority.

You need to have faith in that Name. Many times people start using the Name of Jesus, trying to work up their faith, but faith doesn't come from the Name. Faith comes from hearing God's Word (Romans 10:17).

So, if you're having trouble, go back to the Bible and study the Name of Jesus. Then when you use it, you'll have that sense of authority on the inside that is founded on the living Word.

backup:
Acts 3:12-16

download:
Job 5-6; Revelation 2

voice activate:
At the Name of Jesus every knee shall bow. I have confidence in that Name.
Philippians 2:10

"Enfolded in love, let us grow up in every way and in all things into Him, Who is the Head, [even] Christ, the Messiah, the Anointed One" Ephesians 4:15, AMP

When God's on Your Side

When we give way to love, we begin to look and act like Jesus Himself would if He were living in our bodies—which, of course, He is! Instead of acting worldly, we do what Ephesians 4:15 says and grow up enfolded in love.

It's love that will bring us to our ultimate goal, which is *"the completeness of personality which is nothing less than the standard height of Christ's own perfection—the measure of the stature of the fullness of the Christ, and the completeness found in Him!"* (Ephesians 4:13 AMP).

I'll warn you though, if you decide to walk in love, there will be times when it seems as though love will make you the underdog. There will be times when you're treated wrong, and your old nature will rise up and say, "Now wait a minute! If I just keep on being kind and loving, people will run right over me."

That's not true. When you walk in love, you put yourself in a place where God Himself can protect you. He is a great One to have on your side, because when He is for you, no one can stand against you (Romans 8:31-39).

You can see that in the life of Jesus. He always walked in love—not just when people loved Him, but also when He was mistreated (1 Peter 2:23).

As a result, no one could touch Him. When the people at Nazareth tried to throw Him off a cliff, He just walked through the middle of them. When soldiers came to arrest Him in the Garden, He just said, *"I am He,"* and they all fell to the ground under God's power (John 18:1-6). If Jesus had not willingly given Himself up, He never could have been crucified, for He alone had the power to lay down His life. No one could take it from Him because He lived a life of love.

Love is powerful! If you're being mistreated, or if someone has hurt you, give way to the powerful force of love on the inside of you. Let it rise up in you and overtake that hurt. When you do, not only will you be healed on the inside, but you will also win over whatever Satan's throwing at you on the outside. Remember: God is on your side, so you can't help but succeed. Love never fails!

gloria

backup:
Luke 4:24-32

download:
Job 7-9; Revelation 3

voice activate:
Enfolded in love, I grow up in every way and in all things into Christ. Ephesians 4:15 AMP

"Do not conform any longer to the pattern of this world, but be transformed by the renewing of your mind. Then you will be able to test and approve what God's will is—his good, pleasing and perfect will."
Romans 12:2

july 31

kenneth

Don't Wait for the Doughnuts!

There was a time in my life when I made a decision that I was going to live by faith. I didn't know anything about faith at the time. I just made the decision because the Bible said, *"My righteous will live by faith"* (Hebrews 10:38). From then on, I had to begin making decisions based on what the Bible said rather than what was going on in my life.

I didn't just go charging into life expecting everything to come easily. I began to establish myself in what the Bible said so I'd know what to do when I was faced with difficult situations.

I listened to teaching cassettes for hours upon hours. I thought about my situations and what God promised me. I'd think through what I was going to do. Then sure enough, I'd go right out and run smack into exactly what I'd been praying about just hours earlier.

When that happened, there wasn't any question about what to do. I just took the faith route. Why? I had already made the decision while in prayer!

That's how I conquered a diet problem. I made a rock-solid decision to put sugar out of my life. I could do it because I made the decision in a time of prayer. From that time forward, I refused to listen to the desires of my body. When someone would hand me a piece of pie and my body would say, *Whoa! Look at that! Chocolate!* I wouldn't listen.

Yes, my old nature moaned and groaned for a while, but before long, it lined up with my will and of course, my faith. Now it doesn't bother me at all. My faith took control of my old nature once I made a rock-solid decision.

Look at the things in your life that you want to change. It may not be food, but if it is, waiting until they pass you the doughnuts to decide what to do won't help you. Making a rock-solid decision ahead of time will ensure your success.

backup:
Romans 8:9-13

download:
Job 10-11; Revelation 4

voice activate:
I am not conformed to the pattern of this world. I am transformed as I renew my mind. I am able to test and approve what is the good, pleasing and perfect will of God. Romans 12:2

"There are six things the Lord hates, seven that are detestable to him: haughty eyes, a lying tongue, hands that shed innocent blood, a heart that devises wicked schemes, feet that are quick to rush into evil, a false witness who pours out lies and a man who stirs up dissension among brothers." Proverbs 6:16-19

Don't Judge

You know to keep strife out of your home, but what about your youth group at church?

That is a whole new battleground. Maybe Satan has goaded someone to be rude to you and hurt your feelings. Or maybe he made sure you found out about something someone else has done wrong, and then you talked about it to others.

When he presents you with that opportunity, turn him down—*fast!* Don't give in to that temptation to gossip and stir up strife...because to God, strife in the Church is one of the most serious sins of all (Proverbs 6:16-19).

God considers stirring up strife such a severe sin that He lists it alongside murder. So stay away from it. Ask God to show you if you've been a part of causing strife. He may remind you of a time you passed along some gossip or criticized your youth pastor. If He does, ask for forgiveness and be more alert in the future. Determine that from now on, if you see someone sin, you'll pray for him instead of making the problem worse by talking to everyone about it.

I realize sometimes that seems hard to do. Satan will tempt you to get into

strife by judging someone. Don't give in to that pressure. It's not your job to judge others. (Isn't that a relief?) First Corinthians 4:5 says, *"Therefore judge nothing before the appointed time; wait till the Lord comes. He will bring to light what is hidden in darkness and will expose the motives of men's hearts. At that time each will receive his praise from God."*

If you're in a church where the pastor or youth pastor has done wrong, and you feel you don't want to follow him, that's fine. I don't blame you. Leave that church and go to one with a pastor you can trust and respect, but do it quietly. Don't cause trouble before you go. Most important of all, wherever you go, always be sure to go in love and guard against strife. When you do, you will always keep your faith strong.

backup:
Proverbs 26:20-21; Romans 14

download:
Job 12-13; Revelation 5

voice activate:
I determine to walk in love. I do not stir up dissension among brothers because that is detestable to God. Proverbs 6:16,19

"Wisdom is supreme; therefore get wisdom. Though it cost all you have, get understanding. Esteem her, and she will exalt you; embrace her, and she will honor you. She will set a garland of grace on your head and present you with a crown of splendor."
Proverbs 4:7-9

august 2

kenneth

Supreme Insight

How many times have you prayed and waited...and waited...and waited, and have not received your answer? I can tell you it wasn't because God missed it! The Bible says that when we ask and don't receive, it's because we ask amiss (James 4:3). You need wisdom to ask for the right thing. That means you need to know what God thinks about the situation before you can pray effectively.

You may be crying out to God for healing when what you actually need is a miracle. You may be praying about needing to remember test answers when what you really need is discipline for studying. You may even be causing the problem yourself without knowing it.

You need God's wisdom! How do you get it?

Jesus shows us in Luke 11:49. He began speaking, *"Because of this, God in his wisdom said..."* then He began to quote Scripture. He called the written Word of God the wisdom of God. God's wisdom *is* His Word.

So let the Bible, the wisdom of God, begin to influence your thinking. Soak your mind in it. Don't just scan the pages. Dig into it. Take it seriously.

Then begin to pray. Let the Holy Spirit give you insight. After a while, you'll begin to see your problems in a whole new light.

Remember, wisdom is supreme. God's way of thinking will save your life, pull you out of trouble and put you on the road to success. It will introduce you to possibilities you have never seen before!

backup:
1 Corinthians 2:6-9

download:
Job 14-15; Revelation 6

voice activate:
Wisdom is supreme. Therefore, I get wisdom! Proverbs 4:7

"But seek first his kingdom and his righteousness, and all these things will be given to you as well."
Matthew 6:33

Abraham, Moses, Joshua... and You!

Do you need more faith? Well, you can have as much as you want. How much of God's Word you put in your heart is how much faith you're going to have available when you need it.

It's up to you. No one can keep you from doing it. If you can get a Bible, you can make a deposit into your heart every day by reading the Word.. In fact, you'd better make a deposit every day, because chances are you'll need to make a withdrawal sooner or later. Withdrawals without deposits can leave you stranded without what you need to get the job done.

Some people want to float through life without putting any effort into building up their spiritual account. They want to enjoy the things God has for them, but they don't want to develop the faith it takes to receive those things!

Don't be one of those people! Don't expect to get something from God without faith. It's not going to happen.

Abraham had to act in faith to get Isaac. Moses had to act in faith to get the Israelites to the Promised Land. Joshua had to act in faith to get the walls of Jericho to come down. Rahab had to act in faith to keep her part of the wall around Jericho *from* falling down. If Abraham, Moses, Joshua and Rahab had to have faith, then you're going to have to have faith, too. All of the great victories written in Hebrews 11 happened through faith! That's just the way it is.

That's why the most important thing you can do is to keep your heart full of God's promises—because everything else can be taken care of if your heart account is full. That's what today's verse means.

When you put the Word first, all things will come to you...including more faith. So don't wait any longer! Get into the Bible, put God's promises in your heart and watch your faith account grow!

backup:
Romans 10:14-17

download:
Job 16-17; Revelation 7

voice activate:
I seek first the kingdom of God and His righteousness, and all I need is given to me as well. Matthew 6:33

"Now to each one the manifestation of the Spirit is given for the common good."
1 Corinthians 12:7

august 4

kenneth

You Can Do It All!

When Jesus asked, *"Who do you say I am?"* Peter blurted out, *"You are the Christ [the Anointed One], the Son of the living God"* (Matthew 16:15-16).

Peter, perhaps better than anyone, knew what Jesus and His Anointing could do. As a fisherman, he'd seen Jesus draw every fish in the Sea of Galilee around his boat. Even though Peter had fished all night without catching a thing, when Jesus stepped on board, he caught a net-breaking, boat-sinking load!

Peter had watched Jesus feed thousands with just a few loaves and fishes. He'd seen Him heal countless people and rescue them from demonic oppression. Peter even once pulled money for taxes from a fish's mouth at Jesus' instruction. He'd walked on water at Jesus' word.

Peter knew why Jesus could do those things—He had God's Anointing on Him. He had God's power on Him doing through Him what He as a man could not do Himself!

So when Peter heard Jesus say, "You will be baptized with the Holy Spirit and receive power to tell others about me"

(Acts 1:5, 8), he knew what Jesus was talking about...*Yes! We've got it! He's giving us that anointing! The power that was on Jesus is on us now!*

That had to be what Peter was thinking. That's all he knew.

In light of that, why aren't Christians today charging out into the world and turning it upside down with God's power?

Because many of us don't fully see what can happen when the Anointing of Jesus operates through us. That needs to change. Realize that you are anointed to do all that Peter imagined and more. You are anointed to do all that you dream. You are anointed to change the world you live in today. You can do it!

backup:
Matthew 16:13-19

download:
Job 18-19; Revelation 8

voice activate:
The manifestation of the Spirit is given to me for my common good.
1 Corinthians 12:7

"Do not grieve, for the joy of the Lord is your strength."
Nehemiah 8:10

Go Ahead... Laugh!

Something has been happening to Christians recently. God is pouring out His joy so strongly, it causes people to laugh for hours. Some of them literally end up on the floor, doubled over laughing.

I've seen Ken so filled he could hardly minister. The next day, however, he could not only stand and preach, he felt stronger than he'd felt in ten years.

I have to tell you though, it makes some Christians nervous. As a result, they fold their arms, sit back and say, "I'm not going to be caught acting like that!"...and as a result, they are missing out on a powerful move of God.

Before *you* fold your arms and sit back, know this: We'll truly see God move when we desire God so intensely that we're willing to throw aside our inhibitions and praise Him without reserve.

Why? Because God shows up where He's invited. He shows up where hearts are hungry. He's not going to show Himself to a bunch of people who only want to see Him with half their hearts.

That's why He's finding people who want Him more than anything else life has to offer. He's finding teenagers who want His presence more than they want to be respected by their classmates.

If you are one of those teens, you've probably already found out that some of your friends (or family) don't like it. They might get offended, and they don't want to be around you—especially when you're laughing! You have probably found that it's usually the religious people who have the most trouble with this.

Or, you may be in the other group...you're not too sure about all this laughing. You're not sure you have the strength to face the criticism of others. I have good news for you. You can get that strength. How? By stirring up your joy—because *"the joy of the Lord is your strength!"*

So go ahead. Laugh!

backup:
Psalm 126

download:
Job 20-21; Revelation 9

voice activate:
The joy of the Lord is my strength.
Nehemiah 8:10

"And these signs will accompany those who believe: In my name they will drive out demons; they will speak in new tongues...they will place their hands on sick people, and they will get well."
Mark 16:17-18

august 6

kenneth

Healing *Always* Comes

Today's verse says, "They *will* get well." Not "they *might* get well," but "they *will* get well."

Take the time to let that sink in. It's a very definite promise, and we should believe it—no matter what things look like...because our physical senses can't tell us what's happening in the spiritual world.

Years ago I was in a church service when some people brought in a young girl and asked me to pray for her. She suffered from epileptic seizures. The minute I walked up to her, the Lord told me the seizures were caused by a spirit. So I stood in front of her and said, "In the Name of Jesus, you'll have to take your hands off this girl, Satan. Leave her now!"

Wham! She hit the floor with one of the worst seizures I had ever seen. Four or five people picked her up and carried her out. I never did hear from the girl or her family, so, of course, Satan would harass me and say, *Boy, you sure didn't help things, did you? She went out worse than she came in!*

I'd resist him and say, "No, Satan. The Bible says when I tell you to run, you

run. So as far as I'm concerned, you took off that day."

Years passed. Then one day someone gave me a tape of a Full Gospel Business Men's Fellowship meeting. Do you know what was on that tape? The mother of that little girl giving her testimony of how God rescued her daughter from epilepsy the night I placed my hands on her.

I'm so glad I didn't pull my faith away because she didn't look healed!

God always does His part. He said when we place our hands on the sick, they will get well. Whether someone receives healing is not our responsibility. Our assignment is to place our hands on them, believe God's promises and pray. We can rest assured that when we obey Him in faith, healing always comes.

backup:
Mark 16:15-20

download:
Job 22-24; Revelation 10-11

voice activate:
I am a believer and these signs follow me: In Jesus' Name I drive out demons, I place my hands on sick people and they get well. Mark 16:17-18

"Make every effort to live in peace with all men and to be holy; without holiness no one will see the Lord."
Hebrews 12:14

Sober Up!

The final move of the Holy Spirit has already started. Reports of miracles, signs and wonders are coming in from around the world, and we are going to see more than ever before. God is going to show up in marvelous ways!

Actually, our situation today is much like the one the Israelites found themselves in after Moses led them out of Egypt. When they reached the foot of Mount Sinai, God spoke and told them He was about to show up right in the middle of them (Exodus 19:9-11). Right now, God is saying much the same thing to us. He's telling us to clean up our lives.

It's time we realize that when God shows up, His glory will destroy sin instantly. So those who are clinging to sin will be in trouble.

Do you remember what happened to Ananias and Sapphira in Acts 5? As far as we can tell, they were good members of the New Testament Church. Yet they conspired together to lie to the Holy Spirit and, as a result, they both died in church on the same day!

We haven't seen anything like that today, because God's power hasn't shown up as powerfully among us as it was in the early Church, but it will...and it will even be stronger!

Sin was dealt with quickly in Ananias and Sapphira that day. Of course, it didn't have to be dealt with that way. They could have turned from that sin on the spot. They could have said, "I was wrong. Forgive me!" Instead, they clung to their story. So when God's power extinguished that sin, their lives were extinguished too.

I realize that's a sobering thought, but the Bible instructs us to be sober in these last days. It says we should be serious about holiness. So examine your heart and sober up!

backup:
1 Peter 1:13-16

download:
Job 25-26; Revelation 12

voice activate:
I make every effort to live in peace with all men and to be holy so that I will see the Lord. Hebrews 12:14

august 8

kenneth

"David asked the men standing near him, 'What will be done for the man who kills this Philistine and removes this disgrace from Israel? Who is this uncircumcised Philistine that he should defy the armies of the living God?'"
1 Samuel 17:26

How to Kill a Giant

How do you kill a giant? How do you handle a problem that's so big, you can't see beyond it—and so stubborn it just won't go away?

You stand on the covenant you have with Almighty God! That's how.

When David stood before the Israelite army and called the giant an "uncircumcised Philistine," he knew exactly what he was saying. Circumcision was the mark of the covenant between the Israelites and God. David knew all about that covenant—God's unbreakable promise. He knew that in Deuteronomy 28:7, God said, *"They [your enemies] will come at you from one direction but flee from you in seven."*

David believed that promise. It didn't matter who the enemy was. David knew he would defeat them. He knew he had a covenant with God—and it changed the way he looked at things.

That's why David said, "Goliath is no problem. I can take him."

You too have a covenant with God. It's a covenant bought by the blood of Jesus,

and the Bible says it's a better covenant than even David had (Hebrews 8:6). So if you have a giant of a problem staring you in the face, and all you feel is defeat, you need to check your focus. Where have you been looking lately? Are you looking at the size of the problem—or are you looking at your covenant with God?

When you focus your attention on God's promises to you, everything changes. So go ahead and kill that giant!

backup:
1 Samuel 17:26-50

download:
Job 27-28; Revelation 13

voice activate:
God always causes me to triumph in Christ. 2 Corinthians 2:14

"...be ordering your behavior within the sphere of love, even as Christ also loved you and gave himself up in our behalf and in our stead as an offering and a sacrifice to God for an aroma of a sweet smell."
Ephesians 5:2, Wuest

Decide, Beforehand

There's no question about it, if you are a Christian, you want to walk in love...you can't help it, it's part of who you are now. But *wanting* to do it isn't enough. You have to go a step farther and make a rock-solid decision to *do* it!

You must make up your mind *beforehand* to obey today's verse and constantly walk in love. Notice I said *beforehand*. If you wait until you're facing a tough situation to decide how you want to respond, you'll almost certainly make the wrong choice. Rather than walking in love, you'll end up allowing circumstances or even Satan to influence the way you respond.

So prepare yourself now for what's ahead. If there's a person in your life who is particularly difficult to love, make them a special project. (That kind of person usually needs love more than anyone else). Make plans not just to "put up with them," but to go out of your way to be kind and loving toward them.

"But Gloria," you may say, "You just don't know this person. It would be too hard to love them. I can't do it."

Yes, you can! God has put His very own love inside your heart—the love that never fails. So make a decision to let that love flow from you.

Then start strengthening your spirit by discovering what the Bible says about love. As you think and pray about what the Bible says, it will energize and empower you, making it easier to walk in love. Read scriptures like 1 Corinthians 13. Read them at night before you go to bed. Read them in the morning when you wake up. Print them out from your computer and tape them to your bathroom mirror so you can think about them while you're brushing your teeth.

If you do that, I guarantee you, that Word will come alive in you. It will help you stick with your decision to walk in love.

Then, instead of giving that person a piece of your mind, you'll give him the love of God, and he'll be better off for it.

backup:
Romans 12:9-21

download:
Job 29-30; Revelation 14

voice activate:
I walk in love, even as Christ has loved me. Ephesians 5:2

229

"Submit yourselves, then, to God. Resist the devil, and he will flee from you."
James 4:7

Surviving the Counterattack

We love the moment of success. We love it when our healing shows up. We love it when Satan's attack against our friends or family is stopped for good.

What do you do when that moment comes?

I'll tell you what most Christians do. They breathe a sigh of relief, turn on the TV and say, "Whew! Thank God that battle's over! Now I can relax."

Big mistake.

While they're taking a spiritual vacation, Satan is planning his counterattack, plotting to snatch the victory from under their noses.

I first began to notice how successful many of Satan's counterattacks were years ago. All I had to do was see that many people who were genuinely healed in meetings, went home only to discover that they weren't healed anymore. So what was wrong?

They went to the meeting, heard God's promises to them and, in that atmosphere of faith, found it easy to receive healing. Yet, when they left the meeting, they didn't take that atmosphere

with them. They stepped back into their old, unbelieving lifestyle that had made them vulnerable to sickness in the first place. So when Satan launched his counterattack with a few symptoms, they gave in, saying, "Well, I thought I was healed, but I guess I wasn't."

Instead, they should have said, "Look here, Satan! According to God's Word, I am healed and I'm not going to let you steal it. So take your sickness and go!"

If those people had done that in faith and resisted Satan as it says to in today's verse, they could have defeated the counterattack.

Be prepared for the counterattacks. Lay a foundation of faith in your life, so when Satan comes and throws some lies, pains or tough circumstances your way, your success will not come undone.

b a c k u p :
1 John 5:1-4

d o w n l o a d :
Job 31-32; Revelation 15

v o i c e   a c t i v a t e :
**I resist the devil and he flees from me.
James 4:7**

"For we are God's [own] handiwork (His workmanship), recreated in Christ Jesus, [born anew] that we may do those good works which God predestined (planned beforehand) for us, [taking paths which He prepared ahead of time) that we should walk in them—living the good life which He prearranged and made ready for us to live."
Ephesians 2:10, AMP

Living the Good Life

Every day it touches me how good God is to us. You and I are God's favorites! I know we are because God's mercy and favor are over all His works (Psalm 145:9)—and Ephesians 2:10 says we are all His workmanship!

Psalm 145:8-9 says, *"The Lord is gracious and compassionate, slow to anger and rich in love. The Lord is good to all; he has compassion on all he has made."*

God is *gracious*. Do you know what that means? It means He is inclined to show favors. It's just His nature to bless people. He is also *compassionate*. The word *compassion* doesn't just mean He has pity on us. It means "eager yearning."

Isn't that wonderful? God is eagerly yearning to do you good! In fact, the Bible says He is looking for someone to bless. He is not satisfied unless He can do someone good (2 Chronicles 16:9).

I remember the day I realized that. I was desperate for help. I picked up the Bible and read in Matthew 6:26 that God cared for the birds of the air. What an amazing thought that was to me! No one had ever told me God was good. They had never told me He loved me. They just told me a lot of "do nots."

When I read that scripture, I thought, *Well, if God cares for birds, surely He cares for me!* I gave God my life and asked Him to do something with it, and that's all it took. I gave God an opening and His love flooded through it.

God wants to do you good. He wants you to live the good life! So, the next time someone tells you God wants you to be sick or downtrodden, just remember that God has a good life planned for you, even in this dark world. A life of health. A life of joy. A life of ministering to and helping people. That good life has been set up for you and made ready for you to live. Everything you need—a family, friends, a home, a good job, a future mate—it has all been stored up with your name on it. So go for it! Receive your destiny! Live the good life!

backup:
Matthew 6:25-34

download:
Job 33-34; Revelation 16

voice activate:
I live the good life which God has prearranged and made ready for me to live. Ephesians 2:10, AMP

august 12 | **kenneth**

"So watch yourselves. If your brother sins, rebuke him, and if he repents, forgive him. If he sins against you seven times in a day, and seven times comes back to you and says, 'I repent,' forgive him."
Luke 17:3-4

Serious Business

My forgiving someone doesn't have anything to do with what that person did or didn't do to me. I forgive them because of the blood Jesus shed on the cross for me. God honored the blood and forgave me in the face of my sin, so in the same way He has forgiven me, I forgive others.

For me not to forgive would be to dishonor that blood.

This is serious business we're talking about here! When you dishonor the blood of Jesus, you're stepping out from under its protective covering into Satan's territory. You're stepping out into darkness where he can get a shot at you.

I don't know about you, but I don't want to go out there. I don't care what anyone may do to me, I won't let their bad treatment of me push me out into darkness. No, I'll just honor the blood, forgive them and keep right on walking in the light. If somebody hits me on the cheek, I'll just do what Jesus said: Forgive and turn the other cheek.

Some people think if you do that, you'll get the daylights beaten out of you. They're wrong. If you keep your faith up, when you turn the other cheek, God will protect you from the one who's trying to hit you.

I know of a preacher who experienced that. He was witnessing to a member of a New York street gang who was threatening him with a knife. Instead of fighting back, the preacher just kept telling him Jesus loved him. The guy kept swinging that knife, trying to cut that preacher, but every time he tried, a force he couldn't see stopped him short. He literally couldn't touch him.

As a result, that gang member fell down on his knees and received Jesus. Today he is one of the most outstanding evangelists in the world!

Listen, my friend, forgiveness is one of the most powerful forces in existence. Forgive today!

backup:
Colossians 1:9-14

download:
Job 35-36; Revelation 17

voice activate:
I honor the blood of Jesus by choosing to forgive; therefore, I walk in victory and power. Luke 17:3-4; Revelation 1:5

"Be glad in the Lord and rejoice, you righteous; And shout for joy...Rejoice in the Lord, O you righteous! For praise from the upright is beautiful." Psalm 32:11-33:1, NKJV

Spontaneous Combustion

Never underestimate the power of joy. It's like a blazing fire that captures the attention of people in darkness. In fact, in a dream I had many years ago, God called it "spontaneous combustion."

I didn't even know what the term meant until the next day. When I looked it up in a dictionary, here's what I found: *Spontaneous combustion*— "the process of catching fire and burning as a result of heat generated by an internal chemical reaction."

That's it! Joy—the process of catching fire and burning as a result of heat which comes from the Holy Spirit!

It's time to get excited, to rise up out of our tiredness and put the power of praise into practice. When you do, you'll enter into a place of power, freedom and joy. It's a place that's alive and shining with God's presence.

So throw off those old inhibitions. Take God at His Word. Leap. Shout. Sing. Be ready to obey the Holy Spirit. Let yourself catch fire and never stop burning!

b a c k u p :
Psalm 100

d o w n l o a d :
Job 37-39; Revelation 18-19

v o i c e   a c t i v a t e :
I rejoice in the Lord and am glad. I sing and shout for joy because praise is fitting to all who are upright in heart. Psalm 32:11-33:1

"And now these three remain: faith, hope and love. But the greatest of these is love."
1 Corinthians 13:13

august 14

kenneth

The Three Most Powerful Elements

Wishing won't accomplish anything. *Hoping* will, especially when you couple it with faith and love!

Hope is one of the three most powerful elements in the universe. It is one of the three eternal and living substances that run the entire kingdom of God. I preach a lot about faith. I'm constantly teaching Christians that they can't get anything done without faith. Faith can't get anything done without hope—that is, intense expectation!

Hebrews 11:1 says, *"Now faith is the substance of things hoped for...."* In natural terms you might say faith is the building material and hope is the blueprint. You need hope before faith can begin building anything in your life.

For instance, someone who has cancer might say to me, "I fully expect to be healed of this condition." I might say to them, "What makes you believe that when the doctor just said you're incurable?"

If that person has hope, he'll say, "I'm going to be rescued from this cancer because God's Word says every sickness and every disease is part of the curse of the Law, and Galatians 3:13 says Jesus has rescued us from the curse of the Law, being made a curse for us. In other words, Jesus has already freed me from the curse of this cancer. *That's* why I fully expect to be rescued from it."

When you have a clear, Bible-based image inside you like that, you have real hope—and it's absolutely necessary for anyone who wants to live by faith.

So put hope to work in your life today. Couple it with faith and love. Then you will have the three most powerful elements in the universe working for you!

backup:
Colossians 1:21-24

download:
Job 40-41; Revelation 20

voice activate:
I hope and expect in the mercy and love of God and He delights in me. Psalm 147:11

"Do not store up for yourselves treasures on earth, where moth and rust destroy, and where thieves break in and steal. But store up for yourselves treasures in heaven.... For where your treasure is, there your heart will be also."
Matthew 6:19-21

Your Heavenly Account

Have you ever read anywhere in the Bible where God said, "Since you might forget Me if you get rich, I'm going to keep you poor"?

No, I know you haven't because it's not in there! However, He did say to "always remember that I'm the One Who gives you the power to get wealth" (Deuteronomy 8:18). In other words, remember where you got it!

As Christians, we are *"Abraham's seed, and heirs according to the promise"* (Galatians 3:29). Therefore, we can expect God to put His power behind us. We can expect Him to bless us and give us the power to become wealthy!

"But Gloria," you may say, "I know people who have put God first all their lives, yet they were always broke. God didn't give them the power to get wealth!"

Yes, He did. They just didn't know how to use it.

God's wealth doesn't just hit us on the head. He has specific ways for us to receive it. If we don't know those ways, we'll miss out on what's ours.

That's really not surprising when you think about it. Even things on earth work

that way. For example, you can have a million dollars in a bank account, but if you don't know how to make a withdrawal, you won't enjoy that money.

The same thing is true here. The Bible says you have a heavenly account. It is much like an earthly bank account in that you can make deposits in it. You give to your heavenly account by giving to others. By meeting their needs. By giving to what God is doing in ministries and outreaches—this is above your tithe.

When you do, release your faith. Tell God what you are believing for. Then, you can know that *"God will liberally supply (fill to the full) your every need according to His riches in glory in Christ Jesus"* (Philippians 4:19, AMP).

backup:
Matthew 6:19-21

download:
Job 42; Proverbs 1; Revelation 21

voice activate:
I store up for myself treasures in heaven, for where my treasure is, there will my heart be also. Matthew 6:19-21

"My son, pay attention to what I say; listen closely to my words. Do not let them out of your sight, keep them within your heart...Above all else, guard your heart, for it is the wellspring of life."
Proverbs 4:20-21,23

august 16

kenneth

Change Your Strategy

So many people walk around saying things like, "Well, I'm just so tired...I'm so weak...Things are looking so bad." Then suddenly, they think they're going to jerk their faith out from under the table and raise the dead with it.

Well, that just won't happen, because things don't work that way. Faith needs to be taken out from under the table, all right, but not just so you can get out of a jam and then toss it aside again. You have to keep your faith in action so it can grow.

According to Proverbs 4, God says you must always keep His Word before your eyes, in your ears and in your heart. He says above all else to guard your heart.

Why do you have to do this all the time? Because Satan is coming at you with his junk all the time. He's constantly throwing tricks at you. He works hard to make sure the world is surrounding you with fear and discouragement and sickness and every other kind of garbage he can use to destroy you.

You can protect yourself from those things by speaking the truth. Just arm yourself with a promise from God and speak it out. Make a decision right now to begin responding that way.

Change your strategy today, and make speaking the Word part of your daily life!

backup:
Proverbs 15:1-7,23

download:
Proverbs 2-3; Revelation 22

voice activate:
The Word of God is near me. It is in my mouth and in my heart. Romans 10:8

"Blessed are those who are persecuted because of righteousness, for theirs is the kingdom of heaven. Blessed are you when people insult you, persecute you and falsely say all kinds of evil against you because of me. Rejoice and be glad, because great is your reward in heaven, for in the same way they persecuted the prophets who were before you."
Matthew 5:10-12

Get Excited!

Today's verses hold the secret to overcoming persecution. When persecution comes, don't get depressed. Don't get angry or discouraged. Get excited—*very* excited!

Luke 6:23 takes that command even further. It says, *"Rejoice in that day [of persecution] and leap for joy, because great is your reward in heaven."*

A few days after I first noticed that instruction in the Scripture, someone came into my office and told me about something just plain mean that had been written about Ken and me. So I took that verse literally. I stood up and jumped in excitement. "Glory to God!" I shouted.

I'm sure the person sitting on the other side of my desk was a little surprised, but I didn't care. The Word worked. I discovered you can't jump for joy and give God praise and be depressed at the same time.

Remember that the next time persecution comes your way. It will ruin Satan's whole twisted plan. He thinks he can get persecution to ruin you. He thinks it will discourage you and stop you from living for God.

However, you can turn the tables on him. Get excited and leave Satan as the depressed one. Just think how frustrated he'll be!

august 17

gloria

b a c k u p :
John 15:16-27

d o w n l o a d :
Proverbs 4-5; Psalm 1

v o i c e   a c t i v a t e :
I rejoice when I am persecuted for righteousness' sake, for the kingdom of heaven is mine. Matthew 5:10-12

"'The days are coming,' declares the Lord, 'when the reaper will be overtaken by the plowman and the planter by the one treading grapes. New wine will drip from the mountains and flow from all the hills.'"

Amos 9:13

august 18

kenneth

Time—According to Jesus

Time as we have known it is over. We live in a *different* time now. You and I have entered into a sliver of time, a little, narrow band of time, which is perhaps the most important block of time since God created earth. We have stepped over into a place where we know God can do *"immeasurably more than all we ask or imagine"* (Ephesians 3:20).

John 6:5-13 talks about when Jesus took a basket of just five loaves of bread and two fish and fed thousands of people. Now if there was ever a time when God did immeasurably more than someone could ask or imagine, this was it. There were thousands of people eating until they were full, and twelve baskets filled with leftovers.

People today would say, "Whoa, what an awesome miracle!" The truth is, it was more than a miracle. On that day, *time compressed.* It was tightly compacted, within a short space.

This is what I want you to see: This whole process of Jesus taking the loaves and fish into His hands, blessing it, breaking it and distributing it, is the whole sowing and reaping process condensed into a matter of moments.

A little boy sowed his five bread loaves and two small fish into Jesus' ministry. Jesus received the boy's seed—and *immediately* there was a harvest. Not only was there enough to feed everyone until they were full, there was also plenty left over!

So what happened? The harvester caught up with the sower. Today's verse prophesies that there is a time coming when seedtime and harvest time will run together. That boy sowed his bread and fish into Jesus' ministry that morning, and went home that afternoon with twelve baskets full—all because time compressed in Jesus. That's exciting because that's the kind of time we're living in today!

backup:
John 6:5-13

download:
Proverbs 6-7; Psalm 2

voice activate:
Because of Jesus, time has culminated. The time has come when the plowman has overtaken the reaper. Seedtime and harvest time are running together. Amos 9:13

"I sought the Lord, and he answered me; he delivered me from all my fears."
Psalm 34:4

Who Knows?

Many Christians have what I call a "counseling mentality" today. They think the Bible says, "If there is any troubled among you, let him go for counseling and get the pastor to pray." That's not what the Bible says.

Let me tell you Whose counsel will bring you out of trouble—the counsel of the Lord. Ken and I know that from experience. Some years ago, for instance, this ministry faced serious financial trouble. We were a million dollars in the red and no matter what we did, we just couldn't seem to shake that debt.

So Ken began to seek God's wisdom on the matter. He prayed and said, "What is the problem here, Lord?"

Then he got still and listened. Sure enough, God's counsel came.

God said, *Give the top ten percent of the ministry's gross income away.*

Now, those instructions make no sense in the "natural" way of looking at things. They seem foolish. However, we were just "foolish" enough to follow them. Of course, when we did, God brought us out of that debt.

Let me warn you. You're never going to figure things like that out all by yourself. He is so much smarter than we are that sometimes His wise counsel sounds foolish to us. We have to come to a place where we simply say, "God, I realize that You're smarter than I am, so I'll do whatever You say."

Remember though, God isn't going to interrupt your life and force His wisdom on you. He will wait on you to turn to Him. You must do as Psalm 34:4 says: *"I sought the Lord, and he answered me; he delivered me from all my fears."*

backup:
Psalm 34

download:
Proverbs 8-9; Psalm 3

download:
I seek the Lord and He answers me. He delivers me from all my fears. Psalm 34:4

"For I say, through the grace given to me, to everyone who is among you, not to think of himself more highly than he ought to think, but to think soberly, as God has dealt to each one (the) measure of faith."
Romans 12:3, NKJV

august 20

kenneth

The Measure of Faith

In my years of ministry, I've seen people who will learn a little about faith and put it into practice. Then, if they don't get instant results, they get discouraged. They begin to think they just don't have the kind of faith that people in the Bible had. If that's happened to you, let me assure you, God hasn't shortchanged you. You have everything it takes to live by faith!

The Bible says God has given every Christian the "measure of faith." That means He deposited the same measure of faith inside you that He deposited in me— and every Christian on earth. It's a force inside you that's just as much a part of you as the juices in your stomach that digest your food. It's as real inside your spirit as your brain is inside your head.

No one was ever created with half a measure of faith. Someone might have some kind of deformity in his or her body, but no one has any deformity in his spirit. Everybody's spirit has faith in it. That faith increases as it hears and receives God's promises.

It doesn't matter who you are, where you are or what you are. If you have made Jesus the Lord of your life, you have as much faith capacity in you as any Bible hero you can name.

God hasn't changed. You already have in you all the faith you'll ever need. Now it's up to you to develop and release that faith!

backup:
Mark 10:46-52

download:
Proverbs 10-12; Psalms 4-5

download:
God has given me the measure of faith. My faith grows more and more as I hear the Word. Romans 12:3, 10:17

"Sanctify them—purify, consecrate, separate them for Yourself, make them holy—by the Truth. Your Word is Truth."
John 17:17, AMP

It's Time to Mature

With all God is doing right now, you'd think every Christian on earth would be happy as a pig in the sunshine. You'd think every one of us would be healed and rescued from vices and giving God praise all day long.

Quite frankly, many Christians are more frustrated today than they've ever been. God's miracle-working power is falling around them like rain...yet no matter where they go, they can't seem to get wet! These Christians go from one meeting to the next, hoping God will move in their lives and free them from some habit or sin that has ensnared them.

When they get to the meeting, they make a big display, shouting and hollering and praising God. They run up and down the aisle and have a great time. They even fall on the floor. Yet, by the time they get home, they're find themselves in the same situation. So sadly, they think that God has not done anything for them.

If that has happened to you, I want you to pay close attention. If you've been walking around thinking, *I just don't understand it. I used to be on fire for God. Now even when the most powerful ministers pray for me, nothing happens,* I want you to know something: God has not forgotten you. He is not ignoring you.

It is now time to mature even further.

That's good news! God is letting you know that you're mature enough that you don't need baby food anymore. You don't need to run to a specific minister or a specific meeting for help. You've grown to the point where He expects you to pick up your Bible and get what you need by faith.

Like you, many Christians have reached this same stage of spiritual growth. From now on, if they're going to walk free from sin, discouragement and all the rest of Satan's junk, they'll have to get it from the Word.

Jesus is saying to them, *"You will know the truth, and the truth will (make) you free"* (John 8:32).

b a c k u p :
John 8:31-38

d o w n l o a d :
Proverbs 13-14; Psalm 6

v o i c e a c t i v a t e :
I know the truth and the truth makes me free. John 8:32

august 22 · **kenneth**

"When the people heard this, they were cut to the heart and said to Peter and the other apostles, 'Brothers, what shall we do?' Peter replied, 'Repent and be baptized, every one of you, in the name of Jesus Christ for the forgiveness of your sins. And you will receive the gift of the Holy Spirit.'"
Acts 2:37-38

Continue Daily

When the disciples got together and received the Holy Spirit's power for the first time, thousands of people gathered in Jerusalem to see what all the noise was about. Peter went out and told them to do the same thing he and the disciples had been doing for days: "Repent!" He said, "Do what we've been doing, man! Repent! Then you'll receive the Holy Spirit's power just like we did!"

Sure enough, they did repent and received the power.

"Well now, Kenneth, my youth group had a repentance service back in January. New Year's resolutions, you know. Everybody hugged and cried and, boy, was it great."

I'm sure it was, but the repenting you did six months ago won't put you in the place of God's power today. We have to do like the early Church did. Acts 2:46 says they continued to meet every day, having Communion in their homes.

They didn't stop praying and repenting when God's power came to them. They didn't just have a great meeting and then go back to watching junk on TV and fussing with one another. They stayed in the Word. They stayed in agreement.

When a disagreement cropped up, the disciples took care of it right away—and God's power fell.

What does that mean for you and me? It means that if we'll keep ourselves repentant, if we'll continue to get sin out of our lives daily and get right with our brothers and sisters in Christ, then God will work wonders through us! Not just in church, but at school! At the football game! At the mall!

We will turn into carriers of the healing, transforming, miracle-working power of God. God will use us to bring His presence to the world!

backup:
Acts 2:37-47

download:
Proverbs 15-16; Psalm 7

voice activate:
I continue in the Word; therefore, I am Jesus' disciple. John 8:31

"The Spirit gives life; the flesh counts for nothing. The words I have spoken to you are spirit and they are life."
John 6:63

Life-Giving Force

God's Word actually has the power to heal your body. It actually has *life* in it! Jesus said so in today's verse.

Every time you take the Word into your heart, believe it and act on it, the very *life* of God Himself is released in you. You may have read healing promises over and over again. You may know them as well as you know your own name. Yet, every time you read them or hear them preached, they bring you a fresh dose of God's healing power. Each time, they bring life to you and deliver God's medicine to your body.

That's because the Word is like a seed. Hebrews 4:12 says it is *"alive and full of power—making it active, operative, energizing and effective"* (AMP). It carries within it the power to do what it says it will do!

When you put God's promise about a new life in your heart, then believed and acted on it, that Word released within you the power to become new. In the same way, when you put God's promises about healing in your heart, believe and act on

them, those promises will release God's healing power in you.

When you read the Bible, you'll see that spiritual power has been affecting this physical world ever since time began. In fact, it was spiritual power released in the form of God's Word that brought the universe into existence in the first place.

When you really get that—that God's Word is the force that originally brought about everything you can see and touch—it's easy to believe that the Word is still capable of changing those things you see and touch today...like your body. It makes perfect sense!

So get into the Bible. Speak its life-giving force aloud in faith...and receive your healing! Receive His *life!*

b a c k u p :
Hebrews 4:1-12

d o w n l o a d :
Proverbs 17-18; Psalm 8

v o i c e a c t i v a t e :
The Spirit gives me life. The words that Jesus speaks to me are spirit and life. John 6:63

"The god of this age [Satan] has blinded the minds of unbelievers, so that they cannot see the light of the gospel of the glory of Christ, who is the image of God." 2 Corinthians 4:4

august 24

kenneth

Keep Satan Bound

Do you know how to pray for your family's salvation? Many Christians don't. They just throw prayers around when they pray for the lost. I've met people who've prayed for 20, 30 or 40 years without results.

Knowing how to pray with skill can change that. Here's a bit of insight: No human being who *truly understood* the salvation Jesus offers would reject it. No one!

"Why, then," you ask, "is my brother still unsaved?" Today's verse tells us that Satan is the one who has blinded his mind. Once you realize that it's Satan—not your brother—who's the real problem, your mission becomes clear. You must get Satan out of your brother's way.

Jesus said that in order to carry off a strong man's possessions, you must first tie up the strong man (Matthew 12:29). So tie Satan up! Bind him! Say, "Satan, I know you're blinding my brother to keep him out of heaven. Well, I bind you now. I belong to Jesus Christ. I carry His authority and right-standing with God, and in His Name I command you to stop. I'm rescuing my brother from your hands."

Now, you may not be able to throw Satan entirely out of the situation, because your brother may invite him back in faster than you can throw him out. But by speaking God's promises, you can tie Satan up and keep him bound. It may keep you busy for a few days, but you can do it.

You'll find your next prayer step in Matthew 9:37-38. Jesus said, *"Ask the Lord of the harvest...to send out workers into his harvest field."* Your brother may not listen to you, but God knows whom he will listen to. Pray that the right person shares God's Word with your brother. After all, His Word brings faith for salvation (Romans 10:17).

Once you've prayed for your brother like that, from then on, put your faith in action by treating him like he's a Christian—not like he's no good. Talk to him as if he were already a Christian. Tell him about the good things God is doing. Then just stand back and watch how things change!

backup:
Matthew 9:37-38; 12:29

download:
Proverbs 19-20; Psalm 9

voice activate:
I bind the spirits that blind the minds of my loved ones concerning the gospel of Jesus. I obey the command of Jesus and ask the Lord of the harvest to send out workers into the harvest field. 2 Corinthians 4:4; Matthew 9:37-38

It's About Time

Jesus is coming soon, so get ready. Don't be so caught up in the world's activities that you can't hear what He is telling you to do. Now is the time to dedicate every fiber of your being, every moment of your life and everything you do to the Lord's service. You don't want anything to hold you back.

Jesus taught about being ready in Matthew 25:1-13:

"At that time the kingdom of heaven will be like ten virgins who took their lamps and went out to meet the bridegroom. Five of them were foolish and five were wise. The foolish ones took their lamps but did not take any oil with them. The wise, however, took oil in jars along with their lamps. The bridegroom was a long time in coming, and they all became drowsy and fell asleep.

"At midnight the cry rang out: 'Here's the bridegroom! Come out to meet him!'

"Then all the virgins woke up and trimmed their lamps. The foolish ones said to the wise, 'Give us some of your oil; our lamps are going out.'

"'No,' they replied, 'there may not be enough for both us and you. Instead, go to those who sell oil and buy some for yourselves.'

"But while they were on their way to buy the oil, the bridegroom arrived. The virgins who were ready went in with him to the wedding banquet. And the door was shut.

"Later the others also came. 'Sir! Sir!' they said. 'Open the door for us!'

"But he replied, 'I tell you the truth, I don't know you.'

"Therefore keep watch, because you do not know the day or the hour."

The point of this parable is very clear: You must be prepared—ahead of time. You're the one who has to get yourself ready. You must make sure there's nothing in your life that would cause you to back away from His presence.

So prepare yourself! Keep yourself full of the Word and the Holy Spirit so that when Jesus returns, you'll be ready!

backup:
Colossians 3:1-10

download:
Proverbs 21-22; Psalm 10

voice activate:
I do not know the day or the hour when Jesus will return, so I continue to watch for Him. Matthew 25:13

august 26

kenneth

"These things I have spoken to you, that My joy may remain in you, and that your joy may be full...Ask, and you will receive, that your joy may be full."
John 15:11,16:24, NKJV

Send Satan Running

Whatever is happening in your life today, you need to stir up your joy.

How can you do that?

For starters, you can begin by studying and thinking about God's promises. When you do that, and you gain insight into what God is saying to you, joy comes! It comes because you begin to have a deeper and clearer knowledge of God. It comes because you realize you can go boldly before Him in prayer on the basis of the Word, and be confident your prayers will be answered.

If you've been sad about the direction your brother or sister is heading, for example, you can replace your sad thoughts with an understanding of God's promise to your parents in Isaiah 54:13. When you do, joy will come into your heart. Suddenly, instead of crying over what Satan is doing to your brother or sister, you start getting excited about what God will do. You'll laugh and say, "You might as well forget it, Satan. Just pack it up and go home, because the victory is won. The Lord will teach my brothers and sisters the truth and their peace will be great!"

Then when Satan comes back at you and says, *Maybe so, but aren't you sorry about how much of their life they've wasted?* you can shoot the Word right back at him. You can say, "No, I'm not sorry. I don't have to be sorry because Jesus took up my griefs and carried my sorrows (Isaiah 53:4). So I believe I'll just go ahead and have a good time, thank you!"

Proverbs 15:23 says, *"A man has joy by the answer of his mouth"* (NKJV). When you start answering the troubles you're facing with the promises of God, they will release joy in you and run Satan off. He can't stand the Lord's joy in you!

So stir up that joy. Pray the Word. Really think about what it's saying. Replace wrong thoughts with God's thoughts, and enjoy winning!

b a c k u p :
Isaiah 51:11-16

d o w n l o a d :
Proverbs 23-24; Psalm 11

v o i c e   a c t i v a t e :
I ask and I receive, that my joy will be complete. John 16:24

"For our light and momentary troubles are achieving for us an eternal glory that far outweighs them all. So we fix our eyes not on what is seen, but on what is unseen. For what is seen is temporary, but what is unseen is eternal."
2 Corinthians 4:17-18

None of These Things Move Me

If you want to rob persecution of every last scrap of its power, grab hold of the attitude Paul had in 2 Corinthians 4:17-18. He wasn't concerned about the pressure he was experiencing. Believe me, he was under tremendous pressure.

He'd probably laugh at us talking about persecution these days, we've had so little of it.

Paul's thoughts weren't centered on this short, earthly life. He was thinking about eternity with Jesus. So he didn't grow tired. He didn't crumble under persecutions, tribulations or threats. In fact, in Acts 20:24, KJV he said, *"None of these things move me; nor do I count my life dear to myself, so that I may finish my race with joy."*

Once you grab hold of that attitude, Satan won't be able to manage you at all. He won't be able to find any persecution that will stop you. You'll have your eyes so fixed on running your race and finishing your course, you won't even pay any attention to his junk. Instead of fussing and fuming over all the ugly things other kids are saying about you, you'll be busy looking forward to the day when you will stand face to face with Jesus and hear Him say, "Well done, good and faithful servant."

gloria

b a c k u p :
1 Corinthians 9:24-27

d o w n l o a d :
Proverbs 25-27; Psalms 12-13

v o i c e a c t i v a t e :
I don't fix my eyes on what is seen, but on what is unseen. For what is seen is temporary, but what is unseen is eternal. 2 Corinthians 4:18

august 28

kenneth

"No, this is what was spoken by the prophet Joel: 'In the last days, God says, I will pour out my Spirit on all people. Your sons and daughters will prophesy, your young men will see visions, your old men will dream dreams.'"
Acts 2:16-17

An Awesome Event

The first day the disciples received the power of the Holy Spirit in their lives, 3,000 people made Jesus their Lord, and God continued to move. Throughout the book of Acts, you can see a record of all He did.

Now if the things we see in Acts, wonderful as they are, were only the beginning of what God was doing, can you imagine what is ahead?

Think about that for a moment. This outpouring of God's power on us will contain the Holy Spirit's power as seen in the Old Covenant, plus the Holy Spirit's power as seen on the early Church in the New Covenant. This is all of it together!

Can you imagine someone walking around with the power that Elisha and Elijah had *and* the power that Peter and Paul had—all at the same time? It's about to happen!

If you'll get your act straightened up and get yourself in sync with the Holy Spirit, it will happen to you. It won't matter whether you've been to Bible school or not. If you'll dare to believe

God, you can get in on this awesome event, and when I say awesome, I mean *awesome!*

b a c k u p :
Joel 2:21-29

d o w n l o a d :
Proverbs 28-29; Psalm 14

v o i c e   a c t i v a t e :
In these last days, God is pouring out His Spirit on all people. He is pouring out His Spirit on me! Acts 2:16-17

His Arm Isn't Short

We need to go beyond believing only what is reasonable to our mind. For example, if you're in college, you need to stop being content just to believe God for the money to make your tuition payment each quarter. You need to start believing Him for the money to pay off your entire tuition!

"But Gloria, I don't know how God would get that kind of money to me."

So what! Moses didn't know how God was going to bring in enough food to feed several million Israelites for a month either. So when God said He was going to do it, Moses said, "It would take all our herds and flocks to feed this bunch! It would take all the fish in the sea!" (verse 22).

"And the Lord answered Moses, 'Is the Lord's arm too short?'" Then He proved He was able to do what He said by raining so much quail out of heaven, the Israelites actually got tired of it—just like He said.

When you have a need in your life that seems impossible to meet, think about that. Remember the question God asked Moses, *"Is the Lord's arm too short?"*

No! It wasn't short then and it isn't short now. God knows how to get the job done. He knows how to get you everything you need. So look to Him as your source. Become expectant. Think like He does!

God knows how to do things. You don't have to worry about that. You just focus on your part—believe, speak His promises and walk in His ways. Stop limiting God just because you don't understand how He is going to do what He has promised. If we had to depend on what we could understand, we'd be in great trouble, but we don't! All we have to understand is that God is God and He has all power. He is able to do far beyond what we can imagine!

Whatever you need, GOD IS ABLE! He is able to meet your needs and desires and much, much more. His arm is not short!

b a c k u p :
Numbers 11:16-23, 31-32

d o w n l o a d :
Proverbs 30-31; Psalm 15

v o i c e   a c t i v a t e :
God's arm is not too short, He is able to meet all my needs! Numbers 11:23

"I do not receive honor from men. But I know you, that you do not have the love of God in you. I have come in My Father's name, and you do not receive Me; if another comes in his own name, him you will receive. How can you believe, who receive honor from one another, and do not seek the honor that comes from the only God?"
John 5:41-44, NKJV

Don't Play the Game!

Honor. Godly honor. It keeps its word and standard of integrity no matter what. It never fails—it always succeeds.

Every day, you're required to make commitments of honor. You have choices to make regarding doing what's right or wrong at school, obeying your parents, treating your friends right, keeping your time alone with God—and it's hard. It's a choice between God's honor and man's. One brings true and sure success...and one brings shallow, temporal success that ends in ultimate failure. In other words, it looks good but doesn't last.

In John 5:41-44, Jesus told the religious leaders about honor that comes from God alone. That's the kind of honor we need to stand strong. You can be a powerful force in the earth as a Christian who walks by faith, but to do it, you must operate in His honor.

The world's definition of honor, however, is quite different from God's. It may look like the honor of God, but it is light and shallow—it is a false honor that deceives people. The world's honor is really more of an "honor game." In this

sport, everything is done to gain the prestige, power and authority that people can give. It's temporal, short-lived and dishonorable in view of what some people will do to get it.

In playing the game, people will scheme, beg, swap favors, cheat and "shade the truth" to "win." You may go to school with people like that. These schemers may receive the same privileges, the same "honor" as those who truly deserve them—but they did not come by them with true honor. In the long run, they don't win.

On the other hand, God is faithful to honor you when you act honorably. That's because you are acting in something that He started! He is honorable. So don't play the game! Live honorably with the honor that comes from God alone. Your rewards will be far greater and eternal...He guarantees it.

backup:
Psalm 15

download:
Ecclesiastes 1-2; Psalm 16

voice activate:
As I honor God, He honors me. 1 Samuel 2:30

There Go the Weeds

I believe we've come to the time Peter was referring to when he wrote the words in today's verse. We haven't heard a lot about judgment in recent years, but that's not because the New Testament doesn't teach about it. It does! In fact, Jesus Himself talked about judgment in Matthew 13 where He talks about the separation of the holy from the unholy. It's a separation that will take place in these end times.

According to Jesus, there is coming a time at the end of the world, when the "weeds" are going to be taken out. It's the time when those who live holy will shine with God's glory. It's the time when Jesus will clean His Church so that He can present "a radiant church, without stain or wrinkle or any other blemish, but holy and blameless" (Ephesians 5:26-27).

If you're living an unholy life, that's a frightening thought. But if you've set your heart on being holy, it's exciting. It means that you are going to be a part of that radiant Church.

You may not think you can be holy and blameless, but all of us can. With God's favor on us, we'll be that Church. If these are the end times, then we're all God has, and because He is God, He can make it happen!

God *is* able! So let's believe that. Let's act on it. Let's pray for ourselves and each other as Paul prayed:

"*And may the God of peace Himself sanctify you through and through—that is, separate you from profane things, make you pure and wholly consecrated to God—and may your spirit and soul and body be preserved sound and complete [and found] blameless at the coming of our Lord Jesus Christ, the Messiah. Faithful is He Who is calling you [to Himself] and utterly trustworthy, and He will also do it*" (1 Thessalonians 5:23-24, AMP).

b a c k u p :
Matthew 13:24-30

d o w n l o a d :
Ecclesiastes 3-4; Psalm 17

v o i c e   a c t i v a t e :
The God of peace sanctifies me through and through. My whole spirit, soul and body are kept blameless until the coming of my Lord Jesus Christ.
1 Thessalonians 5:23

september 1

gloria

"Servants, obey in everything those who are your earthly masters, not only when their eyes are on you, as pleasers of men, but in simplicity of purpose (with all your heart) because of your reverence for the Lord and as a sincere expression of your devotion to Him."
Colossians 3:22, AMP

The Path to Promotion

You may not realize it, but if you're a Christian, you have a quality within you that is in great demand in the world today. It's a quality employers prize so highly that they'll promote people who have it—and often pay top dollar for it.

What is this precious quality? The quality of faithfulness.

Employers are desperate for faithful people. The world is full of employees who will do just enough to keep from getting fired. It's a treasure for employers to find a person who works wholeheartedly at his job, who is trustworthy and dependable and honest. So when an employer finds a person like that, he's usually eager to promote him.

The fact is, every Christian ought to be that kind of person. Each of us should live a lifestyle of faithfulness. As Ken says, in every situation we should do what's right, do it because it's right and do it right.

We should follow Colossians 3:22-24. It's God's instruction for employees. Ken and I have seen some of the staff members in our ministry take that attitude

and, as a result, be promoted time and again. One man started out with the job of duplicating tapes for us, but over the years he was so faithful that he eventually became the director over the business affairs of the entire ministry.

You may think, *Well, I don't know if that'll work for me. After all, the world is full of unfair bosses. What if mine won't reward my faithfulness?*

That's no problem. The Scripture doesn't say your reward will come from your employer. It says your reward will come from the Lord!

So make up your mind to put your whole heart into your work, no matter how menial or unpleasant it may seem to be. Do it well. Do it with a smile and enthusiasm. Soon, you will receive a promotion in return...even if that promotion means a different but better job!

b a c k u p :
Galatians 6:7-10

d o w n l o a d :
Ecclesiastes 5-6; Psalm 18

v o i c e a c t i v a t e :
I obey my earthly masters in everything with sincerity of heart and reverence for the Lord. Colossians 3:22

"Now every athlete who goes into training conducts himself temperately and restricts himself in all things. They do it to win a wreath that will soon wither, but we [do it to receive a crown of eternal blessedness] that cannot wither."
1 Corinthians 9:25, AMP

Go the Rest of the Distance

Many Christians have come a long way. They've been rescued from old habits, and have learned to give God first place in their lives. They've trained themselves to spend time with God each day. They aren't living in habitual sin. They know what God wants them to do. They know He has great things for their lives. They have become mature Christians, but they haven't arrived.

"Gloria, what do you mean?"

God is calling all Christians, including mature Christians, to draw closer to Him. He wants us to spend more time in prayer, more time in the Bible. There may not be sin in our lives, but there are little things holding us back. It could be every-day things taking up too much of our time—things that keep us from more of God. Hebrews 12:1 calls them "weights."

The Holy Spirit will show us what adjustments we need to make. Maybe He's telling you to get up earlier like He told me at one point in my life. In fact, I'm thinking of getting up even earlier than I have been. I want more time with God before I go out and live my day.

God speaks to us about what's in our hearts. In love, He says, *Just put that aside for a while. It's taking up too much of your thoughts, too much of your time.*

You need to ask yourself, *What makes me tick? What is it that I think of when I wake up in the morning? What is it that's the center of my attention?*

If it's not God and His Word and living for Him, then you need to make a change. You need to make God your top priority—the center of your life.

So pick up the pace. Go the rest of the distance. You can't win a race with weights attached to your feet! Throw aside those weights and run the race God has set before you.

b a c k u p :
1 Corinthians 9:23-27

d o w n l o a d :
Ecclesiastes 7-8; Psalm 19

v o i c e a c t i v a t e :
I throw off everything that hinders and the sin that so easily entangles me. I run with perseverance the race marked out for me. Hebrews 12:1

gloria

253

September 3

Kenneth

"From the fruit of his mouth a man's stomach is filled; with the harvest from his lips he is satisfied. The tongue has the power of life and death, and those who love it will eat its fruit."
Proverbs 18:20-21

What Are You Becoming?

If you're not sure what you're becoming, let me give you a hint. You're going to be whatever you think about and talk about all the time.

I can listen to you talk for thirty minutes and tell you exactly what you'll become. It doesn't take a prophet to do that. It just takes someone who will listen to your words.

So listen to yourself. If you don't like what you hear, change it. Become something better by beginning to think God's Word, talk God's Word and act on God's Word.

Nobody on earth can determine what you're going to become but you. Yes, you! Don't blame it on Satan. He can't change it. Don't blame it on your parents, your background or your circumstances, and certainly, don't blame God.

Forget your past...and do what Abraham did. The Bible says, *"He did not consider his own body, already dead (since he was about a hundred years old), and the deadness of Sarah's womb"* (Romans 4:19, NKJV).

He just said to himself, *Old man, you don't count. Neither do you, Granny. What counts is God's promise, and I am exactly what God says I am.*

Do you want to become what God says you are? Do you want to be wise? Do you want to be bold? Do you want to be a powerful witness to your classmates? What is your dream?

You can determine your outcome in life by changing your words to match God's words and releasing your faith. You *can* become all you were meant to be.

backup:
Matthew 12:33-37

download:
Ecclesiastes 9-11; Psalms 20-21

voice activate:
My stomach is filled from the fruit of my mouth, and with the harvest of my lips, I am satisfied. Proverbs 18:20

"Worship the Lord your God, and his blessing will be on your food and water. I will take away sickness from among you."
Exodus 23:25

Divine Health

I have some life-changing news for you today. God wants you healthy! Every day!

Oh, I know that, you may quickly think, *I know God will heal me when I get sick.*

Yes, that's true. He will, but that's not what I'm saying. I'm telling you God would rather have you continually living in health. His desire is for you to walk so sure in the power of His Word that sickness and disease are literally pushed away from you. Isn't that good news?

You've probably heard a lot about God's healing power, but there is a difference between *getting* healed and *staying* healed. Years ago, the powerful preacher John G. Lake put it this way, "Divine healing is the removal by the power of God of the disease that has come upon the body. Divine health is to live day by day, hour by hour in touch with God so that the life of God flows into the body just as the life of God flows into the mind or flows into the spirit."

Proverbs 4:20-22 tells us God's Word is life to us and health to our bodies. That word *health* in Hebrew means "medicine."

The Bible has life in it. It is spirit food. As you feed on it, you become strong spiritually and physically.

When you read the Bible and think about what it says, letting it get in your heart, you are taking God's medicine. If you will take it on a regular basis, it will eventually be as hard for you to get sick as it was for you to get well, but it's a process. You can't just read some healing promises once and then go on about your business. You must continually feed on those promises to keep healing in your life. When you do that, you'll *stay* healed every day. You'll be walking in divine health!

backup:
Isaiah 40:28-31

download:
Ecclesiastes 12; Song of Solomon 1; Psalm 22

voice activate:
I worship the Lord my God and He blesses my food and water and takes sickness away from me. Exodus 23:25

September 5

Kenneth

"He could not do any miracles there, except lay his hands on a few sick people and heal them. And he was amazed at their lack of faith."
Mark 6:5-6

No Offense

Prepare yourself. God's anointing—His power—is increasing in the lives of Christians everywhere. It's increasing not only in ministries and churches, but also in the lives of teenagers, parents and kids.

However, there is something that can *block* the power of the anointing, and I want to warn you about it. What is this evil thing? It is taking offense at the message of Jesus.

"But, oh Kenneth, I'd never be offended at Jesus!"

No doubt that's what the people of Nazareth thought, too, before Jesus came to preach at their synagogue. They would have scoffed at the idea of being offended at the Scriptures. After all, they'd been studying them all their lives, yet they became offended.

Those people had been expecting the anointing. They just never expected it to come from the boy who lived around the corner. In their minds, he was just Mary's son, the guy who used to have a carpentry business! They were offended when Jesus said He was anointed (Luke 4:18), and He couldn't do any miracles there. Their unbelief short-circuited the anointing (Mark 6:5-6).

In the Bible, you'll find many times that becoming offended is the thing that stopped God's power from flowing. Sin didn't stop it. Unworthiness didn't stop it. Taking offense did.

In Mark 4, Jesus blatantly pointed out that becoming offended stops God's promises from producing in your life. That's because offense opens the way for Satan to steal the Word, which stops your faith (Romans 10:17). When your faith is stopped, you have nothing to carry you to success when trouble hits.

So check your heart. Make the rock-solid decision to never, ever become offended. These are the end times. God's power is filling the earth, and He's filling it through you...if you'll stop the anointing blocker!

b a c k u p :
Mark 6:1-6

d o w n l o a d :
Song of Solomon 2-3; Psalm 23

v o i c e a c t i v a t e :
I have great peace because I love God's law, and nothing can make me stumble. Psalm 119:165

**...those who seek the Lord lack no good thing."
Psalm 34:10**

God Is Not Broke

God wants us to live well. He has told us that all He has is ours. God put everything in His Word for you and me, and He has no shortage! He wants you to live in a good house. He wants you to have the car that you need. He wants you to be so blessed that you don't even have to think about those things. That way, you can just think about Him.

Now, I know it costs money to live. It costs money to reach people for Jesus— and God's got the money! He's not broke. But He's had a problem getting His people to believe what He says about wealth.

One thing that interferes with our believing is located right between our ears. It's called reason. When Jesus asked Philip how they were going to feed the 5,000, he began to reason. He began to look and see what was possible. "Lord, even if we spent a bunch of money on bread...we still couldn't even begin to do it. There wouldn't be enough to feed the people."

Yet Jesus wasn't looking at anything but God.

That's the same God you and I are connected with today. He knows how to take care of you and me. He knows how to get things done.

What we have a tendency to do is release our faith so that what we can see—with some help from God—might actually come to us. For example, some people have "payment faith" and some people have "car faith."

"Lord, I believe you'll help me make this car payment."

Now, wait. Why don't they just believe to have the car paid off?

Get out beyond what's reasonable. Yes, believe for your car payment, but get your faith out there. Realize God can pay for the whole thing! Base your faith and praying on what the Bible promises, not on just what looks possible to your eyes. According to the Bible, all things are possible with God and all things are possible to whomever believes. God and you make an unbeatable pair!

backup:
Ephesians 3:20; Hebrews 6:12-15

download:
Song of Solomon 4-5; Psalm 24

voice activate:
I seek the Lord and I don't lack any good thing. Psalm 34:10

september 7

kenneth

"Now he who supplies seed to the sower and bread for food will also supply and increase your store of seed and will enlarge the harvest of your righteousness."
2 Corinthians 9:10

Everlasting Harvest

Matthew 14 records how Jesus took one boy's small gift—his seed—and gave it to His disciples to feed thousands of people. Before Jesus did all this, however, He told the disciples, *"Bring them here to me"* (verse 18).

Why do you suppose Jesus told the disciples to give Him the boy's bread and fish? Why did Jesus want to *handle* it? The reason was because that's the way God works. The way He increases your wealth is to have you place your seed into a ministry. Then He has the minister receive it, handle it and distribute it—so it goes out, far more powerful than when you sent it in.

When the boy sowed his small gift into Jesus' ministry—the loaves and fish—Jesus received it, handled it and then distributed it to the thousands there. Then, after everyone was stuffed, Jesus told His disciples to *"Gather the pieces that are left over. Let nothing be wasted"* (John 6:12).

Now why did He do that? Because the 12 baskets full of leftovers belonged to that boy. They were the boy's *immediate* reward, or harvest, from having sown directly into Jesus' ministry. But it didn't

stop there. He also received an eternal reward. He had a part in every future gift given and seed sown from the lives of 20,000 people. *That's* twice-sown seed.

Now, think of all the missionaries who have gone to China, Africa, South America and all those places. They preached and gave their lives, and it looked like Satan had the upper hand.

Well, I have news for you: Every seed sown for the last 2,000 years—every word preached and every drop of blood shed—we're benefiting from today! All 2,000 years' worth of the Word is coming up a hundred times greater than when it was planted, and we're the ones to bring it in. It's time to lead the world to Jesus!

backup:
John 4:35-39

download:
Song of Solomon 6-7; Psalm 25

voice activate:
God supplies seed to the sower and bread for my food. He increases the store of my seed and enlarges the harvest of my righteousness.
2 Corinthians 9:10

"You shall meditate on it [the Word] day and night."
Joshua 1:8, AMP

More Than a History Book

When you meditate on God's Word—that is, study it, think about it and pray about what it says—you're doing more than just reading it. You're taking it into your heart in a very personal way and applying it to your situation.

When you read a scripture about how God wants you to do well in all areas of life, for example, you won't think, *Hey, that sounds nice, but I'll never become good at any of this academic stuff.* Instead, you'll apply it to yourself and say, "That's right! That's God's Word to me. He says I have the mind of Christ (1 Corinthians 2:16). He says He'll give me wisdom liberally (James 1:5), and I'm expecting Him to do that for me in this situation I'm facing!"

If you've been reading the Bible like a history book, make a change and begin to see it as God talking directly to you. Take time to meditate on it. Study it. Think about it. Pray about it. Digest it. Take it so personally that it moves from your head to your heart. Then it will become powerful and active in your life!

gloria

backup:
Psalm 119:73-80

download:
Song of Solomon 8; Isaiah 1; Psalm 26

voice activate:
I meditate on God's Word day and night. I am careful to do everything written in it so I am prosperous and successful. Joshua 1:8

september 9

kenneth

"For God, who said, 'Let light shine out of darkness,' made his light shine in our hearts to give us the light of the knowledge of the glory of God in the face of Christ [the Anointed One and His Anointing]."
2 Corinthians 4:6

Inside-Out

I have studied and prayed about the scriptures that talk about God's glory a lot—and now I am fully expecting His glory to show up in my life. I'm expecting His power to accompany me wherever I go. I'm expecting the same glory that shined like fire on the face of Jesus to shine in me and my situation.

I'm expecting my God to meet all my needs. How? According to His GLORIOUS riches in Jesus!

I'm not looking for that glory to come floating down out of heaven. I'm expecting it to come from the inside of me. I'm expecting it to come from the inside of you. First Chronicles 16:27 (KJV) says, *"Glory and honour are in his [God's] presence,"* and since God Himself lives in us, His glory is inside us!

Our problem up to now has been that we haven't understood that. We haven't understood that God's glory is within us and must be brought out.

God hasn't left us in the dark. He has given us the *"mind of Christ"* (1 Corinthians 2:16) so we can learn how to use His glory that's within us.

There's no need for you to stay tied up in knots over some problem Satan has shoved on you. There's no need for you to be stopped by some mountain of sin or sickness. You have God's glory inside you. Now it just has to come out!

When you put God's Word in your heart and speak it out of your mouth, you can expect the all-powerful goodness of God to show up in your life. Soon, your life will shine with the very light that shines from Jesus' face, the light that illumines all of heaven.

So ask for it! Ask God to teach you about the glory today. James 1:5 promises He will give you wisdom!

backup:
2 Chronicles 7:1-3

download:
Isaiah 2-3; Psalm 27

voice activate:
God's light shines in my heart and gives me knowledge of His glory.
2 Corinthians 4:6

"For where envying and strife is, there is confusion and every evil work."
James 3:16, KJV

Pulling the Plug on Your Faith

Have you ever had everything going smoothly, when suddenly something odd creeps up inside you? Maybe you suddenly felt a little irritated at how well others were doing. Or, maybe you started to feel discouraged about a circumstance that hasn't changed yet.

Watch out! It could be envy or strife trying to enter in. Satan knows that if he can stop your faith from working, he can disrupt everything. One way he may use to stop your faith is to disrupt your love—because faith works *through* love (Galatians 5:6, NKJV). So how does he disrupt your love? By getting envy and strife into your life.

Many Christians don't understand that, so they struggle along, fighting with one another—and then wondering why their faith isn't working. They don't realize that if you want to walk in God's power, you cannot allow envy or strife into your life. Period.

According to James 3:16, envy and strife give Satan an open door into your life. Then, he can really cause trouble.

So what should you do? Shut the door! Resist those pressures and temptations of Satan. Treat strife just like you'd treat a rattlesnake. Don't let it in!

If you've become aware of someone around you who is being more successful than you, don't become envious. Instead, turn the tables on Satan. Start thanking God for that person's success! Then do what you can to help them be even more successful!

In other words, whatever your situation, start walking in love and throwing aside selfishness. If you'll do that, you'll keep the door open for God to bless you. You'll keep Satan from pulling the plug on your faith!

backup:
Genesis 4:1-15

download:
Isaiah 4-6; Psalms 28-29

voice activate:
I walk in love and resist envy and strife. For where envying and strife is, there is confusion and every evil work. James 3:16

September 11

gloria

"Humble yourselves, therefore, under God's mighty hand, that he may lift you up in due time."
1 Peter 5:6

Dare To Step Out

God can take the most simple person in the world, and if that person will dare to believe what is written in the Bible, God will empower him to do any job he is called to do.

I know this because God did that for me. The reason I'm doing so well today is because I am simple enough to believe that God is smarter than I am. When I see something in the Bible that doesn't agree with what I think, I change what I think and believe God's promise instead.

Jesus told us to be like little children. So do that. Humble yourself and just take the Bible as it is written. If God says you'll do something, don't argue, just agree with Him and get busy!

Say, "God, I know that Jesus said, *'Anyone who has faith in me will do what I have been doing'* (John 14:12). I don't know how to do the things He did, but Your Word says I will do them. So I give myself to You. I expect to do what Your Word says!"

Then step out boldly and act on your faith. The bolder we are, the more power that can be released through us. Did you know that? It's when we hesitate and we're afraid of what people might think that nothing happens. So make up your mind now to be bold—whether you want to or not.

That's how it works, but you have to take the first step. Do what the Bible says to do whether you feel like it or not. That's called acting on the Word...aka *faith!*

b a c k u p :
Matthew 18:1-5

d o w n l o a d :
Isaiah 7-8; Psalm 30

v o i c e   a c t i v a t e :
I humble myself under God's mighty hand so He may lift me up. 1 Peter 5:6

"Set a guard over my mouth, O Lord; keep watch over the door of my lips."
Psalm 141:3

What You Compromise To Keep, You Lose

Did you know that Satan can't do anything to you if you won't let him? That's right. If you won't speak words of doubt and unbelief, but instead speak words of faith, he can't keep up his attack.

If you've made Jesus your Lord, Satan doesn't have any authority over you. Satan can't rob you unless you authorize that robbery yourself!

Satan comes to get your words. That's the only way he can get a foot in the door. So refuse to speak words contrary to what you believe. Speak only faith-filled words—even under pressure. No matter what Satan is saying to you in your thoughts, no matter what the people around you are saying, keep agreeing with God's promises to you. Keep saying what God says.

It will be tough sometimes, but you can do it! When things look hopeless, don't give up and start speaking defeat. Double up on speaking faith-filled words!

Learn to immediately answer every doubt with God's Word. Learn to answer every fear with God's Word. Learn to do combat with your words.

Satan will try to intimidate you with threats, but he can only do what you say. He has no way to get into your life unless you let him in. If you won't open the door, he won't be able to carry out even one of those threats. It's when you become timid and fearful with your words that Satan gains the upper hand.

Don't ever allow fear to make you compromise what you say in faith. I learned this long ago: What you compromise to keep, you lose. Stand firm and keep talking faith, and you'll defeat any attack.

gloria

b a c k u p :
Matthew 9:18-26

d o w n l o a d :
Isaiah 9-10; Psalm 31

v o i c e   a c t i v a t e :
The Lord sets a guard over my mouth. He keeps watch over the door of my lips. Psalm 141:3

kenneth

"But I tell you the truth: It is for your good that I am going away. Unless I go away, the Counselor will not come to you; but if I go, I will send him to you."
John 16:7

The Muscle of God

I've found that most Christians seem to think the first time the Holy Spirit did much of anything was after Jesus died and rose again. That's not true. The Holy Spirit has been at work ever since the beginning of time.

When God said "Light be!" the Spirit dove into action and slung this universe into being. He was there just waiting to create.

The Holy Spirit is the muscle of God. Every time power shows up in the Bible, you can be sure the Holy Spirit is there. When the Holy Spirit came on Samson, he single-handedly killed a thousand Philistine soldiers (Judges 15:14-16). He was just an ordinary man who became extraordinary when the Holy Spirit came on him.

The prophet Elijah was the same way. He was just as normal as you or me. When the Holy Spirit came on him, Elijah was a powerhouse. He once called down fire from heaven, killed 450 prophets of Baal, and outran the king's horse-drawn chariot. He did it all in one day (1 Kings 18-19).

Now don't get the idea, however, that the Holy Spirit is simply a mindless source of raw power. Far from it! When He moves in on a situation, He does it with vast wisdom.

"Well then, why hasn't He helped me before now?" you say. "I've needed it!"

He's been waiting for you to give Him something to work with. He's been waiting there inside you, waiting for you to speak God's promises in faith. That's been His role since the beginning—to move on God's Word and deliver the power necessary to make that Word happen. That's what He did at Creation...and that's what He is there to do for you.

Become aware that the Holy Spirit is within you. Stop spending your time thinking about the problems you're facing and start spending it thinking about the power of the One inside you. Release the muscle of God to work for you!

backup:
Judges 15:14-16; 1 Kings 18

download:
Isaiah 11-12; Psalm 32

voice activate:
Because I have received the Holy Spirit, I have received power! Acts 1:8

"I am the Vine, you are the branches. Whoever lives in Me and I in him bears much (abundant) fruit. However, apart from Me—cut off from vital union with Me—you can do nothing. If a person does not dwell in Me, he is thrown out as a [broken-off] branch and withers."
John 15:5-6, AMP

Keep the Union

If you remain in close, constant contact with God, all of the power of heaven is at your disposal.

Did you get that? Think about it for a moment. All the power of heaven! According to Jesus, that kind of prayer power is available to every Christian. It's available to you and to me...*if* we will make our union with God the most important thing in our lives.

So let's do it! Let's stop compromising and allowing the things of the world to eat away at our time with God. Let's get His Word into our hearts so deeply that no one else's opinion seems important.

Then let's start asking. Let's ask Him for what we need. Ask Him for what we want. Ask God to help others, and, of course, ask believing He will do it!

We won't have to be shy about it. We can be bold, knowing that when we give God first place in our lives, He gives us first place in His life. That's what Jesus meant when He said, *"Whoever [really] loves Me will be loved by My Father. And I [too] will love him and will show (reveal, manifest) Myself to him..."* (John 14:21, AMP).

The Lord explained it to Rufus Moseley—a great man of God who went to heaven some years ago—in these words: "Life in Jesus is gloriously easy. It has one responsibility: the responsibility of remaining in union. If you stay in union with Me, I'll take care of everything else."

Isn't that a wonderful, yet simple, instruction? You keep the union. He'll take care of everything else.

b a c k u p :
John 14:21-26

d o w n l o a d :
Isaiah 13-14; Psalm 33

v o i c e   a c t i v a t e :
I remain in Jesus and His words remain in me. I bear much fruit and glorify God. John 15:7-8

september 15

kenneth

"The Lord is with me; I will not be afraid. What can man do to me?"
Psalm 118:6

Supernatural Connection

You don't have to be afraid! It may look as if everything is falling down around your feet, but don't react to it. Just stand your ground. Be like the little guy who came into my office some 20 years ago and said, "Kenneth, I've quit my job. I've decided to live by faith and preach the Bible."

I sat there and looked at him thinking, *He couldn't preach his way out of a paper sack! Lord, it won't be 90 days before this guy will be back wanting money.*

The Lord answered, *Then give him some!* (That ended that right there!)

That young fellow didn't look like he had much going for him, but he had dug into the Word and spent hours upon hours listening to messages and studying his Bible.

Over the next few years, some people told him he couldn't preach. (Not me. I was smart enough to keep my mouth shut.) Still, he wouldn't let go. Others told him he wouldn't amount to a hill of beans. But he wouldn't let go.

He went into one of his first meetings only to find a transformer had blown and the lights wouldn't work. Instead of canceling the meeting, he walked up to the podium and hollered, "Let there be light!"

Sure enough, the lights came on. He just wouldn't give in. He stayed connected to faith.

I asked him once, "What would you have done if the lights hadn't come on?"

"I'd still be standing there hollering at them," he said.

That fellow is still connected to faith today. Just think what a loss it would have been to the Body of Christ if he had disconnected from faith and let fear stop his ministry.

It would be just as great a loss to us all if you stop short of your calling as well. So stay connected to faith— and God's power will stay connected to you!

b a c k u p :
Joshua 10:1-14

d o w n l o a d :
Isaiah 15-16; Psalm 34

v o i c e   a c t i v a t e :
The Lord is with me. I will not be afraid of what man can do to me. Psalm 118:6

"Wisdom is supreme; therefore get wisdom. Though it cost all you have, get understanding. Esteem her, and she will exalt you; embrace her, and she will honor you."
Proverbs 4:7-8

The Best Timesaver of All!

"I'm just too busy!"

That's the number one reason Christians give for failing to spend time with God. Teenagers run from one activity to the next taking care of their social life. Business people rush out the door early every morning and fall into bed exhausted at night. It seems we spend hours thinking how to squeeze more time out of each day. Our schedules are so packed, the demands on our lives are so heavy, that it just doesn't seem we have time to give much attention to the Bible or prayer.

The truth is, we don't have time *not* to!

When your heart is full of God's promises, when trouble comes, His Word is the first thing out of your mouth.

To have your heart full of His promises, you need to do what Joshua 1:8 says: You need to "meditate on the Word." To *meditate* means to fix your mind. So fix your mind on what the Bible says every day. Apply it to yourself personally. Allow the Holy Spirit to make it real to you.

Carefully ponder how what you've read applies to your life. Ask yourself, "What does this say to me? What does it mean in my life? How can it change my situation?"

Then place yourself in agreement with what God says about you in that passage. Make up your mind that you are who God says you are. You can do what God says you can do. You can have what He says you can have. Put yourself in agreement with Him, then receive it.

I know you're busy. There are tremendous demands made on you every day. But God promises that if you'll keep His Word in front of you, you'll know how to succeed in all you do. Now, that sounds like a real time-saver to me!

b a c k u p :
Proverbs 3:1-8

d o w n l o a d :
Isaiah 17-18; Psalm 35

v o i c e   a c t i v a t e :
I get and esteem wisdom. Wisdom exalts me and brings me honor. Proverbs 4:7-8

september 17   kenneth

"And now abide faith, hope, love, these three."
1 Corinthians 13:13, NKJV

Paint Those Pictures!

In today's verse, Paul says hope "abides." To *abide* means to live. So hope is a living thing and you have to guard it and feed it with God's promises so it can grow.

If you'll do that, hope will take the promise of God you want to see happen in your life and show you what your life will look like when it *does* happen. It will show you what you'll look like, healed and successful, with your loved ones serving Jesus, your relationships restored or whatever else you've been hoping for. Hope will paint that picture so clearly inside you and make it so real, you'll begin to ignore what you see on the outside.

As you think about those pictures hope has painted, you'll begin to believe you are what God says you are. You'll begin to realize you're not what the world says you are. You're not what your parents or your friends say you are. You're not even what you think you are. You are what GOD says you are!

Let me give you an example. Say you've prayed for your sister to get free from a drug habit. You can get such a clear picture of what she's going to be like after she has been rescued that she starts looking great to you now—even though she still may be giving you trouble!

You'll actually get to the point where you won't see what a challenge she is being right now because you've seen her the way God sees her. If you'll continue to look at her that way, if you'll refuse to jump up in her face and tell her how sorry she is, one day that sister of yours will look on the outside just like you see her on the inside. She'll be changed! That's what hope does.

So how do you get hope? You go to the same place as you do to get faith: The Bible. You fill your brain and your spirit with God's promises every day. You think about them all the time, wherever you are and whatever you are doing. You listen to recorded messages about faith. In short, you just keep feeding your spirit...and allow the Word to paint those pictures! That's hope at work in you.

backup:
2 Corinthians 3:12-18

download:
Isaiah 19-21; Psalms 36-37

voice activate:
Hope firmly and securely anchors my soul. Hebrews 6:19

"Since we have these promises, dear friends, let us purify ourselves from everything that contaminates body and spirit, perfecting holiness out of reverence for God."
2 Corinthians 7:1

Decontaminate Your Spirit

In today's verse, when it talks about "perfecting holiness," it's simply talking about separating yourself *to* God—and *away from* the world. We do this out of reverence for God, because we respect Him, honor Him and love Him.

It also says we're to cleanse ourselves from everything that contaminates our body and spirit, everything that would prevent us from getting closer to Him.

For example, if you and I believe adultery is wrong, and we have no intention of ever committing adultery, then we should not watch adultery. We should not feed ourselves with adultery that's on television, in a movie or in a book. I like to say it this way, "If you don't want to do it, don't watch it." That applies to everything, not just adultery.

We simply don't have any business contaminating our spirit and mind with the trash the world sells. We're to clean ourselves from *everything* that contaminates our body and spirit, and a lot of things aren't as blatant as adultery. There are subtle ways we can contaminate our spirit.

The greatest sin you and I can commit is to not walk in love. Jesus said, *"A new command I give you: Love one another."* (John 13:34). So when we hate someone or are unforgiving, our spirit is contaminated.

Ken had a vision one time of a water pipe. This pipe was so clogged up, that any liquid in it just dripped out little by little. God showed him that our spirits are the same way. When we're not walking in love, our spirits get so clogged up that God's power can't come through.

We've got to unclog our pipes. We've got to "perfect holiness." We've got to stop contaminating our spirits. Jesus is coming back soon! He's coming for people who have separated themselves *to* Him. He's coming back for you!

b a c k u p :
1 John 2:15-17

d o w n l o a d :
Isaiah 22-23; Psalm 38

v o i c e   a c t i v a t e :
I purify myself from everything that contaminates my body and spirit. I separate myself to God. 2 Corinthians 7:1

269

september 19 *"But we have the mind of Christ."*
1 Corinthians 2:16

kenneth

Change Your Mind

Some people say things like: *"We'll never know the answer to this or that because God's ways and thoughts are higher than ours."*

Yes, the Bible does say His thoughts are higher than ours...but that's not *all* it says. Did you know you can bring the level of your thoughts up, so you're thinking like God thinks? The way it's done is with the Word of God.

In Isaiah 55:11, God says, *"So is my word that goes out from my mouth: It will not return to me empty, but will accomplish what I desire and achieve the purpose for which I sent it."* When you speak God's Word, it does what it says it will do. When you feed it into your mind, it *changes* your mind, to think like God thinks.

"But wait a minute. To think God's supernatural thoughts, you'd have to have a 'supernatural mind,' wouldn't you?"

Yes—and if you're a Christian, you already have one. You have the mind of Christ, the Anointed One (1 Corinthians 2:16). Your mind is under the influence of His power and Anointing.

Just because you've made Jesus your Lord doesn't mean you'll automatically think God's thoughts. You only begin thinking God's thoughts when you begin to fill your mind and heart with His promises.

Romans 12:2 calls that process *"the renewing of your mind"*—and it will transform you. Why does it have such a dramatic effect? Because when you change your mind, you change your choices—and that changes everything.

So learn to stir up the anointing and power of God on the inside of you. Allow it to transform the way you think. Allow it to change your mind!

backup:
Isaiah 55:6-11

download:
Isaiah 24-25; Psalm 39

voice activate:
I have the mind of Christ, the Anointed One. 1 Corinthians 2:16

"We have the same spirit of faith."
2 Corinthians 4:13, NKJV

Nothing Intimidates God

No matter what difficult situation you may be facing today, God can turn it around! The doctors may say you have an incurable disease. The kid at the locker next to yours may be giving you trouble. You may have a friend headed for juvenile detention. Your family's bank account may be empty and the creditors knocking on the door. Your problems may be stacked so high, you feel like you'll never beat them. Don't let Satan fool you. He has never devised a problem that faith in God can't fix! Nothing intimidates God.

Think about that! If you'll dare to believe God's Word, you can have light in the middle of a dark world.

If you want to walk in constant freedom, you must develop a spirit of faith and persevere when Satan is putting pressure on you.

Faith believes God's Word just because God said it—whether what's happening seems to match up with it or not. That means if you want to maintain a spirit of faith in the area of healing, you must start by getting your Bible and finding out what God has said about

healing. Next, you must choose to receive that promise as the truth. Then speak it out! Say, "The Bible says healing belongs to me and I believe it!" Keep putting His promises in your heart day after day until faith rises up within you and your body begins to line up with what God promised.

People with the spirit of faith always receive the good things God has for them. They may go through tests and trials, but they come out winners every time.

I like those odds, don't you? I like to beat Satan *every time*. We can do it if we'll walk continually in the spirit of faith.

Keep your faith stirred up. Dare to believe God. It won't shake Him up! *Nothing* intimidates Him!

b a c k u p:
Exodus 10:16-23

d o w n l o a d:
Isaiah 26-27; Psalm 40

v o i c e a c t i v a t e:
I have the spirit of faith! 2 Corinthians 4:13

kenneth

"And on my servants and on my handmaidens I will pour out in those days of my Spirit; and they shall prophesy: And I will show wonders in heaven above, and signs in the earth beneath."
Acts 2:18-19, KJV

Speak His Word in Prayer

We are on the edge of the greatest move of God this earth has ever seen. Supernatural things are beginning to happen just as the Bible said they would.

Yet many Christians are sitting back, watching these events like spectators at a high school football game. In error, they seem to think God will just hit the earth with miracles and save the day.

Always remember that supernatural things will only happen the way Acts 2 reveals it. If you'll read today's verse, taking out the punctuation that was put in by the translators, you'll see something amazing. You'll see that God is saying when His servants and handmaidens prophesy, then in response, He will work miracles.

That means if this great move of God is to come in all its power, we must start speaking His Word in prayer!

Some years ago, when studying the Bible, I saw over and over how the prayers of God's people paved the way for what God did on earth. Yet I thought God did the most important things on His own.

So one day, I said, "Lord, You brought Jesus into the earth without man doing anything, didn't You?"

No, I didn't, He answered.

"You mean, there were people who prayed for the birth of Jesus?"

Yes, He said. Then He told me about Simeon in Luke 2. I read how Simeon was led by the Holy Spirit to the Temple the day Joseph and Mary dedicated Jesus. He had prayed continually, asking God to send the Redeemer. Then, when Simeon saw Jesus, he immediately recognized Who He was and that He was bringing salvation to the world (verse 32).

We must get on our knees and start praying for this great move of God, coming in full power. We must start praying and speaking out God's Word so He can do miracles. We must start prophesying in prayer!

backup:
Luke 2:25-35

download:
Isaiah 28-29; Psalm 41

voice activate:
I am faithful in prayer. Romans 12:12

"So shall your storage places be filled with plenty."
Proverbs 3:10, AMP

Claim What's Yours

Jesus told us in Matthew 6:19-21 that we're to store up treasure in heaven and not on earth. I call this our heavenly account—and we can deposit and withdraw from this account. How? Well, we make deposits by giving to God's work.

The foundation for that giving is the tithe. When you give the first tenth of your income to the Lord, you open the door for God to come into your finances and move supernaturally. Proverbs 3:9-10 says that when you honor the Lord with your tithe, your storage places will be filled with plenty.

In addition to your tithe, you can also deposit to your heavenly account by giving offerings into what He's doing in the earth. You have to put your seed (money) into good ground if you want a return. (See Mark 4.)

If you are like me, you're already eager to get to the bottom line here. You're saying, "Okay, I know that I have an account. I know where it is, and I know how to make deposits, but when can I get the money? When can I make a withdrawal?"

The answer is in Mark 10:29-30. Jesus was answering the disciples who had asked Him what they were going to get in return for their giving.

He told them they would receive a hundred times their return from their heavenly account—here and now! Although our deposits will bring us rewards for eternity, we don't have to wait until we die and go to heaven to draw on those resources. We can make withdrawals on our heavenly account here and now!

Those withdrawals are made with faith. You do that by believing in faith that what God has already said about financial blessings belong to you. Then you speak those promises out until they become reality in your life (Mark 11:22-24).

Reach out with the hand of faith and claim what's yours!

gloria

⊕ b a c k u p :
Mark 4

⊕ d o w n l o a d :
Isaiah 30-31; Psalm 42

⊕ v o i c e a c t i v a t e :
I honor the Lord with my money and with the first fruits of all my income. My storage places are filled with plenty. Proverbs 3:9-10, AMP

september 23

"So, come out from among (unbelievers), and separate (sever) yourselves from them, says the Lord, and touch not [any] unclean thing; then I will receive you kindly and treat you with favor."
2 Corinthians 6:17, AMP

Favor Everywhere

gloria

I've been following God for a long time, and over the years I have grown to become more dedicated than ever before. Through this, I've learned a valuable truth about God's favor: However much you give of yourself to God, that's how much favor you'll receive in return.

When you do what God says, favor is the result. When you do what He says, things work together for you. The Bible says for those who love God, all things work together for their good (Romans 8:28). Well, who loves God? Jesus Himself taught that those who love God keep His Word and obey it (John 14:23).

The Bible teaches us to give God glory in our body and spirit. Whatever we do, we're to do it to His glory (1 Corinthians 10:31).

Well, you're not going to be sinning and giving Him glory. You give Him glory by walking in love. By giving. By being kind and good. By ministering to others.

We're to worship God...because He's God! We're to serve and obey Him. When we treat Him as God and obey Him and

serve Him and do whatever He tells us to do in our lives, favor comes to us. *Supernatural* favor and blessings can't help but come to us.

So honor Him. Obey Him. Walk with Him. Expect favor from God, and soon you'll have favor wherever you go!

backup:
Psalm 5:11-12

download:
Isaiah 32,33; Psalm 43; Genesis 29-30; Matthew 16

voice activate:
**I am received of the Lord. He shows me kindness and treats me with favor.
2 Corinthians 6:17, AMP**

"Yea, and all that will live godly in Christ Jesus shall suffer persecution."
2 Timothy 3:12, KJV

Shine On!

If you do anything that makes a mark for God in this world, persecution will come. It goes with the territory. Today's verse says so.

Why does living a godly life cause so much trouble? First John 5:19 tells us it's because *"the whole world is under the control of the evil one."* We're living in a world that is ruled by darkness. The brighter our light becomes, the more offensive we are to that darkness.

The reverse is also true. As long as we aren't doing much for God, we aren't bothered much. If we look like the world, talk like the world and act like the world—worldly people will probably think we're all right.

So you might as well know right now, if you're sold out to God, the world isn't going to like you much...and that's an understatement. Jesus put it this way:

"If the world hates you, keep in mind that it hated me first. If you belonged to the world, it would love you as its own. As it is, you do not belong to the world, but I have chosen you out of the world. That is why the world hates you" (John 15:18-19).

You may be thinking, *Well, I'm sure that's true, but it's also not much fun to think about. Why do we have to talk about it?*

We need to prepare ourselves so that when persecution comes, it doesn't slow us down or stop us. That's what persecution is designed to do. It's designed to discourage us and keep us from completing God's plan for our lives.

If we learn how to handle it in advance, it won't even slow us down.

So don't be afraid of the darkness. It may persecute you, but it can't over-come you. Your family may even perse-cute you, but they can't overcome you either. *"For everyone born of God over-comes the world. This is the victory that has overcome the world, even our faith"* (1 John 5:4).

Just turn up your light a little brighter...and shine on!

gloria

b a c k u p :
Matthew 10:16-26

d o w n l o a d :
Isaiah 34-36; Psalms 44-45

v o i c e a c t i v a t e :
Even though I suffer persecution, I con-tinue to live a godly life. 2 Timothy 3:12

"The word of the Lord spread widely and grew in power."
Acts 19:20

kenneth

It Will Work for You

When you speak God's Words, even though you are the one speaking them, they have the same power as if Jesus Himself were speaking them.

"Kenneth, how can that be? I'm not Jesus!"

No, you're not, but when you speak and act in faith on what God promised, His Words always hold His power, just like they did for Jesus.

Peter and John proved that the day they walked up to the lame man, as recorded in Acts 3. When they believed and acted upon what they knew, the Holy Spirit went into action for them just as He had for Jesus—and a miracle happened. When they opened their mouths and said, *"In the name of Jesus Christ of Nazareth, walk,"* that lame man *"jumped to his feet and began to walk. Then he went with them into the temple courts, walking and jumping, and praising God"* (Acts 3:6-8).

They didn't just stop there either. Peter and John and the rest of the disciples moved with what they knew and turned the whole known world upside down! (Acts 17:6).

Since the Word never changes, you can be confident that it will work for you just as surely as it worked for Peter and John. It will work for you as surely as it worked for Jesus. It will work for you as powerfully as when God Himself said, *"Let there be light!"* (Genesis 1:3).

What are you waiting for? You have God's power—His Word—at your fingertips. The more you fill your heart with that Word, the more you act on it and speak it out in faith, the more freely His power can move through you. So stop stalling! Get moving! Grab your Bible, take your stand on it and let's go! God's Word works!

backup:
Acts 17:1-10

download:
Isaiah 37-38; Psalm 46

voice activate:
God's Word spreads widely and grows in power in me. Acts 19:20

"For He has set a day when he will judge the world with justice by the man he has appointed. He has given proof of this to all men by raising him from the dead."
Acts 17:31

A Divine Appointment

"For He has set a day."

God has a timetable set in stone for certain events. Now I know while it's easy to believe that about events that have already occurred, we sometimes aren't too sure about the ones still in the future.

For example, God had a certain time set for the Israelites to come out of Egypt. He set that date in Genesis 15:13 when He told Abraham, *"Know for certain that your descendants will be strangers in a country not their own, and they will be enslaved and mistreated four hundred years."*

Sure enough, after the Israelites went to Egypt, they were enslaved and mistreated. Then, 400 years to the day after Egypt enslaved Israel, God brought the Israelites out just as He promised (Exodus 12:40-41). He wasn't even a day late!

What's more, He saw to it that the Israelites were blessed, equipped and ready to go on that day.

"Well, that's easy to believe, Gloria. It's right there in the Bible."

Yes, it's easy to believe an event that's passed, but what about one that is still to come—like the return of Jesus?

Just as surely as God set an appointment with the Israelites, He has set an appointment with us. Today's verse says, *"For he has set a day."*

The end of things as we know them is drawing near. God has told us through His written Word and by His Spirit that Jesus is coming back for us. It's not just some fairy tale. It will really happen.

Now, we shouldn't fear that day or disbelieve it because we can't understand it. We should be excited about it. God's plans are always good. They always turn out right. This is a plan He set in stone years ago. It's a perfect plan. It's a divine appointment!

backup:
Isaiah 46:9-11

download:
Isaiah 39-40; Psalm 47

voice activate:
I have faith in God that it will happen just as He told me. Acts 27:25

gloria

September 21

Kenneth

"For you know that we dealt with each of you as a father deals with his own children, encouraging, comforting and urging you to live lives worthy of God, who calls you into his kingdom and glory."
1 Thessalonians 2:11-12

Prepare for the Unusual

My friend, we are about to hit a breakthrough that many generations have longed to see! It's not far off either. More and more, prophecies are coming to pass. The more God moves, the more unusual things we'll see.

One of these days, you may be just talking to somebody, asking them how things went at church last Sunday, and they may say, "Oh, it was great! God's glory showed up and 10 crippled people were healed, 30 deaf people had their ears opened, seven cases of cancer were obliterated and Mister Bigmouth and Miss Strife were killed."

I can just hear you thinking, *Whoa! Now hold on a minute, Kenneth. God's glory is a good thing. It doesn't kill people.*

It did in the New Testament Church. Acts 5 tells the story of Ananias and his wife, Sapphira. They lied to the Holy Spirit and withheld part of what they were to give, and they died!

Please understand, I'm not trying to dampen your enthusiasm about this coming move of God. I just want you to realize that willful sin and an unrepentant heart are dangerous things.

A Christian might be able to get away with hanging on to sin when the rest of the congregation is as cold as he is. But when the fire of God begins to burn, he'll have to do one of two things: He'll either have to let go of that sin by repenting, or he'll have to face the consequences.

I realize that's a hard truth, but we need to keep ourselves submitted to God. If we'll do that, we can have a wonderful time like the Church in Acts 5 did.

So prepare yourself. Get ready for the glory. Repent of any sin and get excited when the unusual happens all around you!

backup:
Acts 5:1-11

download:
Isaiah 41-42; Psalm 48

voice activate:
I live my life worthy of God, who calls me into His kingdom and glory.
1 Thessalonians 2:12

"No one will be able to stand up against you all the days of your life. As I was with Moses, so I will be with you; I will never leave you nor forsake you."
Joshua 1:5

What It Takes to Succeed

May I ask you a very direct question? How much do you want to succeed in life?

I've been amazed over the years at the people who have come across God's formula for success only to leave it lying on the table while they stay sick, broke and defeated.

Such people initially think success is easy for those who are gifted with great abilities. When they run into the truth, however, it stops them cold. Because the reality is this: *Real, supernatural success is no picnic for anyone. It takes courage. It takes faith. It has nothing to do with your talents or abilities.*

If Joshua were around today, he could tell you just how true that is. When God called him to lead Israel after Moses' death, he faced an overwhelming task. As Moses' successor, Joshua had some big shoes to fill. Several million people were under his command, and he knew if they didn't stay in line with God, His blessing would not be on them. Without God's blessing, they would never be able to take the Promised Land.

Joshua had to succeed.

"But Gloria, you don't know *me!* I've tried and failed with every formula in the book. I just don't have what it takes to succeed."

If that's what you're thinking, you haven't tried the formula in God's Book. Read again what He said in today's verse. God said the same thing to Moses in Exodus 3:12, *"I will be with you."* In other words, "It doesn't matter who you are, Moses. It matters Who I am. For I am with you!"

That's the great thing about God's success formula. It's not based on our abilities, it's based on His abilities. We may be inadequate in a dozen different ways, but the One Who is with us is more than enough.

backup:
Exodus 3:11-14

download:
Isaiah 43-44; Psalm 49

voice activate:
God is with me. He will never leave me nor forsake me. Joshua 1:5

september 29

kenneth

"For I know that through your prayers and the help given by the Spirit of Jesus Christ, what has happened to me will turn out for my deliverance. I eagerly expect and hope that I will in no way be ashamed."
Philippians 1:19-20

Don't Give Up Hope!

When you have hope, you have a rock-solid expectation that what God has promised will happen in your life. In today's verses, Paul talks about this kind of expectation. He uses two different words from the Greek language, each of which can be translated "hope." One of them means "the happy anticipation of good." The other can be defined as "eager longing, strained expectancy, watching with an outstretched head, an abstraction from anything else that might engage the attention." So, for example, Hebrews 11:1 (KJV) says, *"Now faith is the substance of things hoped [intensely expected] for."*

When you're locked in on God's promises, you can't be distracted from them. Divine hope will come alive in you. I know what that's like. There have been times in my life when I was focused on something God had called me to do, and I was so tuned in to what He said about it, I couldn't think about anything else.

People would try to have a conversation with me and I'd always end up talking about my hope. It would come up so big inside me that, at those times, I was bigger on the inside than I was on the outside. It was, on the inside of me, as though everything I was believing for had already happened.

When your hope gets that strong, it doesn't matter what kind of unbelief, opposition or situation Satan tries to throw your way. You're so one-track-minded, you can't be drawn off course.

So whatever you're believing God for, get your expectancy up for it. Long for it. Stretch your neck out and refuse to be distracted by all the things that would get you off course and tell you it won't happen. Keep God's promise before your eyes. That will keep your hope up, and you will see your desire happen!

backup:
Psalm 16; Proverbs 13:12

download:
Isaiah 45-46; Psalm 50

voice activate:
I eagerly expect and hope that I will in no way be ashamed. Philippians 1:20

"No one engaged in warfare entangles himself with the affairs of this life, that he may please him who enlisted him as a soldier."
2 Timothy 2:4, NKJV

God's Priority

You and I have been called to live true life in Jesus, not to be tied down to the way the world works. All too often we allow ourselves to become tangled up in the temporary affairs of this world instead. We allow those entanglements to drag us into defeat.

Don't let that happen to you. Simplify your life. If you don't have time for God, make time. Don't let your activities, your family or anything else keep you from going on with God.

One thing I can promise you: Every part of your life will be better if you take time to listen to God. There is nothing you can do that is better than hearing from heaven.

Before I consider taking on any new activity, I always ask myself, *Can I afford this?* Not can I afford it financially, but can I afford it spiritually? Can I give time to this activity and still keep my priority time with God? If not, I can't afford it.

There's only one thing you absolutely can't afford to do without—and that's your time spent in prayer and in the Bible. It is your very life. It is where your victory lies. You may forget that, but Satan never does. He'll constantly be sending time-stealers your way. So be alert and don't get caught up in them.

Remember: Ask yourself, "Can I afford this?" Then simplify your life. Make the time you spend with God your first priority every day.

b a c k u p :
2 Timothy 3:14-17

d o w n l o a d :
Isaiah 47-48; Psalm 51

v o i c e a c t i v a t e :
I do not entangle myself with the affairs of this life so that I may please the Lord Jesus. 2 Timothy 2:4, NKJV

"Live such good lives among the pagans that, though they accuse you of doing wrong, they may see your good deeds and glorify God on the day he visits us."
1 Peter 2:12

october 1

kenneth

To Stand or Not To Stand

One time when I was shopping in a convenience store, a preacher came in to purchase some shotgun shells. He tried to talk the clerk into giving him a discount on his shells because he was a minister. It was embarrassing.

It almost made me ashamed for the clerk to know I was a preacher. The clerk didn't have any authority to give the minister a discount even if he had wanted to. I wonder if that preacher has any idea how much damage his obsession with a petty discount might have caused.

Sometimes I get really embarrassed at what dishonorable Christians try to do. It's situations like these and others that often cause the world to look at Christians with a raised eyebrow. They've seen too much dishonor. You can help change that. You can guard the way you live and talk. You can be honorable.

My parents were honorable people. I grew up seeing example after example of what it was to live honorably. That taught me valuable lessons...like the fact that real honor may be hard to find, but it's not hard to recognize. Honor stands out in a crowd.

It takes a decision to be honorable. You must choose between following God's way of doing things or following the world's deceptive ways. If you are honorable, you will stand. If you are dishonorable, you will fall—and bring even more dishonor to the Church. If you don't know how to live honorably, then start learning.

Begin by reading the Bible. As you get into His Word and allow it to get on the inside of you, you'll find yourself *wanting* to walk honorably. You'll feel convicted about even the smallest things...and that's good because you'll know you're tuned in to God. You will become honorable in everything. You'll be honest about the smallest details. You won't exaggerate or walk the fence. Your word will become as good as God's!

backup:
1 Peter 2:1-12

download:
Isaiah 49-51; Psalms 52-53

voice activate:
I will live such a good life that others will see my good deeds and glorify God.
1 Peter 2:12

"Do not let this Book of the Law depart from your mouth."
Joshua 1:8

Change What You're Hearing

Have you ever been frustrated with yourself...because of what you hear coming out of your mouth? Jesus said that out of the overflow of your heart, your mouth speaks (Luke 6:45). If you're focusing most of your attention on watching television, going to the movies, thinking about worldly things, worrying about your schoolwork and family—then that's what you're going to talk about.

What you need to do is refocus your attention. Turn your attention toward God's Word and keep it there.

In everyday terms, Joshua 1:8 says, "Talk the Word."

When I say talk the Word, I don't mean just every now and then when you're feeling spiritual. I mean continually. In Deuteronomy 6:7, God said you should talk His Word, *"when you sit at home and when you walk along the road, when you lie down and when you get up."*

That's pretty much all the time, isn't it? At home, at school, at the mall—wherever you are, keep God's promises in your mouth.

Romans 10:17 (NKJV), tells us that *"faith comes by hearing, and hearing by the word of God."* So when you're continually talking about what God says, what He'll do, and what His promises are, you're going to be growing in faith because you're hearing the Word from yourself all the time.

Isn't that exciting? You can change what you're hearing. Today, start overflowing your heart with God's Word. Listen as your mouth gets in line with what God says about you and your circumstances!

gloria

b a c k u p:
Deuteronomy 6:1-9

d o w n l o a d:
Isaiah 52-53; Psalm 54

v o i c e a c t i v a t e:
I talk the Word wherever I go and in whatever I do. Deuteronomy 6:7

"If you hold to my teaching, you are really my disciples. Then you will know the truth, and the truth will (make) you free."
John 8:31-32

october 3

kenneth

Real Freedom

One afternoon, as I was studying today's scripture, the Lord spoke something to me that nearly knocked me out of my chair. He said, *Jesus was not free because He didn't sin. He didn't sin because He was free.*

Think about that. As Christians, we've been going at things backward. We've thought, *If I could just kick this smoking habit, if I could just get rid of this disease, if I could just get some money, then I'd be free.*

Instead, we need to go after the freedom itself. Once we grab hold of real freedom, those vices will just fall powerless at our feet.

You may say, "Yeah, but people have prayed for me to get me that freedom, and I still don't have it."

Listen, Jesus didn't say that others praying for you would set you free. He said you'd know *the truth, and the truth would make you free!*

I know it's thrilling to have someone pray for you and then feel God's power go through your body. However, it's even more exciting to get your healing by standing in faith in God's Word.

You know you're growing up in Jesus when trouble comes and instead of running to your youth pastor, you pray on your own, open your Bible and find the answer. You begin to read and every promise you find, you write down.

Then, every night before you go to bed, you read those scriptures again— and you believe them no matter how your body feels. Satan may say he'll kill you in the morning, but instead of getting fearful, you just reply, "Shut up, Satan. I don't belong to you and I never will. God says I'm healed and that's the end of it!"

The next morning, you get your Bible and read those scriptures again. Suddenly you catch yourself and think, *Whoa! I got so excited about these verses, I've forgotten to hurt for the last 30 minutes!*

That kind of victory is the best kind there is.

backup:
Luke 8:11-15

download:
Isaiah 54-55; Psalm 55

voice activate:
I know the truth, and the truth makes me free! John 8:31-32

"Every good and perfect gift is from above, coming down from the Father of the heavenly lights, who does not change like shifting shadows."
James 1:17

God Is a Good God

The simple message that *God is a good God* bothers some people. They're uncomfortable hearing that God wants His people healed and living well.

Today, many people are afraid to expect a lot from God, but I want you to know that God wants us to live like royalty. That's what the Bible teaches.

God's plan to bless His people can be seen from Genesis to Revelation. Man has never had to shout up at heaven and say, "Hey God, I want to be blessed so let's make a deal. I'll do these certain things—and You help me in return. Okay?"

No, that's a scene you'll never see in the Bible because God beat man to the punch. Blessings were His idea! That's because *God is good!*

God created the earth and every good thing in it as a gift for man, and when it was finished, *"the Lord God had planted a garden in the east, in Eden; and there he put the man he had formed."* (Genesis 2:8).

I want you to know, man had it made in the Garden. Anything he needed or wanted, he had. He had a close relationship with God Himself. Everything was perfect! If you want to see how blessed God wants us to be, just look at the Garden of Eden. That was His desire for us. That's how He wanted us to live. All man had to do to remain in that environment was believe and obey God.

Well, God never changes. He still operates just like He did in the Garden of Eden. He wants us to live well, all the time. All we have to do is believe and obey Him. Don't listen to Satan like Adam and Eve did. Tell him to get out of your garden! Then live in the good things your good God has for you!

b a c k u p :
Genesis 2:7-25

d o w n l o a d :
Isaiah 56-57; Psalm 56

v o i c e   a c t i v a t e :
Now as always, every good and perfect gift to me is from God, Who never changes. James 1:17

"Be kind and compassionate to one another, forgiving each other, just as in Christ God forgave you."
Ephesians 4:32

october 5

kenneth

Drive Out Unforgiveness

Forgiveness. Many people talk about it. Many fail to actually do it. They try, but trying doesn't get the job done. You can come around and talk to those who try years later, and you'll find they're still carrying around hurts and resentments. They're still saying, "Well, I'm trying to forgive that person, but what they did to me was so bad, I just haven't been able to do it."

That's why the Bible doesn't say anything about "trying" to forgive. It simply commands us to forgive one another *"just as in Christ God forgave you."* Since God has never told us to do anything without giving us the ability to do it, we can be sure He has given every Christian the power to forgive in any and every situation.

You may think it is hard to forgive. It's not. Nothing you do by the power of God is hard. You can make it hard by messing around trying to do it all by yourself. If you'll put your faith in God's promises to you, the struggle will disappear.

If you'll trust God's Word, the Word will fight for you. You won't have to wrestle your problems to the ground and solve them on your own. All you'll have to do is open your Bible and start speaking out God's promises about the situation. Using your faith, believe those promises and they will conquer any problem—including unforgiveness.

God's Word will fight unforgiveness for you. If you'll find out what God has to say—and believe it—it will drive unforgiveness completely out of your life.

backup:
Colossians 3:12-17

download:
Isaiah 58-59; Psalm 57

voice activate:
I am kind and compassionate to others, forgiving others, just as in Christ God forgave me. Ephesians 4:32

"It is for freedom that Christ has set us free. Stand firm, then, and do not let yourselves be burdened again by a yoke of slavery. Mark my words! I, Paul, tell you that if you let yourselves be circumcised, Christ will be of no value to you at all. Again I declare to every man who lets himself be circumcised that he is obligated to obey the whole law. You who are trying to be justified by law have been alienated from Christ; you have fallen away from grace."
Galatians 5:1-4

God Favors You

Did you know it's possible to be a Christian and live without the grace offered by the Holy Spirit? It's true! Read the book of Galatians and you'll see. In today's verses, when Paul said the Galatians had fallen from grace, he didn't mean they had lost their right to go to heaven. He meant they had stopped depending on the Holy Spirit.

Remember—grace is God's favor. They were going back to relying on their traditions, and in doing so, they pulled away from allowing the Holy Spirit to show them God's favor, which they needed every day.

From the day we made Jesus our Lord, the Holy Spirit has been offering God's favor to us in everything we do. When we don't trust and depend on the Holy Spirit, we keep Him from showing it to us.

How can you demonstrate your trust in Him? Simply by being obedient. Do what you know the Bible says to do. The Holy Spirit is the author of the Bible, so you can be sure when you're obeying it, you're in line with the Spirit.

We need to learn to hear the Holy Spirit talking to us. By spending time with God in prayer and reading the Bible, we develop our spiritual hearing and our sensitivity to the Spirit.

Once you know those things, step out and obey His voice. Don't be afraid of making a mistake. He will always lead you the right way.

By following the Holy Spirit day by day in the big things and the small, you won't step out from under God's favor. You'll keep the door open to hearing His voice and knowing what He wants you to do. All that's left is to follow through!

b a c k u p :
1 Corinthians 2:10-16

d o w n l o a d :
Isaiah 60-61; Psalm 58

v o i c e   a c t i v a t e :
I stand firm in God's favor and freedom.
Galatians 5:1-4

gloria

"He could not do any miracles there, except lay his hands on a few sick people and heal them. And he was amazed at their lack of faith."
Mark 6:5-6

october 7

kenneth

He Answers Faith

Would it be possible for someone to starve right in the middle of your school lunchroom? Certainly it would. It would be absurd and unnecessary, but it could happen. A person could be wasting away of hunger, standing at the front of the pizza line, with students offering him milkshakes left and right. But if he refused to receive anything, he would eventually be as dead as can be.

I can just hear you, "That's ridiculous! It would never happen!" Yes, you're probably right. However, in the spiritual realm, things like that happen every day.

Take healing for example. God has already provided healing for all of us. As far as He's concerned, it's done. Yet countless Christians are sick and dying. God's provision isn't helping them because they haven't received it.

"But Kenneth, it's tough to reach out and receive invisible blessings from a God I can't see. If Jesus were here on the earth, I'd have it made."

Would you? Jesus didn't walk around meeting the needs of everyone He met. In a crowd, you might see Him stop and respond to a single individual. What caused Him to single out one person when we know God loves everyone the same (Acts 10:34)? *Faith.*

Jesus did not operate apart from a person's faith. His ministry was not directed by the crowds, nor by His own personal preferences, nor by how much someone needed something. It was directed by the cry of faith.

In fact, the Bible records a couple of times when Jesus said, *"Your faith has made you well"*—not "MY faith has made you well" (Luke 17:19; Mark 10:52). Why did He say that? Because for His power to be given to someone, they had to receive it using *their* faith.

Faith and receiving are intimately connected. If you are starving for something you need, remember: Everything you need has been given to you if you've made Jesus your Lord. All you have to do is believe you receive it. God answers the cry of *faith!*

backup:
Mark 5:25-34

download:
Isaiah 62-63; Psalm 59

voice activate:
God doesn't show favoritism, so I know I have what I need to receive from Him. I have faith! Acts 10:34

"Shun youthful lusts and flee from them, and aim at and pursue righteousness...faith, love, [and] peace...in fellowship with all...who call upon the Lord out of a pure heart."
2 Timothy 2:22, AMP

Spend Time With the Faithful

Living for God was never meant to be done alone. Many people pull away from spending time with other Christians, because they become busy...they're involved in too many activities, they move to a new town, life becomes stressful or whatever.

Being isolated will only lead you down the road to defeat.

If you want to live in victory, you need to spend time with people who know God. Don't try to spend time with the world and live like a winner. It won't work.

We get strength from one another. We also get weaknesses from one another. If you want to grow strong, find someone who is stronger in faith than you are and spend time with them. They'll bring you up.

On the other hand, if you spend time with people who don't live for God, they'll bring you down.

Listen to me. Your life depends on whom you spend time with and where

you go to church. Hang out with people who are strong and walk in power, who preach God's Word and get results when they pray.

You may have to take the initiative. You may be the one to introduce yourself. You may need to go shake hands with the youth pastor...not sit back and wait to see if he notices you. Invite people over for games. Go to the prayer meeting. Go to the Bible study. Go to church!

Spend time with the faithful. If you do, it will help you be the one who ends up living in victory every day.

gloria

b a c k u p :
Hebrews 10:22-25

d o w n l o a d :
Isaiah 64-66; Psalms 60-61

v o i c e   a c t i v a t e :
**I choose to spend time with those who call upon the Lord out of a pure heart.
2 Timothy 2:22**

"And we, who with unveiled faces all reflect the Lord's glory, are being transformed into his likeness with ever-increasing glory, which comes from the Lord, who is the Spirit."
2 Corinthians 3:18

October 9

kenneth

Like a Rocket Headed Home

We're headed for home like a rocket locked on target. Today's verse says as we reflect God's glory, we are being *"transformed into his likeness with ever-increasing glory, which comes from the Lord, who is the Spirit."*

Notice the Word says we're changed as we reflect His glory? How do we do that? By paying attention to God's Word! When you read the Bible, you're changed more and more to be like Him. That's why the Apostle Paul said to be, *"not moved from the hope held out in the gospel.... I have become its servant by the commission God gave me to present to you the word of God in its fullness— the mystery that has been kept hidden for ages and generations, but is now disclosed to the saints. To them God has chosen to make known among the Gentiles the glorious riches of this mystery, which is Christ in you, the hope of glory"* (Colossians 1:23, 25-27).

You have the "hope of glory" inside you. That is, you have an "absolute expectancy" of the glory inside you.

There's something on the inside of you that cries for the glory of God!

It's time for us, as Christians, to find out more about the glory. It's time to get into the Bible, find out what God has already said and then stand on that Word. Say, "That's mine! In Jesus' Name, I fully expect to see God's glory in my life!"

It is your destiny to know the glory of God. Don't let Satan steal it from you. Get into the Bible. Study it out. Take a stand. You'll be like a rocket headed home!

backup:
Isaiah 60:1-3

download:
Jeremiah 1-2; Psalm 62

voice activate:
The hope of glory is inside me!
Colossians 1:27

> "Love...takes no account of the evil done to it—pays no attention to a suffered wrong."
> **1 Corinthians 13:5, AMP**

Living in Love

Did you know that walking in love is good for your health? That's right! I saw a documentary that focused on stress. It explained that researchers had discovered there are two kinds of stress.

The first is the kind you experience when you're working hard to achieve something, pressing yourself to reach a goal. That kind of stress, they said, is natural and good. It doesn't hurt you. The second kind of stress, however, has such a negative effect that it's physically dangerous.

Do you know what they said causes that kind of stress? Hostility. Or, we could say, *not* walking in love.

Now when you think of hostility, you may think of getting angry about "big" things, but according to this documentary, it's the little things that cause the real trouble. When a bully is messing with you, for example. Or when the cafeteria lady puts mustard on your hamburger, especially after you've asked her not to.

In short, what researchers have discovered is what God has been telling us all along. We need to *live* in love.

Just think of all the stress we could avoid if we were quick to forgive. If we truly paid no attention when someone wrongs us. We'd be so healthy! Our bodies weren't made to live with hostility flowing through them. They were designed to live according to love.

So why don't we all live lives of love? Very often, it's because we're still wrapped up in old, worldly habits. We continue to react from the outside instead of from the inside where God (Who is love) lives.

So shake off that stress. Learn to walk in love. Change your way of thinking to agree with God's way of thinking. Choose to walk in forgiveness. Pretty soon you'll be feeling like the new person you are...a person living in love!

gloria

b a c k u p :
Luke 17:1-4

d o w n l o a d :
Jeremiah 3-4; Psalm 63

v o i c e   a c t i v a t e :
I live in love. I take no account of evil done to me. I pay no attention to a suffered wrong. 1 Corinthians 13:5

"We have this hope as an anchor for the soul, firm and secure."
Hebrews 6:19

October 11

kenneth

It's in the Genes

If you focus your hope on a particular problem in your life, it will grow up and become greater. Greater than what? Greater than the problem!

Hope is a very powerful force. It is on the inside of you if you are a Christian. Do you understand that? The moment you received Jesus Christ as your Lord, the Holy Spirit came to live inside you. Your spirit was re-created in His likeness. God literally became the Father of your spirit. Just as your body took on the same genes and traits of your natural mother and father when you were born, your spirit took on the spiritual "genes," so to speak, of your heavenly Father when you were re-created.

Your spirit took on His hope, His faith, His love—and all the other spiritual forces that are part of His character. All of them together are called *life*. The Greek word for it is *zoe*. It's a word that is beyond definition. So the best way I can explain *zoe* is by saying it's the part of God that makes Him *God*. He put *zoe* in your spirit when you made Jesus the Lord of your life.

This isn't a human kind of hope. It's God's kind. It's one of the supernatural forces He used to create the universe, and He put it inside you. Before you can use it, you have to be absolutely certain that you have it.

"But, Kenneth, you don't understand. My circumstances have been bad for so long, I don't have any hope anymore!"

Yes, you do! Hebrews 6:19 says so. You may feel totally hopeless right now, but according to the Bible, you have hope. *God Himself* is your hope. So the first thing you need to do is see that. Say, "Yes! I have hope!" You have to agree with God and His Word.

Hope. You have it living within you right now. Realize that. Use it. Put it to work with God's promises to you and get ready to knock that problem out!

b a c k u p :
1 Peter 3:15-22

d o w n l o a d :
Jeremiah 5-6; Psalm 64

v o i c e   a c t i v a t e :
I have God's kind of hope inside me. It's an anchor for my soul, firm and secure. Hebrews 6:19

"'Therefore come out from them and be separate,' says the Lord. 'Touch no unclean thing, and I will receive you.'"
2 Corinthians 6:17

Separate Yourself!

God has called you to be separate. He wants you to be set apart from your old ways of living. For those who are set apart are called saints.

"Oh, no, not me Gloria. I'm not a saint."

You are if you're a Christian. First Corinthians 1:2 (KJV) says, *"Unto the church of God which is at Corinth, to them that are sanctified in Christ Jesus, called to be saints...."*

In other words, "to them that are made holy, set apart or separated unto God in Christ Jesus, called saints." So you're a saint!

"Well, what does it mean to be set apart for His use?"

It means that whatever He wants you to do, that's what you do. If He asks you to go to your locker partner and tell them about Jesus, or if He asks you to go on summer missions, or become a teacher or a nurse, then you do it!

Why is that? Because you've been *redeemed.*

When you put something in a pawn-shop, you can later go back and redeem it. You buy it back. In the same way, as a Christian, you've been bought back from darkness. You are no longer your own.

You have been paid for by the precious blood of Jesus (1 Corinthians 6:19-20). You now belong to God. If you intend to let God be God in your life, then you will do whatever He asks.

If He calls you to a particular occupation, then that's what you should do. That's obedience. That's being separated unto God. It's not just being separated in your job, but in your lifestyle, in your conduct.

He reveals His will to us "as we go." He may say one day, *This thing is holding you back. Make a change.* Maybe it's not a sin. Maybe it is. What matters is that you obey and get rid of it. That's separating yourself.

So, whatever it is that He's been speaking to you about, make that change. Go where He's saying to go. Do what He's been saying to do. Separate yourself!

backup:
Ephesians 5:1-17

download:
Jeremiah 7-8; Psalm 65

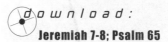
voice activate:
**I am a saint! I am set apart from the world and my old ways of living.
1 Corinthians 1:2, 2 Corinthians 6:17**

"But unto every one of us is given grace according to the measure of the gift of Christ [the Anointed One and His Anointing]."
Ephesians 4:7, KJV

october 13

kenneth

Live in the Anointing

According to today's verse, we're headed toward a time when we'll be walking in God's anointing—His power— to its fullest degree! I want to see that, don't you? I want to see all of us flowing in the anointing so powerfully that the whole earth is filled with God's glory.

I believe with all my heart our generation will see that.

Before we do though, we must put aside the things that block that anointing. We must rid ourselves of old ways of thinking that cause us to believe it's absurd that ordinary Christians like us can operate in the Anointing of Almighty God.

I asked the Lord once what was the greatest problem in the Church. Here's what He told me: *It's your dogged determination to correct one another.*

It's time for us to change that. We must stop strife, stop the criticism and stop getting offended at one another—and we must do it now because these are the end times. God's power needs to flow greater than we've ever dreamed before or seen possible.

We need His anointing in our families, in our schools, in our ministries and in our relationships. It's the anointing that will change things.

So let's rise up together and show the world that what was once true in Jesus' own life and ministry is now true in our lives. Let's dare to believe the Bible and say, "Because I belong to Jesus, the Holy Spirit is upon me and He has anointed me!"

Let's preach—and live—in the Anointed One and His Anointing.

backup:
Ephesians 4:7,11-13

download:
Jeremiah 9-10; Psalm 66

voice activate:
Because I belong to Jesus, the Holy Spirit is upon me and He has anointed me! Luke 4:18

"But solid food is for the mature, who by constant use have trained themselves to distinguish good from evil."
Hebrews 5:14

Continue in the Word

Reading, studying and listening to the Bible is vital to the Christian life. Spending time with God through His Word opens the door to your heart so His character can flow out of you (Galatians 5:22-23).

When you think about it, you can easily understand why. The Word is spiritual food. The more of it you put in your heart, the stronger your spirit becomes. If you'll continue to feed on the Word, eventually your spirit will be so strong that it can overcome your old sinful nature every time (Hebrews 5:14).

The opposite is also true. If you spend your time feeding on teen dramas, romance novels and locker room talk, your old nature will grow stronger and your spirit will weaken. Although you'll still have the inner desire to be loving and kind, your old nature will bully you into acting out of character!

If you're especially wanting to strengthen your spirit with one particular aspect of God's character, the best thing you can do is feed on what the Word has to say about that particular attribute. If you've been running short of joy lately, for example, make it a point each day to read and think about what the Bible has to say about joy. Build yourself up in that area.

Jesus said, *"If you hold to my teaching, you are really my disciples. Then you will know the truth, and the truth will make you free."* (John 8:31-32). Getting into the Bible will help His character flow out of you and set you free from bondage. *"So I say, live by the Spirit, and you will not gratify the desires of the sinful nature"* (Galatians 5:16).

backup:
Galatians 5:16; Hebrews 6:9-14

download:
Jeremiah 11-12; Psalm 67

voice activate:
I live by the Spirit and do not gratify the desires of my old, sinful nature.
Galatians 5:16

"Through Christ Jesus the law of the Spirit of life set me free from the law of sin and death."
Romans 8:2

Living in the Life Cycle

This world is caught in a death cycle. Just look around. Inflation, recession, depression, sin, sickness, disease and death. They're all part of the cycle of death that has been keeping this world in check ever since Adam listened to Satan in the Garden of Eden.

Sadly enough, these things have often kept Christians in check, too. They shouldn't, but they have.

Read today's scripture one more time. This verse means that you and I, as Christians, aren't locked into the death cycle of the world anymore. We can step out of it and into the life cycle of God. We've been set free!

"Kenneth, how can you say we're free? This last swing in the economy ruined my family's business!"

No, it didn't. It was your participation in it that ruined your business.

"Through Christ Jesus the law of the Spirit of life made me free from the law of sin and death."

Yes! We can live debt-free, poverty-free and recession-free right in the middle of a world filled with financial ruin.

"Nobody can do that!"

Yes, Somebody can. In fact, Somebody did...Jesus.

He healed the sick, raised the dead, cast out demons, rebuked the storm. Nothing could control Him—not disease, not circumstances, not criticism, not conspiracy, not demonic forces, not even death itself! Now that's freedom!

You can live the same way if you'll just live the way He did.

So how do you know what He did? By reading the Bible and by spending time with God. He'll tell you what to do and how to do it. He'll teach you how to live in the life cycle—every day.

backup:
Romans 8:1-8

download:
Jeremiah 13-15; Psalms 68-69

voice activate:
Through Jesus, I am made free from the law of sin and death. Romans 8:2

"If you falter in times of trouble, how small is your strength!"
Proverbs 24:10

Strength to Win

These are times of trouble! Whatever you are facing today, you can't afford to be weak. You can't afford to give up. If you do, you'll be in trouble because, as far as this world goes, things aren't going to get better, they're going to get worse.

Don't let that scare you. 1 John 5:4 tells us that *"everyone born of God overcomes the world. This is the victory that has overcome the world, even our faith."*

Did you know that with the Word you can become just as strong as you want to? The only one who can put limits on you is you. If you'll give the Word more time, it will give you more strength.

That's what wise Christians do. They keep themselves strong by spending time reading the Bible every day. They stay strong and ready because they know we live in an evil day.

Wake yourself up to the Word by getting out your Bible every day, reading it and thinking about what it says. Get recorded messages and books by men and women preaching God's Word. Listen to them and read them again and again.

Keep that Word in your heart. Read it and hear it until it changes the way you think. Keep yourself strong and ready and free to do what the Holy Spirit says. Then, when trouble strikes, you'll have supernatural strength to win!

gloria

backup:
Isaiah 40:28-31

download:
Jeremiah 16-17; Psalm 70

voice activate:
I am born of God and overcome the world with my faith. 1 John 5:4

october 17

kenneth

"I urge, then, first of all, that requests, prayers, intercession and thanksgiving be made for everyone—for kings and all those in authority, that we may live peaceful and quiet lives in all godliness and holiness. This is good, and pleases God our Savior, who wants all men to be saved and to come to a knowledge of the truth. "
1 Timothy 2:1-4

Brother Bighead, Mama Smith and You

God cannot sit still when He hears His people cry out! The problem is, most of us are too busy to take time to pray and cry out to Him. We can get so busy being busy for God, we don't make prayer a priority.

In the end, we'll find out it was those who prayed who were behind every success in ministry. Someday in heaven when the rewards are being handed out, Brother Bighead will be sitting on the front row, expecting a huge trophy because he started a church. He'll lean over to the fellow next to him and say, "Oh, yeah, I pastored a church for 47 years. I led 2,000 people to the Lord. I'll tell you all about it as soon as I get my trophy."

Then, when the Lord gives the trophy, instead of calling Brother Bighead's name, He'll say, "Where's Mama Smith?" Then He'll send an angel down to row 7 million to fly Mama Smith up to the front.

When she gets there, He'll put that trophy in her hands and say, "Mama Smith, I want to give you this in honor of those 25 years you prayed before Me. Because of your prayers, I called Brother

Bighead to come start a church. Because of your prayers, thousands of people were saved."

Then He'll turn to the front row and say, "Brother Bighead, I'm rewarding you by allowing you to carry Mother Smith's trophy for her."

I can tell you whose trophies I will get to carry when that day comes. One of them will belong to my mother and the other one will belong to a little woman who used to pray with her all the time.

I'm preaching the good news today because of those two women. I don't get any credit for it. I do have some credit coming for the times I prayed and cried out to God on behalf of someone else. Rewards aren't the reason you pray those kinds of prayers. You pray them because of love. Answer that call!

backup:
Acts 12:1-17

download:
Jeremiah 18-19; Psalm 71

voice activate:
I commit to make prayer a priority and cry out to God! 1 Timothy 2:1

"The good man brings good things out of the good stored up in him, and the evil man brings evil things out of the evil stored up in him. " Matthew 12:35

Faith in All the Right Places

Have you ever heard someone say, "I'd have no problem believing God can heal me if He'd speak to me out loud like He did in Genesis...but He hasn't?"

The correct response is, "No, and He probably won't either." God no longer has to thunder His Word down at us from heaven. These days He lives in the hearts of Christians, so He speaks to us from the inside instead of the outside. What's more, when it comes to issues like healing, we don't even have to wait on Him to speak.

He has already spoken! He has already said, *"By his wounds you have been healed"* (1 Peter 2:24). He has already said, *"I am the Lord, who heals you"* (Exodus 15:26). He has already said, *"And the prayer offered in faith will make the sick person well; the Lord will raise him up"* (James 5:15).

God has already done His part. So we must do ours. We must take the Word He has spoken, put it inside us and let it change us from the inside out. Everything—including healing—starts inside you. Your future is literally stored up in your heart. Matthew 12:35 confirms that.

In other words, if you want things to be better, you'd better start changing your internal condition. You'd better start depositing God's promises in your heart just like you deposit money in the bank. Then you can make withdrawals on them whenever you need. When sickness attacks, you can tap into the healing promises you've put inside yourself and run that sickness off!

Remember: For faith to work, it must be in two places—in your heart and in your mouth. *"For it is with your heart that you believe and are justified, and it is with your mouth that you confess and are saved"* (Romans 10:10).

So get into the Bible. Fill your heart with God's promises...and speak that truth in faith, from your heart. Then you'll have your faith in all the right places!

b a c k u p :
Proverbs 6:20-23

d o w n l o a d :
Jeremiah 20-21; Psalm 72

v o i c e   a c t i v a t e :
I fill my heart with God's promises and speak the truth in faith. This truth guides me, watches over me and speaks to me. Proverbs 6:22

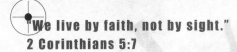

"We live by faith, not by sight."
2 Corinthians 5:7

october 19

kenneth

Get That Bulldog, Never-Give-Up Faith

When I think of the spiritual drive we'll need in the days ahead, I think of a story I once read about a young man who was in pilot training during World War II. He was a bomber pilot training on the Martin Marauder.

One day this young pilot was sitting with his instructor in this airplane at the end of the runway preparing to take off on a training flight. His roommate, who was training in the same kind of plane, was coming in for his final approach. About a quarter of a mile from the end of the runway, right in front of this young pilot's eyes, his roommate flipped that airplane upside down, it hit the ground and exploded in a ball of flames.

Stunned, the young man simply sat and stared in silence. Then he heard the firm voice of his instructor, "Don't just sit there! Take the runway!"

The young pilot was astonished. "Surely we're not going to train today! My buddy just got killed!"

"Take the runway!" the instructor ordered. "We are in the middle of a war. We have no time to grieve. Take the runway!" He taxied through the smoke of his friend's burning airplane and put that bomber in the sky!

I know as well as anyone that living by faith isn't easy. There are times when Satan blindsides you and hurts you so badly that you just want to lie down and cry, but crying won't win the war. You have to keep going.

Walking by faith will win the war, because faith is our link to God's power. Faith releases His power in us—and His power can break and destroy anything Satan throws at you. If you'll keep your faith strong through putting God's promises in your heart, when Satan takes a punch at you, you can rise up.

So commit to live your life by faith. Make a rock-solid decision to live by faith and not by how things look. Determine to keep feeding on the Word, to build that bulldog, never-give-up faith. Just watch...Satan will be the one who gives up!

backup:
1 Kings 17:1-16

download:
Jeremiah 22-23; Psalm 73

voice activate:
I live by faith, not by what I see.
2 Corinthians 5:7

gloria

"Let our lives lovingly express truth.... Enfolded in love, let us grow up in every way and in all things into Him, Who is the Head, [even] Christ, the Messiah, the Anointed One."
Ephesians 4:15, AMP

True Maturity

None of us are happy with old, sinful ways of living. We want to put those old ways behind us and grow up spiritually. We want to be more like Jesus.

The Apostle Paul had that same desire. He prayed for the day when we would all arrive *"at really mature manhood—the completeness of personality which is nothing less than the standard height of Christ's own perfection—the measure of the stature of the fullness of the Christ, and the completeness found in Him"* (Ephesians 4:13, AMP).

Paul not only prayed about that kind of spiritual maturity, he encouraged us to move actively toward it (Ephesians 4:15).

As I've studied God's character, I've come to realize that love is the single most important key to growing up in God. I've seen that if we don't grow up in love, we won't grow up at all.

We won't enjoy as much of God as we want until we start walking in love consistently. Our love life has everything to do with God's presence and power in our lives.

That might come as a surprise to some people. They think that love is so basic, something only beginners need to study. They might consider the gifts of the Spirit—things like healings and miracles—as the things mature Christians should be talking about. According to 1 Corinthians, those aren't the marks of spiritual maturity. As wonderful as those things are, it's character that indicates how mature a Christian is.

So, if you want to know whether you're a spiritual person or not, don't look to see what miracles are happening in your life. Instead, look at the character and integrity in your life. Specifically, look to see if you are walking in love. You simply can't be a mature Christian without being ruled by love. Living a life ruled by God's love is what opens up doors to God's biggest blessings and power!

b a c k u p :
1 Corinthians 3:1-3

d o w n l o a d :
Jeremiah 24-25; Psalm 74

v o i c e   a c t i v a t e :
Enfolded in love, I grow up in every way and in all things into Jesus. Ephesians 4:15

october 21

"Do not let this Book of the Law depart from your mouth; meditate on it day and night, so that you may be careful to do everything written in it. Then you will be prosperous and successful."
Joshua 1:8

kenneth

Turn on the Light

Just because you can't see something doesn't mean it isn't there. For example, you can look out your back window on a moonless night when it's pitch black, and you won't be able to see your patio, but that doesn't mean your patio is gone. It simply means you can't see it. You need to turn on the light.

Sometimes we become concerned that we can't "see" God's promises happening in our lives, but that doesn't mean His Word doesn't work. We just can't see it working because we haven't spent enough time in the Bible for the light to dawn in our hearts. If we'll start reading and praying about those promises, we'll start to see them!

Let me show you what I mean. Let's say God has instructed you to go to a certain college, but you don't have enough cash yet to even pay for the books. Instead of thinking about the problem like, *I'm afraid I'll have to borrow way too much money; I'm afraid I'll be paying it off forever*, make a change. Start thinking about what God said.

Think, *Jesus said, "Give and it will be given to you." I wonder what would happen if I did that?*

If fear tries to rise up (and I assure you it will), just slap it down. You don't have to be afraid. When the "yeah-but-what-ifs" come up, just read what the Bible says again.

Begin to see how your life would change if you became a giver. Let the Holy Spirit use God's promises to paint a picture of how things *can* look.

It will take a while, but if you do this long enough, giving will start looking like the only smart thing for you to do. Courage will overwhelm your fear. You'll find yourself saying, "God said He'd meet my needs! He said if I'd give, it would be given to me. So, I'm going to act on that and He will meet my needs!"

So what happened? What changed? You did. You turned on the light!

backup:
Psalm 119:1-24

download:
Jeremiah 26-27; Psalm 75

voice activate:
I meditate on God's promises day and night, careful to do what He says. I am prosperous and successful! Joshua 1:8

"For if the willingness is there, the gift is acceptable according to what one has, not according to what he does not have."
2 Corinthians 8:12

A Gift of Honor

In God's way of doing things, giving equals receiving. Seeds planted bring a harvest. So why, despite their giving, do a lot of Christians struggle financially?

I believe the difference is in the way people give. You should give in a way that honors God. For example, just because you've been in the habit of setting aside 10 percent for God, it doesn't mean you're a tither. True tithing must be done honorably, with a worshiping heart, not just plunked in the plate.

All our giving must be done in a way that honors God. Here are six principles that will change the way you give:

1) *Start Where You Are*—Some people get discouraged because they can only give small gifts, but every gift matters to God. The poor widow in Mark 12 gave only two mites, yet Jesus said she gave the biggest gift of all.

2) *Give in Faith*—When you give, believe God. You can't tithe in faith and not see results. Expect God to prosper you when you tithe and you will get exactly what you believe for.

3) *Tithe, No Matter What*—Commit to tithe consistently, not just when things are going well financially. You won't increase if you aren't consistent.

4) *Sow What You Want to Reap*—Don't give God your leftovers. Give Him quality gifts (Malachi 3).

5) *Watch Your Words*—When people get under pressure financially, there's a temptation to start spouting their frustration and talking unbelief. Make sure everything you say lines up with God's promises to you.

6) *When You Give, Get Excited!*—Thank God and get excited about all the good things He has given to you (Deuteronomy 26).

This is the kind of giving that honors God. When you give according to these principles, something exciting *will* happen! You can count on it!

backup:
Proverbs 3:9-10; 2 Corinthians 9:7

download:
Jeremiah 28-30; Psalms 76-77

voice activate:
I am a cheerful giver. I honor the Lord with my wealth and he gives me more than enough. 2 Corinthians 9:7, Proverbs 3:9-10

gloria

october 23

"Therefore, since we have been justified through faith, we have peace with God through our Lord Jesus Christ, through whom we have gained access by faith into this grace in which we now stand. And we rejoice in the hope of the glory of God." Romans 5:1-2

kenneth

God's Word + Hope + Faith = Appearance

God's Word + Hope + Faith = Appearance. This spiritual process always works the same way. Hope forms the image, then faith rises up and gives substance to that image, making it a reality in the natural, physical realm.

Now, I have a question I'd like you to seriously consider: In the light of all God has promised us in His Word, what are you and I to expect? What should we be hoping for?

Certainly, healing is great. Financial supply is wonderful. But could it be that God has something even better for us to hope for?

Yes, He does. He tells us what it is in today's verse.

This scripture, in the last phrase, says we're to rejoice in the hope of the glory of God! We're to expect the glory, not just the healing or the finances!

As long as you're just expecting healing, you'll always be battling it out with your old sinful nature, but if you're expecting *the glory*, you'll be raising your spiritual sights to something bigger than healing. You'll be expecting the very presence of God to rise up in you so powerfully that, instead of believing for healing every six weeks, you'll walk in divine health every day!

I've experienced touches of glory, and believe me, I'm eager for more! So start expecting the glory. Raise your expectations to a new level. The results will be glorious!

backup:
Exodus 40:34-38; 1 Kings 8:10-11

download:
Jeremiah 31-32; Psalm 78

voice activate:
I expect the glory of God to shine in my life! Romans 5:2

gloria

"No, in all these things we are more than conquerors through him who loved us."
Romans 8:37

No Fear

Did you know we're not supposed to fear Satan? We're supposed to fear God. We're to have so much reverence and respect for God that we immediately make any adjustment in our lives just to please Him.

When God tells us to do something that friends would think is uncool, we ought to be more concerned about what we will miss if we don't obey Him than what our friends will think if we do.

In other words, when He tells you that you *are more than a conqueror,* and instructs you to march in and take back some part of your life that Satan has stolen from you, you shouldn't sit around debating about whether or not you can do it. You should just start marching!

Well, I just couldn't do that. After all, I've been defeated in that area of my life for so long that I have a poor self-image.

If that's what you're thinking, let me tell you something. If you'll serve God, your poor self-image will begin to change, and you'll start to see yourself as He sees you. We look so much better in Him!

We've got to get away from being so self-conscious, so aware of what we

think we can or can't do. That's what keeps us from winning. Instead of simply obeying God, we start to wonder, *Now what will people think of me if I do that? How will I look?*

It doesn't matter how you look! What counts is that you obey God. Once you do that, your reputation will only get better. It's a funny thing, but once you lose that desire to protect your image, your image gets better. Why? Because then other people can see God in your life rather than just seeing you.

God promised He will be with you (Exodus 3:12). Grab hold of that promise. That's what will cause you to do impossible things. Don't fear Satan and let that fear stop you. You are more than a conqueror! Rise up and obey God!

b a c k u p :
Hebrews 3:12-19

d o w n l o a d :
Jeremiah 33-34; Psalm 79

v o i c e   a c t i v a t e :
I am more than a conqueror through Jesus who loves me. Romans 8:37

october 25

kenneth

"But we have this treasure in jars of clay to show that this all-surpassing power is from God and not from us."
2 Corinthians 4:7

You Have the Treasure

"We're just going to burn ourselves out for God." That's an old, religious cliché, but that's not what God wants for any of us. That's what Satan wants!

Don't give him the opportunity to see you burn out. Take time to feed your spirit so you won't burn out. Keep feeding your spirit until you increase in strength. Burn brighter and stronger every day.

Increase the wattage of your spiritual generator by spending time focusing on God. Begin to work with Him instead of just for Him. Take your focus off the things of the world and look at Him.

Where must you look to see Jesus? First, in the Word. Second, in your own spirit.

For most people, it's easy to see Jesus in the Bible. Yet, we haven't developed our ability to see Him living inside us. That is the key.

You must have that ability to survive the pressure in these last days. You'll need to be able to see Jesus within you just as clearly as you can see Him in the Bible. You'll have to know—not just with your brain, but with every fiber of your being—that God in you is greater than Satan and anything he can throw at you.

Never forget this: Once you truly see that the very Spirit and power of Jesus resides on the inside of you, nothing—no amount of persecution, no disease, no problem of *any* kind—will be able to defeat you. When you see Jesus inside you as bigger than the problems around you, you'll conquer any challenge Satan brings your way.

The answer to everything is inside you right now. Everything you'll ever need is in your spirit. All the strength...all the health...all the wealth...all the wisdom...all of it is in you because that's where Jesus is.

Remember, we have this treasure in jars of clay to show that this all-surpassing power is from God and not from us!

backup:
John 17:20-26

download:
Jeremiah 35-36; Psalm 80

voice activate:
The One Who is in me is greater than the one who is in the world. 1 John 4:4

"I have hidden your word in my heart that I might not sin against you."
Psalm 119:11

Make Those Faith Deposits

Whatever you want to do in life, whether you want to be a surgeon, a construction manager or a schoolteacher, spending time with God and keeping your heart full of His promises is your number-one priority.

That's right. The most important thing you'll do each day is to make those faith deposits. Don't just make them in times of crisis, either. Make them before you need them. Go to Psalm 91 and proclaim the things that belong to you by faith every day.

I remember a letter Ken and I received from a family whose child drowned in the swimming pool. When they came out and found the baby in the pool, he had already turned blue and quit breathing.

Because they had made deposits of God's promises before that time, the moment it happened, they were ready. Nobody said, "Go get the Bible and look up a scripture." Sometimes you don't have time to get your Bible. Immediately that family began to pray and refuse death and command the spirit of that

baby to come back. As a result, that child is alive and well today.

Do you have enough faith in your heart to handle a situation like that? If you don't, start making big deposits of God's Word in your heart now. Start speaking the Word day and night...not just when you're praying or being spiritual, but all the time—at school, at the dinner table, at work, even in your bed at night.

If we'll do that, we will be able to buy back every piece of ground Satan has ever stolen from us. We can enjoy the good things God has for us at last!

backup:
Psalm 18:20-30

download:
Jeremiah 37-38; Psalm 81

voice activate:
I will always make deposits of God's Word into my heart. Psalm 119:11

"In righteousness you will be established."
Isaiah 54:14

october 27

kenneth

You Are Established!

Do you know what it means to be established in righteousness? It means to be in a right place with God. It means being able to stand in the presence of a holy, awesome, almighty, pure God without a sense of guilt or inferiority.

Think about that! What must it be like to be established in righteousness? What must it be like to know beyond the shadow of a doubt that there's absolutely nothing wrong between you and God? No sin. Nothing. Everything is so right that every time you walk in the door, God says, *Yes, yes, yes,* before you can even ask Him for anything.

It's easy for us to believe things are that way between God and Jesus, but realize this: Because of what Jesus did on the Cross, you were placed in right-standing with God, the same as He!

Second Corinthians 5 says, *"Therefore, if anyone is in Christ, he is a new creation; the old has gone, the new has come! God made him who had no sin to be sin for us, so that in him we might become the righteousness of God"* (verses 17, 21).

You have just exactly the same access to God as Jesus does. He loves you just as much as He loves Jesus. (Read John 17:23.)

I know that's hard for you to grasp. It's hard for me too, but we have to keep working on it. We have to keep thinking about it all the time. We have to start seeing ourselves in right-standing instead of in sin. (Hebrews 5:13.)

Do you know what will happen as you do that? You won't be afraid to obey God. You won't be afraid to act like Him. You won't be afraid to boldly claim what is yours in Jesus. You won't be afraid to place your hands on the sick, believing they will recover. You won't be afraid to believe God for your own healing, or for whatever you need!

b a c k u p :
1 Corinthians 1:26-31

d o w n l o a d :
Jeremiah 39-40; Psalm 82

v o i c e   a c t i v a t e :
I am established in righteousness! I'm in the right place with God. Isaiah 54:14

"And without faith it is impossible to please God."
Hebrews 11:6

We're Not Civilians!

A soldier in boot camp will jump out of bed before dawn every morning to run and do push-ups. He may not like it, but he'll do it because his commanding officer has ordered him to do it. He endures the discomfort because he knows it's an inescapable part of military life.

A civilian, on the other hand, might start an exercise program, but when the going gets tough, his muscles feel sore and his schedule gets busy, he'll just quit exercising. If someone asks him about it, he might just shrug and say, "I tried exercise, but it didn't work for me."

Some Christians are like that. They hear about living by faith and they think, *Well, I'll try that.* Then when the hard times come, they give up.

That's not how it should be. After all, we're not civilians. We're soldiers! We don't *try* faith—we make it our lifestyle. We walk by faith, whether it's hard or easy. We don't do it so we'll be blessed. We do it because we're determined to please Jesus. He is our commander in chief, and the Bible says without faith, it is impossible to please Him.

Of course, we will end up blessed if we'll walk by faith. We'll end up healed and doing well in every area of life because God promised we would. That, however, is not our motivation. We're motivated by our desire to serve the Lord. That's what makes us believe His Word, stand strong and endure when the hard times come.

backup:
1 Peter 1:1-7

download:
Jeremiah 41-42; Psalm 83

voice activate:
**I walk by faith and please God.
Hebrews 11:6**

"The Lord is with me; I will not be afraid."
Psalm 118:6

October 29

kenneth

He Will See You Through

Notice in today's verse that David didn't say, "I'll pray for God to take the fear away." He didn't say, "I try not to be afraid." He said, *"I will not be afraid."*

Refusing to fear is first of all a matter of your will. As that verse shows, it is also a matter of choosing to believe that in every situation God is on your side and, by His power, He will see you through.

Of course, to successfully walk by faith and not fear, we need to know exactly how to tap into that power. Second Peter 1:3-4 tells us: *"His divine power has given us everything we need for life and godliness through our knowledge of him who called us by his own glory and goodness. Through these he has given us his very great and precious promises, so that through them you may participate in the divine nature and escape the corruption in the world caused by evil desires."*

God makes everything we could possibly need available through the promises in His Word. If we'll believe them, those promises will show up in our lives.

Satan, however, challenges those promises with fear. He brings us hard times to convince us those promises won't ever happen. He tells us lies. He says, *You'll never make it. Other people can walk by faith because they're stronger than you. There's something wrong with you.*

No matter what, the choice is still yours. You can listen to God's promises or Satan's lies. Which will it be? Just as faith comes by hearing God's Word, fear comes by Satan's lies. Fear comes when you entertain his threats about the future and his boasts about the past.

So make the right choice...even if you have to make it every 30 seconds. Don't let Satan's lies swirl through your head for even a minute. Fill your thoughts with God's promises. Know this: He will see you through.

b a c k u p :
Deuteronomy 31:1-6

d o w n l o a d :
Jeremiah 43-45; Psalms 84-85

v o i c e   a c t i v a t e :
I am not afraid for the Lord is with me. Psalm 118:6

october 30

gloria

In My Name, YOU Will...

Wait a minute, you may be thinking, *I've been saved for 10 years and Jesus has been in me the whole time. He has never preached any sermons or healed any sick people through me.*

That's because you haven't expected Him to do those things. Even though He lives in you, He is not going to be revealed through you unless you use your faith. That shouldn't surprise you. After all, everything we receive from God—even our new lives—must be activated by faith.

So, if you want God to start working through you, you'll have to believe Him for it. You can't just sit back and wait to see what happens. You must grab hold of His promises to you and believe what the Bible says, rather than what your circumstances or experiences say.

You may feel as though you're powerless, but the Bible says, *"Having believed, you were marked in him with a seal, the promised Holy Spirit"* (Ephesians 1:13). In other words, when you made Jesus your Lord, you were stamped with Jesus' likeness. You were made to look like Him on the inside.

What you need to do now is believe that, and let what God put on the inside of you come out! Let Him work through you every day. Let Him have His way. Expect others to see Him in you!

Put your faith into action by spending time with Him. Set your heart on godly things. Desire for Him to show Himself through you so much that you're willing to set aside other things and put Him first.

I firmly believe that the more important Jesus becomes to us, the more He will show Himself through us. So make up your mind to hunger for Him and to give Him His way in you every day. As you do, He'll begin to reach others through you!

backup:
Colossians 1:25-29

download:
Jeremiah 46-47; Psalm 86

voice activate:
God's power works in me and through me! Colossians 1:29

"Submit yourselves, then, to God. Resist the devil, and he will flee from you."
James 4:7

october 31

gloria

Resist Him in the Name of Jesus

How many times have you seen footage on the 6 o'clock news of someone resisting arrest? Have you ever noticed their behavior? They refuse to cooperate. They fight back. They kick, scream, hit and do anything and everything they can *except* what the arresting officer wants them to do. What are they doing? They are resisting. The law calls it "resisting arrest."

Likewise, when you act that way toward Satan, he'll flee from you. James 4:7 guarantees it. The word *flee* in that scripture doesn't just mean he leaves the scene. It literally means he *"runs as in terror."*

The reason he runs is because you're wearing Jesus' Name. That Name strikes terror into every fiber of Satan's twisted being.

If you could see things from the viewpoint of the enemy, you'd see why. Philippians 2:9-10 describes the situation clearly: *"Therefore God exalted him to the highest place and gave him the name that is above every name, that at the name of Jesus every knee should bow, in heaven and on earth and under the earth."* That

includes Satan. He has to bow his knee when he hears the Name of Jesus.

Now you can see why, when you resist Satan in Jesus' Name, he takes off. He has no choice. Jesus is the One Who defeated him. In fact, after Jesus disarmed the powers and authorities of darkness, Colossians 2:15 says He made a public spectacle of them, triumphing over them!

Satan was humiliated in front of all the angels of heaven and the demons of hell. He is a defeated foe and he knows it. Jesus is the One Who defeated him— and it's His Name you're wearing!

So the next time you're tempted, or the next time Satan tries to put something over on you, resist him in the Name of Jesus. Say, "Satan, I resist you in the Name of Jesus and I'll not receive (whatever he's trying to tell you or give you). Colossians 2:15 says you are defeated and I'm victorious! Amen!"

backup:
Colossians 2:9-15

download:
Jeremiah 48-49; Psalm 87

voice activate:
I submit myself to God. I resist the devil and he flees from me. James 4:7

"If any of you lacks wisdom, let him ask of God, who gives to all liberally and without reproach, and it will be given to him."
James 1:5, NKJV

Vote Holy Spirit

As a Christian, I hope you pray for your nation every day. I know I do. It's very important! I regularly pray for the leaders of the United States government from the president down to our local level. I pray that we hold onto our roots in God. I thank God that we are a free nation, that we can worship our God openly.

On the local level, we frequently have the opportunity to vote for elected officials. Every four years, we vote for the next president. (You may even get the opportunity to vote for fellow students taking office in your school). No matter what the level, voting is a tremendous privilege and a tremendous responsibility.

Many Christians are tempted to get discouraged over the things that are wrong with the political system. That is never an excuse not to vote. If you're old enough, you need to vote, because it puts feet to your faith!

So, we should pray *and* vote. Never underestimate the importance of elections. There are spiritual battles that rage over political positions. Satan is always trying to tell people that their vote won't

matter, but that's a lie. Don't listen to his deceptions.

If you don't know whom to vote for, then go to the Lord and ask Him. He will give you the wisdom you need (James 1:5).

Then, as Ephesians 6:13 says, *"Having done all...stand."*

Stand in line to register to vote.

Stand in line to vote.

Stand in faith, believing what God wants will happen.

Then, no matter who wins, pray for them. Your job isn't finished in the voting booth...it continues at home in prayer. You can make a difference before, during and after the elections. Your vote counts and your prayer counts!

kenneth

b a c k u p :
1 Timothy 2:1-4

d o w n l o a d :
Jeremiah 50-51; Psalm 88

v o i c e   a c t i v a t e :
I stand in prayer for those in authority.
1 Timothy 2:1-2

gloria

"For the Lord preserves the faithful. "
Psalm 31:23, NKJV

Lions Go Hungry

It doesn't matter how dark the world is. If we're constantly serving the Lord and doing what is right, God will bring us through as winners.

Just take a look at what He did in Daniel's life. When Daniel was just a young man, he served as one of three presidents directly under the king. Daniel did his job so faithfully that the king considered putting him over the whole realm.

Well, the other presidents became jealous. Immediately, they began looking for something he was doing wrong so they could accuse him.

Do you know what? The Bible says that they couldn't find any fault in him! Since they couldn't dig up any dirt on him, they decided to scheme and trap him. That trap led to Daniel being thrown into the lions' den to be eaten.

Daniel 6:16, 18-20 records the king's words to Daniel as he was being thrown to the lions, and then the morning after he was *not* eaten by the lions. In these verses, the king mentions twice that Daniel continually served God. What stood out to the king was Daniel's faithfulness. He was faithful—both in spiritual things and in everyday things. Because of that faithfulness, God protected Daniel.

What God did for Daniel, He'll do for you. If you'll be faithful with what God has told you to do, He'll protect you. He wants you to be faithful spiritually by spending time with Him every day. He wants you to be faithful with things in everyday life too, so you put yourself in a position of promotion.

For example, if you drive your parents' car, and you want a car of your own, treat their car as if it is yours. Jesus said, *"If you have not been faithful in what is another man's, who will give you what is your own?"* (Luke 16:12, NKJV).

Until now, you may have made mistakes and been a quitter. You can change that today. You have God's own force of faithfulness inside you. Start letting it come out. Then, the next time Satan pressures you to quit or do less than your best, don't stand for it. Make the lions go hungry!

b a c k u p :
Daniel 6:16-22

d o w n l o a d :
Jeremiah 52; Lamentations 1; Psalm 89

v o i c e   a c t i v a t e :
I am faithful, so the Lord preserves me!
Psalm 31:23

"Even so the tongue is a little member, and it can boast of great things. See how much wood or how great a forest a tiny spark can set ablaze!" James 3:5, AMP

A Conditioned Response

Think right now about the most sour lemon you've ever tasted. Picture it in your mind. Pick it up, squeeze it just a little and watch the sour juice just trickle out. Now work up your nerve, put that lemon in your mouth and bite down.

What kind of response are you having right now? Your mouth is watering, right? Your lips are probably puckered up like a prune. Science calls that a conditioned response. It's a physical reaction triggered by a mental stimulus.

Our lives are filled with conditioned responses like that. Every one of us has scores of reactions that, because of our experience, have become totally automatic. Did you know there are certain triggers you can use that will affect your spirit as surely as the thought of that lemon affected your body? It's true! What are those triggers?

Words!

Words are seemingly little things that produce very big results.

Words trigger faith or fear, joy or despair, courage or discouragement. That's a spiritual principle, and it works all the time whether you know it or not.

What's all this got to do with conditioned responses? If you start listening to yourself, you'll find you have many phrases and expressions you use automatically, without even thinking. They could be affecting you without you even knowing it. "Mondays are never good...The only kind of luck I ever have is bad luck...I'll never understand this geometry...." The list goes on and on.

What I want to challenge you to do today is to begin turning those expressions around. Pull a new trigger. Start conditioning yourself to respond to every situation with words of faith instead of words of unbelief. Connect faith words with everything you do all day long. Teach yourself to talk in such a way that every situation becomes a trigger to your faith. It will make a huge difference!

backup:
Hebrews 4:14-16

download:
Lamentations 2-3; Psalm 90

voice activate:
I will make sure the words of my mouth and the meditation of my heart is pleasing in God's sight. Psalm 19:14

"We do not look at the things which are seen, but at the things which are not seen. For the things which are seen are temporary, but the things which are not seen are eternal."
2 Corinthians 4:18, NKJV

november 4

gloria

Seeing Eternal Things

If you want to keep living by faith every day, you'll have to quit thinking about the "impossibilities" that might be piling up around you even now. God is not sweating them, so neither should you. Ken and I have found that out by experience!

More than thirty years ago, Ken was praying down by the riverbed in Tulsa, Oklahoma. Right there, God began speaking to him about preaching to nations. God told him that he would have a worldwide ministry.

It was clear God wasn't thinking about our bank account. We hardly had enough money to get across town—much less go to the nations! We came to realize that God didn't expect us to make it happen. He intended to do it Himself as we put our faith in Him and His promises to us. He intended to provide the power, the resources, the ability—everything! All He expected us to do was believe and obey.

That's all He expects you to do.

Right now you may be thinking, *I really want to do that. I want to live by* faith. The problem is, every time I look at the mess I'm in, I get discouraged!

Then stop looking at that mess!

Instead, focus your attention on God's promises to you. Keep His Word in front of your eyes and in your ears until you can see it happening with the eyes of your spirit.

That's what the spirit of faith does. It doesn't look at the way things are, but at the way things *can* be.

Of course, I'm not saying you should ignore your problems as if they aren't real. They are real, but according to the Bible they are simply *temporary*. They will change if you keep standing on God's Word to you!

backup:
Psalm 108:1-6

download:
Lamentations 4-5; Psalm 91

voice activate:
I look at the things that are eternal. I look at the Word. 2 Corinthians 4:18

"Let us therefore be diligent to enter that rest, lest anyone fall according to the same example of disobedience. For the word of God is living and powerful, and sharper than any two-edged sword, piercing even to the division of soul and spirit, and of joints and marrow, and is a discerner of the thoughts and intents of the heart."
Hebrews 4:11-12, NKJV

The Power of the Word

In a hard situation, I have good news. You don't have to do a thing about it—except live in the Word. The Word can change everything.

God's Word is alive. It will change the way you think, act, feel, live and believe. The Word will turn things around. How can it do that? Because God's Word literally has God's power within it!

Although we put forth the effort to learn God's Word, to spend time in it, speak it and obey it—it is actually the Word itself that brings about the changes in our lives. That's what the writer of today's verse means when he said we must *be diligent to enter that rest.*

We rest on the Word, knowing it will accomplish what God has promised.

Some Christians wear themselves out trying to make something God promised happen. That's not our job! Our job is to let the Word live in us. Our job is to live in Jesus. Our job is to replace our thoughts with His thoughts—to speak and act in line with the way His Word says to speak and act.

It is God Who makes His Word happen. He will make His promises a reality in your life.

What's more, He can do it right in the middle of the worst trouble you may have ever seen. So don't get discouraged! Just set your heart on Jesus. Just let God's Word answer the situation...and you're sure to make it through!

backup:
Psalm 33

download:
Ezekiel 1-3; Psalms 92-93

voice activate:
I rest on the Word, knowing it will accomplish what God has promised, for it is living and powerful in my life. Hebrews 4:11-12

november 6

gloria

"This is what the kingdom of God is like. A man scatters seed on the ground. All by itself the soil produces grain...As soon as the grain is ripe, he puts the sickle to it, because the harvest has come."
Mark 4:26,28-29

A Harvest of Health

People want to be well. No one wants to be sick. However, to be well, you have to make choices. How often have you seen someone with a hacking cough still smoking a cigarette? Or an overweight person eating ice cream?

Our old nature likes to take the easy way. It's much easier to give in to habits than to break them. It's easier to give in and watch television every night like the rest of the world than it is to spend your time putting God's healing promises into your heart.

I heard someone say that people often try to build the third story of a building on a vacant lot. That sounds funny, but it's true. A lot of people want to enjoy the benefits of healing without building the foundation for it from the Bible.

It can't be done. If you want a building, you have to start below ground level and lay a foundation. If you want results, you will have to plant something first.

Everything in this world works that way. Ken calls it the "law of genesis." This "law of sowing and reaping" works in the spirit realm too. It determines your health, wealth and more. Jesus taught about it in Mark 4:26-29.

According to the law of sowing and reaping, if you want health, you need to do more than just want it. You even need to do more than just believe in healing. You need to plant seed—and the seed you plant is God's promises about healing. So look up healing scriptures. Begin putting them into your spirit. Speak them out loud every day. Soon, they will grow up and give you a harvest of health.

backup:
James 1:22-25

download:
Ezekiel 4-5; Psalm 94

voice activate:
I plant the seed of God's promises in my heart and soon they will grow up and give me a harvest. Mark 4:26-29

"'Did I not tell you that if you believed, you would see the glory of God?'"
John 11:40

The Fiery Glory

Today's scripture is what Jesus spoke to Martha when Lazarus died. It is just as true today for you and me as it was for her. If we'll expect God's glory to show up, if we'll study His promises until we truly expect His glory to come, then faith will make it show up right before our eyes.

Does that sound wild to you? Well, it's not! In fact, that's what Christianity is all about—the Bible says so. God intended for us to live with His presence in our lives, because it draws people to Him!

He intended for us to live with His glory so strong in us that sickness and disease take off when we arrive. He intended for us to live in such a way that we have a glimpse of what it will be like in heaven. That's why the Apostle Paul said, *"[For my determined purpose is] that I may know Him...And that I may in that same way come to know the power outflowing from His resurrection...That if possible I may attain to the...resurrection [that lifts me] out from among the dead [even while in the body]* (Philippians 3:10-11, AMP).

I've experienced little touches of that kind of life. More is on the way! Glimpses of His glory are showing up all around the world. A good friend of mine pastors a church where God's glory showed up so powerfully that someone called the fire department. All they were doing was having a prayer meeting—but God's glory came on the scene, and it looked like the church was on fire!

When the firemen arrived, they crawled up in the attic and, sure enough, the fiery glory of God was still blazing up there. Those firemen couldn't figure it out. They knew it wasn't fire, but they didn't know what it was. Finally they left, because they didn't know what to do!

More and more, that kind of glory will show up as we start expecting to see it and start walking in it. Sickness and disease will run and God's presence will flow from us!

b a c k u p :
John 11:18-44

d o w n l o a d :
Ezekiel 6-7; Psalm 95

v o i c e   a c t i v a t e :
I believe, so I will see the glory of God!
John 11:40

november 8

gloria

Riches—From Genesis to Revelation

We've been told that God wants us to do well (3 John 2). What many Christians haven't heard is how their everyday decisions to obey, or not to obey God's commands directly impact their financial wellness.

You see, you can't separate God's financial principles from any of His other principles. All of them work together. So you have to live according to the entire Bible to have a good foundation for godly prosperity.

For example, the primary commandment Jesus gave us is to *"love one another"* (John 15:12). Now, that commandment may seem to have nothing to do with money, yet to have true riches, love must be the guiding force of your life.

Think of it this way. Every action you take, every decision you make, every time you go love's way, you're putting another block on your foundation of prosperity.

When you pray for your enemies instead of hating them, when you turn away from immorality, when you see things in your life that you know aren't right and you correct them, you're preparing yourself to handle greater finances.

Today's verse, for example, proves that faithfulness and riches are tied closely together. Wherever you find one, you'll find the other.

According to *Webster's Dictionary*, a *faithful* man is one who "adheres to duty, of true fidelity, loyal, true to allegiance, and constant in the performance of duties or services."

Luke 16:10 says, *"He who is faithful in a very little [thing], is faithful also in much; and he who is dishonest and unjust in a very little [thing], is dishonest and unjust also in much"* (AMP). So if you want to be trusted with more and be promoted to a better job, you have to be faithful and honest in the job you have right now.

If you really want to prosper... follow *all* God's commands for living right—from Genesis to Revelation.

b a c k u p :
1 Peter 3:8-11

d o w n l o a d :
Ezekiel 8-9; Psalm 96

v o i c e a c t i v a t e :
I will be richly blessed because I am faithful. Proverbs 28:20

"I in them and you in me. May they be brought to complete unity to let the world know that you sent me and have loved them even as you have loved me."
John 17:23

Dare To Believe It!

You are a winner in God! You are more than a conqueror in Jesus! You are everything to the Father that Jesus is. Today's verse says God loves you as much as He loves Jesus.

"But Kenneth," you may say, "how could He?"

I don't know! You'll have to ask Him. I just know that's what He said, and I believe it. His victory is my victory because He said it was. If I don't believe it, then He wasted His time. If I don't believe it, then Jesus went through hell to win a victory He already had. He didn't need victory over the world. I did. He won it to give it to me. The moment I believe it, that victory is mine. Until I do believe it, I don't have any victory at all.

Once you dare to accept that fact, your life will be forever changed. You'll no longer be satisfied to just sit around whining and wanting things to be different. You'll want to step up into all Jesus has given you, to take your place beside Him, and learn to operate the way He does.

If we'll receive that message, if we'll dare to believe it, if we'll dare to put it into action, the world around us will never be the same again!

backup:
Hebrews 2:5-18

download:
Ezekiel 10-11; Psalm 97

voice activate:
God loves me as much as He loves Jesus.
John 17:23

321

november 10

gloria

"The time has come for my departure. I have fought the good fight, I have finished the race, I have kept the faith. Now there is in store for me the crown of righteousness, which the Lord, the righteous Judge, will award to me on that day—and not only to me, but also to all who have longed for his appearing."
2 Timothy 4:6-8

A Victorious Soldier

In every army there are good soldiers and sloppy soldiers. There are soldiers who win battles and conquer enemy territory, and there are soldiers who fail and lose ground. I want to be a good soldier, driving Satan back and advancing God's kingdom. Don't you?

The Apostle Paul was that kind of soldier. He was a man of victory. He won in every circumstance. Satan tried to stop him again and again with persecutions, beatings and trouble of every kind, but Paul kept marching forward, preaching the good news, healing the sick and working miracles.

Eventually, Paul was put in prison, in chains. Imagine how terrible the prison conditions must have been in those days! No doubt, Satan expected that to stop Paul—but it didn't. Instead of lying down and feeling sorry for himself, Paul used his time in prison to pray and write letters to minister to people. He didn't know he was writing letters that would become a major part of the New Testament. Prison didn't even slow him down.

It was during this time that he wrote *"I have fought the good fight, I have finished the race...."*

Aren't those wonderful words? I want to be able to say words like that when I come to the end of my life on earth. I want to know that I have fought the good fight—and won!

Someone might say, "Well, Gloria, that was the Apostle Paul! He was special. We can't all be like him."

Why not? We have the same Savior Paul had. We're filled with the same Holy Spirit. Yes, you can be a victorious soldier like Paul. You can conquer enemy territory, push Satan back, and advance God's kingdom!

backup:
2 Corinthians 11:22-33

download:
Ezekiel 12-13; Psalm 98

voice activate:
I will fight the good fight, finish the race and keep the faith all my life.
2 Timothy 4:7

"Be strong and courageous…Be strong and very courageous…Be strong and courageous."
Joshua 1:6-7,9

Be Courageous!

After reading the book of Joshua many times, I'm convinced that as God began to give Joshua His instructions, Joshua was deeply shaken by how big a task he faced.

Yet God didn't speak to Joshua about the impossibilities. He simply kept repeating to him, "Be strong and very courageous!"

God didn't tell Joshua to do a lot of things. He didn't say, "Go figure out how to get across the river."

He didn't say, "Check your military might and see if you have firepower to conquer this land."

He just said, *"Be strong and very courageous."* In other words, "Joshua, your part in this assignment is to be strong and courageous. I'll take care of everything else. I'll win the battles. I'll keep the people in line. I'll show you how to divide the land. You just be courageous!"

"Well, Kenneth, He's never said that to me!"

Yes, He has. In fact, He had it written for you in the New Testament.

"God has said, *'Never will I leave you; never will I forsake you.'* So we say with confidence, *'The Lord is my helper; I will not be afraid. What can man do to me?'"* (Hebrews 13:5-6). Therefore, *"be strong in the Lord and in his mighty power."* (Ephesians 6:10).

For whatever impossible challenge that may be set before you, God has already given you your instructions. "Be strong and very courageous." If you'll do that, He'll take care of the rest.

b a c k u p :
Joshua 1

d o w n l o a d :
Ezekiel 14-15; Psalm 99

v o i c e   a c t i v a t e :
I am strong and very courageous!
Joshua 1:7

"Fight the good fight of the faith."
1 Timothy 6:12

november 12

gloria

Fight On!

"I'm tired of fighting! As soon a I whip one problem, there's two more!"

Some years ago a friend of mine said those very words to the Lord. She was tired from the constant pressure of pushing back the powers of darkness in her own life and in the lives of others. I'll never forget the Lord's response to her.

What is an army for, if not to fight? You'll either be fighting or retreating from now until Jesus returns!

Those words shock many Christians. They don't want to be warriors. They want a comfortable, easy life. They want to lie back and go on a spiritual vacation, but that's not what we as Christians are called to do.

We're called to *"fight the good fight of the faith."* We are an army and we are at war, *"not against flesh and blood, but against the rulers...authorities...powers of this dark world and against the spiritual forces of evil in the heavenly realms"* (Ephesians 6:12).

God has given us spiritual weapons (2 Corinthians 10:4) and His own armor (Ephesians 6:10-18). He has equipped us to be spiritual soldiers!

Right now you may be thinking, *Whoa—I'm not sure if I can do all that.*

Yes, you can! Just focus your attention on the truth that Jesus is alive and you are in Him! When He rose from the dead, you arose. When He defeated Satan, you defeated Satan. His victory is your victory!

Think about that when Satan is telling you that you're not going to make it. Then turn the tables on him and tell him a few things for a change!

Say: *Satan, I am Jesus' representative here on the earth. I have His power and act in His Name. All I have to do is stand in the victory Jesus has already won. The only way you can defeat me is by convincing me to quit, and that's the one thing I won't do! I will stand until I win!*

Or, if you are short on time, just say, "Get out in the Name of Jesus!"

b a c k u p :
2 Corinthians 10:1-6

d o w n l o a d :
Ezekiel 16-18; Psalms 100-101

v o i c e   a c t i v a t e :
I fight the good fight of faith.
1 Timothy 6:12

"For as he [a man] thinks in his heart, so is he."
Proverbs 23:7, NKJV

Paint Your Destiny!

How many times have you heard someone say, "I sure do wish God would do something for me?" You just know they want to add: "but He probably won't."

That's not faith. That's unbelief. Unbelief works the same way faith works—only backwards. Fear is actually faith going the wrong way. When someone is thinking negative thoughts or worrying, he or she is developing inner pictures. Not pictures of hope, but pictures of despair.

Just as fear is the flip side of faith, despair is the flip side of hope. It's an inner image of failure, sickness, lack or whatever else Satan wants to throw in. Despair is actually the opposite of hope, and fear, like faith, brings it to pass.

Do you see how powerful this process is? It literally controls the course of your life. These inner images, whether they are of hope or despair, become the blueprint for your faith or fear, and ultimately control your destiny.

What you must do is dig into God's Word and begin building your hope. Start developing God's pictures within you. As long as you have an image of your own defeat on the inside of you, you're des-

tined to be defeated. If you change that inner image with God's promises, no demon in hell will be able to stop you.

Jesus came to change the inner man. *"If you hold to my teaching,"* He told us, *"you are really my disciples. Then you will know the truth, and the truth will (make) you free."* (John 8:31-32).

Get that truth working on the inside of you. Put it in there until hope paints new pictures in your heart. Then hang on to those pictures as tight as you can. Don't ever let them go. Eventually, faith will make those pictures as real on the outside as they are on the inside.

"For as a man thinks in his heart, so is he." It's the pictures inside you that determine your destiny. Paint some new pictures. God's Word is full of them. The question is—are you?

Kenneth

backup:
Titus 3:4-7

download:
Ezekiel 19-20; Psalm 102

voice activate:
I am as I think in my heart. Therefore I choose to think about things that are true, noble, right, pure, lovely and admirable. Philippians 4:8

november 14

gloria

"Throw off everything that hinders and the sin that so easily entangles"
Hebrews 12:1

Victory Is a Sure Thing

God has called us all to holiness. He has called us to a life that is set apart to Him. I'll warn you though, some of the things the Lord may ask you to get rid of may not necessarily be sinful. They may simply be the "hindrances" referred to in today's verse.

What are hindrances? They are natural interests or pursuits that take up your time or energy and hold you back. They are earthly distractions that may not necessarily be bad, yet they keep you from going higher in spiritual pursuits.

Hindrances are also anything that takes God's place in your heart. God is supposed to be your first love. He is not meant to be one of many treasures in your life. He is meant to be *the* treasure of your life.

Colossians 3:1-2 says, *"Since, then, you have been raised with Christ, set your hearts on things above, where Christ is seated at the right hand of God. Set your minds on things above, not on earthly things."*

If you don't devote much time to the Lord, you will find it very difficult to overcome your natural desires. You will find yourself throwing them aside one day and picking them back up the next because spiritually you're just not strong enough to do what you know you should do.

When you find yourself in that condition, immediately start spending more time studying the Bible and praying. Your union with the Lord is what makes your spirit strong, so focus on maintaining that union. You'll soon find you have more than enough strength to overcome that stubborn sin, or turn off that television program, or set aside that baseball game, or cancel that trip to the mall when the Lord prompts you to spend time with Him.

Remember this: God can take care of any situation if you'll give Him enough of your time. As you spend time with Him, you'll get stronger inside. Once you get victory on the inside, victory on the outside is a sure thing!

b a c k u p :
1 John 3:1-3

d o w n l o a d :
Ezekiel 21-22; Psalm 103

v o i c e   a c t i v a t e :
I set my affection on the things of God. Colossians 3:2

> "For therein is the righteousness of God revealed from faith to faith: as it is written, The just shall live by faith."
> **Romans 1:17, KJV**

The Greatest Satisfaction

Several years ago I was snow-skiing down a mountain when suddenly I hit a patch of ice and went down like a derailed freight train. My goggles flew one way, and my skis, poles and hat flew every other direction. By the time I landed, it looked like I was having a yard sale!

I landed on my right shoulder. Man, it hurt! After I finally stood up, I hit another patch of ice. Wham! I fell, hitting that same shoulder.

By the time I got back home, I could hardly use my right arm. However, every time it would hurt, I'd say, "This injury is not what God truly wants for me, so I don't have to have it. I am healed." Then I'd read God's promises about healing.

During those first few days, not much seemed to be happening. A little later, I went to preach in New Orleans. That morning I read more of God's promises to me, spoke them out and thanked God that I was healed. Then I tried to comb my hair...and I still couldn't raise my arm high enough to do it.

All kinds of doubtful thoughts ran through my mind, but I just threw aside those thoughts, thanked God for His faithfulness, and walked across the street to the conference where I was to preach.

When I walked in, the praise and worship had already started. So I stepped up on the platform, put my Bible down in the chair and just threw both arms up in the air and started praising God!

I never did feel a thing. No goose bumps or tingling power. Yet I want you to know, victory—when it comes by faith—brings a satisfaction like nothing else.

It's so satisfying because you're getting His blessing. You're living by faith, just like Jesus did!

Next time you're faced with a challenge, just stand on the Word...and when the victory comes, you'll have a satisfaction you've never known! You'll have acted like Jesus!

backup:
Psalm 19:7-14

download:
Ezekiel 23-24; Psalm 104

voice activate:
I live by faith. Romans 1:17

november 16

gloria

"Live by the Spirit, and you will not gratify the desires of the sinful nature...The acts of the sinful nature are obvious:...envy...."
Galatians 5:16,19,21

Envy—Satan's Virus

We've all experienced it, but most people think it is no big deal. They see it as just a harmless, human emotion. They are gravely mistaken.

As innocent as it may seem, envy is actually Satan's own poison, designed to turn love into hate and stop faith from working in your life.

"That sounds awful! Good thing I'm not envious of anyone."

That may be true, but let me encourage you to search your heart carefully just to be sure, because many times, we don't even know when envy is there. We may feel it stirring within us, but we don't identify it as envy because it just feels "natural." That's what's so bad about envy. It can slip in silently.

Suppose you go to a soccer game, for instance, and you see Cool Phil with a new car. Suddenly a thought comes to your mind: *Why does he get a new car? He didn't even need it. I'm the one who needs a new car.* Then, you begin to resent the fact that he has a new car.

Or suppose you see Sweet Sally in a new dress. As you sit down next to her, you notice how raggedy your dress feels compared to hers. Suddenly, you feel ugly and self-conscious. You resent that you don't have a dress as nice as hers.

You may not think much more about it. But later, you notice you're a little irritated or depressed. You can't quite put your finger on why you feel that way. After all, you were having a good day until a little while ago. What happened?

Envy crept in and poisoned you with discontentment because of something good that happened to someone else. Envy made a move on you.

If you're a Christian, envy is not part of your nature. It's something Satan dangles it in front of you like bait on a hook, hoping you'll take a bite. Don't do it! It will bring hate into your life. It will stop the force of faith in your life. It will stop your success cold. So get rid of envy. Make a decision never to allow it in again. It's Satan's personal poison. Let him keep it to himself!

b a c k u p :
James 3:13-18

d o w n l o a d :
Ezekiel 25-26; Psalm 105

v o i c e   a c t i v a t e :
I will not be envious. I live by the Spirit and don't gratify the desires of my old nature. Galatians 5:16-21

"I have been crucified with Christ and I no longer live, but Christ lives in me. The life I live in the body, I live by faith in the Son of God, who loved me and gave himself for me."
Galatians 2:20

Red-Hot Faith

There are so many things in our lives that can be solved by simply making rock-solid decisions. They can't be solved by begging God, "Oh, God, take this habit away from me!"

If God were going to do it that way, He'd have done it already!

"But Kenneth, making a decision to get rid of this habit isn't easy!"

No, it isn't, but it is possible to do, and I can tell you how to get started.

First, dig into the Bible and find some of God's promises to you. Spend some time finding out what belongs to you in Jesus.

The phrases "in Christ," "in Him" or "in Whom" are used more than 100 times in the New Testament. Search them out. Read every book from Acts through Revelation looking for them. As you find them, make a decision right then and say, "That's mine. I'm in Christ and He's in me and I take hold of that promise now. That verse is talking about me."

Then begin to see yourself the way God sees you. See power, love, discipline and self-control in your life (2 Timothy 1:7, AMP). See yourself making rock-solid decisions.

Instead of considering the way things look or feel, consider what the Word says! Fix your mind on His promises. Start programming yourself with them. Decide—in advance—that no matter what happens, you are going to choose Jesus and His Word instead of what the situation or your feelings say.

If you'll do that, when trouble hits, your spirit will take over and see you through, and the temperature of your faith will rise and rise!

backup:
2 Corinthians 5:17-21

download:
Ezekiel 27-28; Psalm 106

voice activate:
I have been crucified with Christ and I no longer live, but Christ lives in me. I live by faith in Jesus who has given me power, love, discipline and self-control.
Galatians 2:20, 2 Timothy 1:7

november 18

gloria

"Do you not say, 'Four months more and then the harvest'? I tell you, open your eyes and look at the fields! They are ripe for harvest."
John 4:35

The Final Frontier

I believe living in holiness is the "final frontier" for us to cross before Jesus comes. I believe these are the last of the last days. As we get our lives in order, as we separate ourselves to God, I believe more people are going to turn to God than we've ever seen. It's starting now.

I'm telling you, it is going to shake the world. The things God is going to do will be awesome. The prophets have prophesied about it, they've seen visions of it and I'm expecting it.

One person has prophesied that God's power from the Old Covenant, plus God's power from the New Covenant, plus the multiplying of the power of this age is all coming together—and that's what we're going to see!

People are hungry to see God. You know that every time there's some kind of phenomenon, some kind of miracle—godly or evil—thousands of people will go to see it. People are hungry for spiritual power.

Before the end they are going to see plenty of it. Miracles this world has never seen will happen. People from all over the world will make Jesus their Lord. It's harvest time. There's a harvest of souls to get in before Jesus comes. God is going to get the people in, and then the end will come.

So our part is to be ready. We should be ready for God to use us whenever He needs us. That's what holiness is. It's when you separate yourself apart to God for His use. So get ready. All those people you've been praying to find Jesus—your friends, your family, your classmates—they're coming to God!

backup:
Romans 10:9-13; 2 Timothy 2:19-22

download:
Ezekiel 29-30; Psalm 107

voice activate:
I keep myself ready for God's use. My eyes are open and I see the harvest!
John 4:35

330

"Blessed are those who have not seen and yet have believed."
John 20:29

Head Faith Versus Heart Faith

Miracles. If you haven't seen them in your own life or in the lives of Christians around you, you soon will because they are happening everywhere.

I love it! I love to watch God work. There's nothing more exciting. It's so much fun, in fact, that if we're not alert—we can get so caught up in watching miracles that we neglect spending time with God and we allow our faith to slip.

"Whoa! Wait a minute now, Kenneth. How could my faith slip while I'm watching miracles? Don't they make my faith even greater?"

Not according to the Bible. Romans 10:17 says faith comes by hearing and hearing by the Word of God. It doesn't say anything about faith coming by what you see or feel.

Some people might argue with that. They might think that since they saw a miracle, faith filled their heart. What actually happens when you see something and then believe it is that faith comes to your head!

"Head faith" and "heart faith" are two totally different things. Heart faith—the

God kind of faith—operates in the realm of the spirit. It takes hold of God's promises in the unseen realm and makes those promises happen in the natural world. It a powerful force that changes things!

Head faith, on the other hand, has no real power. It doesn't change things. In fact, just the opposite happens: Things change *it!* Everybody in the world has head faith. They believe certain things just because they can see them or because they've experienced them. Your spirit doesn't have to do a thing to believe things you see.

So what kind of faith do *you* have? The God kind generates spiritual power and life in your life. It's believing before you see it with your natural eyes. It comes by hearing God's promises and believing them. So get into the Bible and watch the right kind of faith come alive!

backup:
John 4:43-54

download:
Ezekiel 31-33; Psalms 108-109

voice activate:
My faith is heart-faith, not head-faith. I believe what the Word says. John 20:29

november 20

gloria

"If you belong to Christ, then you are Abraham's seed, and heirs according to the promise."
Galatians 3:29

The Unstoppable Blessing

Once, when there was a famine in the land, Isaac considered moving to Egypt to escape it. Then, the Lord appeared to him and said, *"Do not go down to Egypt.... Dwell temporarily in this land, and I will be with you and will favor you with blessings...and I will perform the oath which I swore to Abraham your father"* (Genesis 26:2-3, AMP).

Keep in mind, famines back then were just as awful as today. Yet right in the middle of it all, *"Isaac sowed seed in that land, and received in the same year 100 times as much as he had planted, and the Lord favored him with blessings"* (verse 12).

I want you to know, that's what the blessing of Abraham will do. It will enable you to be successful, no matter what's happening around you. If you're Abraham's seed—and you are if you've made Jesus your Lord—you don't have to worry about the way things are happening in the world around you. Those things don't have to affect you. You are dependent *only* on your covenant with God—and that never changes! He never changes what He says, and He has said you are BLESSED!

What's more, He's said you're a BLESSING! That means the school you attend or the company you work for will be blessed just because you're there.

That's what happened in Genesis 41. Abraham's great-grandson, Joseph, started out as a slave in the ungodly nation of Egypt. However, because he was Abraham's seed—just like you are—he ended up saving that nation from being destroyed by famine. Not only that, he became the most powerful man in the nation next to the Pharaoh himself. The entire country was blessed because of Joseph!

You were re-created to live above the circumstances of this world—not in slavery to them. Put your name in the Bible's promises and speak them to your circumstances. The truth is, nothing can stop God from blessing you!

backup:
Genesis 41

download:
Ezekiel 34-35; Psalm 110

voice activate:
Belonging to Christ, I am Abraham's seed and an heir according to the promise. I am a blessing! Galatians 3:29, Genesis 26:12

"Be not afraid, O land; be glad and rejoice. Surely the Lord has done great things. I will show wonders in the heavens and on the earth, blood and fire and billows of smoke. The sun will be turned to darkness and the moon to blood before the coming of the great and dreadful day of the Lord. And everyone who calls on the name of the Lord will be saved."
Joel 2:21,30-32

Prepare for Glory

You need to understand that when those verses talk about *"blood, and fire and billows of smoke,"* they aren't talking about destruction. No, those come *before* the day of destruction. They're talking about the miracles coming in these end times. Notice the next line: *"And everyone who calls on the name of the Lord will be saved."* That's not destruction. That's restoration!

I asked the Lord one time, "Lord, how will You do that? How will You make the sun stop shining?"

He told me He will block out its light with the cloud of His glory. You can see where God showed up in this cloud in both the Old and New Testament. In the Old, Israel saw it as a pillar of smoke in the daytime and a pillar of fire at night. In the New, that same fire was manifest on the Day of Pentecost.

God said to me, *I'll make that cloud get so thick on whole cities, that people can't see the sunshine.* Then He added, *That's the reason you need to be ready.*

What He said to me, I'm saying to you. If you want to be in on this, you need to get ready. You need to quit criticizing your fellow Christians and get the sin out of your life. You need to pray and learn how to lead people to Jesus. Go practice! Learn how because when God's power hits and His glory cloud hits a whole city at one time, people everywhere—yes, even in your school hallways—will fall under the power of it, crying out to God.

Then when it hits, they'll be looking for answers...and the only ones who will have the Answer are you and me. The Lord will speak to you clearer than you've ever heard in your life. He'll begin to tell you what to do, what to say, how to pray, and we'll see thousands upon thousands turn to Him. We'll see homes put back together, and God's glory will cover the land!

backup:
Acts 2:14-21

download:
Ezekiel 36-37; Psalm 111

voice activate:
I'm not afraid—I'm excited! When God's glory hits, I'll be ready. I am saved because I called on the Lord. Joel 2:21, 30-32

333

november 22

gloria

"But you shall (earnestly) remember the Lord your God; for it is He Who gives you power to get wealth."
Deuteronomy 8:18, AMP

Pass the Test

The very idea of wealth scares some Christians. They think having a lot of money is ungodly—but that's not what the Bible says. God doesn't object to us having money. On the contrary, He *"takes pleasure in the prosperity of His servant"* (Psalm 35:27, AMP). What God doesn't want is for *money* to have *us!* He doesn't want us to love money and make it our god.

So He gave us a safeguard. In the Bible, He gave us a foundational instruction that enables us to be wealthy and godly at the same time: *"Seek for (aim at and strive after) first of all His [God's] kingdom, and His righteousness [His way of doing and being right], and then all these things taken together will be given you besides"* (Matthew 6:33, AMP).

That is the foundation of biblical prosperity. It's based on God's way of working. Wealth comes to those who operate according to God's system of life, instead of the world's system.

The world's system has money for its god. It loves and seeks after money. On the other hand, God's system has *God* for its God, and in His economy, you can't become truly wealthy unless you

put Him and His ways first place in your life.

Granted there are times when godly people begin to prosper and then get off track. They fail the prosperity test. They start out putting God first, but when they begin to experience His financial blessings, they become overly occupied with the things that He's given them. Their hearts begin to grow cold toward God because they don't continue to give Him first place in their lives.

God doesn't want that to happen to His people. That's why He told the Israelites not to forget Him when they entered the Promised Land and started living in goodly houses and enjoying material abundance...*"But remember the Lord your God, for it is he who gives you the ability to produce wealth."*

b a c k u p :
Deuteronomy 8:11-18

d o w n l o a d :
Ezekiel 38-39; Psalm 112

v o i c e   a c t i v a t e :
The Lord gives me power to get wealth.
Deuteronomy 8:18

"[I will] not in any degree leave you helpless, nor forsake nor let [you] down!"
Hebrews 13:5, AMP

Make That Decision

If God has called you to do something, something that you think is impossible, chances are Satan has been bombarding you with thoughts of doubt, fear and discouragement.

Don't let him lead you down that road. Don't let him keep you from remembering that God has the ability and faithfulness to get the job done. Resist the temptation to think about your problems and inabilities—resist the temptation to worry.

Stop struggling and start resting. Relax. God knows that what He has called you to do is impossible. He knows you are having a problem with that fact. He doesn't mind waiting while you draw on His promises and develop the courage you need for the task.

You don't have to panic. Just keep reminding yourself that as long as you have your Bible and your faith, you can do anything God tells you to do.

Put thoughts about your own weaknesses behind you and focus instead on God's awesome ability. Start saying to yourself, *God is with me! He will not, He*

will not, HE WILL NOT leave me help-less, forget me nor let me down!

Then open your Bible and choose to believe what it says about you. Treat it as God's blood-sworn oath to you. Keep it in front of your eyes. Keep it in your ears. Keep it coming out of your mouth. Make a rock-solid decision to stick with it until the strength of God Himself rises up within you and overwhelms the fear.

Once you make that decision, there's no turning back. It's on to bigger and better things!

backup:
Philippians 4:4-9

download:
Ezekiel 40-41; Psalm 113

voice activate:
The Lord won't leave me helpless at all. He won't forget me or let me down. Hebrews 13:5

november 24

gloria

"Be holy, because I am holy."
1 Peter 1:16

I'm Doing the Best I Can

When Max, our grandson, started kindergarten, he had quite a surprise waiting. He was surprised to find out that in kindergarten he wasn't the center of attention. He couldn't believe he was actually expected to sit still!

For the first few weeks, Max just didn't seem to be able to do it. He got in trouble again and again. One day, his mother talked to him about it, and he threw his hands up and said, "I'm doing the best I can."

"Well, Max, you're going to have to do better," his mother replied.

"I told you, I'm doing the best I can!" he said again.

Within a few weeks, Max got tired of having to stay on the sidewalk during recess—his penalty for misbehaving in his class. That's when he discovered he *could* do even better.

I think about Max when God is dealing with me about giving some area of my life to Him. Max has ruined the old excuse, "Lord, I'm doing the best I can!" Now I say to myself, *Gloria, you're just doing the best you want to do!*

Many of us act that way. When it comes to being holy, and getting rid of sin, we haven't done all we know to do. We've just done what we wanted to do. We may have thrown out what we considered to be major sins and even many minor sins, but there are worldly hindrances we've held on to because our old, sinful nature enjoys them.

When God tells us to make a change, we must obey.We can't feed on the garbage of the world and at the same time be set apart to God, fit to do good work (2 Timothy 2:21).

I realize this is a bit uncomfortable...but we're told to put our misdeeds to death (Romans 8:13). We're to purify ourselves and set ourselves apart to God (2 Corinthians 6:14-7:1).

When you do that, then you can truthfully say, "I'm doing the best I can!"

backup:
1 Corinthians 6:9-20

download:
Ezekiel 42-43; Psalm 114

voice activate:
I will live holy because the Lord is holy.
1 Peter 1:16

336

"Your attitude should be the same as that of Christ Jesus: Who, being in very nature God, did not consider equality with God something to be grasped, but made himself nothing, taking the very nature of a servant, being made in human likeness"
Philippians 2:5-7

Get Beyond the Requirements!

More than any other man, Paul knew what it was to be free. He was born a free Roman citizen. Then he made Jesus his Lord and God showed him how he had been rescued from the rulership of darkness, and brought into a new life in Jesus. Yet he bowed his knee to Jesus and said, "I give away my freedom. I give away my will. I give it all away to serve You. I'll live for You and I'll die for You."

Jesus Himself set the pattern for such servanthood when He was on earth, and Philippians 2:5-7 encourages us to follow His example.

As a servant, your attitude will be like Jesus' attitude: *"Not my will, but yours be done"* (Luke 22:42). You'll say, "I don't care what it takes, I will obey God. If He wants me to lock myself up in my closet and pray all weekend, that's what I'll do, because I'm His servant!"

Some people like to argue that God would never require such sacrifices from us.

That's just proof that those people aren't servants, because true servants aren't interested in doing only what God requires. True servants want to be totally committed to God and His Word. They want everything they do to be led by Him. As a result, God rewards them. He gives them His gifts. He gives them His power, and He uses them to do great things in His Name.

If you want God to give His gifts to you, if you want to do great things in His Name, then you'll first need to become a servant—one who goes beyond the requirements.

b a c k u p :
Philippians 2:5-11

d o w n l o a d :
Ezekiel 44-45; Psalm 115

v o i c e a c t i v a t e :
Lord, not my will, but Yours be done in my life. Luke 22:42

november 26

kenneth

"For everything God created is good, and nothing is to be rejected if it is received with thanksgiving, because it is consecrated by the word of God and prayer."
1 Timothy 4:4-5

Stop! Before You Take Another Bite

Have you ever wondered why on earth we pray over our food?

I don't pray over my meals because my church or religion says that's what I should do. I pray over my food because I have to eat it!

The Bible says our food is conse-crated (set apart for good) by the Word, by giving thanks and by prayer. I pray over my food because it's right to do. I've eaten all over the world in all kinds of places. I've eaten stuff that I didn't have any idea what it was – and I didn't want any more of it, either!

I was in a place one time when they came out and honored me at 4:30 in the morning with a breakfast they had pre-pared. I sat down in front of something green on my plate. I have no earthly idea what it was. I looked at it and thought, *I'm not going to eat this. I'm going to start a fast right now.*

The Holy Spirit said, *What does My Word say?*

"I knew You would ask me that. The Bible says when you're out in the field, eat whatever is set before you. It also says no deadly thing will hurt you. It says the food is consecrated. Okay, I know, I know. I got the message."

Then He added, *That means do it with a smile on your face.*

So I did, and then I went on a fast the next day.

When you pray over your food, do it in faith. Receive it, giving thanks. Jesus broke Satan's power to contaminate your food. Praying in faith over your food allows it to minister nourishment and strength to your body, rather than pain and sickness. When we receive it, giving thanks in Jesus' Name, it is sanctified, set apart for our use.

So stop right now before you take another bite of fast food, your mom's cooking, or the school cafeteria mystery special. Pray, *"Father, thank You for this food. I receive it blessed and set apart for my use according to Your Word. In Jesus' Name. Amen."*

b a c k u p :
Exodus 23:25

d o w n l o a d :
Ezekiel 46-48; Psalms 116-117

v o i c e   a c t i v a t e :
The food I receive is blessed and set apart for my use according to God's Word. 1 Timothy 1:4:4-5

"I will praise you, O Lord, with all my heart; I will tell of all your wonders. I will be glad and rejoice in you; I will sing praise to your name, O Most High. My enemies turn back; they stumble and perish before you. For you have upheld my right and my cause; you have sat on your throne, judging righteously."
Psalm 9:1-4

Go to War With Praise

Praising God and giving Him thanks are integral parts of prayer. After you made the decision to believe for something, then you need to praise God for the answer. Thank God that what you prayed for will happen.

Offering praise and thanks involve more than just speaking nice words to God. There is power in praise. Praise was set apart by God for a definite reason.

Psalms 8 and 9 point out some things about praise that every Christian should know. Psalm 8:1-2 says, *"O Lord, our Lord, how majestic is your name in all the earth! You have set your glory above the heavens. From the lips of children and infants you have ordained praise because of your enemies, to silence the foe and the avenger."*

From these scriptures, we see that God ordained praise—He brought it into existence. Why? *"To silence the foe and the avenger."* Praise stops Satan cold. It is strength. It's a weapon we can use to stop whatever Satan's throwing at us.

Psalm 9:1-4 says, *"I will praise you, O Lord, with all my heart; I will tell of all*

your wonders. I will be glad and rejoice in you; I will sing praise to your name, O Most High. My enemies turn back; they stumble and perish before you. For you have upheld my right and my cause; you have sat on your throne, judging righteously."

When you praise, your enemies will turn back! Remember: Our struggle is not against flesh and blood, but against Satan's forces (Ephesians 6).

Whatever trouble is challenging you today, begin to praise God. Exercise this vital weapon against Satan and his forces. Your enemies will have to turn back. They will fall and die before you, and the peace and victory that Jesus bought for you will be yours.

b a c k u p :
2 Chronicles 20:20-30

d o w n l o a d :
Daniel 1-2; Psalm 118

v o i c e a c t i v a t e :
As I praise God, my enemies turn back, fall and die before me! The peace and victory Jesus has for me is mine.
Psalm 9:1-4

gloria

"Let patience have its perfect work."
James 1:4, NKJV

The Pressure Is On

You've prayed in faith. You believe you have what you've prayed for. You are speaking God's promises, but instead of getting better, you grow worse.

Soon all you can think about is how fed up you are with waiting for your answer to come. You've had it and you're about to say those two words that cost more Christians their success than anything else in the world: *I quit!*

Sound familiar? Sure it does. Every Christian has gone through times like that. Tough times. Maybe those times have tripped you up in the past. Maybe Satan has used them to pressure you into letting go of what you're believing for. It doesn't have to be that way.

There is a force so powerful, it can carry you through those hard times. It is a force so dynamic, Satan cannot stop it. It's the force of patience.

Patience keeps you from falling under pressure. It is the quality that never surrenders to circumstances.

"That sounds great, Gloria, but I don't have that kind of patience!"

Yes, you do! It's part of God's character and He equipped you with it the moment you made Jesus your Lord. He placed it into your re-created human spirit right along with other character-building material (read Galatians 5:22-23).

God didn't give you just any old type of patience, either. He gave you His very own patience, and *The Amplified Bible* says He is *extraordinarily* patient (2 Peter 3:9). God has what it takes to get through hard times, and He has given you that power too!

Just as water won't flow from a faucet unless you open the valve and let it through, God's patience inside you won't flow out unless you release it on purpose. You have to make a decision.

I know that the pressure is on, and it can be intense, but patience will see you through. Open that valve, and let patience go to work!

backup:
Luke 8:5-15

download:
Daniel 3-4; Psalm 119:1-24

voice activate:
I let patience have its perfect work in my life. James 1:4

"The Lord will grant you abundant prosperity—in the fruit of your womb, the young of your livestock and the crops of your ground—in the land he swore to your forefathers to give you.... You will lend to many nations but will borrow from none."
Deuteronomy 28:11-12

From Galatians to the Garage

There was a time in my life when I had none of the blessings listed in Deuteronomy 28. That chapter lists all the promises to Abraham—promises God says belong to me through Jesus. For *"if you belong to Christ, then you are Abraham's seed, and heirs according to the promise."* (Galatians 3:29).

No, there was no doubt in my mind that these blessings were mine. The only question I had was, "How can I get hold of them?!"

As I dug into the Word, I found the answer. To enjoy the blessings of Abraham, I was going to have to walk in the same kind of faith he did. Faith opens the door to God's promises. It did in Abraham's day, and it will today. To me, that was good news.

Not everyone sees it that way, however. Some people want the blessings without having to live by faith, but it doesn't work that way.

"Well," you say, "I'd be happy if it did!"

No, you really wouldn't. God didn't set up the system of faith and prayer in order to make things difficult for you. He did it because Satan is always trying to steal our blessings. God's system is designed to keep him from doing that.

God's promises belong to you. To access them, you'll have to learn the procedures. You'll have to study the Bible and discover His ways.

My eagerness to do that was about all I had going for me, but it was enough. I was so desperate to learn faith that I locked myself in my garage with cassette teachings from Kenneth Hagin, where he talked about our inheritance in Jesus. I stayed out there with those tapes hour after hour. I couldn't get enough.

I'm the same way today. I still can't get enough. I don't care what else is going on in the world, I'm going to stick with the Word. It has taken me through everything that has ever come my way...and it will do the same for you.

backup:
Isaiah 48:15-19

download:
Daniel 5-6; Psalm 119:25-49

voice activate:
The Lord provides more than enough for me, for I belong to Him and I am Abraham's seed. Deuteronomy 28:11, Galatians 3:29

"I will rebuke the devourer for your sakes."
Malachi 3:11, KJV

gloria

It Takes Faith

Do you realize how wonderful it is to have our finances connected to God's heavenly economy? It means we can sleep peacefully at night when the rest of the world is tormented by fear of financial failure. We give our tithes and the Bible says Satan cannot devour our money.

Oddly enough, some Christians shrink back at such bold words. "Well, I just don't know," they protest. "I give my tithe, but I'm still not doing as well as the sinner down the street. So I'm not sure tithing does that much good."

The people in Malachi's day said exactly the same thing. They said, *"It is useless to serve God; and what profit is it if we keep His ordinances?... And now we consider the proud and arrogant happy and favored; evildoers are exalted and prosper."* (Malachi 3:14-15, AMP).

God didn't like those words. He said they were hard and stout against Him. Why? Because they were words of unbelief instead of words of faith.

God wants us to tithe because of our love for Him...and He wants us to use our faith! It takes faith to please Him (Hebrews 11:6).

If you don't have faith that God will prosper you, then get your Bible and study the promises He has made to you *because* you tithe. Study that Word, so you can tithe believing that God will keep His end of the promise and bless you with more than enough.

God loves it when you tithe with that kind of confidence, trusting Him to take care of you. So, the next time you drop your tithe in the offering, use your faith. Stand on God's promises for those who tithe...and receive the blessings that God wants to give to you!

backup:
Hebrews 7:1-9

download:
Daniel 7-8; Psalm 119:50-72

voice activate:
I will tithe and I know the Lord rebukes the devourer from stealing from me.
Malachi 3:11

"I have given you authority to trample on snakes and scorpions and to overcome all the power of the enemy; nothing will harm you."
Luke 10:19

Don't Buy the Lie!

Satan can't force you to do anything. He doesn't have the power. All he can do is make a sales pitch and try to sell you the lies he's peddling. He can't make you buy them. He can only present them. It's your choice as to whether you take him up on his sorry deal or refuse to give him the time of day.

So when he makes you a sales pitch, don't toy with it. Don't take the bait. Instead, learn to immediately turn away from his doubts and start thinking about God's promises instead. Ask yourself, *What does God say that's the opposite of what Satan just tried to sell me?*

Get in the Bible and find out the truth. That's where your power is—in the truth. Satan will lie to you, cheat you, trick you, deceive you and tie you up if you'll let him. However, God will always tell you the truth, and that truth will make you free.

So don't buy Satan's lies. Once you know the truth, you won't spend your days crying about how bad things are. You'll spend your days telling those problems exactly where to go.

Instead of whining, you'll be more than a conqueror in Jesus. You'll kick Satan out of your affairs with the words you say. As you stand strong, with your needs met, your body healed and your heart excited, you can laugh right in the face of that snake as he slinks away complaining about his defeat.

backup:
Luke 4:1-13

download:
Daniel 9-10; Psalm 119:73-96

voice activate:
I have authority to overcome all the power of the enemy! Luke 10:19

december 2

gloria

"The night is far gone [and] the day is almost here. Let us then drop (fling away) the works and deeds of darkness and put on the [full] armor of light. Let us live and conduct ourselves honorably and becomingly as in the [open light of] day; not in reveling (carousing) and drunkenness, not in immorality and debauchery...not in quarreling and jealousy. But clothe yourself with the Lord Jesus Christ, the Messiah, and make no provision for [indulging] the flesh."
Romans 13:12-14, AMP

Live in the Light

In this day and hour we need to receive everything God wants us to have, because time is getting short. It's time for us to wake up. It's time we quit allowing Satan to darken our homes, our schools, our churches and our lives with strife and envy. It's time we started living in the light!

You may be thinking that what I am talking about is easier said than done, but you can do it.

Learn to watch over yourself. Pay attention to your state of mind. When you find yourself depressed or downcast, don't just ignore those feelings. Think back. Ask yourself, *What started me feeling this way?*

You may realize that a particular situation sparked feelings of aggravation, jealousy or strife within you. If so, look at that situation through God's eyes and then speak to it (see Mark 11:23).

Say, "That situation has no power over me. I refuse to allow it to bring envy and strife into my life. I give the forces of love and joy rule in my life."

Then give God praise. Throw in a CD that will lift you up, and force yourself to sing along. Before long, God's love will burst out from within you again and you'll be singing from a pure heart.

Jesus is coming soon. We want Him to find us standing tall—full of love, faith and power—walking in everything Jesus bought for us.

We want Him to find us living in the light!

b a c k u p :
Proverbs 10:12, 14:30, 20:3

d o w n l o a d :
Daniel 11-12; Psalm 119:97-120

v o i c e   a c t i v a t e :
I fling away the works and deeds of darkness and put on the full armor of light! Romans 13:12

"So [as the result of the Messiah's intervention] they shall [reverently] fear the name of the Lord from the west, and His glory from the rising of the sun. When the enemy shall come in like a flood, the Spirit of the Lord will lift up a standard against him and put him to flight—for He will come like a rushing stream which the breath of the Lord drives."
Isaiah 59:19, AMP

You Can Flood the Earth

Think about that for a minute. What do you have if something stretches "from the west" to "the rising of the sun?" You have something without boundary.

What happens when water gets out of bounds? It becomes a flood! It's no longer just a lazy, old river. You have an unstoppable force that is roaring throughout the countryside with such power that nothing can stand in its way!

Now, with that in mind, I want you to move the comma in the next portion of today's verse. The translators put that comma in to make the verse read, *"When the enemy shall come in like a flood, the Spirit of the Lord will lift up a standard against him."*

That could not possibly be correct. How could Satan be a flood? He is containable. Not only is he containable—he has been contained!

Satan wasn't a flood when he came against Jesus. He wasn't even a drop in the bucket. Jesus is the One Who came in like a flood. Jesus was the One Who was uncontainable. No matter what Satan tried to do, he couldn't contain Him.

Everything Jesus did and said left Satan completely helpless.

So put that comma where it should be and read what that verse really says: *"So they shall fear the name of the Lord from the west, and His glory from the rising of the sun. When the enemy shall come in, like a flood the Spirit of the Lord will lift up a standard against him."*

Now, that's something to shout about! Jesus flooded Satan! What's even better news is that the same Holy Spirit flood that flowed through Jesus is now flowing through you and me! You can flood Satan. You can cast out demons and pray for others and watch them be set free!

So get started. Flood the earth today with His glory, His mercy and His love for everyone around you.

backup:
Isaiah 59:16-21

download:
Hosea 1-3; Psalm 119:121-144

voice activate:
When the enemy comes against me, like a flood the Spirit of the Lord will lift up a standard against him and put him to flight! Isaiah 59:19

"Here I am, I have come to do your will."
Hebrews 10:9

For the Sake of the Glory

God wants to pour out His glory in us and upon us. He wants us to place our hands on the sick and see them recover. He wants us to cast out demons and raise the dead. He wants us to have so much of His power flowing through us that He can do miracles through us. That is our destiny as His sons and daughters.

He cannot fully do everything He wants to do until we are living holy lives before Him. He cannot do it until we surrender everything in our lives to Him and obey every prompting he puts in our hearts. He needs us so submitted that we can say as Jesus did, *"Here I am, I have come to do whatever You will."*

I'm telling you, God is going to have children who say that to Him. He is going to have people who hunger after Him so much that they are willing to set aside anything in their lives that might hinder it. He is going to have children who have heard and followed the words Jesus spoke to His first disciples: *"If anyone would come after me, he must deny himself and take up his cross and follow me. For whoever wants to save his life will lose it, but whoever loses his life for me and for the gospel will save it"* (Mark 8:34-35).

I have determined in my heart once and for all that I am going to be one of those people. I will walk this road of holiness day by day. I want God's glory in my life. I have made up my mind that when I stand before Jesus, I will hear Him say, *"Well done, good and faithful servant."*

I urge you to make that same commitment today. Don't put it off another moment, for the time is very short. Bow your heart before the Lord and say:

Lord Jesus, I give everything I have and everything I am to You today. I determine to set my heart on You, and, by the energizing power of Your Spirit, I put aside every sin that would hinder me. Here I am. I have come to do Your will. Enlighten my heart, speak to me and tell me what changes I need to make in my life. I'm ready to hear and obey Your voice. In Jesus' Name, Amen.

b a c k u p :
Matthew 25:14-30

d o w n l o a d :
Hosea 4-5; Psalm 119:145-176

v o i c e   a c t i v a t e :
Lord, here I am. I have come to do your will. Hebrews 10:9

"Let it be to me according to your word."
Luke 1:38, NKJV

Connected to the Power

If you spend much time with the Lord, what I'm about to say is no surprise to you. You've already sensed it in your spirit: These are the end times.

Things have sped up and a new time is about to be born. Everyone is having to move fast. All of us have a role to play—and this is no false alarm.

Every one of us needs to get in position and do what God has called us to do. Yet everyone seems to have some kind of excuse that would keep them from doing what God called them to...but it's not time for excuses! It's time for us to say what Mary said when the angel told her she would have a baby supernaturally by God's power. She said, *"Let it be to me according to your word."*

Wow, what faith! Mary didn't know how it would work. It was beyond anything she had ever heard. Yet she just said, "Yes, Lord. Let's go!"

Do you know what happened when Mary released her faith in response to God's promise to her? It connected her to the supernatural. It connected her to a place where nothing is impossible (Luke 1:37).

That truth hasn't changed. A person without faith in action is stuck, living in this natural, material world of what's possible. A person *with* faith in action connects themselves to the Holy Spirit's power—or what I like to call "the muscle" of God—and impossible things happen in his or her life!

That's how Jesus did all the impossible things He did when He was on earth. He fulfilled His calling the same way you and I have to do it—by using His faith to connect Himself to supernatural power.

Remember this: It doesn't matter how impossible something may be, when you're connected by faith to the supernatural, you're connected to God...and all things are possible to Him!

"Everything is possible for him who believes" (Mark 9:23).

backup:
Luke 1:26-38

download:
Hosea 6-7; Psalm 120

voice activate:
Everything is possible to me, because I believe! Mark 9:23

december 6

kenneth

"If you remain in me and my words remain in you, ask whatever you wish, and it will be given you."
John 15:7

Thinking Like Him

Your choices can affect others. They can be far-reaching. You can make certain choices that can either damage or enrich lives all around you. What may not seem like a very important decision to you may ultimately make vital differences in your future, in your family's future, and in your friends' future. Just think how things would change if you made different choices.

If you allow your choices to be filtered through what God has said, those choices will separate you from the destructive bent of this world and take you into the track of His blessings.

God sees the whole picture. He knows what's around the corner that you can't see. So when you change your choices to match the choices God would make, things start working. All the pieces of the puzzle start coming together.

You can save yourself so much heartache and headache it isn't even funny, just by spending some quality time with God and in His Word. If you'll let Him, He will help you with every choice you make.

In order to have true life on this death-bound planet, you'll have to live a supernatural lifestyle by making supernatural choices every day of your life!

So start now getting God's promises into your heart. Start now letting what God says direct your choices—big and small. Let God begin to lift you up to His way of thinking.

b a c k u p :
Deuteronomy 30:11-20

d o w n l o a d :
Hosea 8-9; Psalm 121

v o i c e   a c t i v a t e :
I remain in God and His Word remains in me. John 15:7

"It is written: 'I believed; therefore I have spoken.' With that same spirit of faith we also believe and therefore speak."
2 Corinthians 4:13

A Winning Spirit

The spirit of faith speaks! It calls things that aren't as though they are. It speaks aloud about faith—not because it's "supposed to," but because it's so eager and confident, it can't keep its mouth shut!

The spirit of faith says, "I don't care what God has to do; He'll turn the world upside down if He has to, but He will change this situation for me."

Every time I talk about the spirit of faith, I think about my high school football team. For years the school had losing teams. Then, something happened to the bunch on my team. A winning spirit got into us.

When we were sophomores, we were on the B-squad. We were the nothings, but somehow, we got the idea that we could win. Every year the B-squad would have to scrimmage the varsity team, and usually the varsity just beat the daylights out of the sophomores.

The year our B-squad played them, that changed. We didn't just beat them, we had them down by several touchdowns, just daring them to get the ball

when the coach called off the game. He was so mad at the varsity team, he didn't even let us finish.

What happened to that little B-squad? We reached the point where we expected to win. We saw ourselves as winners, and it eventually took the best team in the state to beat us.

If a varsity giant is staring you in the face today, get that winning spirit in you. See yourself as the real winner. Stir up the spirit of faith. Speak over that situation, "I don't care what God has to do; He'll turn the world upside down if He has to, but He will change this situation for me. I am more than a conqueror in Jesus!" Then, celebrate the victory because you're a winner!

b a c k u p :
Romans 4:16-21

d o w n l o a d :
Hosea 10-11; Psalm 122

v o i c e   a c t i v a t e :
I believe and speak with the spirit of faith. 2 Corinthians 4:13

"[God] is able to do immeasurably more than all we ask or imagine, according to his power that is at work within us."
Ephesians 3:20

december 8

gloria

What Time Is It?

If you're a Christian and you've been struggling financially, scraping along with just barely enough—it's time for that to change. It's time for you to wake up to the riches that belong to you in Jesus, kick the limits off your faith and receive your financial inheritance.

Even if you haven't been struggling, even if your family's bills are paid and your major needs are met, you can still "step up." We all need to do that, because God has more in store for every one of us than we own right now. He is able to do "immeasurably more than all we ask or imagine, according to his power that is at work within us."

What's more, time is coming to a close. Jesus is coming soon. God wants to pour out His glory more than ever before—not just in our hearts, lives and youth group services, but in our finances as well.

Some time ago, the Lord began to speak to me about that. I began to hear, *Do you know what time it is? It's exceedingly-abundantly-above-all-that-you-can-ask-or-think time!*

I don't mind telling you, I was thrilled when I heard those words! I've become even more excited about them as time has passed. I believe it with all my heart!

We are in the end times. God is teaching us how to draw great riches from our heavenly account so we can glorify Him and get the good news preached to the world. He is showing us how we can have enough to give to every good work and have plenty left over to enjoy! He *"richly provides us with everything for our enjoyment!"* (1 Timothy 6:17).

So stand up and stretch your faith. Believe God for more than you need! Believe God for what the Church needs to minister life to the world!

b a c k u p :
1 Kings 10:1-24

d o w n l o a d :
Hosea 12-13; Psalm 123

v o i c e   a c t i v a t e :
God is able to do immeasurably more than all I ask or imagine, because His power is at work within me. Ephesians 3:20

> "Now faith is being sure of what we hope for and certain of what we do not see."
> **Hebrews 11:1**

Faith...or Desperation?

Did you know you can make your faith lose its aim? You can have all the faith you need, yet not get results. How? By losing your hope.

The fact is, faith won't function without hope. Hope is the "blueprint" of faith—it gives it direction. When hope is lost, faith loses its aim. It no longer has a mission to accomplish. It just scatters.

I remember one time when that happened to me. I had given my airplane to another preacher at God's instruction, and then ordered another to replace it.

I joined my faith to God's promises, and I was going along fine as it was being manufactured, believing God for the full amount I needed to pay for it. Then, just a few days before the plane was to be delivered, I was $20,000 short.

I got alarmed. I started speaking as fast as I could: "Thank God I have that $20,000. In Jesus' Name, I have it. I have it. I have it." That sounded like faith, but it wasn't. It was desperation.

I knew something had to change, so I grabbed my Bible, got in my boat, and went out to the middle of the lake so I could be totally alone. I was still saying,

"Thank God, I have that $20,000. In Jesus' Name, I have it. I have it."

Suddenly the Lord spoke up on the inside of me: *Kenneth, be quiet!* He said, *I'm tired of hearing that. Just hush and let Me show you what I can do.*

When He said that, hope came alive inside me again. Suddenly I was expectant instead of desperate. I started eagerly anticipating what God was about to do, instead of fearing what would happen if He didn't come through.

Sure enough, the $20,000 came in, but it wouldn't have happened if I hadn't stopped and let the Holy Spirit rebuild hope inside me. Hope is what took me from desperation to faith.

If you're facing serious circumstances, get alone with God, and let that hope come alive inside you. It will stop the desperation...and get your faith on target again.

backup:
Romans 8:18-25

download:
Hosea 14; Joel 1; Psalm 124

voice activate:
Hope is alive in me. My hope is in God. 1 Peter 1:21

kenneth

december 10

gloria

"I will praise you, O Lord, with all my heart; I will tell of all your wonders. I will be glad and rejoice in you; I will sing praise to your name, O Most High. My enemies turn back; they stumble and perish before you."
Psalm 9:1-3

Now, That's Power!

Together, joy and praise release strength on the inside of you and power on the outside. Psalm 22:3 says God inhabits our praises. When God's presence comes into our lives, our enemies fall back. They can't stand His presence.

Psalm 68:1-3 says, *"May God arise, may his enemies be scattered; may his foes flee before him. As smoke is blown away by the wind, may you blow them away; as wax melts before the fire, may the wicked perish before God. But may the righteous be glad and rejoice before God; may they be happy and joyful."*

Now, that's power! When God's people rise up in praise and worship, His enemies are scattered.

No wonder Satan has tried so hard to get God's people to sit still. No wonder he tries to make you feel stupid when you're the only one in your youth group raising your hands in praise. Satan doesn't want us to worship God!

That day is over. I'm telling you, when the Holy Spirit begins to move, your inhibitions will leave. That's what happened to the disciples on the Day of Pentecost. They had been hiding out only a few days before, but when the Holy Spirit came upon them, suddenly they were on the streets acting so wild, everyone thought they had been drinking. They had lost their inhibitions—by supernatural means!

Listen, God wants you free. He doesn't want you bound up with fear of what other people might think. He wants you to be free to laugh. He wants you to be free to leap and praise and sing. He wants you to be free to enjoy Him. He wants you so free that other people won't understand it— they'll just want it!

backup:
Psalm 98

download:
Joel 2-3; Amos 1; Psalms 125-126

voice activate:
I will praise God with *all* my heart! Psalm 9:1

"The joy of the Lord is your strength."
Nehemiah 8:10

More Than Laughter

If you've been in many church services where the Holy Spirit is moving in recent years, you've probably heard laughter—lots of laughter. You've seen and, perhaps, experienced spontaneous outbreaks of joy that range from a few, quiet chuckles to uproarious laughter that literally leaves Christians rolling in the aisles.

It's wonderful. There's no denying that, but what is it all about? The answer to that question is even more thrilling than the laughter itself.

Jesus is building us up, arming us with the spiritual might we will need to march out of every bondage and crush Satan under our feet—once and for all.

Now I want to show you something: The word *glory* in the Old Testament literally means to be heavy laden with everything that is good. That's God's presence. On the other hand, the word for *grief* is the exact opposite. It means to be heavy laden with everything that is bad.

Grief is the direct opposite of glory. So when God's glory—His goodness—comes on you, grief—anything bad—doesn't stand a chance. When God's glory comes, the joy of the Lord that's in you just starts bubbling out.

Of course, that's a lot of fun; we all enjoy it. But actually, the Lord is not just out to give laughter. He has a greater purpose. He wants us to be full of joy because it's the force that will make us strong enough to carry out His plan. It will give us the spiritual, mental and physical strength to rise up and lead others to Him.

Listen to me: We will not leave this earth like a whipped dog. No, God will make us winners. God will make *you* a winner. I don't care what low-level devil is harassing you with an aggravating problem...that low-level devil doesn't have the final say.

So rise up and laugh at what the devil thinks he can do! The victory is yours but the battle is the Lord's. God always wins!

backup:
Psalm 105:37-43

download:
Amos 2-3; Psalm 127

voice activate:
The joy of the Lord is my strength. Nehemiah 8:10

gloria

"But as to the suitable times and the precise seasons and dates, brethren, you have no necessity for anything being written to you. For you yourselves know perfectly well that the day of the Lord['s return] will come [as unexpectedly and suddenly] as a thief in the night."

1 Thessalonians 5:1-2, AMP

God Wants Us Handy

There is a shout going out...a prophetic shout...a shout that is shaping the life of every Christian on the face of the earth.

"JESUS IS COMING!"

The signs of Jesus' return are all around us. Never before has there been a time like this. Never before has it been so crucial that you and I be ready.

Some would say, "Oh, Gloria, you can't be sure Jesus is coming soon. After all, the Bible says nobody knows when Jesus is coming. His return will surprise us like a thief in the night."

If that's what you've been thinking, you'd better go back to the Bible and read today's scripture again. First Thessalonians 5 goes on to say that only those living in darkness will be caught by surprise. It says we are to keep wide awake, alert, watchful, cautious and on our guard.

If you're a Christian who is ready, Jesus' return will not take you by surprise. You're living in the light and you'll know. You may not know the *exact time*, but you will know the season.

In fact, I just suspect that those who are ready will be *so* ready that on the day Jesus returns, they'll sense something great is about to happen. A spiritual excitement will sound in their hearts.

There is no question about it. You and I have to be ready. Just like the military forces of our nation stay ready for combat, we also must be ready all the time. We must be ready, too, because there's an enemy out there. If we let him catch us off guard, he can make a serious mark on our lives. However, if we're ready and we resist him, he will shoot away like lightning.

We must be ready! We ought to be handy for God to use at any time. He wants us willing! He wants us ready!

backup:
1 Thessalonians 5:1-6

download:
Amos 4-5; Psalm 128

voice activate:
I am alert and ready for the Lord's return. I won't be caught by surprise. 1 Thessalonians 5:4-6

> "For since He Whom God has sent speaks the words of God...God does not give Him His Spirit sparingly or by measure, but boundless is the gift God makes of His Spirit!"
> John 3:34, AMP

Operate in Full Power

"Oh, God, I need more power! Please...please give me more power!"

Have you ever prayed a prayer like that? I have. In fact, years ago I was praying like that, asking God to give me greater power to minister. It sounded very spiritual. However, the Lord interrupted me right in the middle of it.

Kenneth, He said. *Where would I go to get you more power?*

The question stopped me cold.

No one has more power than I do, He continued. *I've already filled you with My Spirit. I've put within you the same miraculous force that created heaven and earth, the same supernatural strength that raised Jesus from the dead. Where am I going to go to find something greater that that?*

His point was clear. We don't need more power. We need to use what we've been given. We need to allow the Holy Spirit to work through us. If we're not seeing miracles in our lives, it isn't God's fault. He isn't limiting us. We are!

That may not sound like good news to you, but it is. If you're the one who is keeping the lid on God's power in your life, then you're the one who can take that lid off! You can make a decision to increase the flow of God's power in your life—starting today!

"Well, I don't believe we can turn God's power on just *whenever!*"

I don't either. Thank God, we don't have to! His power is always on! He is just waiting for us to start using it to do the things Jesus did, and even more (John 14:12). How? By operating in the same unlimited power that Jesus did—the same power He had because He spoke God's Word.

Jesus *always* spoke God's Word—in everything He did (John 8:28). That was what brought God's presence on the scene without limits.

So quit asking God to give you more power. He couldn't, even if He wanted to. He doesn't have any more to give. You already have it all...just turn it on! Speak out His promises every day, all day long, and operate in full power.

backup:
John 14:8-14

download:
Amos 6-7; Psalm 129

voice activate:
God has given me His power. I will start to use it by doing the same things Jesus did...and more! John 14:12

december 14

gloria

"From the days of John the Baptist until now, the kingdom of heaven has been forcefully advancing, and forceful men lay hold of it."
Matthew 11:12

Spiritual Aggression

What does it take to be a winner? Everyone everywhere wants to know the answer to that question. Everyone wants to win, but when it comes right down to it, not everyone is willing to pay the price to do it.

During some recent Olympic games, I listened to the athletes being interviewed. They talked about how hard they worked to compete in the games.

None of them just woke up one morning and said, "Hey! I think I'll be in the Olympics this year." They trained for years to get there.

I heard one champion tell how she got out of bed every morning to run. She ran in the cold. She ran in the rain. Sometimes she would push herself so hard, she would get sick. Even then, she refused to quit. She was determined to win and she gave her very best.

That kind of commitment is what it takes to be a winner, not just physically, but spiritually. Jesus said so in today's verse. When He said those words, He wasn't talking about going to

heaven. I believe He was talking about laying hold of the good things God has for us on earth—taking hold of the promised blessings like healing, prosperity and peace.

You can have those blessings here and now, but it's not easy. You have to grab hold of them with all your might. You have to become spiritually aggressive, using your faith and putting God's Word in your heart.

So start training for your race now. Don't waste another minute. Get into the Bible. Build up your faith. Get aggressive with it. Do whatever it takes. Just like the Olympic runner, it will be worth it all!

backup:
1 Timothy 6:11-12

download:
Amos 8-9; Psalm 130

voice activate:
**I am a spiritually aggressive person who grabs hold of God's promises.
Matthew 11:12**

"Rejoice in the Lord always. I will say it again: Rejoice!"
Philippians 4:4

Overloaded With Joy

Joy...it's a traditional part of the Christmas season. In December, people who hardly crack a smile all year send out cards with messages about joy. Carolers chirp out "Joy to the World!" as grumpy shoppers push their way through crowded malls. Glittering banners wave the word "JOY" over city streets jammed with irritated drivers who just want to get home.

The truth is, with all the pressures people face this time of year, it's easy to let joy slip through your fingers, but don't do it. Instead, get a true understanding of joy that you can hang onto all year 'round.

Joy used to be my weakest area. I spent so much time focusing on faith that I didn't pay much attention to it; however, the Lord taught me that you can't live by faith without joy. That's because it takes strength to live by faith. The natural pull of the world is always negative. When you leave things alone and don't work against that negative flow, they always get worse.

To move toward life, you must constantly swim upstream. If you ever get too weak spiritually to do that, you'll find yourself being swept back toward defeat. So you can never afford to run out of strength.

No wonder the Apostle Paul wrote to rejoice in the Lord always! To rejoice means to *re-joy*, to back up and get another load!

Paul understood the link between joy and strength. That's why he prayed for the Colossians to be *"strengthened with all might, according to His [God's] glorious power, for all patience and longsuffering with joy"* (Colossians 1:11, NKJV). The heart of that sentence says we are strengthened with might and joy!

Paul reaffirmed this basic truth: The joy of the Lord is our strength (Nehemiah 8:10)! So back your truck up...and get another load!

b a c k u p :
Acts 20:16-24

d o w n l o a d :
Obadiah; Jonah 1; Psalm 131

v o i c e   a c t i v a t e :
I rejoice in the Lord always!
Philippians 4:4

"The backsliding of the simple shall slay them, and the careless ease of [self-confident] fools shall destroy them. But whoso hearkens to me [Wisdom], shall dwell securely and in confident trust, and shall be quiet without fear or dread of evil."
Proverbs 1:32-33, AMP

gloria

Hearing From Heaven

There is nothing—absolutely nothing!—on this earth that's as valuable as God's wisdom. It is the key to success, health, long life, peace and security. All of these are available to those who learn from and live by His wisdom.

Oddly enough, many Christians don't seek God's wisdom until their backs are against the wall. They wait until trouble hits, and then, in desperation, they listen hard for God's voice. All too often they are unable to hear it.

Why? Because, as the voice of Wisdom says in Proverbs 1:24-28: *"I have called and you refused [to answer],...you have treated as nothing all my counsel, and would accept none of my reproof, I also will laugh at your calamity; I will mock when the thing comes that shall cause you terror and panic, When your panic comes as a storm and desolation, and your calamity comes on as a whirlwind, when distress and anguish come upon you. Then they will call upon me [Wisdom], but I will not answer; they will seek me early and diligently, but they will not find me"* (AMP).

Don't ever let yourself get caught in a situation like that. Don't ever let yourself get to the point where you're unable to hear from heaven.

Hearing from heaven is the most important thing in your whole life! That's because you can never come up with a problem too big for God to solve. The important thing to remember, however, is that you can't turn God's wisdom on and off like a water faucet. Hearing from heaven must be part of your lifestyle.

If you want to be sure that God's wisdom will be there for you when a crisis hits, you need to start listening for His guidance now. Learn to seek His wisdom, to listen for His instructions on the little, everyday matters of life. That way, when the big problems come, you'll be ready. You'll be in the habit of hearing from heaven.

b a c k u p :
Proverbs 4:7-9

d o w n l o a d :
Jonah 2-3; Psalm 132

v o i c e   a c t i v a t e :
Because I listen to God's wisdom, I am secure and confident, without fear or dread. Proverbs 1:33

"Whatever is true, whatever is noble, whatever is right, whatever is pure, whatever is lovely, whatever is admirable—if anything is excellent or praiseworthy—think about such things."
Philippians 4:8

Thinking God's Thoughts

When you begin to study God's Word, the first thing you discover is that it goes absolutely contrary to the way you're used to thinking. The only way for the Word to live in you is to choose it over your old, worldly thoughts.

How do you get a grip on worldly thoughts and turn them into thoughts that line up with what God says? By *replacing them* with His thoughts and His Words (2 Corinthians 10:4-6).

Think about this: God isn't worried, is He? He's not filled with anxiety about your problems. No! He has more than enough power to get you through every circumstance. So when you think His thoughts, you won't be afraid either. You'll be full of His peace.

If you're going to live in God's peace, you have to close the door to thoughts that don't line up with His Word. You have to throw aside every thought that disagrees with the Word and choose to think God's thoughts instead. You literally have to select what your mind thinks.

You have to be like my daughter Kellie when she was a little girl. One day I took her by the hand, led her into her room,

opened the door of her closet (which was piled full of junk) and said, "Kellie Dee Copeland, this closet of yours is a mess! Now you're going to get in there and clean it up."

She just looked up at me and said, "That's not my thought."

She wouldn't accept that thought. Even when she went ahead and cleaned up the closet, it wasn't her thought. The only reason she did it is because her parents made her.

That's the way we need to treat Satan. When he comes around with a worried thought, we need to tell him, "That's not my thought. I'm not touching that with my thought life." Then we need to immediately replace that thought with one of God's promises. We need to think like He thinks!

backup:
Psalm 119:40-64

download:
Jonah 4; Micah 1-2; Psalms 133-134

voice activate:
I think like God thinks. I think about whatever is true, noble, right, pure, lovely, admirable, excellent or praiseworthy. Philippians 4:8

"He who sent me is reliable, and what I have heard from him I tell the world…I do nothing on my own but speak just what the Father has taught me."
John 8:26,28

Imitate Him

Just about everything I know, I learned from copying someone else. Take skiing, for example. Gloria and I love to ski. We had a good ski instructor. He did everything right. He always looked so great coming down the mountain.

I learned to ski by imitating him. I kept listening to everything he told me to do and then I went out there and did it. It worked! I didn't look as smooth as he looked, of course, but I skied.

Every year I ski a little better. Could someone accuse me of copying that ski instructor? Of course, they could! That's exactly what I'm doing. I'm doing everything I possibly can to look just like him. Why? Because he's a better skier than I am!

There was a guy once who was criticizing me. "That Copeland just runs around acting like a little Jesus," he said. He didn't realize it, but as far as I'm concerned, that's a great compliment. That's exactly what I'm trying to do!

Jesus told me to do it. He said, *"I do nothing on my own but speak just what the Father has taught me."* In other words, "I'm standing here copying the Father. Now you copy Me."

Know this: You *will* act like somebody. You'll copy what you see on television or what you read in magazines or what you hear from the world—or you'll copy Jesus.

The question is, who will you choose to imitate? If you choose to be like Jesus, you'll change your words to say what He says. You'll change your actions to do what He does. The more skilled you become with disciplining yourself, the more you'll live like Jesus did. He's the best teacher and example you'll ever know. Imitate Him!

b a c k u p :
John 8:25-29

d o w n l o a d :
Micah 3-4; Psalm 135

v o i c e a c t i v a t e :
My words and actions are following after God's. John 8:28

"The person who is united to the Lord becomes one spirit with Him."
1 Corinthians 6:17, AMP

Get a Reputation

Jesus trained His disciples, *"As you go, preach this message: 'The kingdom of heaven is near.' Heal the sick, raise the dead, cleanse those who have leprosy, drive out demons. Freely you have received, freely give"* (Matthew 10:7-8).

"Well, yes, but that was back then. Maybe He has a different plan for us."

No, He doesn't! His last words before He went to heaven were the same instructions—and His Word never changes: *"Go into all the world and preach the good news to all creation...And these signs will accompany those who believe: In my name they will drive out demons...they will place their hands on sick people, and they will get well"* (Mark 16:15, 17-18).

Praise God! We have the same God, the same Holy Spirit and the same commission those first disciples had. Do you remember what happened to them after Jesus left?

They kept right on doing what Jesus had done—and the crowds treated them just like they had treated Jesus. They brought the sick so they could be healed.

Why did they do that? They heard if you could get to where the Christians were, you could get healed. The Christians had a reputation. It was the same reputation Jesus had. As a result, thousands became Christians every day!

That's the way it should be for us.

"But I can't heal the sick!" you say. "I can't cast out devils!"

Maybe not, but God *in* you can. Jesus said, *"On that day you will realize that I am in my Father, and you are in me, and I am in you"* (John 14:20).

You and Jesus are one. You are His instrument in the earth. Dare to believe that. Be bold enough to speak the words the Bible speaks and do whatever Jesus tells you to do. Believe me, people will come to you for help. The Holy Spirit will empower you—and great things will happen!

backup:
Ephesians 2:18-22

download:
Micah 5-6; Psalm 136

voice activate:
I am one with Jesus! 1 Corinthians 6:17

kenneth

"For the kingdom of God is not a matter of eating and drinking, but of right-eousness, peace and joy in the Holy Spirit."
Romans 14:17

Connected to the Holy Spirit

One way to stir up your joy is to spend time with the Holy Spirit. According to Romans 14:17, there is joy in the Holy Spirit! So stay connected with Him! Pray and sing in the language He gives you. Start with praise and giving thanks for all He has done for you.

Thank Jesus for dying on the Cross and rising again. Thank Him for washing away your sin. Thank Him that you're on your way to heaven. If you can't think of any other reason, just think about those few things. Keep shouting, "Yes! My sins are washed away!" until joy rises up in you.

"I can't do that. I just don't feel like it."

That doesn't matter! Expressing your joy is a matter of choice, not feeling. In Psalm 27:6, King David wrote, *"Then my head will be exalted above the enemies who surround me; at his [God's] taberna-cle will I sacrifice with shouts of joy; I will sing and make music to the LORD."*

If you're having problems with someone at school, don't stay up all night worrying about what's going to happen tomorrow. If you're going to stay up, give God praise. Sing. Dance. Give thanks. Shout out God's promises and laugh at Satan until joy comes. Then keep on being joyful until you're so filled with God's strength that nothing can stop you.

Keep doing it until your body is well. Keep doing it until every chain Satan has used to keep you in bondage snaps like a thread. Keep doing it until people start coming to you saying, "Hey, I want some of that joy!"

Think about it. Wouldn't it be won-derful if we started expressing our joy this Christmas and just kept on every day? I believe with all my heart that's what God is calling us to do.

Let's connect with the Holy Spirit and get that joy!

b a c k u p :
Romans 14:17

d o w n l o a d :
Micah 7; Nahum 1-3; Psalm 137

v o i c e a c t i v a t e :
The Holy Spirit gives me joy. Romans 14:17

"Love [God's love in us] does not insist on its own rights or its own way, for it is not self-seeking."
1 Corinthians 13:5, AMP

Center Your Life Around God

God loves the unlovely. No matter how bad, mean or ornery someone might be, if they'll turn to Him, He'll cleanse them and forgive them.

That's the way God loves us, and that's the way He expects us to love each other. In 1 Corinthians 13, He gives us a detailed description of that kind of love. According to the Bible, it's God's love that sets you apart. You and I have a high calling. We're called to live a life of love just like Jesus did.

We must die to our own selfish tendencies and desires. We must stop centering our lives on what we want and what we feel. We must stop looking out for ourselves all the time. Walking in love means we set aside our own rights and look out for the other person's instead.

That may sound tough, but it's actually the easiest way to be blessed—because when you walk in love, God takes care of you! The Bible says, *"The eyes of the Lord run to and fro throughout the whole earth, to show Himself strong in behalf of those whose heart is blameless toward Him"* (2 Chronicles 16:9, AMP).

When you walk in love, blessings are coming your way!

Not only that, when you stop being selfish, you'll be a happier person. When you're self-centered, you're always thinking about yourself. You're always thinking about someone who did you wrong...or how much you have to do.

It's impossible for a selfish person to stay happy because everything centers around him. We're not made to live that way. We're not big enough or powerful enough for everything to center around us.

As a Christian, you've been rescued from selfishness. You don't have to center your life around yourself. You have the power to center your life around God instead. You can keep your mind on obeying His Word and living a life of love! He will take care of everything else (Matthew 6:33).

backup:
Ephesians 4:1-3

download:
Habakkuk 1-3; Psalm 138

voice activate:
I walk in love. I seek God and His ways, and He takes care of everything else. Matthew 6:33

kenneth

"In righteousness you will be established."
Isaiah 54:14

Be a Strong Oak

Jesus is the very picture of established righteousness. He always knew He had right-standing with God. At Lazarus' funeral, He was the only One not dressed in black. That's because He hadn't come to a funeral...He had come to a raising! He was so established in righteousness that He boldly said, "Roll the stone away from the door of the tomb" (John 11:39).

He commanded, *"Lazarus, come out."* Then, God backed Him up. When Righteousness speaks, there's nothing Satan can do but bow and leave.

"Sure, Jesus could speak like that," you say, "but I'm not Jesus!"

No, but you're in right-standing with God because of Him. He's given you righteousness! That's why that angel shouted at Jesus' birth, *"I bring you good news of great joy that will be for all the people"* (Luke 2:10).

What was so joyful about that good news? Those angels were talking to Hebrew people who were living their lives by the Law. They'd forever struggled to please God so they could be in right-standing with Him, but they couldn't do it. So the coming of the Righteous One was the best news they had ever heard.

All too often, Satan tries to trick us out of it. He tells us that we're *not* in right-standing. He's tells us God is mad at us. Why? So we're willing to accept whatever he has to offer: oppression, fear and doubt.

God says we are *"oaks of righteousness, a planting of the Lord for the display of his splendor"* (Isaiah 61:3). So be a tree of righteousness planted by God. Not just any old tree, but a strong oak! Stand there tall because God put you there. Then, when Satan comes along, you tell him, *"No! According to God's Word I am in right-standing with God! I won't accept what you're trying to give me!"*

So stand strong, Oak Tree! Just keep standing there digging your roots into the promises God has for you. Keep acting the same way Jesus did. You'll be living proof that there truly is peace on earth, good will toward men!

b a c k u p :
Luke 2:1-20

d o w n l o a d :
Zephaniah 1-3; Psalm 139

v o i c e   a c t i v a t e :
I am established in right-standing with God. Isaiah 54:14

"Therefore, since the promise of entering his rest still stands, let us be careful that none of you be found to have fallen short of it."
Hebrews 4:1

It's Time To Rest

Ephesians 2:6 says God has *"raised us up with Christ and seated us with him in the heavenly realms in Christ Jesus."* In Hebrews 3 and 4, we are commanded to enter God's rest...and then stay there.

Now I'll be the first to admit that entering into God's rest—His peace—has been one of the harder things for me to do in ministry. In my personal life, when faced with Satan's attack, I have taken God's promises for peace, stood on them, believed God and entered into His rest.

I'm seeing that God intends for us to rest over *every* situation—particularly with all we have facing us in these end times.

When those hungry people came up to Jesus in Matthew 14:19-21, He didn't fall on His face and start sobbing and kicking the dirt, saying, "Oh, God! Oh, God! I just don't know what I'm going to do. There are 5,000 of them—and that's just the men. We don't have enough money. Besides, we're out here in the middle of nowhere!"

No, Jesus just rested in God. He trusted in His Father.

Today, our goal is to walk in God's promises with such faith that, no matter what challenge or need comes our way, we do just like Jesus did when that huge crowd came to Him: We just smile and say, "Bring me the bread and fish."

Then we take our seed, look to God, give thanks for it, bless it, break it and *expect* God to move—and we just rest.

backup:
Psalm 37:7; Hebrews 3-4

download:
Haggai 1-2; Psalm 140

voice activate:
The peace of God guards my heart and mind. Philippians 4:7

december 24

kenneth

"In the beginning was the Word, and the Word was with God, and the Word was God…Yet to all who received him, to those who believed in his name, he gave the right to become children of God…The Word became flesh and made his dwelling among us."
John 1:1,12,14

The Bridge Between Two Worlds

Everyone knows heaven is a great place. It has everything—wealth so immense that the streets are made of gold, health so strong that sickness can't exist there, joy so plentiful it forever extinguishes all sorrow.

Christians everywhere dream of going there when they die. I want you to imagine for a moment how wonderful it would be if you could have access to heaven right now. Think what it would be like if God would build a bridge between heaven and earth so that those boundless heavenly supplies could come down and meet the needs in your life today. It's a wonderful thought, isn't it? Do you know what's even more wonderful? The bridge has been built!

Most people can't even believe such a thing is possible. That's because, in their minds, heaven isn't quite real. So they can't understand how the "reality" of this physical world and the "unreality" of the spiritual world could ever connect.

I used to think that way too. Then years ago, God began to change my way

of thinking. He told me that reality includes *both* the spiritual world and the physical world. He also informed me that, contrary to popular belief, the spiritual world is not only just as real as this physical world, but it is *more* real!

Two thousand years ago, an angel exploded with joy announcing the good news: "Peace on earth. Good will toward men!" (Luke 2:14, KJV). Jesus was born! The Word that brought life to Adam had come again. Immediately, Heaven and Earth reconnected…the bridge for your salvation was built…the separation that had existed since Adam's disobedience to God was over.

Because of that, today, you can have all your needs met—and more. Yes, Jesus is born! You have been given a Savior. Invite Him into your heart today…and walk across the bridge between two worlds.

backup:
John 1:1-14

download:
Zechariah 1-3; Psalms 141-142

voice activate:
The Word has come and given me the right to be a child of God! John 1:12

> "I bring you good news of great joy that will be for all the people. Today in the town of David a Savior has been born to you; he is Christ the Lord."
> Luke 2:10-11

Merry Christmas!

St. Nicholas should be an inspiration to us all. He was a godly man whose reputation for giving to people caused him to be a great example of what compassion and giving are all about. He was not a jolly, fat man who climbed down chimneys, and he didn't have flying reindeer!

Stories of his life—a life full of Christian beliefs and values—are the real background for today's mythical Santa Claus. So much of what Nicholas was—and what Santa Claus has become—has been distorted. What has been done to weaken and contort the testimony of this godly man is wrong.

Born in Turkey in 280 A.D., Nicholas was raised by Christian parents who considered him a gift from God. They diligently taught him devotion to God and to be very generous to the poor.

At nineteen, Nicholas was ordained a priest. His uncle, a bishop, prophesied that Nicholas would offer guidance and consolation to many people, and that he would eventually become a bishop. All of this was fulfilled in Nicholas' lifetime.

Many accounts have been written about his dedicated life. It has been said that he would spend all night studying the Bible to bring it to the people. He was known for helping the poor, praying, fasting and standing steadily in faith and goodness.

The true story of St. Nicholas is a beautiful picture of the giving that Christmas is all about. The greatest gift of all is the gift of Jesus to us from God the Father. Jesus is our hope, redemption and victory. He will never leave us. In Him we have the joy of living a heavenly life on earth.

He is the true meaning of Christmas. He is the One St. Nicholas served. He is our triumphant Savior, Jesus the Christ, the Lord of lords and King of kings! Now, that's a merry Christmas!

kenneth

backup:
Matthew 1-2

download:
Zechariah 4-5; Psalm 143

voice activate:
God loves me so much, He sent Jesus to earth to save me! John 3:16

367

december 26

kenneth

"And afterward, I will pour out my Spirit on all people. Your sons and daughters will prophesy, your old men will dream dreams, your young men will see visions. Even on my servants, both men and women, I will pour out my Spirit in those days. I will show wonders in the heavens and on the earth, blood and fire and billows of smoke."
Joel 2:28-30

Ask for True Understanding

Some people think the fire and smoke in that verse refers to destruction, but it doesn't. Fire and smoke are just a couple of the ways God's glory shows up. That scripture is talking about the greatest movement of God ever seen on this earth.

We are already in the beginning stages of what God is doing. Where is it coming from? It's coming from within Christians like you and me. It will keep getting bigger and bigger as His love and anointing power move from our hearts into our homes, our schools, our neighborhoods and our world.

Let me warn you, this isn't going to happen while we sit around watching TV, playing football and filling our time with the ordinary details of life. It's going to come as we dig into the Bible and build our faith in what God can do. The more we learn to expect Him to move through us, the more we line our lives up with His ways, the more we will see.

So get out your Bible and start studying. Every time you see the word *Christ,* translate it and think about the fact that it means "the Anointed One and His Anointing." Learn how to protect the anointing and how to live your life in such a way that the Holy Spirit can work freely through you.

In other words, ask God for a true understanding of what it really means to be anointed with the Anointing of Jesus—God's own world-changing, healing, rescuing, explosive, supernatural, universe-creating power. Ask for a true understanding of what it really means to be a Christian.

Once you see the full picture, the world around you will never be the same again.

b a c k u p :
John 7:37-39

d o w n l o a d :
Zechariah 6-7; Psalm 144

v o i c e   a c t i v a t e :
I can do all things through the Anointed One and His anointing! Philippians 4:13

"What if some did not believe and were without faith? Does their lack of faith and their faithlessness nullify and make ineffective and void the faithfulness of God and His fidelity [to His Word]? By no means! Let God be found true though every human being be false and a liar."
Romans 3:3-4, AMP

God Is Not a Liar

Everything that has to do with people, everything in this natural world, is subject to change, but God's Word is not. The Bible is true even when everything else around you is telling you otherwise. Notice that today's verse says you must let God be true in your life.

To do so, you must settle forever in your heart and mind, that there is no fault in God. He doesn't change His mind. There's no weakness or shortcoming in what He says.

You will never catch God in a lie. You will never get in a situation where you exercise faith in a promise of God and He fails to keep His Word. Never! The Bible says that God is active and alert, watching over His Word to perform it (Jeremiah 1:12, AMP).

Understand, however, that it's not enough just to know what the Bible says. It must be reality to you—more real than the problem you face.

For example, maybe you have experienced recurring symptoms of an illness for a long time. If so, you need to sit down and ask yourself, *Do I really believe that according to 1 Peter 2:24, by His stripes I was healed?*

However you honestly answered that question in your heart makes the difference in your situation. You have to choose to believe that God cannot lie and that His Word is true...regardless of what the circumstances are telling you. You can't try to put faith in His Word based on head knowledge. That's not enough!

That's why we must constantly focus on God's Word—because it's that Word that produces faith in our hearts. In fact, you cannot deepen your faith in God without deepening your trust in His Word.

Let God be found true...if you believe in His Word, His promises will become reality in your life!

backup:
Psalm 119:89; John 17:17

download:
Zechariah 8-9; Psalm 145

voice activate:
God's Word is truth. It always does exactly what it promises. John 17:17, Jeremiah 1:12

Kenneth

369

december 28

gloria

"I am convinced and sure of this very thing, that He Who began a good work in you will continue until the day of Jesus Christ—right up to the time of His return—developing [that good work] and perfecting and bringing it to full completion in you."
Philippians 1:6, AMP

Get Caught Up!

From the moment you made Jesus your Lord, God began to peel things away from you that were holding you back, things that were stopping Him from moving powerfully in your life.

He's still doing that. You're still growing. You keep growing and allowing God to talk to you and deal with you. He keeps speaking to you about things you need to change, things you need to drop out of your life.

Still, it's not only about dropping things, it's about taking on new things. We grow by learning the truth of God's Word and applying it. Your old habits and old lifestyle will soon lose their hold on you.

The more you get to know God, the less you want the old things. The more you know God, the more of the old is peeled away.

You could just say, "Okay, I'm not going to smoke cigarettes anymore. I'm not going to do it anymore. I just won't."

That's better than saying you will do it, but there is a MUCH better way.

The best way is to get so caught up in serving God that God's Spirit and His power begin to throw those things off you. You have to make a decision—you have to *choose* to do what's right. When you do, His power will change you.

So get in the Word. Think about what it says. Listen to recorded teachings of the Word preached. Don't ever stop. Remember, you should always be growing. Just get caught up in Him!

backup:
2 Corinthians 5:17; Ephesians 4

download:
Zechariah 10-11; Psalm 146

voice activate:
God started a work in me, and He will keep developing it and perfecting it until it is fully completed. Philippians 1:6

> "We are hard pressed on every side, but not crushed; perplexed, but not in despair; persecuted, but not abandoned; struck down, but not destroyed."
> 2 Corinthians 4:8-9

Inner Strength

Remember the class bully when you were in elementary school? He was nothing but a 4 ½-foot, 100-pound heap of trouble who scared everyone silly. Well, you're over that situation by now, but trouble is still around.

In this life, Satan takes every opportunity he gets. Even the Apostle Paul said he was troubled by circumstances on every side, but Paul didn't focus on the trouble around him. Instead, he fixed his attention on the promises of God he knew...because that's where God's power is.

Perplexed...persecuted...struck down. There's no doubt about it, Paul was under more pressure than most of us will ever experience, but he handled it. You can also handle it if you'll do the following three things:

ONE: Remember where the pressure is coming from—the outside! Also, remember where your strength comes from—the inside!

TWO: Stop running on too little. Feed your spirit with God's Word.

THREE: Focus on Jesus inside you until your inner picture of Him is bigger than the outside situations you're facing.

If you'll build up your spirit in those three ways, when pressure comes, it won't affect you like it does today. Soon, the problems that are knocking you flat will blow away with the wind.

Remember the bully? He couldn't even make you blink today, now that you're six feet tall. What happened? What changed? You grew. You're stronger now. That little kid's no longer a threat. That's what happened to Paul. He grew! He kept feeding on the Word until the image of Jesus within him grew bigger than the pressures around him. So just keep feeding your spirit on the Word. Get strong on the inside, and don't let the bullies get you down!

backup:
2 Corinthians 4:8-12

download:
Zechariah 12-13; Psalm 147

voice activate:
Satan can't get me down. God is on my side! 2 Corinthians 4:8-9, Romans 8:31

gloria

"I believed; therefore have I spoken."
2 Corinthians 4:13

Why Didn't You Say Something?

Consider the following scenario:

"Where should we eat?" you ask your friend, walking through the mall.

"Oh, I don't care. Anywhere you want to go is fine," your friend says.

Taking your friend at his word, you go to your favorite restaurant. The problem is, your friend really doesn't like it. Once you get there and start to order, your friend seems a bit aggravated.

"What's wrong?"

"Oh nothing," he snaps.

"What is it?"

"I didn't want to eat here. I want to eat somewhere else."

"Well, why didn't you say something?" you ask in exasperation.

Now, that's just a small example, but it illustrates a very real truth. Someday, when we stand before Jesus, someone might say, "Lord, I really needed wisdom for my schoolwork when I was on earth...I really needed healing for my body...I really needed rescuing from my circumstances."

I can hear Jesus saying to us just what you said to your friend: "Well, why didn't you *say* something?!"

Those words may shock you. You may be sitting around in the middle of a crisis waiting for God to act—when all the time, He's waiting for you. Jesus is waiting for each one of us to take the power and authority He gave us and use it to put those Satan-generated crises where they belong—under our feet!

Jesus said, *"All authority in heaven and on earth has been given to me. Therefore [you] go..."* (Matthew 28:18-19). In other words, *I'm giving you My authority, so use it!*

Whatever troubles you're facing right now, if you want a change, why don't you *say* what you want? Jesus said you can have what you say!

b a c k u p :
Matthew 28:16-20

d o w n l o a d :
Zechariah 14; Malachi 1; Psalm 148

v o i c e   a c t i v a t e :
I only speak what I believe.
2 Corinthians 4:13

> "But solid food is for the mature, who by constant use have trained themselves to distinguish good from evil."
> **Hebrews 5:14**

Living Right

Whatever you're exposed to, that's what you will practice. You can practice living right just as easily as you can practice living wrong.

If you've ever smoked a cigarette, the first time you smoked, you probably got sick. You probably coughed and spit and carried on, because it's unnatural to put smoke inside your lungs. You had to learn how to do that. You had to practice until you could handle smoke in your lungs.

That doesn't make any sense at all, but it seemed sensible to you when you were in darkness.

"I've got to learn how to get this smoke in my lungs so it will cut my life short and I can't breathe well."

Now, that's nonsense, but it made sense before you made Jesus your Lord.

If you've ever taken a slug of beer—I imagine it got you good. It was hard to swallow, and tasted downright nasty. You had to learn how to drink it by repeating the procedure. Because it tastes *bad.*

Well, that's exactly what happens to you in living right before God. You learn by practice.

When you first start out, you might say to yourself, *I'm not going to smoke anymore.* Then you might fail. Ken quit smoking a lot of times, and so did I. Then one day, we quit for good.

If you mess up, what do you do? You turn from that thing and say, "Lord, I'm hanging on to You. Help me to do this! I believe I'm rescued from it."

It's not just willpower. Your willpower is there to make the choice. God's power empowers you to stand for what you know God wants you to do.

Say, "Listen up, old nature! You are not going to have your way here. I'm serving God. I'm not going to do and practice the things that are displeasing to God. I'm going straight ahead into living right!"

b a c k u p :
Colossians 3:1-17; 1 John 3:2-9

d o w n l o a d :
Malachi 2-4; Psalms 149-150

v o i c e   a c t i v a t e :
I am a child of God and because His seed remains in me, sin has no place in my life. 1 John 3:9

Topical Index to Devotions

"For the earth shall be full of the knowledge of the Lord, as the waters cover the sea" (Isaiah 11:9).

JANUARY

1   Genesis 1-3; Matthew 1-2
2   Genesis 4-5; Matthew 3
3   Genesis 6-7; Matthew 4
4   Genesis 8-9; Matthew 5
5   Genesis 10-11; Matthew 6
6   Genesis 12-13; Matthew 7
7   Genesis 14-15; Matthew 8
8   Genesis 16-18; Matthew 9-10
9   Genesis 19-20; Matthew 11
10 Genesis 21-22; Matthew 12
11 Genesis 23-24; Matthew 13
12 Genesis 25-26; Matthew 14
13 Genesis 27-28; Matthew 15
14 Genesis 29-30; Matthew 16
15 Genesis 31-33; Matthew 17-18
16 Genesis 34-35; Matthew 19
17 Genesis 36-37; Matthew 20
18 Genesis 38-39; Matthew 21
19 Genesis 40-41; Matthew 22
20 Genesis 42-43; Matthew 23
21 Genesis 44-45; Matthew 24
22 Genesis 46-48; Matthew 25-26
23 Genesis 49-50; Matthew 27
24 Exodus 1-2; Matthew 28
25 Exodus 3-4; Mark 1
26 Exodus 5-6; Mark 2
27 Exodus 7-8; Mark 3
28 Exodus 9-10; Mark 4
29 Exodus 11-13; Mark 5-6
30 Exodus 14-15; Mark 7
31 Exodus 16-17; Mark 8

FEBRUARY

1   Exodus 18-19; Mark 9
2   Exodus 20-21; Mark 10
3   Exodus 22-23; Mark 11
4   Exodus 24-25; Mark 12
5   Exodus 26-28; Mark 13-14
6   Exodus 29-30; Mark 15
7   Exodus 31-32; Mark 16
8   Exodus 33-34; Luke 1
9   Exodus 35-36; Luke 2
10 Exodus 37-38; Luke 3
11 Exodus 39-40; Luke 4
12 Leviticus 1-3; Luke 5-6
13 Leviticus 4-5; Luke 7
14 Leviticus 6-7; Luke 8

15 Leviticus 8-9; Luke 9
16 Leviticus 10-11; Luke 10
17 Leviticus 12-13; Luke 11
18 Leviticus 14-15; Luke 12
19 Leviticus 16-18; Luke 13-14
20 Leviticus 19-20; Luke 15
21 Leviticus 21-22; Luke 16
22 Leviticus 23-24; Luke 17
23 Leviticus 25-26; Luke 18
24 Leviticus 27; Numbers 1; Luke 19
25 Numbers 2-3; Luke 20
26 Numbers 4-6; Luke 21-22
27 Numbers 7:1-48; Luke 23
28 Numbers 7:49-78; Luke 24

MARCH

1   Numbers 7:79-89; 8; John 1
2   Numbers 9-10; John 2
3   Numbers 11-12; John 3
4   Numbers 13-14; John 4
5   Numbers 15-17; John 5-6
6   Numbers 18-19; John 7
7   Numbers 20-21; John 8
8   Numbers 22-23; John 9
9   Numbers 24-25; John 10
10 Numbers 26; John 11
11 Numbers 27-28; John 12
12 Numbers 29-31:1-24; John 13-14
13 Numbers 31:25-54; 32; John 15
14 Numbers 33; John 16
15 Numbers 34-35; John 17
16 Numbers 36; Deuteronomy 1; John 18
17 Deuteronomy 2-3; John 19
18 Deuteronomy 4-5; John 20
19 Deuteronomy 6-8; John 21; Acts 1
20 Deuteronomy 9-10; Acts 2
21 Deuteronomy 11-12; Acts 3
22 Deuteronomy 13-14; Acts 4
23 Deuteronomy 15-16; Acts 5
24 Deuteronomy 17-18; Acts 6
25 Deuteronomy 19-20; Acts 7
26 Deuteronomy 21-23; Acts 8-9
27 Deuteronomy 24-25; Acts 10
28 Deuteronomy 26-27; Acts 11
29 Deuteronomy 28-29; Acts 12
30 Deuteronomy 30-31; Acts 13
31 Deuteronomy 32-33; Acts 14

APRIL

1	Deuteronomy 34; Joshua 1; Acts 15
2	Joshua 2-4; Acts 16-17
3	Joshua 5-6; Acts 18
4	Joshua 7-8; Acts 19
5	Joshua 9-10; Acts 20
6	Joshua 11-12; Acts 21
7	Joshua 13-14; Acts 22
8	Joshua 15; Acts 23
9	Joshua 16-18; Acts 24-25
10	Joshua 19-20; Acts 26
11	Joshua 21-22; Acts 27
12	Joshua 23-24; Acts 28
13	Judges 1-2; Romans 1
14	Judges 3-4; Romans 2
15	Judges 5-6; Romans 3
16	Judges 7-9; Romans 4-5
17	Judges 10-11; Romans 6
18	Judges 12-13; Romans 7
19	Judges 14-15; Romans 8
20	Judges 16-17; Romans 9
21	Judges 18-19; Romans 10
22	Judges 20-21; Romans 11
23	Ruth 1-3; Romans 12-13
24	Ruth 4; 1 Samuel 1; Romans 14
25	1 Samuel 2-3; Romans 15
26	1 Samuel 4-5; Romans 16
27	1 Samuel 6-7; 1 Corinthians 1
28	1 Samuel 8-9; 1 Corinthians 2
29	1 Samuel 10-11; 1 Corinthians 3
30	1 Samuel 12-14; 1 Corinthians 4-5

MAY

1	1 Samuel 15-16; 1 Corinthians 6
2	1 Samuel 17-18; 1 Corinthians 7
3	1 Samuel 19-20; 1 Corinthians 8
4	1 Samuel 21-22; 1 Corinthians 9
5	1 Samuel 23-24; 1 Corinthians 10
6	1 Samuel 25-26; 1 Corinthians 11
7	1 Samuel 27-29; 1 Corinthians 12-13
8	1 Samuel 30-31; 1 Corinthians 14
9	2 Samuel 1-2; 1 Corinthians 15
10	2 Samuel 3-4; 1 Corinthians 16
11	2 Samuel 5-6; 2 Corinthians 1
12	2 Samuel 7-8; 2 Corinthians 2
13	2 Samuel 9-10; 2 Corinthians 3
14	2 Samuel 11-13; 2 Corinthians 4-5
15	2 Samuel 14-15; 2 Corinthians 6
16	2 Samuel 16-17; 2 Corinthians 7
17	2 Samuel 18-19; 2 Corinthians 8
18	2 Samuel 20-21; 2 Corinthians 9

19	2 Samuel 22-23; 2 Corinthians 10
20	2 Samuel 24; 1 Kings 1; 2 Corinthians 11
21	1 Kings 2-4; 2 Corinthians 12-13
22	1 Kings 5-6; Galatians 1
23	1 Kings 7-8; Galatians 2
24	1 Kings 9-10; Galatians 3
25	1 Kings 11-12; Galatians 4
26	1 Kings 13-14; Galatians 5
27	1 Kings 15-16; Galatians 6
28	1 Kings 17-19; Ephesians 1-2
29	1 Kings 20-21; Ephesians 3
30	1 Kings 22; 2 Kings 1; Ephesians 4
31	2 Kings 2-3; Ephesians 5

JUNE

1	2 Kings 4-5; Ephesians 6
2	2 Kings 6-7; Philippians 1
3	2 Kings 8-9; Philippians 2
4	2 Kings 10-12; Philippians 3-4
5	2 Kings 13-14; Colossians 1
6	2 Kings 15-16; Colossians 2
7	2 Kings 17-18; Colossians 3
8	2 Kings 19-20; Colossians 4
9	2 Kings 21-22; 1 Thessalonians 1
10	2 Kings 23-24; 1 Thessalonians 2
11	2 Kings 25; 1 Chronicles 1-2; 1 Thessalonians 3-4
12	1 Chronicles 3-4; 1 Thessalonians 5
13	1 Chronicles 5-6; 2 Thessalonians 1
14	1 Chronicles 7-8; 2 Thessalonians 2
15	1 Chronicles 9-10; 2 Thessalonians 3
16	1 Chronicles 11-12; 1 Timothy 1
17	1 Chronicles 13-14; 1 Timothy 2
18	1 Chronicles 15-17; 1 Timothy 3-4
19	1 Chronicles 18-19; 1 Timothy 5
20	1 Chronicles 20-21; 1 Timothy 6
21	1 Chronicles 22-23; 2 Timothy 1
22	1 Chronicles 24-25; 2 Timothy 2
23	1 Chronicles 26-27; 2 Timothy 3
24	1 Chronicles 28-29; 2 Timothy 4
25	2 Chronicles 1-3; Titus 1-2
26	2 Chronicles 4-5; Titus 3
27	2 Chronicles 6-7; Philemon
28	2 Chronicles 8-9; Hebrews 1
29	2 Chronicles 10-11; Hebrews 2
30	2 Chronicles 12-13; Hebrews 3

JULY

1	2 Chronicles 14-15; Hebrews 4
2	2 Chronicles 16-18; Hebrews 5-6
3	2 Chronicles 19-20; Hebrews 7

4	2 Chronicles 21-22; Hebrews 8		22	Proverbs 15-16; Psalm 7
5	2 Chronicles 23-24; Hebrews 9		23	Proverbs 17-18; Psalm 8
6	2 Chronicles 25-26; Hebrews 10		24	Proverbs 19-20; Psalm 9
7	2 Chronicles 27-28; Hebrews 11		25	Proverbs 21-22; Psalm 10
8	2 Chronicles 29-30; Hebrews 12		26	Proverbs 23-24; Psalm 11
9	2 Chronicles 31-33; Hebrews 13; James 1		27	Proverbs 25-27; Psalms 12-13
10	2 Chronicles 34-35; James 2		28	Proverbs 28-29; Psalm 14
11	2 Chronicles 36; Ezra 1; James 3		29	Proverbs 30-31; Psalm 15
12	Ezra 2-3; James 4		30	Ecclesiastes 1-2; Psalm 16
13	Ezra 4-5; James 5		31	Ecclesiastes 3-4; Psalm 17

4   2 Chronicles 21-22; Hebrews 8
5   2 Chronicles 23-24; Hebrews 9
6   2 Chronicles 25-26; Hebrews 10
7   2 Chronicles 27-28; Hebrews 11
8   2 Chronicles 29-30; Hebrews 12
9   2 Chronicles 31-33; Hebrews 13; James 1
10   2 Chronicles 34-35; James 2
11   2 Chronicles 36; Ezra 1; James 3
12   Ezra 2-3; James 4
13   Ezra 4-5; James 5
14   Ezra 6-7; 1 Peter 1
15   Ezra 8-9; 1 Peter 2
16   Ezra 10; Nehemiah 1-2; 1 Peter 3-4
17   Nehemiah 3-4; 1 Peter 5
18   Nehemiah 5-6; 2 Peter 1
19   Nehemiah 7-8; 2 Peter 2
20   Nehemiah 9-10; 2 Peter 3
21   Nehemiah 11-12; 1 John 1
22   Nehemiah 13; Esther 1; 1 John 2
23   Esther 2-4; 1 John 3-4
24   Esther 5-6; 1 John 5
25   Esther 7-8; 2 John
26   Esther 9-10; 3 John
27   Job 1-2; Jude
28   Job 3-4; Revelation 1
29   Job 5-6; Revelation 2
30   Job 7-9; Revelation 3
31   Job 10-11; Revelation 4

AUGUST
1   Job 12-13; Revelation 5
2   Job 14-15; Revelation 6
3   Job 16-17; Revelation 7
4   Job 18-19; Revelation 8
5   Job 20-21; Revelation 9
6   Job 22-24; Revelation 10-11
7   Job 25-26; Revelation 12
8   Job 27-28; Revelation 13
9   Job 29-30; Revelation 14
10   Job 31-32; Revelation 15
11   Job 33-34; Revelation 16
12   Job 35-36; Revelation 17
13   Job 37-39; Revelation 18-19
14   Job 40-41; Revelation 20
15   Job 42; Proverbs 1; Revelation 21
16   Proverbs 2-3; Revelation 22
17   Proverbs 4-5; Psalm 1
18   Proverbs 6-7; Psalm 2
19   Proverbs 8-9; Psalm 3
20   Proverbs 10-12; Psalms 4-5
21   Proverbs 13-14; Psalm 6

22   Proverbs 15-16; Psalm 7
23   Proverbs 17-18; Psalm 8
24   Proverbs 19-20; Psalm 9
25   Proverbs 21-22; Psalm 10
26   Proverbs 23-24; Psalm 11
27   Proverbs 25-27; Psalms 12-13
28   Proverbs 28-29; Psalm 14
29   Proverbs 30-31; Psalm 15
30   Ecclesiastes 1-2; Psalm 16
31   Ecclesiastes 3-4; Psalm 17

SEPTEMBER
1   Ecclesiastes 5-6; Psalm 18
2   Ecclesiastes 7-8; Psalm 19
3   Ecclesiastes 9-11; Psalms 20-21
4   Ecclesiastes 12; Song of Solomon 1;
     Psalm 22
5   Song of Solomon 2-3; Psalm 23
6   Song of Solomon 4-5; Psalm 24
7   Song of Solomon 6-7; Psalm 25
8   Song of Solomon 8; Isaiah 1; Psalm 26
9   Isaiah 2-3; Psalm 27
10   Isaiah 4-6; Psalms 28-29
11   Isaiah 7-8; Psalm 30
12   Isaiah 9-10; Psalm 31
13   Isaiah 11-12; Psalm 32
14   Isaiah 13-14; Psalm 33
15   Isaiah 15-16; Psalm 34
16   Isaiah 17-18; Psalm 35
17   Isaiah 19-21; Psalms 36-37
18   Isaiah 22-23; Psalm 38
19   Isaiah 24-25; Psalm 39
20   Isaiah 26-27; Psalm 40
21   Isaiah 28-29; Psalm 41
22   Isaiah 30-31; Psalm 42
23   Isaiah 32-33; Psalm 43
24   Isaiah 34-36; Psalms 44-45
25   Isaiah 37-38; Psalm 46
26   Isaiah 39-40; Psalm 47
27   Isaiah 41-42; Psalm 48
28   Isaiah 43-44; Psalm 49
29   Isaiah 45-46; Psalm 50
30   Isaiah 47-48; Psalm 51

OCTOBER
1   Isaiah 49-51; Psalms 52-53
2   Isaiah 52-53; Psalm 54
3   Isaiah 54-55; Psalm 55
4   Isaiah 56-57; Psalm 56
5   Isaiah 58-59; Psalm 57
6   Isaiah 60-61; Psalm 58

7	Isaiah 62-63; Psalm 59		25	Ezekiel 44-45; Psalm 115
8	Isaiah 64-66; Psalms 60-61		26	Ezekiel 46-48; Psalm 116-117
9	Jeremiah 1-2; Psalm 62		27	Daniel 1-2; Psalm 118
10	Jeremiah 3-4; Psalm 63		28	Daniel 3-4; Psalm 119:1-24
11	Jeremiah 5-6; Psalm 64		29	Daniel 5-6; Psalm 119:25-49
12	Jeremiah 7-8; Psalm 65		30	Daniel 7-8; Psalm 119:50-72
13	Jeremiah 9-10; Psalm 66			
14	Jeremiah 11-12; Psalm 67			

7 Isaiah 62-63; Psalm 59
8 Isaiah 64-66; Psalms 60-61
9 Jeremiah 1-2; Psalm 62
10 Jeremiah 3-4; Psalm 63
11 Jeremiah 5-6; Psalm 64
12 Jeremiah 7-8; Psalm 65
13 Jeremiah 9-10; Psalm 66
14 Jeremiah 11-12; Psalm 67
15 Jeremiah 13-15; Psalms 68-69
16 Jeremiah 16-17; Psalm 70
17 Jeremiah 18-19; Psalm 71
18 Jeremiah 20-21; Psalm 72
19 Jeremiah 22-23; Psalm 73
20 Jeremiah 24-25; Psalm 74
21 Jeremiah 26-27; Psalm 75
22 Jeremiah 28-30; Psalms 76-77
23 Jeremiah 31-32; Psalm 78
24 Jeremiah 33-34; Psalm 79
25 Jeremiah 35-36; Psalm 80
26 Jeremiah 37-38; Psalm 81
27 Jeremiah 39-40; Psalm 82
28 Jeremiah 41-42; Psalm 83
29 Jeremiah 43-45; Psalms 84-85
30 Jeremiah 46-47; Psalm 86
31 Jeremiah 48-49; Psalm 87

NOVEMBER
1 Jeremiah 50-51; Psalm 88
2 Jeremiah 52; Lamentations 1; Psalm 89
3 Lamentations 2-3; Psalm 90
4 Lamentations 4-5; Psalm 91
5 Ezekiel 1-3; Psalms 92-93
6 Ezekiel 4-5; Psalm 94
7 Ezekiel 6-7; Psalm 95
8 Ezekiel 8-9; Psalm 96
9 Ezekiel 10-11; Psalm 97
10 Ezekiel 12-13; Psalm 98
11 Ezekiel 14-15; Psalm 99
12 Ezekiel 16-18; Psalms 100-101
13 Ezekiel 19-20; Psalm 102
14 Ezekiel 21-22; Psalm 103
15 Ezekiel 23-24; Psalm 104
16 Ezekiel 25-26; Psalm 105
17 Ezekiel 27-28; Psalm 106
18 Ezekiel 29-30; Psalm 107
19 Ezekiel 31-33; Psalms 108-109
20 Ezekiel 34-35; Psalm 110
21 Ezekiel 36-37; Psalm 111
22 Ezekiel 38-39; Psalm 112
23 Ezekiel 40-41; Psalm 113
24 Ezekiel 42-43; Psalm 114

25 Ezekiel 44-45; Psalm 115
26 Ezekiel 46-48; Psalm 116-117
27 Daniel 1-2; Psalm 118
28 Daniel 3-4; Psalm 119:1-24
29 Daniel 5-6; Psalm 119:25-49
30 Daniel 7-8; Psalm 119:50-72

DECEMBER
1 Daniel 9-10; Psalm 119:73-96
2 Daniel 11-12; Psalm 119:97-120
3 Hosea 1-3; Psalm 119:121-144
4 Hosea 4-5; Psalm 119:145-176
5 Hosea 6-7; Psalm 120
6 Hosea 8-9; Psalm 121
7 Hosea 10-11; Psalm 122
8 Hosea 12-13; Psalm 123
9 Hosea 14; Joel 1; Psalm 124
10 Joel 2-3; Amos 1; Psalms 125-126
11 Amos 2-3; Psalm 127
12 Amos 4-5; Psalm 128
13 Amos 6-7; Psalm 129
14 Amos 8-9; Psalm 130
15 Obadiah; Jonah 1; Psalm 131
16 Jonah 2-3; Psalm 132
17 Jonah 4; Micah 1-2; Psalms 133-134
18 Micah 3-4; Psalm 135
19 Micah 5-6; Psalm 136
20 Micah 7; Nahum 1-3; Psalm 137
21 Habakkuk 1-3; Psalm 138
22 Zephaniah 1-3; Psalm 139
23 Haggai 1-2; Psalm 140
24 Zechariah 1-3; Psalms 141-142
25 Zechariah 4-5; Psalm 143
26 Zechariah 6-7; Psalm 144
27 Zechariah 8-9; Psalm 145
28 Zechariah 10-11; Psalm 146
29 Zechariah 12-13; Psalm 147
30 Zechariah 14; Malachi 1; Psalm 148
31 Malachi 2-4; Psalms 149-150

"Read Through the Bible in a Year Plan"
written by Marilyn Hickey. Used
by permission.

Prayer for Salvation and Baptism in the Holy Spirit

Heavenly Father, I come to You in the Name of Jesus. Your Word says, *"Whosoever shall call on the name of the Lord shall be saved"* (Acts 2:21, KJV). I am calling on You. I pray and ask Jesus to come into my heart and be Lord over my life according to Romans 10:9-10, KJV. *"If thou shalt confess with thy mouth the Lord Jesus, and shalt believe in thine heart that God hath raised him from the dead, thou shalt be saved. For with the heart man believeth unto righteousness; and with the mouth confession is made unto salvation."* I do that now. I confess that Jesus is Lord, and I believe in my heart that God raised Him from the dead.

I am now reborn! I am a Christian—a child of Almighty God! I am saved! You also said in Your Word, *"If ye then, being evil, know how to give good gifts unto your children: HOW MUCH MORE shall your heavenly Father give the Holy Spirit to them that ask him?"* (Luke 11:13, KJV). I'm also asking You to fill me with the Holy Spirit. Holy Spirit, rise up within me as I praise God. I fully expect to speak with other tongues as You give me the utterance (Acts 2:4).

Begin to praise God for filling you with the Holy Spirit. Speak those words and syllables you receive—not in your own language, but the language given to you by the Holy Spirit. You have to use your own voice. God will not force you to speak. Worship and praise Him in your heavenly language—in other tongues.

Continue with the blessing God has given you and pray in tongues each day.

You are a born-again, Spirit-filled believer. You'll never be the same!

Find a good Word of God preaching church, and become a part of a church family who will love and care for you as you love and care for them.

We need to be connected to each other. It increases our strength in God. It's God's plan for us.

About the Authors

Kenneth and Gloria Copeland are the best-selling authors of more than 60 books such as the popular *Walk With God, Managing God's Mutual Funds* and *God's Will for You*. Together they have co-authored numerous other books including *Family Promises*. As founders of Kenneth Copeland Ministries in Fort Worth, Texas, Kenneth and Gloria are in their 32nd year of circling the globe with the uncompromised Word of God, preaching and teaching a lifestyle of victory for every Christian.

Their daily and Sunday *Believer's Voice of Victory* television broadcasts now air on more than 500 stations around the world, and their *Believer's Voice of Victory* and *Shout!* magazines are distributed to more than 1 million adults and children worldwide. Their international prison ministry reaches an average of 60,000 new inmates every year and receives more than 17,000 pieces of correspondence each month. Their teaching materials can also be found on the World Wide Web. With offices and staff in the United States, Canada, England, Australia, South Africa and Ukraine, Kenneth and Gloria's teaching materials—books, magazines, tapes and videos—have been translated into at least 22 languages to reach the world with the love of God.

Learn more about Kenneth Copeland Ministries
by visiting our Web site at www.kcm.org.

Books Available From Kenneth Copeland Ministries

by Kenneth Copeland
* A Ceremony of Marriage
  A Matter of Choice
  Covenant of Blood
  Faith and Patience—The Power Twins
* Freedom From Fear
  Giving and Receiving
  Honor—Walking in Honesty, Truth and Integrity
  How to Conquer Strife
  How to Discipline Your Flesh
  How to Receive Communion
  Living at the End of Time—A Time of
    Supernatural Increase
  Love Never Fails
  Managing God's Mutual Funds
* Now Are We in Christ Jesus
* Our Covenant With God
  Partnership, Sharing the Vision—Sharing the Grace
* Prayer—Your Foundation for Success
* Prosperity: The Choice Is Yours
  Rumors of War
* Sensitivity of Heart
* Six Steps to Excellence in Ministry
* Sorrow Not! Winning Over Grief and Sorrow
* The Decision Is Yours
* The Force of Faith
* The Force of Righteousness
  The Image of God in You
  The Laws of Prosperity
* The Mercy of God
  The Miraculous Realm of God's Love
  The Outpouring of the Spirit—The Result of Prayer
* The Power of the Tongue
  The Power to Be Forever Free
  The Troublemaker
* The Winning Attitude
  Turn Your Hurts Into Harvests
* Welcome to the Family
* You Are Healed!
  Your Right-Standing With God

by Gloria Copeland
* And Jesus Healed Them All
  Are You Listening?
  Are You Ready?
  Build Your Financial Foundation
  Build Yourself an Ark
  Fight On!
  God's Prescription for Divine Health
  God's Success Formula
  God's Will for You
  God's Will for Your Healing
  God's Will Is Prosperity
* God's Will Is the Holy Spirit
* Harvest of Health
  Hidden Treasures
  Living Contact
  Living in Heaven's Blessings Now
* Love—The Secret to Your Success
  No Deposit—No Return
  Pleasing the Father
  Pressing In—It's Worth It All
  Shine On!
  The Power to Live a New Life

The Unbeatable Spirit of Faith
* Walk in the Spirit
  Walk With God
  Well Worth the Wait

Books Co-Authored by Kenneth and Gloria Copeland
  Family Promises
  Healing Promises
  Prosperity Promises
  Protection Promises

* From Faith to Faith—A Daily Guide to Victory
  From Faith to Faith—A Perpetual Calendar

One Word From God Series
• One Word From God Can Change Your Destiny
• One Word From God Can Change Your Family
• One Word From God Can Change Your Finances
• One Word From God Can Change Your Formula
    for Success
• One Word From God Can Change Your Health
• One Word From God Can Change Your Nation
• One Word From God Can Change Your Prayer Life
• One Word From God Can Change Your Relationships

Over The Edge—A Youth Devotional

Pursuit of His Presence—A Daily Devotional
Pursuit of His Presence—A Perpetual Calendar

Other Books Published by KCP
  The First 30 Years—A Journey of Faith
    The story of the lives of Kenneth and
      Gloria Copeland.
  Real People. Real Needs. Real Victories.
    A book of testimonies to encourage your faith.

  John G. Lake—His Life, His Sermons, His Boldness
    of Faith
  The Holiest of All by Andrew Murray
  The New Testament in Modern Speech by Richard
  Francis Weymouth

Products Designed for Today's Children and Youth
  Baby Praise Board Book
  Baby Praise Christmas Board Book
  Noah's Ark Coloring Book
  The Best of *Shout!* Adventure Comics
  The *Shout!* Joke Book
  The *Shout!* Super-Activity Book

*Commander Kellie and the Superkids*_{SM} Books:
  The SWORD Adventure Book
  *Commander Kellie and the Superkids*_{SM} Series
    Middle Grade Novels by Christopher P.N. Maselli

    #1 The Mysterious Presence
    #2 The Quest for the Second Half
    #3 Escape From Jungle Island
    #4 In Pursuit of the Enemy

*Available in Spanish

World Offices of Kenneth Copeland Ministries

For more information about KCM and a free catalog, please write the office nearest you:

Kenneth Copeland Ministries • Fort Worth, Texas 76192-0001

Kenneth Copeland
Locked Bag 2600
Mansfield Delivery Centre
QUEENSLAND 4122
AUSTRALIA

Kenneth Copeland
Private Bag X 909
FONTAINEBLEAU
2032
REPUBLIC OF SOUTH AFRICA

UKRAINE
L'VIV 290000
Post Office Box 84
Kenneth Copeland Ministries
L'VIV 290000
UKRAINE

Kenneth Copeland
Post Office Box 15
BATH
BA1 3XN
ENGLAND U.K.

Kenneth Copeland
PO Box 3111 STN LCD 1
Langley BC V3A 4R3
CANADA

We're Here for You!

Believer's Voice of Victory Television Broadcast

Join Kenneth and Gloria Copeland and the *Believer's Voice of Victory* broadcasts Monday through Friday and on Sunday each week,* and learn how faith in God's Word can take your life from ordinary to extraordinary. This teaching from God's Word is designed to get you where you want to be—*on top!*

You can catch the *Believer's Voice of Victory* broadcast on your local, cable or satellite channels.

*Check your local listings for times and stations in your area.

Believer's Voice of Victory Magazine

Enjoy inspired teaching and encouragement from Kenneth and Gloria Copeland and guest ministers each month in the *Believer's Voice of Victory* magazine. Also included are real-life testimonies of God's miraculous power and divine intervention into the lives of people just like you!

It's more than just a magazine—It's a ministry.

Shout! ...The dynamic magazine just for kids!

Shout! The Voice of Victory for Kids is a Bible-charged, action-packed, bimonthly magazine available FREE to kids everywhere! Featuring *Wichita Slim* and *Commander Kellie and the Superkids, Shout!* is filled with colorful adventure comics, challenging games and puzzles, exciting short stories, solve-it-yourself mysteries and much more!!

Stand up, sign up and get ready to *Shout!*

To receive a FREE subscription to *Believer's Voice of Victory,* or to give a child you know a FREE subscription to *Shout!,* write:

Kenneth Copeland Ministries • Fort Worth, Texas 76192-0001

Or call: • 1-800-600-7395 • (9 a.m.-5 p.m. CT)

Or visit our Web site at: www.kcm.org

If you are writing from outside the U.S., please contact the KCM office nearest you. Addresses for all Kenneth Copeland Ministries offices are listed above.

The Harrison House Vision

Proclaiming the truth and the power

Of the Gospel of Jesus Christ

With excellence;

Challenging Christians to

Live victoriously,

Grow spiritually,

Know God intimately.

If this book has changed your life, we would like

to hear from you. Please write us at:

Harrison House Publishers

P.O. Box 35035 • Tulsa, Oklahoma 74153

You can also visit us on the web at

www.harrisonhouse.com